Developing and Using Decision Support Applications

Steven C. Ross
Richard J. Penlesky
Lloyd D. Doney
Marquette University

West Publishing Company
St. Paul New York Los Angeles San Francisco

Copyeditor: John Thomas
Cover Design: T. Randall Productions

50 West Kellogg Boulevard
P.O. Box 64526
St. Paul, MN 55164-1003

Printed in the United States of America

Library of Congress Cataloging-in-Publication Data

Ross, Steven C.
Developing and using decision support applications.

(The Microcomputing series)
Includes bibliographies and index.
1. Decison support systems. I. Penlesky, Richard James, 1951- . II. Doney, Lloyd D. III. Title. IV. Series.
T58.62.R67 1988 658.4'03 87-13289
ISBN 0-314-30124-0

CONTENTS

PUBLISHER'S NOTE

This book is part of THE MICROCOMPUTING SERIES. We are proud to announce that this unique series is now entering its third year, and currently includes four different types of books:

1. A core concepts book, now in its second edition, teaches basic hardware and software applications concepts. This text is entitled *Understanding and Using Microcomputers.*

2. A series of introductory level, hands-on lab manuals for a wide variety of specific software packages. These provide both self-paced tutorials and complete reference guides. Each book's title begins with *Understanding and Using* . . . .

3. Several larger volumes combine DOS with three popular software packages. Two of these volumes are called *Understanding and Using Application Software,* while the third is titled *Understanding and Using Shareware Application Software.* These versions condense components of the individual lab manuals while increasing the coverage of DOS and the integration of the different application packages.

4. An advanced level of hands-on lab manual with a strong project/systems orientation. These titles all begin with *Developing and Using* . . . .

Our goal has always been to provide you with the maximum flexibility in meeting the challenging needs of your courses through this "mix and match" approach. We remain committed to offering the widest variety of current software packages.

We now offer these books in THE MICROCOMPUTING SERIES:

Understanding and Using Microcomputers, second edition — by Steven M. Zimmerman and Leo M. Conrad

OPERATING SYSTEMS

Understanding and Using MS-DOS/PC DOS: The First Steps
by Laura B. Ruff and Mary K. Weitzer

Understanding and Using MS-DOS/PC DOS: A Complete Guide
by Cody T. Copeland and Jonathan P. Bacon

PROGRAMMING LANGUAGES

Understanding and Using MICROSOFT BASIC/IBM-PC BASIC
by Mary L. Howard

WORD PROCESSORS

Understanding and Using Displaywrite 3 and Displaywrite 4
by Patsy H. Lund and Barbara A. Hayden

Understanding and Using Microsoft Word
by Jonathan P. Bacon

Understanding and Using Multimate
by Mary K. Weitzer and Laura B. Ruff

Understanding and Using PC-Write
by Victor P. Maiorana

Understanding and Using pfs:WRITE
by Mary K. Weitzer and Laura B. Ruff

Understanding and Using WordPerfect
by Patsy H. Lund, Barbara A. Hayden, and Sharon S. Larsen

Understanding and Using WordStar
by Steven C. Ross

Understanding and Using WordStar 4.0
by Patsy H. Lund and Barbara A. Hayden

SPREADSHEET PACKAGES

Understanding and Using ExpressCalc (including PC-CALC)
by Victor P. Maiorana and Arthur A. Strunk

Understanding and Using Lotus 1-2-3
by Steven C. Ross

Understanding and Using Lotus 1-2-3 Release 2
by Steven C. Ross

Understanding and Using SuperCalc 3
by Steven C. Ross and Judy A. Reinders

Understanding and Using SuperCalc 4
by Judy A. Reinders and Steven C. Ross

DATABASE PACKAGES

Understanding and Using dBASE III (Including dBASE II)
by Steven C. Ross

Understanding and Using dBASE III PLUS
by Steven C. Ross

Understanding and Using PC-FILE III
by Victor P. Maiorana and Arthur A. Strunk

Understanding and Using pfs:FILE/REPORT
by Laura B. Ruff and Mary K. Weitzer

Understanding and Using R:BASE 5000 (Including R:BASE System V)
by Karen L. Watterson

INTEGRATED SOFTWARE

Understanding and Using AppleWorks
by Frank Short

Understanding and Using Educate-Ability
by Victor P. Maiorana and Arthur A. Strunk

Understanding and Using FRAMEWORK
by Karen L. Watterson

Developing and Using Office Applications with AppleWorks
by M. S. Varnon

Understanding and Using Symphony
by Enzo Allegretti

COMBINATION VOLUMES

Understanding and Using Application Software, Volume 1:
DOS, WordStar 4.0, Lotus 1-2-3 Release 2, and dBASE III Plus
by Steven C. Ross, Patsy H. Lund, and Barbara A. Hayden

Understanding and Using Application Software, Volume 2:
DOS, WordPerfect, Lotus 1-2-3 Release 2, and dBASE III Plus
by Steven C. Ross, Patsy H. Lund, and Barbara A. Hayden

Understanding and Using SHARE-WARE Application Software:
DOS, PC-Write, ExpressCalc, and PC-FILE
by Victor P. Maiorana and Arthur A. Strunk

ADVANCED BOOKS

Developing and Using Advanced Lotus 1-2-3 Applications
by Steven C. Ross

Developing and Using Decision Support Applications
by Steven C. Ross, Richard J. Penlesky, and Lloyd D. Doney

Developing and Using Microcomputer Business Systems
by Kathryn W. Huff

We are delighted by the popularity of THE MICROCOMPUTING SERIES. We appreciate your support, and look forward to your suggestions and comments. Please write to us at this address:

West Publishing Company
College Division
50 W. Kellogg Blvd.
P.O. Box 43526

ABOUT THE AUTHORS

Robert L. Armacost contributed Units 11 and 14, and Appendix C. He received a B.S. degree in Engineering from the U. S. Coast Guard Academy, an M.S. degree in Operations Research from the U. S. Naval Postgraduate School, and a D.Sc. degree in Operations Research from The George Washington University. He is a retired Coast Guard officer, having served in numerous managerial and analytical functions in field and headquarters commands. Currently, Dr. Armacost is an Assistant Professor of Management Science at Marquette University where he teaches statistics and management science. He also consults with businesses and non-profit organizations to improve the quality of decision information using analytical methods.

Charles H. Breeden contributed Units 5 and 8. He holds a B.S.B.A. degree in Accounting from the University of Florida and an M.A. and Ph.D. in Economics from Virginia Tech. Currently, he is an Associate Professor of Economics at Marquette University where his teaching is concentrated in graduate and undergraduate classes in Managerial Economics. In those classes, Dr. Breeden integrates the microcomputer into course work through the use of statistical software packages for data manipulation and for regression and time series analysis.

Lloyd D. Doney contributed Units 4, 9, and 13 and participated in the editing of the entire book. He earned a B.S. degree from Michigan Technological University and M.B.A. and Ph.D. degrees in Accounting from Louisiana State University. He is a Certified Data Processor (CDP) and a Certified Data Educator (CDE). Currently, Dr. Doney is a Professor of Accounting at Marquette University. At Marquette he has taught both the basic computing course and several upper division and graduate courses where he has used the computer extensively. Dr. Doney is the author of over forty articles in professional journals, many dealing with the use of computers in management decision-making, and has consulted with several firms in the use of computers in planning, cost estimating and accounting.

Adrienne S. Kim prepared part of Units 1 and 2. She holds a B.S. degree in Psychology from the University of Wisconsin—Madison and an M.B.A. degree from Marquette University. Ms. Kim has been involved in sales and marketing of microcomputer technology to businesses of varied types and sizes, which fostered her interest in software applications designed to support business decision making.

Richard J. Penlesky contributed Units 6, 10, and 12, part of Unit 1, and participated in the design and editing of the entire book. He holds both an Honors Bachelor of Science degree in Mechanical Engineering and an M.B.A. degree from Marquette University. He received his D.B.A. degree from Indiana University in Operations Management with minors in Quantitative Analysis and Management Information Systems. Dr. Penlesky has been on the faculty of the Management Sciences Department at the University of Minnesota, and he is currently an Assistant Professor of Operations Management at Marquette University. Dr. Penlesky is a member of the American Production and Inventory Control Society (APICS), the Decision Sciences Institute (DSI) and The Institute for Management Science (TIMS). He has published articles in the *Conference Proceedings of the Decision Sciences Institute* and in *AIIE Transactions.*

Steven C. Ross contributed Appendices A and B, parts of Units 1 and 2, and directed the design and editing of the entire book. He earned a B.S. degree in History from Oregon State University and M.S. and Ph.D. degrees in Business Administration from The University of Utah. Currently, he is an Assistant Professor of Management at Marquette University. At Marquette, he has been responsible for the introduction of microcomputers into the primary computer course and for the integration of computer applications throughout the curriculum. Dr. Ross also consults with businesses of all sizes to integrate microcomputers into the managerial operations of those organizations. He is the author of six other books in THE MICROCOMPUTING SERIES and is currently working on three that will appear in 1988-89.

Thomas S. C. Soon contributed Unit 3. He holds a B.S. degree in Management Sciences from the National Chiao Tung University, Taiwan, Republic of China and is currently completing a Ph.D. in Management Sciences at Ohio State University. Mr. Soon has taught database management and microcomputer courses at Marquette University, and he has also consulted with business organizations.

Rajesh Srivastava contributed Unit 7. He received a B.Tech. degree in Electrical Engineering from the Indian Institute of Technology, Kampur, India, an M.B.A. from the University of Wisconsin—Whitewater, and a Ph.D. in Business Administration from Ohio State University. Currently, he is an Assistant Professor of Management at Marquette University. Dr. Srivastava teaches Operations Management at the graduate and undergraduate levels.

PREFACE

Developing and Using Decision Support Applications is about the design of computer models to support typical business decisions. Decision Support Systems are employed in situations where a combination of executive judgment and quantitative analysis are required. The decision support applications presented herein are designed to support judgment by providing the quantitative analysis. The book contains specific tools as well as a discussion of how the mathematical models developed here relate to the organization's database and how both may be combined in a "user-friendly" system.

WHY THIS BOOK?

Although there are books that discuss "Decision Support Systems for Microcomputers," these books generally concentrate on the computer programming and not on how the systems actually support business decision making. In *Developing and Using Decision Support Applications*, we strike a balance between *developing* — programming — and *using* — understanding the basic concepts underlying a model and interpreting the results of that model. To the best of our knowledge, this book is unique in its dual focus.

To create such a book, we assembled a team of persons familiar with various business disciplines — Accounting, Economics, Finance, Management, Operations, and Management Information Systems — each of whom has used microcomputer models in his teaching and research. Each person developed one or more applications based on a specific decision situation. All team members were involved in reading and editing the work of other team members, with the desire to achieve a book that presents a unified approach to diverse topics.

Because of the dual focus of the book — developing and using — it may be used in two different types of courses. Those who enjoy development will find a series of interesting and challenging models, complemented by sufficient theory to understand why the model is developed as it is. Those who are more interested in using models will find a diverse set of decision aids that may be applied to a number of situations. Thus, this book may be used in courses ranging from Advanced Spreadsheet Modeling to Decision Support Systems to Managerial Economics to Accounting Information Systems to Operations Management to Business Policy.

HOW TO USE THIS BOOK

The topics in this book are generally independent of each other; you may proceed in just about any order you choose. We recommend that you read Unit 1 before starting on the applications so that you have a general appreciation of what the book is about. Unit 2 discusses the realm of microcomputer software. Unit 3 details database management considerations for decision support, but you may skip that unit if your primary focus is on using rather than developing. Units 4 through 14 present the various applications. These may be completed in any order, except that Unit 11 builds on the application developed and used in Unit 6.

The application units (4-14) are organized in a consistent manner. Each unit includes:

- **Learning Objectives**: what you should know and what you should be able to do after completing the unit.
- **Basic Concepts**: an introduction to the theory or technique discussed in the unit. This section usually includes a discussion of the mathematical operations necessary to solve the problem.
- **Gathering the Data**: a discussion of sources for the data used with the technique. Generally the data is found both within the company and external to the company.
- **The Problem**: a specific problem to be analyzed using the technique presented in the unit. The sample problems in this book are all drawn from a fictitious organization: The EZRydr Motor Company.
- **Developing the Spreadsheet**: general and specific factors to be considered in developing a spreadsheet model of the problem.
- **Checking the Model**: procedures for determining whether or not the model has been correctly entered into the computer.
- **Using the Spreadsheet**: the steps to analyze the specific problem, as well as extensions to additional types of problems.
- **Enhancements to the Application**: features that may be added to make the model easier to use, and additional considerations such as transfer of data from a database.
- **Exercises**: questions that require further analysis using the model.
- **Review Questions**: designed to test your knowledge of the material presented. The answers to selected questions are found in Appendix D.
- **Additional Reading**: references for further information about a technique.
- **Application-Specific Software Packages**: a list of specialized software packages available for some techniques, such as simulation and linear programming. This section is not found in all units.

Additional features of *Developing and Using Decision Support Applications* are

- **Appendix A Glossary of Lotus 1-2-3 Commands, Functions, Features**: because the examples in the book are developed using Lotus 1-2-3, we provide this glossary for those who are not familiar with that package, or are using a different package and need to "translate" from Lotus.

- **Appendix B Transferring Data between Lotus 1-2-3 and dBASE III Plus**: this appendix deals with the specific problem of transferring data between these two packages, as well as more general issues of data transfer between applications software programs.

- **Appendix C Random Numbers and Probability Distributions**: this appendix provides fundamental information about its topic as well as suggestions for incorporating probability features into decision support applications.

- **Data Disk**: this disk is available to instructors and includes solutions to the problems and exercises as well as a database for EZRydr that can be accessed for additional data to be used with the applications.

A NOTE OF THANKS . . .

to Rich Wohl, Cheryl Wilms, and Jayne Lindesmith of West Publishing Company. Your guiding comments and gentle prodding hastened the development of this manuscript.

to the reviewers of this text, Eileen Bechtold Dlugloss (Cuyahoga Community College), Ronald A. Guillemette (University of Wisconsin—Milwaukee), Ram Monan R. Kasuganti (Youngstown State University), Terry D. Lundgren (Utah State University), and Edward J. Szewczak (Southern Illinois University—Carbondale). Your comments were very helpful as we developed and refined the concept and focus of the book.

to our Marquette colleagues, whose comments ranged from "You're going to do what? With whom?" to "Haven't you finished that thing yet?" to "Bully for you!" Your support through these rather trying months has been most appreciated.

and finally, to our families — spouses, parents, siblings, and children — no decision support system will ever measure the value of your love.

S.C.R. et al.
Milwaukee
September, 1987

PART

1

FOUNDATIONS

This book is about *Developing and Using Decision Support Applications* using popular personal computer (PC) software. In Parts 2, 3, and 4, the book presents a series of models that have been developed by business-school faculty members, each working in his area of expertise. Before the models are presented, however, we introduce general concepts of decision support, problem solving, and data management, as well as a summary of the various types of software available for decision support applications. In this part we also introduce "EZRydr Motor Company," a fictitious organization whose decisions we are supporting.

UNIT

1 AN INTRODUCTION TO DECISION SUPPORT ON PERSONAL COMPUTER SYSTEMS

In this unit we set the stage for *Developing and Using Decision Support Applications* using popular personal computer (PC) software. Before we delve into the models presented in the book, we must introduce the concept of decision support systems (DSS) and different problem-solving techniques that are used for decision support. In this first unit, we also provide some general information about "EZRydr Motor Company," the fictitious organization whose decisions form the need and the basis for the decision support applications we develop.

LEARNING OBJECTIVES

At the completion of this unit you should know

a. the general differences among EDP, MIS, and DSS,

b. what the technological levels of a DSS are,

c. different methods of decision making that are used in DSS.

WHAT IS DSS?

DSS versus MIS versus EDP

DSS . . . MIS . . . EDP . . . It all sounds like Captain Marvel's secret code, but these are acronyms for three types of computer systems. Although experts do not agree on the exact meanings of the terms, we begin by providing some generally-accepted definitions. These are important because this book deals with DSS issues, and by defining DSS, MIS, and EDP, we provide a basic introduction to what this book covers, and what it does not.

Contributed by Steven C. Ross,
Richard J. Penlesky, and Adrienne S. Kim

In the beginning, there was EDP, *Electronic Data Processing*. EDP facilitated efficiency within an organization by using computers to perform calculations and data retrieval formerly done by hand. Then, there were MIS, *Management Information Systems*, which provided more information to managers at most levels within an organization by tabulating and summarizing the data maintained within the EDP system. Now, there are DSS, *Decision Support Systems*. DSS is the relatively new term describing an information system that encompasses and draws upon traditional EDP and MIS departments. In its broadest sense, DSS is a new phase of information management that offers managers at all levels of an organization information to support their decision-making processes. Both DSS and MIS draw on the database, but DSS is more forward-looking in perspective while MIS is more historical.[1]

Consider the following example. A small manufacturer has 50 employees in its job shop. Each employee might work on two to three different jobs per day and will fill out a time ticket for each of those jobs. Even in this small organization, the payroll department will receive as many as 750 time tickets per week. Because the employees are paid semimonthly, the payroll department has the following EDP needs:

- to process the time tickets and produce paychecks efficiently,
- to maintain tax information (withholdings, exemptions, social security numbers),
- to produce W-2 statements easily at the end of the year.

EDP focuses on data storage and processing and functions at the operational level of the organization. Transaction processing is efficient due to batch processing, a method by which the operator posts hundreds of entries at one time. In a manual accounting system, payroll processing requires the clerk to make at least three entries; one to update the employee record, another to update the payroll journal and a third to update the general ledger. In addition, a job costing system requires that labor hours spent on each job be recorded. In a computerized system, transaction processing means that all the updating happens automatically when payroll hours are input. To batch process payroll transactions means that the operator can input payroll data from each time ticket at one sitting, and the computer will update the necessary data files. The payroll staff of this company will schedule Wednesday afternoons as the day to batch process the time tickets. In other words, time tickets will accumulate weekly and be entered into the computer on Wednesdays. These payroll transactions are posted to the accounting system which can then be used to produce paychecks, payroll summary reports and W-2 statements at the end of the year. Computer time is optimized by scheduling computer runs (in this case Wednesday afternoons).

Middle management at this company has the following MIS needs:

- to evaluate whether the labor costs incurred for each job were estimated accurately,
- to evaluate current levels of work in process inventory,
- to evaluate the efficiency of the laborers.

---

1 For a concise review of the role of DSS, see the article by Sprague listed in the Additional Reading for this Unit.

Transactions processed by the payroll department flow through the accounting system to update payroll and job costing data files. Summary reports produced by the payroll department should meet the MIS needs listed above. MIS is aimed at middle level managers and ideally, allows on-line, real-time inquiry using structured data files. Real-time inquiry means that the user can look at the desired information through a terminal rather than having to wait for a printout. Typically, however, managers receive stacks of reports and the promise of MIS is not realized. Consider how the EDP information is used in our example organization. The payroll summary report shows the number of hours each laborer worked and year-to-date pay, while the job costing summary report shows the number of hours each employee contributed to various jobs. Managers become frustrated with these reports because what they really want to know is the number of hours each job has accumulated, how this accumulated number of hours compares to the number of hours estimated, and how much longer until the job will be complete. This information must be extracted manually from various summary reports. The managers dream of a system that would allow them to retrieve this information easily from the computer system, "All the information I need is in that computer, it's just a matter of getting it out in the form I need!"

MIS evolved from EDP because managers wanted more control over information concerning their department. MIS often emphasizes integration by business function, such as Marketing MIS, Production MIS, or Operations MIS. To a certain extent, this emphasis has relieved the processing load in the main computer department (which we call the "management information systems department" in this book). Since each business function handles information specific to itself, the MIS department need not concern itself with processing this information. In addition, managers have their own terminals or personal computers so they can satisfy their information needs independently of the MIS department. However, the success in decentralizing computer operations is offset by the information redundancy that occurs among departments. In this example, note how labor hours are important to the payroll department, the job costing center, and the operations department. A decentralized computer system requires that three departments input the labor hours into their own system in order to get the necessary reports, or that the MIS department must manage the transfer of data among the departments, adding back some of the workload that was supposedly removed by departmental data processing.

Other levels of management might have the following DSS needs, which tend to be broader than MIS needs:

- How many times per year are special consultants hired temporarily, and should the firm consider a permanent position?

- Which of the customized jobs are particularly profitable, and is there more business opportunity in this type of customization?

- How much will an incentive program cost that is based on the number of jobs that an employee helps complete?

Note that these DSS needs combine a need for data from historical records (e.g., hiring of special consultants) with some sort of a model (e.g., cost of a permanent position versus cost of temporary consultants) to support a decision, which may be influenced by other factors that are not quantified in the model (e.g., projected need for such expertise in the future, or an organizational hiring freeze). DSS is aimed at top managers and decision makers, but some DSS applications are appropriate for other levels of management.

DSS emphasizes flexibility, adaptability, and quick response. Although fundamental set-up work must be accomplished by the MIS department, a DSS is user initiated and controlled, offering support for personal styles of decision making. DSS attempts to coordinate decision making across levels of management. DSS is designed to strike a balance between human judgment and computer calculation. DSS attempts to address *semistructured* tasks: those in which part of the analysis is based on historical data and quantitative models but part of the analysis is not yet reduced to computer-analytic models. In this example, the manager needs the computer to store information about each job completed, but the manager must actually decide whether a specific type of customization is a profitable business opportunity. The manager designates the criteria used to evaluate the profitability of the job, and the characteristics that differentiate a particular job as a better business opportunity. The criteria and characteristics are programmed into an application, and the relevant data, such as labor hours, cost and profit margins, are extracted from the available information system. An ideal DSS system would allow the decision maker to call the information needed from the appropriate data files to the current application being used. DSS does not mean the elimination of the programming staff. Generally, we still need the expertise of a programmer, but he or she will program the criteria and characteristics that the manager asks for, not what the programmer thinks the manager needs.

This example illustrates that the same piece of information, labor hours, is utilized by various levels of the company for different purposes. Specifically, labor hours are used in order to produce paychecks and other statements: an "EDP" task. Labor hours are also used to measure the accuracy of sales staff quotations to the customer as well as the timeliness of job completion and staff efficiency: an "MIS" task. Finally, labor hours are used as a factor in decision making in the broader context of the firm's personnel staffing, business opportunities and employee benefits: "DSS" tasks. In a well-designed DSS system, once a piece of information is put into the system decision makers at all levels can easily access and use the information to support their decision-making process.

In summary, each of the three words in DSS is important. A DSS is a system that supports the organization's decision-making process. To be a *system*, the DSS includes data, models (usually mathematical in nature), and a method of interaction with the user. *Supporting* decisions is different from making decisions or controlling processes: a DSS provides some, but seldom all, of the data analysis to the decision makers who must incorporate other considerations. Finally, DSS support *decisions*, not routine data processing or reporting for control purposes. Sometimes, of course, data processing and reporting are a necessary part of the decision support process, but a true DSS views these tasks as a means, not an end.

Levels of DSS

DSS can be divided into three technological levels: Specific DSS, DSS Generators, and DSS Tools. *Specific DSS* is the application model or programs that actually assist with the decision-making process. In the example above, an application model or program that would assist a manager in assessing new business opportunities would constitute a Specific DSS. The second level, *DSS Generators*, are hardware and software packages that provide capabilities to allow the creation of Specific DSS quickly and easily. Managers as well as the programming staff use DSS Generators. The DSS Generator the manager might use to create this application could be an electronic spreadsheet, such as Lotus 1-2-3. The third and most fundamental level of DSS is called *DSS Tools*. These are the hardware and software elements that facilitate the development of Specific DSS or DSS Generators. Tools can be personal, mainframe, or mini-computers, as well as programming languages and operating systems. The DSS Tools used in our example would include the accounting software and the programming language that facilitates the extraction of the necessary information.

This book is designed to give you practice in developing Specific DSS, which we call *Decision Support Applications*. The DSS Generators used in our examples to create Specific DSS are Lotus 1-2-3 and dBASE III, but the discussion is general enough that you should be able to accomplish the same result with many other DSS Generators (i.e., spreadsheet and database management packages). The DSS Tool we use is a personal computer, but the work could be done on any computer that supports the necessary software. Our focus is on those application models or programs that a manager would use in order to facilitate decision making in the business environment.

In conclusion, the focus of the topics presented in this book is on Specific DSS, or those application models that support the decision-making process. The title of this book, *Developing and Using Decision Support Applications* is appropriate because you will learn how to create Specific DSS or application models with spreadsheet and database management software, then use those models to analyze decisions for a hypothetical company.

THE PROCESS OF DECISION MAKING

Decision making is a unique combination of art and science. In MIS, the study and development of *expert systems* and *artificial intelligence* (AI) has led to a greater understanding of the decision-making process. There are nine general stages that can be identified in the process of making a decision:

1. **Awareness**. In this stage of the decision-making process, key organizational members begin to feel that a problem exists. Often the symptoms of a problem are noticed but the exact nature of the problem (or opportunity) is vague. For example, lower earnings per share in the recent quarter or the knowledge of a new form of technology are often sufficient to sensitize decision makers.

2. **Identification**. In this stage, the focus of the decision-making situation becomes more clearly defined as the decision maker attempts determine the cause of the symptoms. For instance, managers try to discern why earnings per share have decreased or what specific opportunities the new technology provides.

3. **Specification**. In this stage, the decision maker develops a clear statement of the problem or opportunity. This statement should include:

    a. the *objectives* being pursued. The objectives are used to identify the criterion (or criteria) used to select among the alternatives.

    b. the *variables* that impact the decision. These generally include personnel, materials, time, money, demand, and so on.

    c. the *constraints* imposed by limited availability of some resources (e.g., $100,000 available for investment) and minimum standards imposed by other variables (e.g., fair-labor standards).

d. the *boundary* of the decision-making situation. The boundary must be defined so that issues relevant to the decision can be separated from those that are irrelevant or unimportant.

4. **Generation of Alternatives**. There is usually more than one way to achieve the objectives, given the variables, constraints, and boundary of the situation. The process of generating alternatives varies from one situation to another. Sometimes, alternative courses of action are obvious, in other cases alternatives can be identified through a systematic process, otherwise alternatives must be generated by brain storming or other creative process.

5. **Model Selection and Formulation**. Decision-support models are often used to facilitate the decision-making process, to maintain consistency from one decision to the next, and to permit objective analysis of hunches and intuition. There are a variety of characteristics in decision-making situations that influence the selection of a decision-support model. These characteristics include:

   a. *Data Inquiry* versus *Computational Modeling* — Data inquiry focuses on data retrieval and simple data analysis. For example, the answer to the question, "Should we order more units of raw material X?" could be answered by comparing the stock position of the item to its reorder point. Thus, the decision is made based on the value of the stock position and reorder point which are retrieved from a data file. On the other hand, the answer to the question "What is the best quantity in which to order raw material X?" is analyzed via a computational model (an inventory control model, see Unit 7) because the answer to the question requires a number of mathematical calculations.

   b. *Stochastic* versus *Deterministic* — In a stochastic decision-making situation, a variety of possible outcomes exist for each alternative (e.g., "If we manufacture product Y, will we sell 50, 100, or 200 units per month?") and the decision maker assigns probabilities to each of those outcomes occurring. In a deterministic situation there is no uncertainty regarding outcomes (e.g., "It will cost us $153 to build each unit of product Y."). Some models contain both stochastic and deterministic components. For example, while the cost parameters in a decision tree situation are assumed to be deterministic, the outcomes are normally stochastic.

   c. *Single Criterion* versus *Multi-criterion* — Most decision-making models are single criterion models. They attempt to minimize cost *or* maximize profit *or* maximize quality. Multi-criterion models are those that attempt to satisfy a number of objectives simultaneously such as minimizing cost *and* maximizing quality.

   d. *Generic* versus *Specific* — Generic decision support models can be used to analyze a wide variety of situations in all of the functional areas of a business. For example, linear programming can be used in finance and marketing just as easily as it can be used in operations management. Specific decision support models are designed and used to analyze fairly unique decision-making situations, such as inventory control, aggregate planning, cost accounting, and so on.

e. *Heuristic* versus *Optimizing* — For some problems, determining the best solution is either very difficult because of the nature of the problem or not possible given current technology. In such cases, heuristic decision support models are used. Heuristic models generally use a "rule of thumb" to produce an adequate solution. On occasion, a heuristic model may in fact produce the best possible (i.e., optimum) solution to a problem, but there is no guarantee that it will do so. The Weighted Factor Approach (see Unit 12) is a heuristic technique that allows the decision maker to consider both quantitative and qualitative criteria simultaneously in arriving at a decision. An optimizing model is one that produces the best possible solution under the stated conditions of a problem. Linear programming (see Unit 14) is an optimizing technique. Remember that the solutions provided by optimizing techniques under the simplified assumptions of the model seldom produce optimal results in the more complex "real world." The notion of optimum is a theoretical abstract.

Table 1-1 categorizes the models presented in this book according to the characteristics listed above. Where a model has elements of both characteristics in a given dichotomy, the application is categorized according to the predominant characteristic.

TABLE 1-1 Characteristics of Decision Support Models Developed in this Book

	Unit											
	3	4	5	6	7	8	9	10	11	12	13	14
Data Inquiry	x											
Computational Modeling		x	x	x	x	x	x	x	x	x	x	x
Stochastic								x	x			
Deterministic	x	x	x	x	x	x	x			x	x	x
Single Criterion		x	x	x	x	x	x	x			x	x
Multi-criterion	x								x	x		
Generic	x							x	x	x		x
Specific		x	x	x	x	x	x				x	
Heuristic	x	x		x					x	x		
Optimizing			x		x	x	x	x			x	x

Unit	Topic
3	Databases
4	Cost Allocations
5	Production Analysis
6	Aggregate Planning
7	Inventory Analysis
8	Demand Analysis
9	Breakeven Analysis
10	Decision Trees
11	Simulation
12	Weighted Factor Approach
13	Financial Analysis
14	Resource Allocation

5. **Data Collection.** Collecting data relevant to a particular decision can be a complex undertaking. Each of the application models presented in this book discusses "Gathering the Data" and suggests appropriate sources internal and external to the firm.

6. **Analysis.** The model and the data are then used to analyze the decision-making situation. Normally, the model is solved using the original set of parameters (costs, etc.) and the robustness of the recommendation provided by the model is then tested by evaluating its sensitivity relative to changes in the parameters. With linear programming models, this is called sensitivity analysis. With spreadsheet models, this is usually called what-if analysis.

7. **Decision.** The decision-support model is but one tool that the decision maker uses in choosing among alternative courses of action. Ultimately the decision maker chooses an alternative by combining the objectivity provided by the model with the intangibles — hunches, assumptions, intuition, managerial prerogative, horoscope, and so on — brought to the situation by the person or persons making the decision. Remember that we are developing decision *support* models, not decision *making* models.

8. **Implementation.** Many elegant, precise, and optimal solutions have no impact on the organization because they are poorly implemented, if at all. Once the decision has been made, it must be clearly communicated to those who are to carry it out, and progress toward implementation must be monitored.

9. **Feedback.** Decisions may fail to achieve the intended results because of factors overlooked in problem formulation or changes in the environment. Results must be monitored. Over the short term, results indicate the effectiveness of the decision-making process (e.g., was the right problem identified or the right model used?). Over the long term, results suggest when the decision-making process must be repeated (e.g., the initial solution no longer provides the desired effect).

DECISION SUPPORT APPLICATION MATRIX

Decision making occurs throughout the organization. For this book, we have developed a "generic" organization structure that includes the following functional staff areas:

Accounting and Finance
Economics and Long-Range Planning
Human Resources
Marketing and Logistics
Management Information Systems
Operations Planning and Control
Executive Officers

Each unit begins with a matrix that identifies which functional areas would be most likely to use the decision support application, and which areas would provide input or be impacted by the application. Some of the applications are rather broad, and could be used in all departments, while some are rather specialized and are of interest to only a few departments. We hope that the matrix helps you put a specific technique in the proper perspective within the overall operation of a business organization. The entire matrix is illustrated in Table 1-2.

TABLE 1-2 Decision Support Application Matrix

Unit/Topic	Accounting & Finance	Economics & Long-Range Planning	Human Resources	Marketing & Logistics	Management Information Systems	Operations Planning & Control	Executive Officers
3 Databases	¤	¤	¤	¤	■	¤	¤
4 Cost Allocations	■		¤			■	¤
5 Production Analysis	¤	■	¤	¤	¤	■	¤
6 Aggregate Planning	¤		¤	¤		■¤	¤
7 Inventory Analysis	¤			■¤		■¤	¤
8 Demand Analysis	¤	■¤		■¤		¤	¤
9 Breakeven Analysis	■		¤	■	¤	■	¤
10 Decision Trees	■¤	■¤	■¤	■¤	■¤	■¤	■¤
11 Simulation	■¤	■¤	■¤	■¤	■¤	■¤	■¤
12 Weighted Factor Approach	■¤	■¤	■¤	■¤	■¤	■¤	■¤
13 Financial Analysis	■		¤			■	¤
14 Resource Allocation	■¤	■¤	■¤	■¤	■¤	■¤	■¤

■ Departmental area(s) in which the technique is or can be used. In these departments, people develop methods and make decisions using this technique.

¤ Departmental area(s) that provide input to or are impacted by the technique. Although these departments are not normally responsible for developing and using the technique, they usually provide information and may be responsible for implementing the decisions.

EZRydr MOTOR COMPANY

The decision support applications developed in this book center around EZRydr MC (EZRydr Motor Company). Although the applications are general enough to be used in practically any organization, we feel that it is useful to provide one company situation as a unifying element. An in-depth knowledge of EZRydr or any other manufacturer is not important, but a general understanding of the problems faced by business persons is essential to the development of computer applications for decision support.

EZRydr MC was founded as the Easy Rider Company and later renamed Easy Rider Motor Company. Easy Rider was a family-owned bicycle company that began making motorcycles in World War II under contract to the Army. At the end of the war the company again turned to the consumer market, deciding to continue to manufacture motorized vehicles. The last non-motorized vehicle was produced ten years ago — now the only products of EZRydr are motorized vehicles.[2]

EZRydr occupies a solid niche as a US manufacturer of highway-class and heavy-duty off-road motorcycles. In recent years, EZRydr has ceased most fabrication operations, instead concentrating on assembling parts (such as motors, wheels, frames) produced by other organizations to EZRydr's specifications. The high quality of EZRydr's cycles is obtained by careful design and close liaison and inspection of suppliers' materials. Every machine is carefully tested by EZRydr personnel before it earns the right to the EZRydr logo.

[2] In fact, there is only *one* company in the United States that produces motorcycles: Harley-Davidson. We have avoided using any special knowledge we may have of Harley-Davidson in developing this book, and any similarity between EZRydr's decisions and specific practices of that company is unintended.

Even though most of EZRydr's business is for the consumer market, there are still some contracts with governmental agencies. The Army and Marines have tested and purchased a limited number of EZRydr's Buffalo Scout models for reconnaissance operations; and a number of metropolitan police forces use the Boss Hog model for freeway patrols. In most cases, the basic models are further customized for the purchasing agency. These government contracts tend to be less predictable and in smaller volume than consumer sales, but are more profitable.

EZRydr is still a family-owned firm, and is motivated by many of the managerial goals common to such firms. The management of EZRydr desires to stabilize employment to protect their workers, some of whom are descendants of the first employees of the firm. The firm has followed a no-layoff policy for most of its life, a "nice" policy but one which leads to excess capacity during late summer and early fall when demand for its products drops. Also, the firm is looking to expand its operations to become a larger company so it can employ more family and long-term employees in managerial positions.

As with most US businesses, EZRydr feels competition from both Europe and Asia as well as from within the country. To meet the challenge of Harley-Davidson, BMW, and Honda, among others, EZRydr has attempted to contain costs while continuing to maintain actual and perceived quality. The move to assembly was one step in that direction, and the adoption of other manufacturing techniques, such as a variation of just-in-time purchasing, is another. EZRydr's most recent move has been to acquire a number of personal computers for use by managerial and staff personnel to support decision making.

The hope of EZRydr management is that these computers will allow EZRydr management to apply modern management techniques from the fields of operations management, managerial economics, financial management, marketing, and human resource management to both ongoing operations and strategic planning. You have been hired by EZRydr to help the managers develop the computer applications that will make this hope a reality.

The topics in this book are divided into three phases in EZRydr's life. The first group of topics, in Part 2, deals with the current on-going operation of EZRydr's motorcycle production process. We first discuss how to organize data for decision support. Then we deal with methods of allocating costs, determining production levels, planning production targets, controlling inventory, the relationship between variable cost and level of production, and finally, the forecast of demand for products.

In Part 3, we introduce techniques for supporting the decision of whether or not to enter a new line of business — snowmobiles and all terrain vehicles (ATVs). We discuss profit planning for the product, a decision tree method for determining whether or not the product line should be expanded, and a simulation of the various outcomes of the product line expansion.

In Part 4, we assume that EZRydr has decided to expand the product line, and we discuss models useful as the company prepares to produce snowmobiles and ATVs. The weighted factor method is used to determine the best plant location, a model to help decide whether to purchase or replace existing equipment is discussed, and finally a model to help determine the allocation of resources to the product lines is developed.

DATA FOR THIS BOOK

All units in this book have data that have been estimated by the departments responsible for making decisions in each respective area. These estimates have served well in the past, and you may choose to use this estimated data as you design and develop the decision support applications. We have used these data in developing the examples in this book.

There is another source of data that is newly available to EZRydr's managers. This set of data is contained in a centralized database (maintained using the dBASE III software package). This data crosses departmental boundaries and, in many cases, is more current than the data available in any given department. The MIS department is responsible for managing the database, but much of the data is entered by the different functional departments.

The data in the database can replace some, but not all, of the data currently held in the department. For instance, you can inquire the database to determine productivity data that may be more accurate then the departmental estimates. On the other hand, some data is not available in this database, such as the number of working days per month. Furthermore, some of the information is based on goals established by managers (such as target inventory levels) or legal contracts (such as overtime pay rates).

As you work through the units, you will be presented with the estimated data and told how to inquire the database to obtain data from that source. Your instructor will tell you which set of data to utilize as you develop and use the decision support applications.

REVIEW QUESTIONS

Answers to the questions marked with an * (asterisk) can be found in Appendix D.

*1. Briefly state the general differences among EDP, MIS, and DSS.

2. Think of a professional sports or entertainment organization (e.g., football team, symphony orchestra, etc.). Suggest what EDP, MIS, and DSS needs the organization might have.

*3. What are the technological levels of a DSS?

4. List and describe the primary stages of the decision-making process.

*5. Outline the different types of decision-making models that are used in DSS, listing pairs of alternatives and how they differ.

ADDITIONAL READING

Keen, P. G. W., and M. S. Scott Morton. *Decision Support Systems, an Organizational Perspective.* Reading, MA: Addison-Wesley, 1978.

Sprague, R. H., Jr., "A Framework for the Development of Decision Support Systems." *MIS Quarterly*, 1980, **4**(4). This and several other excellent articles are reprinted in Sprague, R. H., Jr., and E. D. Carlson. *Building Effective Decision Support Systems.* Englewood Cliffs, NJ: Prentice-Hall, 1982.

UNIT

2 SOFTWARE FOR DECISION SUPPORT APPLICATIONS

This unit deals DSS generators, the software used to create decision support applications. A decision support application must contain three features: models, data, and communication. The most well-known and popular DSS generators are the spreadsheet packages, and these are used extensively in this book. Spreadsheets are used to build and perform the calculations required by many decision support application models. Occasionally they are also used for data storage and retrieval. In many cases, the data management aspect of decision support is handled by a database management system (DBMS). A well-designed decision support application will use a DBMS to retrieve current data to facilitate timely decision making. A decision support application must communicate with the user, for both input and output. Word processing and graphics software extend spreadsheet and DBMS capabilities to achieve this function. Several other types of software are used in one or more of the tasks of decision support.

LEARNING OBJECTIVES

At the completion of this unit you should know

a. the three components of a decision support system,

b. common and variable features of spreadsheet and related software packages,

c. features of database management software,

d. bases for choosing either spreadsheet or database software for a specific task,

e. how word processing, outlining, communications, quantitative analysis, graphics, and programming language software support the development of decision support applications.

Contributed by Adrienne S. Kim
and Steven C. Ross

THREE COMPONENTS OF A DECISION SUPPORT SYSTEM

As you develop the decision support applications in this book, remember that all applications are composed of three components: models, data, and user interface. In this book the emphasis is on the models, but we discuss both data and user interface issues as well.

Models

Models are mathematical representations of the system about which you are making decisions. A simple model is a cash flow statement: money comes in, money goes out, and a balance is maintained. The mathematics are simple — addition and subtraction — and the application is easy to develop. A more complex model is the economic production function, where total output is a function of the product of labor usage, capital expenditures, and other factors (see Unit 5). Determining the mathematical form of this function requires logarithmic transformations and multiple regression and the application takes longer to develop.

As you develop the applications in this book, you will find that the models discussed rely on a variety of disciplines: economics, accounting, statistics, and so on. Remember that every model has certain assumptions, and that an application based on a model is only as good as the fit between the model, its assumptions, and the "real-world" system that is being modeled.

Data

Data are the facts and figures that models manipulate. Elegant models with inaccurate data will provide no better solutions than simple models with inaccurate data. (This is the GIGO — garbage in, garbage out — principle.) In some cases, the needed data are managerial or staff estimates of future events (e.g., sales goals) and are readily entered into the application. In other cases, the relevant data are a long series of numbers (e.g., labor and capital utilization for the last 50 months) whose entry is rather tiresome. A third case is the situation where the database contains detailed numbers (e.g., a general ledger) and the model requires only summary data (e.g., total expenditures for vehicle maintenance). Managing the data and entering that data into the application is often the most tedious part of decision support. A good database management system (DBMS) and model can be designed to work with each other to extract the required information from the database and insert it into the model.

As you work with the applications in this book, you will see many types of data. We have developed a database for EZRydr that contains much of the data needed for the applications, and we provide several suggestions for how to incorporate DBMS technology into the decision support system.

User Interface

User interface is the most-neglected aspect of the decision support applications that we have seen in business organizations. The applications are normally developed by persons with substantial expertise in using the computer. When a less-experienced person attempts to use the application, he or she is usually lost without the guidance of the developer who knows which keys to push. Also, the jumble of numbers that a computer can produce may conceal the important results.

In this book we suggest many means by which the user interface of the applications can be improved, including menus, graphics, and windowed displays. As you work through the examples, put yourself in the place of a naive user, and ask "How do I know what to look at, and what to do next?"

THE ELECTRONIC SPREADSHEET

Lotus 1-2-3 and SuperCalc 4 are two of many popular electronic spreadsheets that have been the best selling type of applications software in the computer industry for the past few years. Because valuable time is saved by the use of a spreadsheet, it is a tremendously powerful software tool for any person who even occasionally works with numbers. Many computers have been sold for the sole purpose of spreadsheet analysis. Consider the following example of how a spreadsheet can save time, money, and preserve staff attitude:

> One of the critical tasks performed by every department in every organization is the preparation of a budget. You, the manager, have had your staff preparing facts and figures for a report in order to justify your budget request. As you proofread the thirty page report the morning of your meeting, you notice that transposed digits on page four have caused the final figure to understate the needs of your department. In order to correct this error, all figures related to the one in error must be recalculated. There are two likely scenarios to follow. The first is that you panic, rush to your secretary and demand that the report be retyped within the hour. To your dismay, your secretary replies, "Can I just white-out the mistakes and type over them?" Or perhaps your secretary used a word processor to prepare the report. Thus, instead of retyping thirty pages, only twenty six pages must be edited and all related budget figures recalculated. Not only is your staff's productive time wasted repeating work, there is no guarantee that another error will not occur during the rushed recalculations. In scenario two, you calmly sit down at your PC, recall the spreadsheet containing the budget model, and correct the error that you spotted on page four of your report. This correction causes the worksheet to automatically recalculate all related figures on subsequent pages. You print the report with enough time left to proofread it and go to lunch. Your time as a manager is valuable to both you and your company. The less time you spend reworking figures, the more time you have to analyze and interpret information. While the example just described may sound simplistic, the scenarios are very common occurrences in the business environment.

Because spreadsheets come equipped with built in functions that allow rapid design of application models for decision making, an electronic spreadsheet is considered a DSS Generator. A spreadsheet can total a column of numbers. Or the numbers can be graphed in order to look for patterns. Because the user defines the logic and calculations of the spreadsheet, business people have discovered that spreadsheets assist them with information control and answers.

All spreadsheets can handle mathematical computations, but spreadsheets vary in their relative power. Some spreadsheets are sophisticated enough to run regression analysis, calculate mathematical and financial statistics, sort data according to specified criteria, and graph data for dramatic emphasis of trends or changes. For example, to maintain a portfolio, you might like to know which investments have rates of return greater than 10%. Using spreadsheet features called database functions, investments that meet or exceed this criterion can be listed. Rates of return can be graphed to illustrate the success of these investments. Additionally, a spreadsheet that calculates financial statistics is especially useful to the business manager. Lotus 1-2-3 can calculate net present value, future value, and internal rate of return. A manager can easily ascertain the net present value of an investment under different depreciation schedules using these functions. The payment function is another useful feature that allows the calculation of payments on a loan given the principle amount, interest rate, and number of payments.

Another characteristic that differentiates levels of power between spreadsheets is one that allows you to specify the solution. Here, the spreadsheet calculates values of the variables so that they are consistent with the desired end result. This *goal seeking* feature gives the user power above and beyond basic numeric analysis because the user sets the bottom line result and then the computer determines the performance levels necessary to meet that end result. Goal seeking allows you to answer questions like, "How many units must be produced so that unit cost is $45.00?" or "What price should I charge so that my income is $40,000 in the first quarter and $90,000 in the second quarter?" Contrast these problems to the more usual spreadsheet problems like "What will my gross profit be if I sell 100,000 units at $40.00 each?" or "If my labor costs increase 10%, how much will my net income decrease?" Notice that usual problems are solved in a "top to bottom" fashion, while goal seeking type problems are solved in a "bottom to top" fashion.

Spreadsheets also vary in modeling style. For example, IFPS is a spreadsheet that is commonly used on a mainframe computer. Its style is similar to writing a BASIC program. IFPS allows you to define relationships using plain English in an arithmetic format. For example, "Sales = Cash + Credit" tells IFPS that there are three variables; cash, credit and sales. The sum of the variables, cash and credit, is equal to the variable sales. Once you specify the cash and credit values (the values can be formulas or fixed numbers), IFPS transforms the relationship into a columnar worksheet, repeating variable values and formulas across columns as often as necessary. In contrast, Lotus 1-2-3 uses an on-screen modeling style. The user is presented with a blank worksheet on the screen, and defines the value of each cell. The value of each cell can be numeric, text or a formula. Relationships between cells are established using the functions of the worksheet.

Electronic spreadsheets have both advantages and disadvantages. Any managerial problem that is primarily numeric can be quickly and easily solved using a spreadsheet. The ability to extract specific data from the spreadsheet based on selective criteria gives the manager control over relevant and irrelevant information. Finally, a spreadsheet with graphics capability allows the manager to communicate more effectively with persons who are not as fluent with numbers as with pictures.

The disadvantages of a spreadsheet become apparent when the particular application is not well suited to the spreadsheet environment. An application that involves filing data is not a good use of a spreadsheet. Selecting data based on criteria can be cumbersome if the spreadsheet is large (150 rows or more) or if the selection is based on several criteria. In addition, it is easy to create a large spreadsheet and find that your personal computer has reached its memory capacity. Even with expanded memory, you are likely to exceed memory capacity if the spreadsheet file is large.

In summary, electronic spreadsheets are powerful tools for managers and offer a variety of features that make data computations and analysis easy. Spreadsheets are not the be-all and end-all; they are merely one of the tools available to the developer of decision support applications.

DATABASE MANAGEMENT SYSTEMS

Many software packages provide a data-management feature. Word processors enable you to keep and update lists, and print-merging enhancements to these packages provide a report generation feature. All spreadsheets provide some amount of data management and several of the newest versions provide the capability to select data that meet a criterion. There are software packages called *file managers* and *list managers* that allow for input, change, and reporting of simple data sets. More powerful than all of these, however, are the programs called *database management systems* (DBMS). A DBMS allows the maintenance of data in multiple files and sophisticated entry, query, and reporting functions.

The most simple form of a database is a single file system, which could be implemented in several different ways. For example, you can automate your address book using a database or spreadsheet. In a spreadsheet, each record appears horizontally in a row of the spreadsheet, with one variable per column. In this case, variables would include last name, first name, address, city, state, zip code, phone number, birthday, and anniversary date. These 10 cells would probably extend past the length of your computer screen. In order to view your data, you would have to scroll the screen left and right. Using most database software, each record would appear individually on the screen, in a format that you have designed. For example, each address record could look like a three by five index card.

Customized display is only one advantage of a DBMS over a spreadsheet. The commands to list the names and addresses of all those who live in St. Louis are cumbersome in a spreadsheet environment because you must define the data area (all the address records), the criterion area (where city is St. Louis), and a range where you want the list to appear. Using a database, you would type a one-line command to receive the listing. An address file is an example of an application that is more appropriate for a database than it is for a spreadsheet because there is little computation involved, there are many records involved (you may have 500 friends), and the purpose of the application is to track and compare information as opposed to mathematically manipulate information.

Now imagine that the address book is really your customer base with 5,000 names. You sell various types of shoes and maintain two files with customer data. One file contains the customer's name, address, city, state, zip code, and some identifying code (perhaps telephone number, which is unique for a given family). In another file you keep purchase information, such as date of purchase, shoe size purchased, style number and manufacturer of the purchase, amount of purchase, and a code (again, telephone number) that links the purchase record to the name and address record. One of your manufacturers, SuzieShoes, is having a special promotion. The promotion is unique because the manufacturer will assume the cost of the promotional mailing, and has asked you to provide the names and addresses of customers you think will be interested in the promotion. The greater the percentage of customers that respond to the mailing, the greater will be your sales of SuzieShoes. Thus, you want to provide qualified prospects. You can provide this list easily by querying your database for customer name and address when the manufacturer name, SuzieShoes, appears in the purchase record (methods for accomplishing this are discussed in Unit 3). Such a report would be extremely difficult to accomplish if your customer data were maintained in a spreadsheet file, but is fairly easy when the data are maintained in a database managed by a DBMS.

A DBMS is more than an electronic filing system. Suppose further that you also maintain an order file to track manufacturer name, date of last shipment, style number, and quantity of each style received. In another file, style number, size and quantity in stock are maintained. The relational aspect of a database allows you to define a link between independent data files. In this case, a relationship between the customer purchase file and the manufacturer file based on manufacturer name could be established. In addition, a relationship between the manufacturer and the inventory file based on style number could be established. These relationships link all three data files and enable you to update files simultaneously. Thus, when you update the customer purchase file with a purchase of size 7 SuzieShoes sandals (style 100), the inventory file can be reduced by one pair of size 7 SuzieShoes (style 100) using the manufacturer file as the link.

Databases also provide some computational functions. For example, you could compute the total and average sales amount for all customers who had purchased SuzieShoes. Or you could count the number of customers who have bought SuzieShoes in order to determine how many brochures to order from the manufacturer. Some DBMS programs can also calculate natural logarithms, square roots, and exponential functions (which will not help you sell shoes, but do help you analyze a stock portfolio).

The most powerful aspect of a database is the relational database feature described previously. This feature gives the manager the power to handle many data files and a choice as to how to view the data. In addition, some databases allow the user to write command files or subroutines. Most decision support application models use command files so that the data entry person need not understand the details of software operations. Furthermore, the data file is protected from "unauthorized" changes when command files are used because the subroutine typically prompts the user for input. Thus, the program handles updating the appropriate records, avoiding inadvertent record changes.

The advantages of using a database include its ability to handle many records efficiently, its relational features, and command file creation. Since most decision support application models tend to be generated from a spreadsheet, the typical way to use a database is as a supporting source of information for the spreadsheet. Often the DSS application requires information that can be easily obtained through database manipulation. The biggest disadvantage of a database is that most people are intimidated by database software. Even the most straightforward database requires some use of special syntax, and most people do not want to learn another set of instructions.

SPREADSHEET, DBMS, OR BOTH?

The basic distinction between a spreadsheet and a database is that a spreadsheet gives the user power to handle extensive calculations while a database gives the user power to handle extensive filing needs. As you develop a decision support application, you will probably find that one consideration dominates the other, or that both are important but at different points in the usage of the application. The challenge is to match the software to the task.

Where the task is data management, a DBMS is the most common choice. A spreadsheet becomes too cumbersome with many records, while most databases are written specifically to handle large volumes of data. In contrast to a database, a spreadsheet has very limited relational features. With most popular spreadsheet programs, information on one spreadsheet cannot be linked to information on another to permit identifying, viewing, and updating of records related to one another.

Where the task is computation, spreadsheets are the major DSS generators. DBMS computations are generally limited to within-record tasks (e.g., net revenue for a year is gross revenue less returns for that year) or within-field (e.g., sum gross revenue for all years). Spreadsheets offer more sophisticated mathematical operations (e.g., multiple regression and computation of internal rates of return) and more flexibility in selecting data to be included in a given computation.

Where the task is display, the choice is less obvious. Display of data is often best handled by DBMS, but spreadsheets are usually used when the need is to emphasize differences or similarities pictorially. In some cases, graphics needs can be met by using a database to transfer the relevant information from the data file to a graphics software package.

Often, the application calls for data retrieval, computation, and display. If the retrieval, computation, and display tasks are simple, then either type of package is sufficient. If the tasks are fairly complex, then you may have to develop an application that transfers data from one type of software to another (see Appendix B of this book).

OTHER SUPPORTING SOFTWARE

In addition to the two primary DSS generators, there are other types of software that support DSS development. These assist in one or more of the DSS functions, as noted below.

Word Processing

Word processing software is a necessity for any business person. It is the means by which you communicate your decisions to others in a DSS environment. Besides the fact that documents can be easily created, revised, and printed using a word processor, valuable time can be saved because many documents are similar and can easily be modified. For example, you may send a weekly memo to your sales staff in order to provide feedback on the previous week's sales performance. Each memo is similar except that the performance statistics change. Using a word processor, all the secretary must do is change the date and the sales statistics as opposed to completely retyping the same memo every week. In addition, this data can usually be transferred directly from database or spreadsheet files, further reducing the difficulty of revising the memo. Furthermore, word processing software can include a spelling corrector and thesaurus, designed for people who hate to use a dictionary.

Beyond preparing written correspondence, word processing software has several other features valuable in the DSS environment. Because it is a powerful editor, a word processing package is often used to create command files (programs) for other types of software. Word processing can also be used for some data entry tasks. Recently-available word processing packages include some data-management and computation features, and some decision support applications could be written entirely in a word processor!

Outlining

Working closely with word processors are computer software packages that are designed to manage phrases, words, and sentences in an outline format. ThinkTank and Ready! are two examples of this type of software. These packages allow you to quickly record notes and ideas, and then rearrange them in a logical order. Moving a major topic to another place in the outline also moves all subtopics. Working in an outline format can be very efficient for large or complicated projects and presentations. For example, a department meeting to develop marketing objectives and goals for a new product line could record ideas as they are generated, add headlines and subordinate lines, and rearrange sections as necessary. At the conclusion of the meeting, a neatly typed copy of the plan can be provided to each person. They can refer to the outline during the week and fill in gaps so that the plan can be completed during the next meeting. An outline is a concise way to summarize discussion. It is also a valuable format to use when generating new ideas and plans. Because ideas can easily be erased, rearranged, and changed, employees and coworkers will be more likely to generate ideas since they do not need to be in final form.

Some outlining software packages reside in memory while you use your word processor or spreadsheet. Thus, ideas can be written using the outliner and used later after the word processing or spreadsheet session is finished. You can also transfer files to a word processor or spreadsheet. Outlining software is a DSS generator designed to facilitate creativity in developing new ideas and organizing projects.

Communications

Communications software enables a computer to communicate with other computers. In order to use your computer to communicate with others, you need three things: a communications software package, a modem or other transmission device, and a computer to call. Communications software manages the transfer of data between computers, allowing entire files to be transferred, and may also make your computer appear to be a certain type of terminal to the other computer (this feature is called *terminal emulation*). Computer communications can be tricky because of *communication protocols.* Because there are several combinations of speed (*baud rate*), data arrangement (*word size*, *start bits*, and *stop bits*), and error checking (*parity*), it is important that the software package be flexible and easy to set, and that you know what the other computer expects.

Communications software is valuable because it permits access to information sources that may be too costly to maintain in a department or company. For example, you may subscribe to *The Wall Street Journal* because it is not feasible for you to keep a department that monitors business activities across the nation. Similarly, you can subscribe to a computer service such as *CompuServe* or *Dow Jones News Retrieval* for up-to-the-minute stock market information and general business news. Computer communications also allow the transfer of data among distant offices. We have seen instances where "headquarters" develops a skeleton spreadsheet for the annual budget, telecommunicates that to all "branches" for them to fill in the details, and then receives the completed spreadsheets for consolidation into a master budget. With typical equipment, a large (100K) spreadsheet or database can be transmitted from one computer to another in less than fifteen minutes, while more modern high-speed modems can cut that time to less than three minutes. This is certainly faster, and usually costs less than express mail services.

Software for Quantitative Analysis

Quantitative analysis includes statistical analysis and linear, integer, and quadratic programming. While a few spreadsheets can run regression analysis, it may be better to use a statistical package that has more features to perform the regression analysis, and then transfer the coefficients into your spreadsheet model. As personal computers have become more popular, statistical software for PCs has become more powerful and less expensive. For example, statistics software packages offer summary statistics such as arithmetic, harmonic, and geometric means, as well as variance, standard deviation, skewness, and kurtosis. Time series analysis and graphics of the data such as histograms, scatterplots, and pie charts are also available. Finding the appropriate statistics package depends upon your specific needs. Software packages vary, not only in the types of statistical procedures available, but in ease of use, speed of calculations and the number of variables that can be processed. Statistical software offers support to your specific DSS application model. For example, forecasting demand for a specific product is an involved and sometimes overwhelming task. But once the data are collected, a statistics package can quickly turn this raw data into meaningful information. Using regression analysis and the diagnostic statistics, you can determine whether or not your demand model is acceptable. Assuming success, you can transfer the coefficients into your spreadsheet model and generate further demand estimations (see Unit 8).

As business becomes more sophisticated and resources become more limited, linear programming has become a popular allocation tool (see Unit 14). Some software packages like What's Best! and Vino work in conjunction with Lotus 1-2-3 to find the best solution based on the constraints you have specified. Thus, these software packages play all the what-if scenarios for you and record the best solution on your spreadsheet model. This type of quantitative analysis is invaluable to the manager with limited resources. As DSS generators, What's Best! and Vino optimize specific DSS application models. For example, once a demand estimation model is developed and used to develop an aggregate planning model, you may need to allocate resources to two plants. Each plant has different overhead and cost characteristics. Linear programming software allows you to develop a plan to meet the aggregate demand and minimize the total cost of production at both locations.

In addition to statistical and linear programming packages, quantitative analysis packages that help solve decision trees (see Unit 10) and create simulations (Unit 11) also exist. In this book, we have limited ourselves to spreadsheet and database software for the DSS generators, but you should become familiar with these other modeling packages as you develop more sophisticated systems.

Business Graphics

Graphics software allows you to display numeric and other data on the screen or on paper in graphic form. Many spreadsheet and some other software packages provide graphics in addition to their primary purpose, but dedicated graphics software is designed to give the user more flexibility and control to create professional graphics presentations. Many dedicated graphics software packages have an interface with spreadsheet, database, and other types of files, allowing you to input, retrieve, and analyze with one package and display with another. When developing a decision support application that will be viewed by upper managers and persons not familiar with numeric displays, consider employing a specialized graphics program for added effect.

Programming Languages

Each of the packages discussed above represents an attempt by a software manufacturer to provide the developer of decision support applications with an alternative to writing programs in one of the computer languages. Sometimes, however, it is easier to write a simple program using a language such as BASIC to accomplish your goal rather than try to force a canned software package to accomplish your goal. Additionally, some experience with a programming language can be helpful in creating your own DSS environment. For example, writing a command file in dBASE III is very similar to writing a BASIC program. Similarly, learning a spreadsheet like IFPS will be easier if you have knowledge of a programming language. In an environment with thousands of software packages readily available, it is easy to ignore programming languages like BASIC, FORTRAN, COBOL, or Pascal, but these languages are also DSS Generators and should not be forgotten.

There are new *fourth-generation* languages that will see even more use as DSS generators. The most readily available of these for PCs is called Prolog, a language that allow the processing of lists of data instead of the more-common numeric processing methods. Look for future growth in the use of this and similar programming languages in decision support applications.

REVIEW QUESTIONS

*1. What are the three components of a decision support system?

2. What common features do most spreadsheet and related software packages share? What features are found in some but not in all packages?

*3. What are the features of database management software?

4. State some simple criteria for choosing between spreadsheet and database software for a task.

*5. What other types of software are used as DSS generators? Give an example of how each may be used.

UNIT

3 DATABASES FOR DECISION SUPPORT APPLICATIONS

Information required for decision making is usually generated from data — records of facts relevant to the decision. The quality of information is judged by its accuracy, relevancy, and timeliness. To assure high-quality information for decision making at the data level, decision makers require that all the relevant data be available and accurate, and that retrieval and processing of data be conducted easily and in a timely manner. Decision support requires both high-quality data, the topic of this unit, and powerful analytic techniques, discussed in the later units of this book. Database systems can provide both the conceptual guidelines and the practical operations needed to improve the quality of data in a decision-making environment. A well-designed and organized database is therefore the foundation of successful decision support applications.

DECISION SUPPORT APPLICATION MATRIX

Accounting & Finance	Economics & Long-Range Planning	Human Resources	Marketing & Logistics	Management Information Systems	Operations Planning & Control	Executive Officers
¤	¤	¤	¤	■	¤	¤

■ Departmental area(s) in which the technique is or can be used.

¤ Departmental area(s) that provide input to or are impacted by the technique.

LEARNING OBJECTIVES

1. After completing this unit you should know

   a. the basic concepts about data, files, and databases,

   b. the basics of database design and implementation,

Contributed by Thomas S. C. Soon

c. how to maintain and manipulate data for a decision support task.

2. After completing this unit you should be able to

   a. design a database,

   b. define a database,

   c. maintain a database,

   d. manipulate data in a database.

INTRODUCTION TO DATABASE CONCEPTS

In this unit we discuss the fundamentals of designing and developing a database for decision-making applications. There are three general types of database architectures: network, hierarchical, and relational. Only the relational database is emphasized in this unit because it has a clear, simple, yet powerful structure and because its conceptual structure is implemented in most of the microcomputer database management software. This unit discusses three issues: first, how to determine what to store in the database; second, how to organize the data in a database; third, how to extract information from the database through database operations.

Issues of Database Design

The primary purpose of a database is to store records about facts in a decision-making environment. As a database designer, one must first determine what the important facts are, for both practical and economic reasons. We certainly could store everything that we can observe in the environment in the database. However, the cost of maintaining a huge amount of data can easily outweigh the benefit of making even perfect decisions. In practice, only the most relevant facts are stored in the database, and these are usually determined through careful analysis of the decision requirements for the decision support tasks. In this unit we demonstrate how system analysis techniques can be applied for that purpose.

The next issue faced by the database designer is how to organize the data in a database. The reason for organizing data in a database is the same as the reason for organizing data on documents in a file cabinet. Just imagine how chaotic it would be if facts were recorded randomly on documents, then saved without any order in a file cabinet. You could not find the data needed unless, theoretically, you had checked through an average of half of the data items in the entire file cabinet. Although a computer can search for a piece of data much faster than a human can, efficient retrieval of information still relies on well-structured organization of the data.

There are three levels of organization to consider in a file cabinet system:

1. Which data should be grouped on which document.

2. Which document should be placed in which file folder.

3. How the file folders should be arranged in the file cabinet.

Similarly, database design involves grouping individual data items into records, collecting records into files, and finally organizing files into a database.

In addition to facilitating the retrieval of information, a well-designed database provides two more important benefits:

1. Data redundancy is minimized; most data items are stored only once in the database.

2. Update anomalies are eliminated; most data items are inserted, deleted, or changed only once as the content of the database changes.

Both benefits are discussed later. We also examine how normalization theory can be applied to database design.

The third issue of database design concentrates on how to extract information from a database for decision-making purposes. Database users are usually provided with three powerful conceptual operations to retrieve information from the database: select, project, and join. In addition, database software typically provides other supportive features such as statistical summary and report formatting operations. We discuss how select, project, and join can be used for decision applications and for database maintenance purposes. In this unit, implementation of the design is illustrated in dBASE III. For more information about this microcomputer database management system, consult *Understanding and Using dBASE III* by S. C. Ross.

Basic Terminology

Data versus Information. *Data* are the factual records about the environment in which events, objects, ideas, and phenomena exist. *Information* is processed data that is valuable for decision making. The value of information is demonstrated by either reducing risks or increasing payoffs in executing the decision made. In a business organization, we collect data about people, transactions, and resources to provide management with a better picture of the state of the business. We process the data with analytic techniques to extract information to support a decision-making task. For example, we collect market survey data to understand market behavior, and we collect accounting records to provide a picture of business operations. By summarizing the market survey data, we obtain information to evaluate the effectiveness of several promotion alternatives; by processing the accounting records, we obtain information to formulate internal control schemes.

Attribute, Data Item, Record, and Field. An *attribute* is a single characteristic (e.g., color) of an object, event, idea, or phenomenon. There is no smaller piece of data than the value of an attribute, which is called a *data item* (e.g., "maroon" is the color of a particular object). We generally use a set of attributes to describe an object (e.g., color, motor size, frame size to describe motorcycles). A *record* refers to a particular object and is the collection of data items for that set of attributes. The attributes in a record are usually called *fields*.

Example. The sales department maintains a list of the dealerships for order-validation purposes. Each dealership is described by the following characteristics: dealership name, dealer ID number, location, credit limit, and outstanding balance. The location contains building number, street, city, state, and zip code. We may organize the characteristics in a data structure description as follows:

Data Structure	Data Item
DEALERSHIP RECORD	
DEALERSHIP NAME	Wild West Motorcycle
DEALER ID NUMBER	24002
LOCATION	
BUILDING NUMBER	375
STREET	Elm Street
CITY	Chicago
STATE	IL
ZIP CODE	61382
CREDIT LIMIT	$50,000.00
OUTSTANDING BALANCE	$0

Corresponding to the list, attributes are DEALERSHIP NAME, DEALER ID NUMBER, BUILDING NUMBER, STREET, CITY, STATE, ZIP CODE, CREDIT LIMIT, and OUTSTANDING BALANCE. Notice that LOCATION is the label of a group of attributes. It is not itself considered an attribute because it can be described by the items in an address. Only an attribute can have observed data. While LOCATION is a record in itself, here it is also part of a record. Thus a record can be a composite of several records. To display the components of a composite record, we list the attributes of a subordinate record as the second-level attributes. Such a list of attributes in several levels is called a *record structure*. In the above example, the record structure is presented as an attribute list organized in two levels. Record structure is sometimes called *data structure* by information professionals.

File and File Organization. A *file* is a collection of *homogeneous* records; that is, all records in a file contain data items for an identical set of attributes. Therefore a file is frequently a collection of records to describe many occurrences of the same event or many objects of the same type. A file can also be viewed as a two-dimensional table in which a record is a row in the table. The number of rows is the number of records in the file. The number of columns is the number of fields (attributes) in the file.

A file can be specified with the record structure. For example, the DEALERSHIP file is a collection of DEALERSHIP records — thus the file specification based on the record structure is

```
DEALERSHIP FILE
    DEALERSHIP RECORD*
        DEALERSHIP NAME
        DEALER ID NUMBER
        LOCATION
            BUILDING NUMBER
            STREET
            CITY
            STATE
            ZIP CODE
        CREDIT LIMIT
        OUTSTANDING BALANCE
```

Notice the * (asterisk) after DEALERSHIP RECORD. This symbol indicates replication. The file specification should be read as "The DEALERSHIP file specification is a replication of DEALERSHIP RECORD structures." The records in the file may look like the following:

Dealership Name	Dealer ID #	Building Number	Street	City	State	Zip Code	Credit Limit	Outstanding Balance
Wild West Motorcycle	24002	375	Elm Street	Chicago	IL	60601	50,000	0
Phaser Motorcycle	15764	10	5th Ave.	St. Paul	MN	55101	75,000	50,000

How the records are structured into a file and how they can be stored and retrieved in the computer storage devices is referred to as *file organization.* The physical arrangement of data on a storage device limits the way that data can be retrieved. Two basic file organizations are introduced here: sequential organization and random access organization. With *sequential organization* records are stored and accessed in the order in which they were entered in the database. To retrieve a target record, the computer must scan forward or backward from its current record position through all records until the target record is located. It is easy for the computer to retrieve the next or previous record in a sequential organization. In *random access organization*, records are stored randomly on a storage device. A record can be located directly if the record identification information, usually referred to as the *record address*, is provided to the computer. Using the record address, the computer can access the record directly. Random access is a more efficient way to retrieve a specific record. It is also more expensive, however, because it requires a more complicated storage structure, larger storage capacity, and larger computer operating system overhead. There are several other file organizations that are not discussed here because they are not usually supported by microcomputer systems.

There are two major types of storage devices for massive amounts of data in modern computer systems: *direct access storage* devices, such as hard and floppy disk drives; and *sequential access storage* devices, such as tape drives. Direct access storage devices can support both sequential and random access file organization. Sequential access storage devices can support only sequential file organization.

Key Attributes and Relations. The set of attributes whose values uniquely determine every single record in a file are called the *key attributes.* Key attributes allow users to retrieve specific records from a file. In order to retrieve these records, the user first needs to specify which records are desired. There are two ways to specify a record in a file: either by the order of the record, for example, the first record, the twelfth record, and so on; or by the content of the record, for example, the record whose value of attribute A is *xyz*. When the second method is used to specify a record, the record specification may not be unique; that is, there may be several records that satisfy the specification. In order to achieve a unique specification, we may need to combine specifications on two or more attributes; for example, the record whose value for attribute A is *xyz* and whose value for attribute B is *abc*, and so on.

It is important that the key attribute be determined by the database administrator (i.e., at the semantic level), instead of by the data itself (i.e., at the data level). Semantics is the study of the contextual meaning of language. *Semantic*, as used in database design, refers to the process of determining structure and symbols that capture, in a simple but meaningful fashion, the detail and the relationships in the environment represented by the database. The semantic level is more abstract than the data level, often relying on symbols or codes assigned by the database administrator rather than on common terms used by the general populace. The following example explains this concept further.

Example. In the dealership file, DEALER ID NUMBER is chosen as the key attribute for the file. The decision is made at the semantic level, because the organization assigns a unique DEALER ID NUMBER to each of the dealerships. It is not good practice to select the key attribute at the data level. That is, it would not be good practice to look through the file records, find that no two records have the same DEALERSHIP NAME, and then decide to use DEALERSHIP NAME as the key. Although it is unlikely that two dealerships would have the same name, such a possibility does exist. To avoid any possible confusion, it is much better to use the ID NUMBER as the key. In this way, the key is based on your decision rather than on a decision made by others (i.e., the dealer's chosen name for his or her company), and you are able to eliminate duplicates.

A *relation* is a file satisfying the following two restrictions:

1. There is no missing value for any key attribute in the relation.

2. The value of any field is data observed for a single attribute; no field may have a record or relation as its value.

The first condition is referred to as the *key integrity rule* and the second restriction is called the *atomic characteristic* of a relation.

Database and Database Management System. A *database* is a collection of files with minimum redundancy. Physically, it is an integrated and shared repository for stored data. Logically, the entire database can be viewed as a single file, or two conceptually related files, or many conceptually related files, as long as the users are able to use the data as necessary. The key point here is that the collection of data should be flexible enough to let the user define his or her own view of the data. In contrast to a file-processing system, in which each file is both a logically and a physically independent unit of data stored in a storage device, a file in a database system is a logically defined file meaningful to the user who defines it. Physically, a database file need not be stored as a distinct physical file; it may be stored in two or more independent physical units.

A *database management system* (DBMS) is a software package that allows users to define, access, and maintain data at the logical level without having knowledge about how and where the data are stored physically in the system. Usually a DBMS provides a set of high-level commands to let users interact with the database. The commands fall into two categories: data definition language and data manipulation language. Users may define the files with the data definition language and retrieve or summarize data with the data manipulation language.

DATABASE DESIGN AND IMPLEMENTATION CYCLE

In this unit we use the following four steps to introduce the database development cycle:

1. Specification of data in the database.

2. Refinement of the design.

3. Data definition and maintenance.

4. Data manipulation.

The reason we stress *cycle* is that a *perfect* database system or any *perfect* application software system (it is difficult, of course, to define what a *perfect* system is) is usually developed after repeated review and modification. Readers should therefore realize that a first pass through the development steps does not represent the end of database development. As a database designer, one should closely monitor system performance and users' reactions to the system and coordinate with users to improve the system.

Step 1: Specification of Data in the Database

The first step of database design is to specify the data in the database. The specification is usually expressed by a list of attributes about the facts relevant to a decision. In this section, we introduce an approach based on system analysis concepts.

Basic Terms. System analysis is a technique used to describe and design the data operations in a business organization. The analyses of each business unit or department are integrated to form the design of the entire business operation. It is sufficient to describe business data operations by the following components: source and destination of data, data flow, data store, and process.

Source and destination of data describes the unit that initially generates or ultimately receives data. For example, a customer places an order which is represented by some data in the system. The customer initiates the order; therefore the customer is considered the source of the data. As another example, a department manager receives a department performance report. The performance report contains data, and the department manager is the person who ultimately receives the data; therefore the department manager is represented as a destination of data in the system.

Data flow is used to describe the movement of data. The start of a data flow can be a data source, a process, or a data store. The end of a data flow can be a data destination, a process, or a data store.

A *data store* represents an accumulation of data in the system. It is necessary to store data under certain circumstances. After a customer places an order and before the order is actually shipped, for example, the order should be stored in the system. Such a deposit of data is called a data store.

A *process* is a functional unit (or operation) that transforms input data flow into output data flow. For example, the sales department receives a customer's order, checks the customer's credit standing and the inventory level, and then sends a shipping bill to the warehouse. In this short description, the order can be viewed as the input data flow, the shipping bill as the output data flow, and both the credit and inventory checking can be regarded as the process.

After the source and destination, data flows, data stores, and processes are identified in a system, a data flow diagram can be used to describe the system graphically. In a data flow diagram, sources and destinations of data are represented as rectangles, data flows as arrows, data stores as open-end boxes, and processes as circles. A data flow diagram of an order-processing operation is illustrated in Figure 3-1. Each of the components in the diagram is numbered for identification (note that each *type* of component has its own numbering scheme). Order validation is the process of verifying the information about the dealership on an order:

the quantity of each item ordered is confirmed; the credit standing of the dealership is verified; the order number is assigned; a copy of the approved order is filed in the pending order file; the approved orders are passed to the production department; and the unapproved orders are returned to the sales department for further investigation.

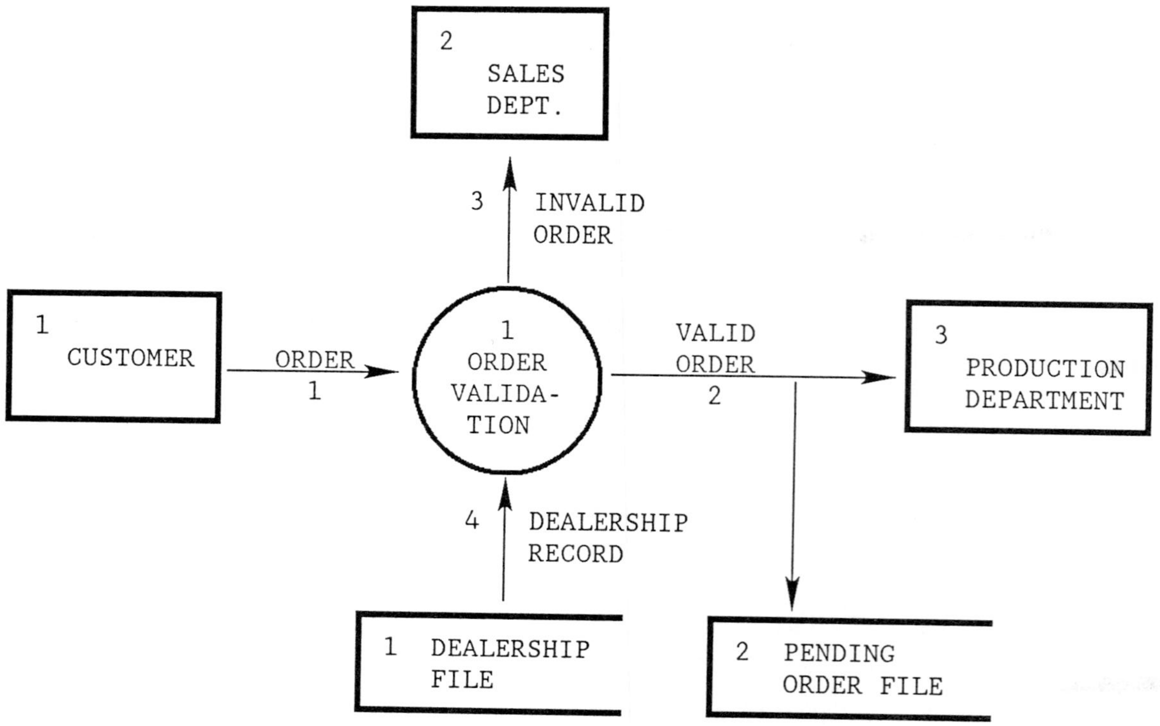

FIGURE 3-1 Data Flow Diagram of an Order-Processing Operation

A *data dictionary* is built to describe the contents of data flows and data stores by means of record and data structure specification. The following is a sample data dictionary for data flow number 1 — ORDER, and data store number 2 — PENDING ORDER.

DATA FLOW #1

```
ORDER
        ORDER DATE (the date when the order is received)
            DAY
            MONTH
            YEAR
        DEALERSHIP_NAME
        DEALERSHIP_ADDRESS
            BUILDING_NUMBER
            STREET
            CITY
            STATE
            ZIP_CODE
        ORDER_ITEM*
            MODEL_NUMBER
            QUANTITY
```

DATA STORE #2

```
PENDING_ORDER_FILE
        PENDING_ORDER_RECORD*
            ORDER_NUMBER (assigned by the process)
            ORDER_DATE
                DAY
                MONTH
                YEAR
            DEALERSHIP_NAME
            DEALERSHIP_ADDRESS
                BUILDING
                STREET
                CITY
                STATE
                ZIP_CODE
            ORDER_ITEM*
                MODEL_NUMBER
                QUANTITY
                SCHEDULED_DELIVERY_DATE (to be assigned)
                    DAY
                    MONTH
                    YEAR
                UNIT_PRICE (assigned by the process)
                ITEM_PRICE (assigned by the process)
            ORDER_TOTAL_PRICE (assigned by the process)
```

The record structure of the dealership file in the "File and File Organization" section of this unit (i.e., DEALERSHIP FILE) can be used in the data dictionary to describe the contents of data store DEALERSHIP FILE. Data flow VERIFIED ORDER has the same content as the data store PENDING ORDER. The data dictionary specifications for these items are omitted here.

Notice that the data dictionary provides an initial list of attributes for relevant facts involved in the operations. The most important component in the analysis is the data description of the data stores in the system. Each data store is a file in the database. In the order-processing operation, there are two data stores: DEALERSHIP FILE and PENDING ORDER FILE. The initial list of attributes in each of the data stores can be refined in the next step to derive the database design.

Step 2: Refinement of the Design

The purpose of design refinement is to eliminate the update anomalies of database operations. The database is a data repository for recording events in the environment. Because the environment is changing, constant modification of records is required to keep accurate descriptions of the environment. After a customer order has been validated, a new record is added to the data store PENDING ORDER FILE. When a shipping bill is assigned to an order, the corresponding record in the data store should be removed. If a customer calls in to change an order, the corresponding record should be adjusted. Because such updates are constantly performed on database files, some database designs suffer from *update anomalies*. To avoid the update anomaly problem in a design, we introduce *normalization theory*. The basic concept of normalization is to regroup the file attributes such that each file contains the simplest possible semantic form. The semantic form of a file is determined by the relationships among all attributes in a file. The most important types of relationships are *one-to-one*, *one-to-many*, *many-to-one*, and *many-to-many*. To determine the relationship between any two attributes, we must examine all possible values of the attributes. The collection of all possible values for an attribute is called a *domain*. The type of relationship between two attributes is classified according to the correspondence of the values in the respective domains.

One-to-one relationship: Customer ID number versus Customer Phone Number. Each customer has a unique ID number; no two customers (represented by customer ID numbers) have the same phone number. (As with all examples, we can think of exceptions to the rule; here we assume the "normal" case.)

Many-to-one relationship: Tenant versus Apartment Building. Each apartment building has a unique address. Several tenants live in one apartment building, but no tenant lives in two different apartment buildings.

One-to-many relationship: Automobile Serial Number versus Part Serial Number. Several parts, represented by the part serial numbers, make up the automobile, represented by the automobile serial number. A particular part cannot be installed in two automobiles. Thus one part serial number corresponds to an automobile serial number, but one automobile serial number corresponds to several part serial numbers.

Many-to-many relationship: Teacher versus Student. A teacher teaches many students and a student is taught by many teachers.

A simple method of determining the type of relationship is to select a value from the first domain, examine its corresponding relationship with each of the values in the second domain, and then do the opposite with a selected value from the second domain.

We describe the many-to-one and one-to-one relationships as *functional relationships.* If A has a one-to-one or many-to-one relationship with B, we say *B functionally depends on A*, or, *A functionally determines B*. We also call A the *functional determinant*, or *determinant* for short. If we know the value of A, we can determine the value of B; but knowing the value of B does not necessarily allow us to determine the value of A. We can graphically express a many-to-one functional relationship as A -> B, and a one-to-one relationship as A <-> B. In a one-to-one relationship, each item is the determinant of the other. (Knowing either phone number or customer ID allows us to determine the other item by searching in the file for the item we already know.) In a many-to-one relationship, knowing any of the "many" items allows us to determine the "one" item, but the converse is not true for a one-to-many relationship. (Knowing the part serial number, we can locate the automobile serial number in the file; but knowing the automobile serial number does not allow us to determine the part serial number in a file, we can only determine a set of part serial numbers which are contained in the automobile.)

Normalization Theory. The theory used to determine efficient file design is called *normalization theory.* This theory refers to several types of relations (normally, each relation is a separate file) in a hierarchy of *normal forms.* In this unit, we discuss only first, second, and third normal forms because these forms are sufficient for most decision support applications.

First normal form: A relation is in first normal form (1NF) if and only if every field has atomic value, that is, the value of any field is data observed for a single attribute and no field has a record or relation as its value. The value of each field is the value observed or assigned for the corresponding attribute.

Second normal form: A relation is in second normal form (2NF) if it satisfies two conditions: first, it is in first normal form; second, every non-key attribute is fully functionally dependent on the primary key, as we explain below.

There may be many attributes that qualify as key attributes. Because only one key attribute is required for unique record identification, the term *primary key* refers to the attribute selected from among all those that qualify. Once the primary key is determined, every attribute not part of the primary key is a *non-key attribute.*

The following example shows why a relation in the second normal form is simpler in its semantic structure than a relation in the first normal form, and illustrates how a second normal form relation suffers fewer update anomalies. More importantly, the example demonstrates that a first normal form file can always be decomposed into files in the second normal form. We begin the example with a description of a portion of the operations performed in the EZRydr production division. For better production control, records are needed to track the manufacturing activities.

In an EZRydr factory, there are storage areas for basic parts and for major components, several work centers, and assembly lines. The storage areas are monitored by the inventory control department. Each of the assembly lines has several workers and is supervised by a foreman. Several inspectors are assigned to the assembly lines according to the type of major components assembled. Each of the inspectors is assigned to inspect only one type of major component; an inspector who inspects engine assemblies does not also inspect brake assemblies.

The basic parts are placed in storage bins. Each of the storage bins has a unique bin number. A storage bin log is attached to the bin to record the current part contents. When needed, the bin is moved to the assembly line, where the required parts are removed. On receiving the storage bin, the assembly line foreman records the storage bin number and receiving time on the assembly line log, and then he registers his foreman ID, the part ID number, and the quantity of parts removed from the bin in the bin log. When the used storage bin is returned to the inventory control department, the contents of the bin are checked by the inventory control personnel. An updated bin log is attached before the bin is returned to the storage area. Once a major component is completed on an assembly line, a completion label with a component name and serial number is attached to the finished component. The foreman records the assembly line ID, foreman ID and completion time on the label. An inspector inspects the component and writes the inspector ID and inspection results on the same label. The finished major component is then transferred to the component inventory area and placed at a proper location for final product assembly.

From the above description, we can identify many file attributes to support the operations. To manage the storage bins and their contents, for example, we need the storage bin number, bin contents, and bin locations. Suppose that the specification for storage bins in the data dictionary is as follows:

```
STORAGE_BIN_FILE
    STORAGE_BINS* (the file is a repetition of storage bin records)
        BIN_NUMBER (unique for each bin)
        BIN_LOCATION (location is specified by an aisle, side, and level)
            AISLE_NUMBER
            SIDE
            LEVEL_NUMBER
        BIN_CONTENTS
            PARTS* (repetition of parts in a bin)
                PART_ID (unique for each part)
                NAME (part name, may not be unique)
                UNIT_COST (unit cost of the part)
                QUANTITY (quantity of the part in the bin)
```

Do not confuse the logical specification of the storage bin with the bin log. The bin log is a form that serves as a message carrier for operational purposes. The data dictionary of the storage bin is a logical specification to describe the entity *storage bin* in the information system.

Some facts about EZRydr's storage bins:

- Bin number 1 is stored in aisle 4 on the north side at level 3; it contains 100 units of part 1001001, 30 units of part 1001002, and 10 units of part 2001001.

- Bin number 2 is stored in aisle 3 on the south side at level 5; it contains 50 units of part 3001001 and 15 units of part 3001002.

- Bin number 3 is stored in aisle 3 on the south side at level 4; it contains 30 units of part 3001001.

- Part 1001001 is 1/4" pipe.

- Part 1001002 is 3/8" pipe.
- Part 2001001 is 1/4" T-joint.
- Part 3001001 is Model A front brake disk.
- Part 3001002 is Model B front brake disk.

The data in the file, before it has been normalized, are

BIN_NUMBER	AISLE	SIDE	LEVEL	PART_ID	NAME	QUANTITY	U_COST
1	4	N	3	1001001	1/4 PIPE	100	12.00
				1001002	3/8 PIPE	30	16.50
				2001001	1/4 T JOINT	10	8.50
2	3	S	5	3001001	BRAKE DISK A	50	85.00
				3001002	BRAKE DISK B	15	65.25
3	3	S	4	3001001	BRAKE DISK A	30	85.00

The key of the file is the combination of BIN_NUMBER and PART_ID. There are missing values in the key field. Thus the above file is not in first normal form. To normalize the file, we need to eliminate the missing values by repeating the data in the missing columns. Thus we have the following normalized file (in 1NF):

BIN_NUMBER	AISLE	SIDE	LEVEL	PART_ID	NAME	QUANTITY	U_COST
1	4	N	3	1001001	1/4 PIPE	100	12.00
1	4	N	3	1001002	3/8 PIPE	30	16.50
1	4	N	3	2001001	1/4 T JOINT	10	8.50
2	3	S	5	3001001	BRAKE DISK A	50	85.00
2	3	S	5	3001002	BRAKE DISK B	15	65.25
3	3	S	4	3001001	BRAKE DISK A	30	85.00

The data dictionary of the normalized file can be rewritten as follows (notice that the repeating group PARTS is no longer a part of the record):

STORAGE_BINS_FILE
    PARTS_IN_STORAGE_BINS*
        BIN_NUMBER and PART_ID *(unique for each part in bin)*
            AISLE_NUMBER
            SIDE
            LEVEL_NUMBER
            NAME
            UNIT_COST
            QUANTITY

The above file contains redundant data; for example, every time part 3001001 is placed into a bin, the part name and part cost are duplicated, even though they have been recorded in the file already. If an empty bin is stored in a location, it cannot be recorded in the file without violating the key integrity rule. This is an *insertion anomaly*. If the above file is the only place where the data of part number, part name, and part cost are stored, then when all of the parts in a bin are removed we lose all of the information about those parts. To record the event of removing all the parts from bin 1, for example, the first three records are deleted from the file. As a result of the deletion, we lose the information about part 1001001, part 1001002 and part 2001001 forever. This is a *deletion anomaly.* Now, if bin 1 is moved to a new location, say aisle 6, south side, and level 2, then the aisle, side, and level must be updated to the new values for the first three records in the file. If the person who revises the data to reflect the new location misses any one of the nine data items, then data inconsistency occurs. This is a *revision anomaly.*

To eliminate these problems, we may convert the above 1NF file into second normal form files. First let us make sure the file is not already in 2NF. We know that the BIN_LOCATION is fully functionally dependent on the BIN itself. PART_NAME and PART_UNIT_COST depend on the PART_ID only. But QUANTITY is the *only* attribute that fully functionally depends on the combined key, and thus the file is not in 2NF. Figure 3-2 is the functional dependency diagram of the attributes in the 1NF file.

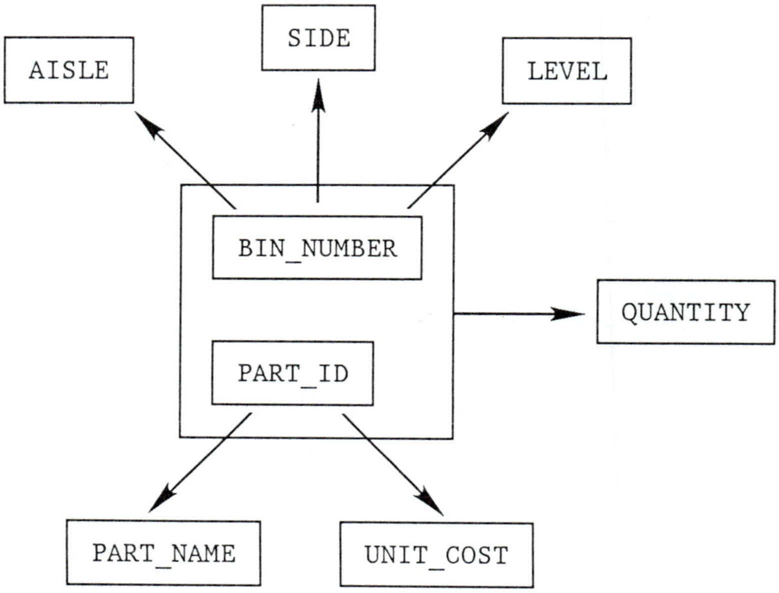

FIGURE 3-2 Functional Dependency Diagram of the 1NF File

If we group the attributes with their common determinants, we have the following new groups:

(BIN_NUMBER, PART_ID, QUANTITY)
(BIN_NUMBER, AISLE_NUMBER, SIDE, LEVEL_NUMBER)
(PART_ID, NAME, UNIT_COST)

Each group of attributes should be a file. The keys of the files are BIN_NUMBER and PART_ID for the first file, BIN_NUMBER for the second file, and PART_ID for the third file. In each file, every non-key attribute is fully functionally dependent on the primary key. Therefore all of the files are in 2NF.

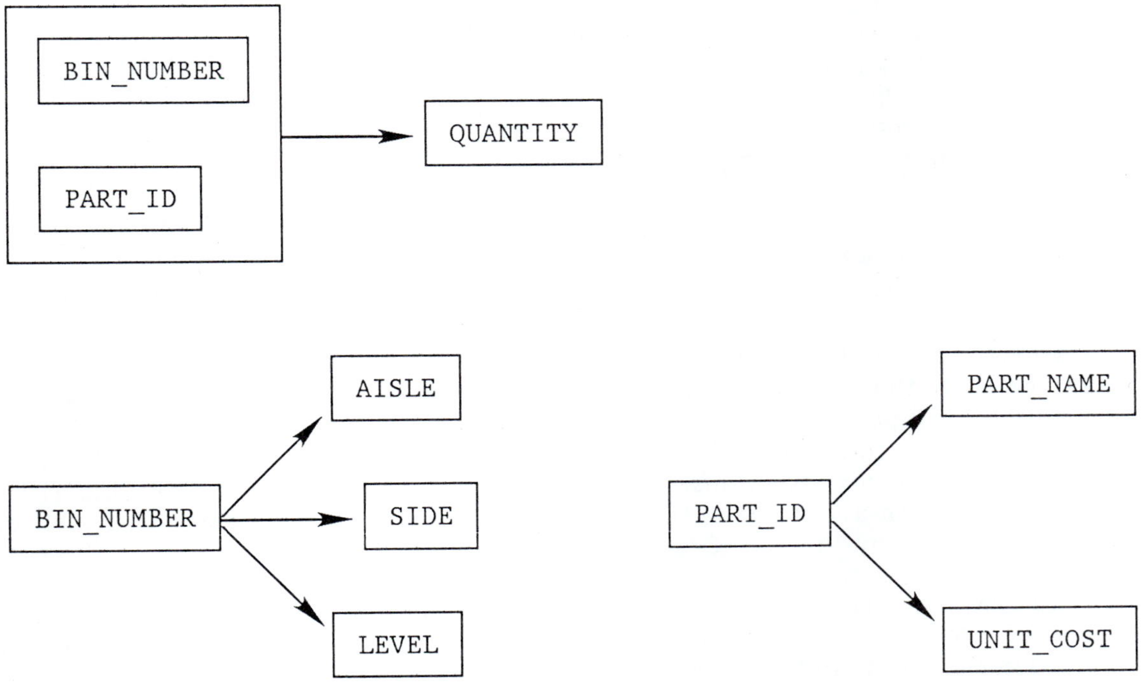

FIGURE 3-3 Functional Dependency Diagram of 2NF Files

Figure 3-3 contains the functional dependency diagrams of the 2NF files. Compare the functional dependency diagrams of the 1NF file and the 2NF files. Notice that in each of the 2NF files there exists a functional relationship only between the key and each of the non-key attributes. On the other hand, in the 1NF file, there are functional relationships between key and non-key attributes and functional relationships between two non-key attributes. Therefore, the semantic form in the 1NF file is more complicated than that in the 2NF files. According to the new file specification, data can be rearranged as follows to record the same set of facts:

BIN_NUMBER	PART_ID	QUANTITY
1	1001001	100
1	1001002	30
1	2001001	10
2	3001001	50
2	3001002	15
3	3001001	30

BIN_NUMBER	AISLE	SIDE	LEVEL
1	4	N	3
2	3	S	5
3	3	S	4

PART_ID	NAME	UNIT_COST
1001001	1/4 PIPE	12.00
1001002	3/8 PIPE	16.50
2001001	1/4 T JOINT	8.50
3001001	BRAKE DISK A	85.00
3001002	BRAKE DISK B	65.25

Now let us compare these two file specifications. Both specifications can record the same set of facts. But in the new specification, data redundancy is eliminated in each of the files — there are no duplicated data items even though we do have more files. If we have an empty bin stored in a location, this fact can be recorded directly in the second file without violating the key integrity rule; that is, no insertion anomaly exists. If a bin is moved into a new location, it needs to be updated in only one place, the second file. Therefore the chance of having data inconsistency (i.e., the revision anomaly) is significantly reduced. If the contents of a bin are completely removed, we just delete the corresponding records from the first file. We do not lose information about parts, thus the deletion anomaly can be avoided. All of the update anomalies suffered by the 1NF file have been eliminated.

Third normal form: A relation is in third normal form (3NF) if it is in second normal form and every non-key attribute is not transitively functionally dependent on the primary key. If A functionally determines B, and B functionally determines C, we say that A *transitively functionally* determines C, or that C is transitively functionally dependent on A.

The third normal form was developed to reduce the anomalies from which the second normal form suffers. As expected, a file in second normal form can always be decomposed into files in the third normal form. The process of converting a file into a higher normal form (e.g., from 1NF to 2NF, 2NF to 3NF, and so on) is called *normalization.*

The difference between 2NF and 3NF files is that a 2NF file allows transitive dependency whereas a 3NF file does not. The following example is used to explain the difference. EZRydr's sales department classifies the distribution areas into four main sales regions (REGION): East, Midwest, West, and South. Every region has a unique regional sales manager (R_MANAGER). States (STATE) are assigned to regions. In each state, there are several distribution centers, each identified by the ID number of the distribution center (DIST_ID). Each of the distribution centers has a manager (D_MANAGER). However, several distribution centers may be managed by the same manager. Let us group attributes R_MANAGER, D_MANAGER, REGION, STATE, and DIST_ID into a single file and examine whether the file is in 2NF. The relationships among attributes can be described in the following diagram:

DIST_ID -> STATE -> REGION <-> R_MANAGER
DIST_ID -> D_MANAGER

Notice that the key attribute in the file is DIST_ID, and every non-key attribute is fully functionally dependent on the key. For example, the relationship between DIST_ID and R_MANAGER is DIST_ID -> R_MANAGER. Because every distribution center is classified into a region and every region has a regional manager, there is a many-to-one relationship between DIST_ID and R_MANAGER. Other relationships between a non-key attribute and the DIST_ID follow. Notice that there exist several transitive dependencies among the attributes, for example, DIST_ID and REGION via STATE, STATE and R_MANAGER via REGION, DIST_ID and R_MANAGER via STATE and REGION. Data in the file may look like the following:

DIST_ID	D_MANAGER	STATE	REGION	R_MANAGER
W964131	SALLY PARK	WA	W	SAM OAKLAND
W936101	BOB DOLES	CA	W	SAM OAKLAND
W901101	BOB DOLES	CA	W	SAM OAKLAND
M548192	STEVE BATES	WI	M	JOE PHILPS
M613001	JACK SMITH	IL	M	JOE PHILPS
E201101	DAVID HEAPS	NY	E	LARRY COOKS
S791001	ED SHOULER	OK	S	ALAN ROBERSON

EZRydr is considering expanding into Oregon. Although a distribution center has not yet been established, Oregon is classified into the West region under the supervision of regional manager Sam Oakland. The fact that Oregon belongs to the West region under the supervision of Sam Oakland cannot be inserted into the file because there is no distribution center in Oregon. This is an insertion anomaly. (What would be wrong if we put data into incomplete records and forced those records into the file?) Southern states are not a stronghold of EZRydr and the only distribution center in the southern states is in Oklahoma. For financial and geographic reasons, the distribution center is being closed and new distribution centers will be opened in Texas. As a result, the last record should be deleted from the file. However, the deletion of this record will remove more facts than just the closing of distribution center S791001 in Oklahoma. The information about the regional manager will be deleted, too. This is certainly an undesirable loss of information, but it will occur if the deleted record is the only place recording the fact that Alan Roberson is the regional manager. This illustrates the deletion anomaly. Besides the anomalies mentioned above, you may find redundant data that could cause a revision anomaly; for example, Sam Oakland and Joe Philps appear several times as regional managers. Therefore, if a new regional manager is assigned to a region, R_MANAGER must be revised at every occurrence of the region, and the chances of having a revision anomaly are increased.

A solution is to regroup the attributes according to the 3NF definition. New groups are suggested as follows:

(DIST_ID, D_MANAGER, STATE)
(STATE, REGION)
(REGION, R_MANAGER)

Reorganizing data, we have the following data files:

DIST_ID	D_MANAGER	STATE
W964131	SALLY PARK	CA
W936101	BOB DOLES	CA
W901101	BOB DOLES	CA
M548192	STEVE BATES	WI
M613001	JACK SMITH	IL
E201101	DAVID HEAPS	NY
S791001	ED SHOULER	OK

STATE	REGION
WA	W
CA	W
WI	M
IL	M
NY	E
OK	S

REGION	R_MANAGER
W	SAM OAKLAND
M	JOE PHILPS
E	LARRY COOKS
S	ALAN ROBERSON

Identify the key in each of the files. Are the files are in 3NF? Have the update anomalies been alleviated?

Observe from these examples that we may always decompose the low normal form file into higher normal form files. Notice that the final third normal form files contain the same information as the first normal form file. This shows that decomposition does not eliminate any information from the file. It simply restructures the files such that certain update anomalies can be avoided. Actually, we benefit from normalization: data redundancy in the third normal form files is less than in the first normal form file. The conclusion is that files which suffer fewer update anomalies are always simpler in their relationship structure among attributes. Yet a logical question remains unanswered: Are the third normal form files free from update anomalies? Unfortunately, the answer is no; however, the third normal form is sufficient for most decision support application databases and we will not discuss stronger normal forms in this book.

Heuristic Normalization Rules. The following set of rules can be used to group attributes into 3NF files. By *heuristic*, we mean that these rules do not guarantee to produce files that are free of update anomalies in all cases. In most situations, however, they do provide satisfactory results.

1. Identify *all* functional relationships in a given application situation.

2. Identify the set of attributes whose functional relationships form a closed loop regardless of the direction. For examples, A -> B, B -> C, and C -> A, or X -> Y, X -> Z, and Y -> Z, are two sets of attributes which form closed loops.

3. Break the loop by removing the redundant relationships. If the loop is circular, you may remove any relationship to break the loop. You can test for circular loops by starting from any attribute in the loop and moving according to the direction of the functional relationship to the next attribute. If eventually you come back to the initial attribute, then the loop is circular; otherwise the loop is not circular. For example, A -> B, B -> C, and C -> A form a loop. Starting from B and moving along the direction of the functional relationships, we come to C, and then to A, and then to B again. Thus the loop is circular. In a circular loop there is one and only one redundant relationship. This relationship can be any relationship in the loop. Usually we delete the relationship whose attributes have the fewest relationships with the attributes not in the loop. In the case that the loop is not circular, the redundant relationships are the implied relationships. For example, A -> B and B -> C implies A -> C. Thus A -> C can be removed.

4. Collect the attributes with their immediate determinants to form a group. Therefore, in each of the groups, there is only one determinant and its dependents. Such groups represent files in 3NF, with the determinant as the key attribute. After grouping all dependents with their determinants, you may find attributes which do not belong to any group. Each of these attributes is a separate group by itself.

Further references are provided at the end of this unit for more information, such as how to determine the redundant relationships in a large set of attributes and relationships. In practice, normalization to higher than the third normal form is seldom necessary, but users should be aware of the nature of the problems.

Step 3: Data Definition and Maintenance

Once we have developed a normalized design, each database file can be described by the key specification and the list of attributes. The following is a refined design of the two previous examples:

```
BIN(BIN_NUMBER, PART_ID, QUANTITY)
LOCATION(BIN_NUMBER, AISLE_NUMBER, SIDE, LEVEL_NUMBER)
PART(PART_ID, NAME, UNIT_COST)

DIST_CENTER(DIST_ID, D_MANAGER, STATE)
REGION(STATE, REGION)
R_MANAGER(REGION, R_MANAGER)
```

Each of the relations is given a name for identification purposes. The key attribute in each relation is underlined.

Specifying the file description for a database is usually referred to as *data definition*. This can be done through the data definition commands provided by the DBMS. In dBASE III, the command to define a database file is **CREATE {database file name}**. Besides the database file name and field names, we also need to specify the data type and field width to complete the database file definition. Note that dBASE III does not require explicit key specification. An implicit key for any dBASE III database file is the record number. Once the file has been created, it is opened for subsequent operations by the command **USE {database file name}**.

Another feature of dBASE III allows users to index a database file. Indexing is a procedure for establishing direct access capability based on the value of the index key, which may be composed of one or more fields. Searching for a record according to the value in an indexed field takes less time than searching based on an unindexed field. If a database file is not indexed, searching is conducted sequentially.

dBASE III permits modification of the database file definition through **MODIFY STRUCTURE {database file name}**. Users may delete a field, insert a new field, and change the field name and field width in an existing database file. Before using these operations, however, you should test the operations thoroughly. For example, dBASE III truncates the data in a field if the field width is changed to a smaller number. Without a clear understanding of the consequences, users may lose data unexpectedly by performing these operations.

dBASE III supports three data input methods: interactive data input (e.g., **EDIT, BROWSE, CHANGE**, and **APPEND**); input from an ASCII file (e.g., **APPEND FROM, IMPORT** [dBASE III Plus only]); and input controlled by command files. dBASE III command files provide flexible facilities to customize input/output procedures. This capability is particularly important for processing a transaction involving multiple database files.

The database file structure in dBASE III (obtained with the **DISPLAY STRUCTURE** command) is sufficient for internal operations but not complete enough to describe all of the data definition details. We strongly recommend that users establish a database file to store all of the data dictionary details for each of the database files defined in the system. dBASE III allows a memo data type to store a long text field to support such an application. Good database system documentation, including a data dictionary, is an essential component of a successful database system.

Step 4: Data Manipulation

The relational database approach suggests three basic operations for data retrieval: select, project, and join. These operations are performed on the records satisfying a record-specification expression. A *record-specification expression* is a logical specification that allows users to indicate criteria by which to select the records to be retrieved.

Both select and project operate on a single database file. *Select* retrieves specified records from a database file, operating as a row-retrieval operation; for instance, you could select (create a list of) all dealers in the state of California. *Project* picks up the specified fields from a database file, acting as a column-retrieval operation; for instance, you could project a list of dealership names. Combining these two operations, the user can retrieve any particular set of data in the file, for instance, the dealership names of all dealerships in California. *Join* operates on two database files, and it serves the purpose of combining the information stored in two separate files. Besides these three basic operations, a stand-alone database management system such as dBASE III also provides many supportive commands, such as commands for statistical functions, sorting, and report generating to aid users in summarizing, organizing, and presenting information in the database.

Record Specification Expression. The format of the simplest record-specification expression is

{attribute name} {comparison operator} {constant value}

The attribute (usually a field name or expression) must exist in the file that is being manipulated. The constant value can be a numeric value or a character value, and it should be consistent with the value type of the attribute. The comparison operator can be one of the following:

=	*Equal to.*
>	*Greater than.*
<	*Less than.*
>=	*Greater than or equal to.*
<=	*Less than or equal to.*
<>	*Not equal to.*

Examples of simple record specification expressions:

```
C_LIMIT > 10000
BALANCE <= 2000
NAME = 'Wild West Motorcycle'
```

The simple record specification expression can be combined by parentheses and logical operators such as **.NOT.**, **.AND.**, and **.OR.**. Examples of combined record specification expressions:

```
.NOT. C_LIMIT < 10000
C_LIMIT < 10000 .AND. BALANCE > 5000
STATE <> 'WI' .OR. .NOT. ( C_LIMIT < 10000 .AND. BALANCE > 20000)
```

Relational Database Operations. We will illustrate these operations using the following sample database:

DIST_CENTER FILE: (dBASE III file name: DISTCNTR)

DIST_ID	D_MANAGER	STATE
W964131	SALLY PARK	CA
W936101	BOB DOLES	CA
W901101	BOB DOLES	CA
M548192	STEVE BATES	WI
M613001	JACK SMITH	IL
E201101	DAVID HEAPS	NY
S791001	ED SHOULER	OK

REGION FILE: (dBASE III file name: REGION)

STATE	REGION
WA	W
CA	W
WI	M
IL	M
NY	E
OK	S

RMANAGER FILE: (dBASE III file name: RMANAGER)

REGION	R_MANAGER
W	SAM OAKLAND
M	JOE PHILPS
E	LARRY COOKS
S	ALAN ROBERSON

For the following examples, we provide both generic database management commands and commands specific to dBASE III. If you are using a different DBMS, the combination of the two should provide sufficient information for determining the necessary commands.

Operation: Select

Generic Format: SELECT WITH {record-specification expression}
FROM {file name}
TO {resultant file name} *(This is optional.)*

Purpose: To create a file that contains records satisfying the record-specification expression from the specified file.

Example: SELECT WITH STATE = 'CA'
FROM DIST_CENTER, STATE

Result:

DIST_ID	D_MANAGER	STATE
W964131	SALLY PARK	CA
W936101	BOB DOLES	CA
W901101	BOB DOLES	CA

dBASE III Implementation:

USE DISTCNTR
LIST FOR STATE = 'CA'
or
DISPLAY FOR STATE = 'CA'
or
COPY TO DISTATE FOR STATE = 'CA'

Operation: Project

Generic Format: PROJECT ON {attribute list}
FROM {file name}
TO {resultant file name} *(This is optional.)*

Purpose: To create a file containing the columns whose corresponding attributes are in the list from the specified file.

Example:

```
PROJECT ON D_MANAGER
FROM DISTCNTR
```

Result:

D_MANAGER	STATE
SALLY PARK	CA
BOB DOLES	CA
BOB DOLES	CA
STEVE BATES	WI
JACK SMITH	IL
DAVID HEAPS	NY
ED SHOULER	OK

dBASE III Implementation:

```
USE DISTCNTR
LIST DMANAGER,STATE
   or
DISPLAY ALL DMANAGER,STATE
   or
COPY TO MGRSTATE FIELDS DMANAGER,STATE
```

The purpose of select is to retrieve data horizontally from a database file, and the purpose of project is to retrieve data vertically from a database file. Combining these two operations, one can retrieve any single piece of data in a database file. Thus these two operations are logically sufficient for retrieval of data from a single database file. In dBASE III, these two operations are implemented as one command — **LIST**, **DISPLAY**, **COPY**, and a few others. Users should be aware of the delicate difference between the conceptual operations and the dBASE III commands. To retrieve the manager's name of distribution center M548192, for example, we give the following dBASE III commands:

```
USE DISTCNTR
LIST DMANAGER FOR DIST_ID = 'M548192'
```

This command sequence is equivalent to the generic commands which select the record which matches the specific distribution center:

```
SELECT WITH DIST_ID = 'M548192'
FROM DIST_CENTER
TO RESULT
```

Followed by a project of the specific field:

```
PROJECT ON D_MANAGER
FROM RESULT
```

We have discussed normalization and the heuristic rules as a technique to find the simplest semantics in each of the normalized files. Sometimes, however, we encounter questions whose answers involve data in two different database files. If we wish to know the regional manager of Bob Doles, for example, there is no single file in the database which directly provides the answer. However, from the DIST_CENTER file, we may find that Bob Doles manages a distribution center in CA; from the REGION file, we know CA belongs to region W; and from RMANAGER, the answer that Bob Doles's regional manager is Sam Oakland can be derived. The example shows that the answer cannot be derived without combining the information in different files. To combine the information in two different files, we introduce the JOIN operation.

Operation: Join

Generic Format: JOIN WITH {record-comparison specification}
FROM {file one} {file two}
TO {resultant file name} *(This is optional.)*

Purpose: To combine two files according to the record-comparison specification. A record in the resulting file is the horizontal concatenation of the records in the two joining files.

Example: JOIN WITH REGION.REGION = RMANAGER.REGION
FROM REGION, RMANAGER

REGION.REGION indicates the field REGION in file REGION; RMANAGER.REGION means field REGION in file RMANAGER.

Result:

STATE	REGION	R_MANAGER
WA	W	SAM OAKLAND
CA	W	SAM OAKLAND
WI	M	JOE PHILPS
IL	M	JOE PHILPS
NY	E	LARRY COOKS
OK	S	ALAN ROBERSON

Let us examine how the result is conceptually derived, step-by-step. First, the first record from the first file is selected and combined with the first record in the second file, and a record is output to the resultant file. Then, the first record in the first file is combined with the second record in the second file. Again, a record is output to the resultant file. When the records in the second file are exhausted, the process selects the next record in the first file and repeats the process with each of the records in the second file. This procedure is repeated until the records in the first file are exhausted. After this step the intermediate result is

	REGION		RMANAGER	
	STATE	REGION	REGION	R_MANAGER
➤	WA	W	W	SAM OAKLAND
	WA	W	M	JOE PHILPS
	WA	W	E	LARRY COOKS
	WA	W	S	ALAN ROBERSON
➤	CA	W	W	SAM OAKLAND
	CA	W	M	JOE PHILPS
	CA	W	E	LARRY COOKS
	CA	W	S	ALAN ROBERSON
	WI	M	W	SAM OAKLAND
➤	WI	M	M	JOE PHILPS
	WI	M	E	LARRY COOKS
	WI	M	S	ALAN ROBERSON
	IL	M	W	SAM OAKLAND
➤	IL	M	M	JOE PHILPS
	IL	M	E	LARRY COOKS
	IL	M	S	ALAN ROBERSON
	NY	E	W	SAM OAKLAND
	NY	E	M	JOE PHILPS
➤	NY	E	E	LARRY COOKS
	NY	E	S	ALAN ROBERSON
	OK	S	W	SAM OAKLAND
	OK	S	M	JOE PHILPS
	OK	S	E	LARRY COOKS
➤	OK	S	S	ALAN ROBERSON

The second step is to eliminate records that do not satisfy the record-specification condition. The record-specification condition in the example requires the value in field REGION from file REGION be the same as the value in field REGION from file RMANAGER. Those qualified records are marked with a ➤ (this symbol is not contained in the file, it was added by us to point out qualifying records). Eliminating records that do not qualify, we obtain the following file:

REGION		RMANAGER	
STATE	REGION	REGION	R_MANAGER
WA	W	W	SAM OAKLAND
CA	W	W	SAM OAKLAND
WI	M	M	JOE PHILPS
IL	M	M	JOE PHILPS
NY	E	E	LARRY COOKS
OK	S	S	ALAN ROBERSON

The file contains a column of redundant data, REGION. After eliminating the redundant column and renaming the file, we obtain the resultant file of the join operation:

STATE	REGION	R_MANAGER
WA	W	SAM OAKLAND
CA	W	SAM OAKLAND
WI	M	JOE PHILPS
IL	M	JOE PHILPS
NY	E	LARRY COOKS
OK	S	ALAN ROBERSON

The dBASE III implementation is fairly straightforward:

```
SELECT 1
USE RMANAGER
SELECT 2
USE REGION
JOIN WITH RMANAGER FOR REGION = RMANAGER->REGION TO RESULT
```

The join operation in dBASE III always creates a new joined database file. This may cause a problem when the available disk storage is limited. Another facility, **SET RELATION**, which provides similar joining capability by indexing, can be used when a new file is not required.

Maintenance of the Database System

Constant review is one of the key factors of successful database design. To review the database, designers should first document current database systems. A good document should contain a careful list and description of each of the database files, cross-referenced with the supported decision-making processes. After the database is in operation, designers should observe and investigate whether the data in the system can support the intended decision-making processes properly and efficiently, and whether the data in the system are redundant in terms of the decision support applications. Results of the investigation should be carefully studied and included in an improved database design.

DATABASE OPERATIONS FOR DECISION SUPPORT APPLICATIONS

Throughout the remainder of this book, we use data as input to our decision support applications. In some cases, the data are be lists of facts, such as the population and income of an area over time. In other cases, the data are be summarized into a few key figures, such as the number of hours required to produce an item or the total inventory on hand. To develop the required lists and summary figures, you use select, project, and join operations as discussed in this unit. In most of the applications in this book, you do not have to specify the database design: that has been done for you.

Transferring Data between Database Files and Spreadsheet Files

The creation of a database file with the desired information through select, project, or join operations is only the first step in using data in decision support operations. Once the appropriate data are assembled, it is often necessary to transfer the data from a database file to a spreadsheet file. Specific techniques for accomplishing this task are presented in Appendix B, "Transferring Data Between Lotus 1-2-3 and dBASE III Plus."

REVIEW QUESTIONS

*1. What is an attribute? What is a record structure? Describe the products carried in a grocery store, listing the attributes and organizing them in a record structure.

2. What is a key attribute? Is there a set of attributes which can be used as a key in the record structure in Question 1?

*3. Define one-to-one, many-to-one, one-to-many, and many-to-many relationships. What is a functional relationship?

*4. Identify all the attributes in data stores DEALERSHIP_FILE and PENDING_ORDER_FILE in this unit. What are the key attributes in DEALERSHIP_FILE and PENDING_ORDER_FILE, respectively?

5. Refine the record structure of data stores DEALERSHIP_FILE and PENDING_ORDER_FILE into a 3NF database design. Draw the functional relationship diagram first, then specify the design with new groupings of the attributes.

ADDITIONAL READING

To learn more about database design and use, and about dBASE III, consult the following books:

Date, C. J., *An Introduction to Database Systems, Volume 1*, 4th edition. Reading, MA: Addison-Wesley, 1986.

Kroenke, D., *Database Processing*, 2nd edition. Chicago: Science Research Associates, 1983.

Ross, S. C., *Understanding and Using dBASE III (Including dBASE II)*. St. Paul: West, 1986.

Ross, S. C., *Understanding and Using dBASE III Plus*. St. Paul: West, 1987.

PART

2 CURRENT OPERATIONS

In this part we discuss a series of models that are relevant to the current operations of a business. The topics range from the cost-accounting question of how to assign overhead costs to products that are produced to the economic-planning question of what the demand for a product will be, given certain assumptions about price and the economic environment. Other units in this part address the relationship between labor, capital, and production, planning for operations, and control of inventory. Although these units discuss EZRydr in particular, they also provide a broad base for extensions of these models to other organizations.

UNIT

4 COST ALLOCATIONS— WHO ABSORBS THE OVERHEAD?

A manufacturing firm must determine the total cost of producing its products in order to comply with financial reporting requirements. First, the cost of goods sold must be reported in the periodic income statement. Second, the cost attached to products remaining in inventory at the end of the period must be ascertained and reported as a current asset under the inventory classification. Where there are both producing and service departments involved in the manufacturing effort, cost allocations are necessary. The capabilities of a spreadsheet software package provide an effective tool for calculating the appropriate allocations for these purposes.

DECISION SUPPORT APPLICATION MATRIX

Accounting & Finance	Economics & Long-Range Planning	Human Resources	Marketing & Logistics	Management Information Systems	Operations Planning & Control	Executive Officers
■		¤			■	¤

■ Departmental area(s) in which the technique is or can be used.

¤ Departmental area(s) that provide input to or are impacted by the technique.

LEARNING OBJECTIVES

1. After completing this unit you should know

    a. why cost allocations are necessary,

    b. the difference between the direct method and the step-down method,

    c. how to calculate appropriate allocations using the direct method,

Contributed by Lloyd D. Doney

d. how to calculate appropriate allocations using the step-down method,

e. how to partially check your allocations for correctness,

f. how spreadsheet software can facilitate cost allocation computations,

g. how to use spreadsheet graphic capabilities to reveal how allocations differ among allocation methods.

2. After completing this unit you should be able to

   a. create cost-allocation spreadsheets using both the direct method and the step-down method,

   b. develop a graph that reveals the differences in allocations between the two methods.

BASIC CONCEPTS

A major task of the cost accounting system in a manufacturing firm is to accumulate, allocate, and summarize the costs of producing the products for the period. Depending on the nature of the product, this is accomplished by using a job-order or a process costing system. In a job-order system, costs are traced through departments to particular jobs. In a process system, cost are traced through departments to particular batches of the product. In either case, in addition to producing departments that have a direct role in manufacturing the product, there are typically several service departments, that have no direct role in the manufacturing activity, but are essential to the overall manufacturing effort.

Many manufacturing costs, such as direct materials and direct labor can be traced directly to producing departments, and thus, to products, by sophisticated record-keeping systems. These costs are defined as *direct costs*. Other costs, like those incurred by a service department, are not directly traceable to producing departments or products. These costs, defined as *indirect costs*, must be allocated to the producing departments so that the costs attached to products within producing departments reflect the total or complete manufacturing cost.

Cost allocation is both a science and an art. The science is represented by the mathematical calculations that are made. The art is represented by the selection of the basis of cost allocation and the selection of the method used to allocate the costs. While the calculations reflect precision, the guide for the selection of an appropriate basis of allocation is that it be "reasonable." Once the allocation basis has been selected, the method must be chosen. Obviously, different combinations of bases and methods lead to different outcomes in terms of allocations. Once a basis and method have been selected, the same basis and method are used in ensuing periods in order to comply with the principle of consistency in accounting. Some examples of a reasonable basis of allocation include the following:

- Allocation of maintenance service department costs to producing departments on the basis of machine hours used in the producing departments.

- Allocation of plant medical department costs to producing departments on the basis of the number of employees in each of the producing departments.

- Allocation of custodial department costs to producing departments on the basis of the size, in square feet, of each of the producing departments.

After the basis of allocation has been selected, there are three different methods of accomplishing the allocations: (1) direct method; (2) step-down method; and (3) simultaneous equations method. Due to their relative ease of application and understanding, the direct and step-down methods are the most commonly used. The simultaneous-equations method is beyond the scope of this unit, but simultaneous equations are applied to a similar problem in Unit 14.

The direct method allocates the cost of each service department directly to producing departments. There is no allocation of cost from one service department to another service department, even though a plant cafeteria may serve the employees of the maintenance department — another service department. The direct method is the simplest of the two methods explored in this unit. Once an appropriate basis of allocation has been selected, the cost of the service department is allocated to producing departments, using appropriate ratio computations.

The step-down method does take into account the fact that service departments may serve other service departments. In this method, some service department costs are allocated to other service departments as well as to producing departments. The service departments are considered, one after the other, in a step-by-step fashion, until the costs of all service departments are allocated to producing departments. The step-down method is a one-way street, however, in that once the cost of a service department has been allocated, there are no further reallocations from other service departments back to that department, even though there may be services provided in that direction. The only method that fully takes into account services between service departments in both directions is the simultaneous-equation method. The step-down method is a compromise between the direct method, which recognizes no service between service departments, and the equation method, which recognizes all services between service departments.

In addition to selecting appropriate, reasonable bases of allocating the cost of service departments using the step-down method, the user also must pick an order in which the cost of the service departments will be allocated. This choice is a final "artistic" touch in the process of cost allocation. In most cases, a different sequence of choices results in different costs allocated to producing departments. After the choices of bases and order of allocations have been made, the amounts to be allocated are made using appropriate ratio computations in much the same way as in the direct method.

GATHERING THE DATA

Within the Company

The data used in making cost allocations come primarily from the firm's accounting information system. These data are aggregate amounts rather than detailed amounts, however, and do not require any substantial retrieval or preliminary manipulation of numbers from the firm's database. Depending on the allocation bases selected, some aggregate measures related to operations for the period are also required. If machine hours are to be used as a basis of allocation, then it is necessary to retrieve the total machine hours used in each of the producing departments from the operating statistics for the period.

External to the Company

All data required for cost allocations are available within the firm.

THE PROBLEM

The manufacturing function at EZRydr is organized into two producing departments, fabrication and assembly. In addition, there are two service departments, security and maintenance. At the end of each accounting period it is necessary to allocate the costs of security and maintenance to fabrication and assembly. Until now the company has simply been assigning half of the service department costs to each of the producing departments. In response to a recommendation from their auditor, management is interested in implementing a more sophisticated and more appropriate method of cost allocation. For this reason they would like to see the differences in cost allocations between the current 50-50 method, the direct method, and the step-down method for the most recent period. Initially, management would like you to answer the following questions:

1. What is the total cost of each producing department, after allocations, using the current 50-50 basis of allocation?

2. What is the total cost of each producing department, after allocations, using the direct method?

3. What is the total cost of each producing department, after allocations, using the step-down method?

Departmental Data

The costs in Table 4-1 have been compiled from the most recent operating period for purposes of the analysis. The data have been gathered in view of the decision to base the allocation of maintenance costs on machine hours used and the allocation of security costs on the basis of square feet occupied.

TABLE 4-1 Cost Allocation Data

	Service Depts.		Producing Depts.	
	Maintenance	Security	Fabrication	Assembly
Department Direct Cost	$250,000	$120,000	$5,400,000	$4,250,000
Machine Hours Used	-	-	600,000	100,000
Square Feet Occupied	5,000	3,000	100,000	150,000

Data in the Database

The following information can be derived from the database. All data relevant for this application are maintained in a data file named OPERATNS.DBF. The database data are for monthly periods, and you must sum or average the data as appropriate if you intend to analyze the data on a quarterly or yearly basis. The fields relevant to this application are DEPARTMENT, MONTH, YEAR, DIR_COST, MACH_HOURS, and FLOOR_AREA. In this section, we assume that you would like the data for the third quarter (July, August, September) of 1987.

Department Direct Cost. This is the sum of DIR_COST for each department for the desired months.

Machine Hours Used. This is the sum of MACH_HOURS for each department for the desired months. For the service departments considered here, this should equal zero.

Square Feet Occupied. This figure should be computed as the *average* for each department for the desired months.

DEVELOPING THE SPREADSHEET

To answer the questions raised by EZRydr's management, we must build a spreadsheet for the current 50-50 method of allocation as well as for allocations resulting from the direct method and the step-down method. In addition, it is well to include a reconciliation of costs at the end of the spreadsheet to serve as a partial check on the accuracy of the results obtained.

Start with a blank spreadsheet. In the upper left corner of the spreadsheet, enter the operating data given for each of the four departments, using one column for each department. Include appropriate labels to the left of the columnar display.

Next, use the operating data entered to create a tabular computation of the allocations resulting from the current 50-50 allocations method, as shown in Figure 4-1. In the first row (row 11) record the department direct cost by making appropriate relative cell references to those costs included in the operating data, that is, C5, D5, E5, and F5. In row 12 show the allocation of the maintenance department cost by subtracting the cost in cell C12 and entering one-half of the cost in cell E12 and the other half in cell F12. In row 13 do a similar allocation of the security department cost. Draw a line across the departmental columns in line 14. After completing the allocations, add the amounts in each of the departmental columns on line 15. These amounts represent the departmental costs after allocation. The amount is zero for each of the service departments because their costs have been allocated. The costs of the producing departments have each been increased by their shares of the allocated service department costs.

The spreadsheet is completed by constructing similar allocation tables for each of the two proposed methods. In each case, the first row of the table shows the department direct costs, carried down from the appropriate cells in the operating data table.

```
A1: 'COST ALLOCATION                                                          READY


        A          B           C             D            E            F
1   COST ALLOCATION
2
3   OPERATING DATA:
4                         Maintenance     Security  Fabrication     Assembly
5   Dept. Direct Cost        $250,000     $120,000   $5,400,000   $4,250,000
6   Machine Hours Used                                  600,000      100,000
7   Square Ft. Occupied         5,000        3,000      100,000      150,000
8
9   COST ALLOCATION -- CURRENT 50-50 METHOD:
10
11  Dept. Direct Cost        $250,000     $120,000   $5,400,000   $4,250,000
12  1/2 Maint Cost          ($250,000)                 $125,000     $125,000
13  1/2 Security Cost                   ($120,000)      $60,000      $60,000
14                      -----------------------------------------------------
15  Cost After Allocation          $0           $0   $5,585,000   $4,435,000
16
17
18
19
20
```

FIGURE 4-1 EZRydr's Current Method for Allocating Costs

In the direct method, the maintenance costs are allocated to producing departments on the basis of the machine hours used in each producing department in row 20 (see Figure 4-2). Subtract the maintenance cost in the maintenance department column, C20, and calculate the appropriate allocations in cells E20 and F20. The direct-method allocation computation is as follows:

$$\text{Allocated cost} = \frac{\text{Departmental Machine Hours}}{\text{Total Machine Hours}} \times \text{Maint. Dept. Cost}$$

For the fabrication department, enter the appropriate formula in cell E20 (use relative and absolute cell addressing if your spreadsheet package supports this feature). Maintenance cost of $214,286 is allocated to the fabrication department on the basis of this computation:

$$[600000 / (600000 + 100000)] \times 250000 = 214286$$

Copy the formula in cell E20 to cell F20 to compute the appropriate allocation of maintenance cost to the assembly department, $35,714.

Next allocate the security department cost to producing departments on the basis of square feet occupied. Subtract the cost in the security department column and enter appropriate formulas in cells E21 and F21 to compute the allocations. Please note that in the formula for these allocations the denominator excludes the 5000 square feet in maintenance and the 3000 square feet in security, since no cost is being allocated to these departments. In each instance, the denominator in the allocation formula is (100,000 + 150,000), the total square feet in the two producing departments that are receiving the allocated cost. Failure to exclude the square feet in the two service departments results in an allocation to producing departments that is less than the total cost to be allocated.

Complete the direct method allocation table by drawing a line and summing the departmental costs as shown in Figure 4-2. Note that, in the direct method, the order of service department allocation could have been reversed (i.e., allocate security before maintenance) without having any affect on the final allocations.

In the next section of the spreadsheet, enter the table of allocations for the step-down method. Since service department costs are allocated to other service departments in this method, order is important. We allocate the security department first in this case because security serves maintenance as well as the producing departments, whereas maintenance does not serve security. The basis for choice of order may vary. Some suggest that service departments be allocated in order of cost, that is, the one with the highest cost first, the one with the next highest cost second, and so on. In other cases the service department serving the most other service departments is allocated first, and so on.

After entering the department direct cost on the first line of the table, allocate the security department cost by subtracting it from the security department column. Enter the proper formulas for allocations to the maintenance, fabrication and assembly departments, using the basis of square feet. Exclude the 3000 square feet occupied by security in the denominator of the allocation formula for the reasons stated above. Note that in Figure 4-2 the following allocations result:

Maintenance	$2,353
Fabrication	47,059
Assembly	70,588

Before allocating the cost of the maintenance department, add the allocated cost from the security department to the direct cost of the maintenance department. This results in a cost to be allocated of $252,353. Allocations of the maintenance department cost to producing departments will include this amount in the allocation formula. The allocation of maintenance department cost may now be completed based on machine hours. Again, sum the allocated cost for each of the departments.

Although it is not necessary, it is well to include the reconciliation of costs shown at the bottom of the spreadsheet. On the first line, sum the departmental direct costs for the four departments as given in the operating-data section of the spreadsheet. On the remaining lines add the costs after allocations for the two producing departments for the 50-50 method, the direct method, and the step-down method as computed in each of the allocation tables. All totals should agree. Although this does not insure the correctness of the allocations, it does insure that all costs have been allocated.

A1: 'COST ALLOCATION READY

	A B	C	D	E	F
1	COST ALLOCATION				
2					
3	OPERATING DATA:				
4		Maintenance	Security	Fabrication	Assembly
5	Dept. Direct Cost	$250,000	$120,000	$5,400,000	$4,250,000
6	Machine Hours Used			600,000	100,000
7	Square Ft. Occupied	5,000	3,000	100,000	150,000
8					
9	COST ALLOCATION -- CURRENT 50-50 METHOD:				
10					
11	Dept. Direct Cost	$250,000	$120,000	$5,400,000	$4,250,000
12	1/2 Maint Cost	($250,000)		$125,000	$125,000
13	1/2 Security Cost		($120,000)	$60,000	$60,000
14		----------	----------	----------	----------
15	Cost After Allocation	$0	$0	$5,585,000	$4,435,000
16					
17	COST ALLOCATION -- DIRECT METHOD:				
18					
19	Dept. Direct Cost	$250,000	$120,000	$5,400,000	$4,250,000
20	Allocate Maint	($250,000)		$214,286	$35,714
21	Allocate Security		($120,000)	$48,000	$72,000
22		----------	----------	----------	----------
23	Cost After Allocation	$0	$0	$5,662,286	$4,357,714
24					
25	COST ALLOCATION -- STEP-DOWN METHOD:				
26					
27	Dept. Direct Cost	$250,000	$120,000	$5,400,000	$4,250,000
28	Allocate Security	$2,353	($120,000)	$47,059	$70,588
29		-------------			
30	Sum Maint Cost	$252,353			
31	Allocate Maint	($252,353)		$216,303	$36,050
32		----------	----------	----------	----------
33	Cost After Allocation	$0	$0	$5,663,361	$4,356,639
34					
35					
36	RECONCILIATION:				
37	Total Dept. Direct Cost Before Allocation				$10,020,000
38	Total Prod. Dept. Cost After Alloc. - Present Method				$10,020,000
39	Total Prod. Dept. Cost After Alloc. - Direct Method				$10,020,000
40	Total Prod. Dept. Cost After Alloc. - Step-Down Method				$10,020,000

FIGURE 4-2 The Completed Spreadsheet

CHECKING THE MODEL

Before using the spreadsheet to answer EZRydr's questions, you should perform two checks to ensure that the logic of the model is correct. First, compare the results you obtain with those illustrated in Figure 4-2. Any deviation indicates an error. Second, enter the following simple operating data. Manually compute the expected result for each method and compare your results with the spreadsheet.

	Maintenance	Security	Fabrication	Assembly
Department Direct Cost	90	50	10	10
Machine Hours Used	-	-	6	4
Square Feet Occupied	10	5	20	20

USING THE SPREADSHEET

This cost allocation spreadsheet was prepared in response to questions raised by EZRydr's management in their attempt to implement more suitable allocation methods. It is now possible to use the spreadsheet to answer each of the questions raised.

1. What is the total cost of each producing department, after allocations, using the current 50-50 basis of allocation? Inspection of the spreadsheet reveals that the 50-50 method results in the following costs after allocations:

Fabrication	$5,585,000
Assembly	4,435,000

2. What is the total cost of each producing department, after allocations, using the direct method? The direct method results in the following costs after allocations:

Fabrication	$5,662,286
Assembly	4,357,714

3. What is the total cost of the producing departments, after allocations, using the step-down method? The spreadsheet reveals these costs after allocations:

Fabrication	$5,663,361
Assembly	4,356,639

Note that the differences between the total cost of the producing departments, after allocations, is not large. The largest difference is between the current 50-50 method and each of the two proposed methods. The difference between the direct and the step-down method, in this instance, is very slight.

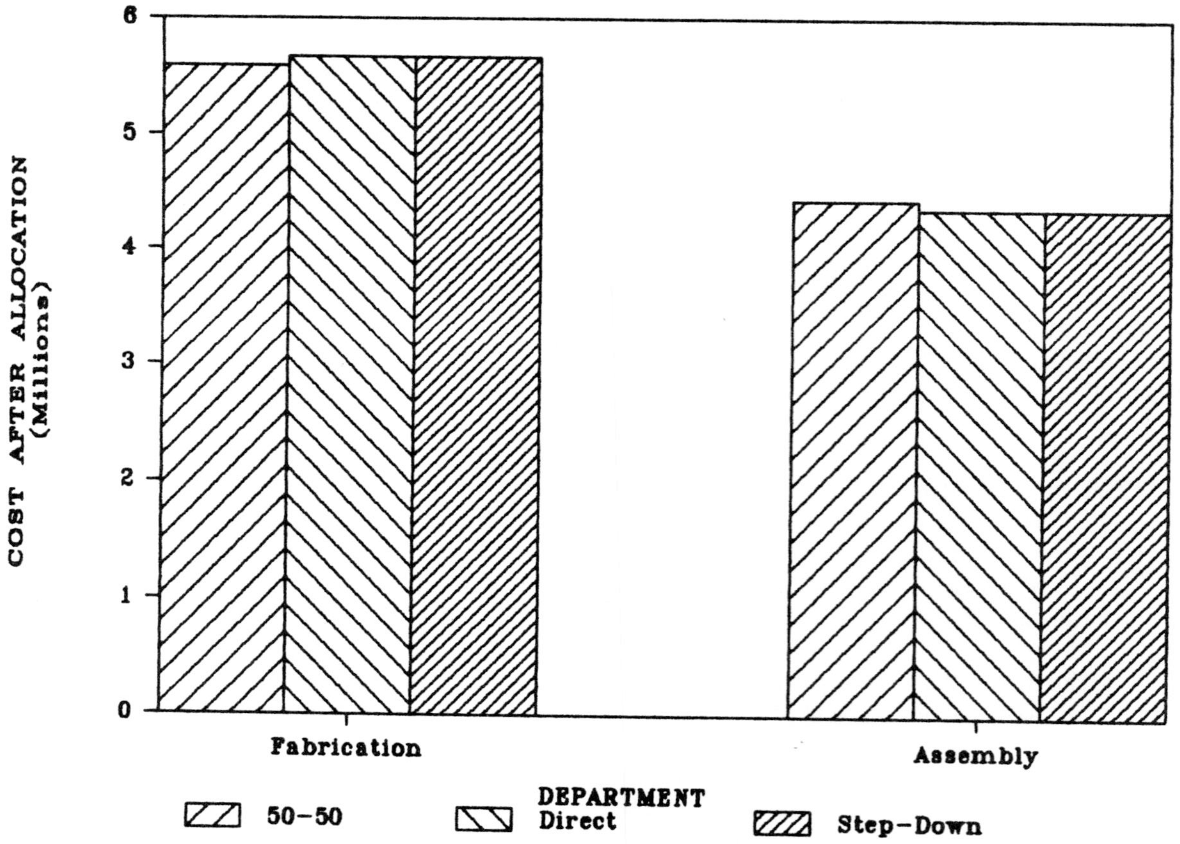

FIGURE 4-3 Comparison of the Three Methods

A visual summary of the results of the allocation methods can be prepared easily by using the graphic capabilities of most spreadsheet software packages. Such a graph, developed using Lotus 1-2-3, is illustrated in Figure 4-3. Using your spreadsheet package, prepare a similar graph, including professional touches such as legends and titles. Once completed, note that the graph reveals the very slight differences of cost after allocations in this case, though the difference between the current 50-50 method and either of the other methods is larger than the difference between the direct method and the step-down method.

EXERCISES

The cost allocation spreadsheet was developed in response to specific questions raised by EZRydr's management. Once the choice of allocation method has been made, a spreadsheet using the method elected can be prepared and used at the end of each period to compute the proper amounts of allocation. Prior to leaving the current spreadsheet, however, complete Exercise 1, below.

1. Below the current spreadsheet create a three-row by two-column arrangement of cells containing the total amount of indirect cost allocated to the fabrication and assembly de-

partments, using each of the three methods. Then use the graph capabilities to produce a bar graph, similar to Figure 4-3, showing the differences in the amounts of indirect cost allocated using the three different methods. Because this cost excludes the substantial amount of producing department direct cost, in each instance, it may reveal the differences in allocations of indirect cost more dramatically than Figure 4-3. Does it?

2. Assuming that management has elected the step-down method and the bases of allocations previously used, create a cost allocation spreadsheet that uses only the step-down method. Use the operating data section so that each time the spreadsheet is used, appropriate allocations may be accomplished by entering the current operating data only. When the spreadsheet is completed, make allocations for the two periods below:

Period 1	Maintenance	Security	Fabrication	Assembly
Department Direct Cost	$300,000	$140,000	$5,000,000	$4,000,000
Machine Hours Used	-	-	500,000	90,000
Square Feet Occupied	5,000	3,000	100,000	150,000

Period 2	Maintenance	Security	Fabrication	Assembly
Department Direct Cost	$200,000	$100,000	$4,000,000	$3,000,000
Machine Hours Used	-	-	300,000	50,000
Square Feet Occupied	5,000	3,000	100,000	150,000

3. Which allocation method would you recommend and why?

ENHANCEMENTS TO THE APPLICATION

There are a few enhancements that would make this spreadsheet easier to use. In this section, we point out some changes. You and your instructor may determine additional enhancements that may be made.

1. Use the cell-protection feature to protect all cells except those in which the periodic data are entered.

2. Using features such as Lotus's /RangeInput and macro commands, develop a data-entry system for this spreadsheet.

3. Create a database command file that will extract the necessary data and place it in an interim file. Add a feature to your spreadsheet that will import data from that interim file into the proper positions on the spreadsheet. (There are many methods for accomplishing this, depending on the particular software available to you.) This feature is an alternative to Enhancement 2.

4. Revise the model to allow the retention of more than one period's data.

REVIEW QUESTIONS

*1. Why are cost allocations necessary?

2. Define the following terms as they are used in this unit.

   a. direct costs

   b. indirect costs

   c. allocated costs

   d. service department

   e. producing department

*3. Why can cost allocations be characterized as an art form?

4. Describe the direct method.

*5. Describe the step-down method.

6. Which allocation method takes into account the fact that a service department can offer service to other service departments as well as to producing departments.

7. Suggest a suitable basis for allocating the following service department costs in a manufacturing firm.

   *a. employee cafeteria

   b. plant medical services

   *c. inventory control

   d. plant manager's office

ADDITIONAL READING

This unit explores the cost allocation methods most frequently used in business. Additional information regarding cost allocation methods can be found in most managerial accounting or cost accounting texts; see, for example,

Horngren, C. T., and G. Foster, *Cost Accounting: A Managerial Emphasis*, 6th edition. Englewood Cliffs, NJ: Prentice-Hall, 1987.

Horngren, C. T., and G. L. Sundem, *Introduction to Management Accounting*, 7th edition. Englewood Cliffs, NJ: Prentice-Hall, 1987.

Killough, L. N., and W. E. Leininger, *Cost Accounting Concepts and Techniques for Management*, 2nd edition. St. Paul: West, 1987.

Magee, R. P., *Advanced Managerial Accounting*. New York: Harper and Row, 1986.

Matz, A., and M. Usry, *Cost Accounting Planning and Control*, 8th edition. Cincinnati: South-Western, 1984.

Rayburn, G. R., *Principles of Cost Accounting: Managerial Applications*, revised edition. Homewood, IL: Irwin, 1983.

UNIT

5 PRODUCTION ANALYSIS—PUTTING RESOURCES TO WORK

A firm has a variety of means at its disposal for analyzing its production system and its operations. The majority of these production analysis techniques rely on internal accounting and engineering formulas that relate inputs to outputs on some quantitative basis. The economic approach to production analysis postulates output as the result of inputs. Expressed in mathematical form, as below, output (Q) is represented as a function of representative input variables, typically labor (L), capital (K), energy (E), and others:

$$Q = f(L, K, E, \ldots)$$

This approach does not inquire into the actual physical or mechanical combination of inputs into output. Instead, the economic approach analyzes statistical data relating to output and input utilization levels over time. Various statistical software packages that allow easy estimation of the production parameters from organizational data are available. Once estimated, the model can be used to assist in predicting or controlling production activities. In this unit we demonstrate the use of a spreadsheet to estimate production relationships.

DECISION SUPPORT APPLICATION MATRIX

Accounting & Finance	Economics & Long-Range Planning	Human Resources	Marketing & Logistics	Management Information Systems	Operations Planning & Control	Executive Officers
¤	■	¤	¤	¤	■	¤

■ Departmental area(s) in which the technique is or can be used.

¤ Departmental area(s) that provide input to or are impacted by the technique.

Contributed by Charles H. Breeden

LEARNING OBJECTIVES

1. After completing this unit you should know

   a. the logic behind a production function,

   b. the basic approach to building a production model,

   c. the uses of production parameters estimated for the firm.

2. After completing this unit you should be able to

   a. use a spreadsheet to estimate the parameters of a simple production function,

   b. use a spreadsheet to estimate the output effects of changes in input usages,

   c. determine if there are increasing or decreasing returns to scale in an operation,

   d. develop graphic presentations of total, marginal and average product curves.

BASIC CONCEPTS

The primary purpose of production analysis is to understand the firm's operations by modeling the relationship between input usage and the associated output. A secondary purpose is to prepare a foundation for the study of costs. The focus of production analysis is on units of input used in various periods and the units of output associated with them. Production analysis is necessary when a firm has questions about its basic operations, such as whether there are returns to scale in operations that are not being realized.

The simplest relationship in a firm's operations is between production level and time. Figure 5-1 depicts a production process over time. Notice that total product (units of output) rapidly increases after 1978, which may reflect the addition of new productive capacity.

Another basic relationship in a production function is between one input variable and output, given a set of fixed factors. The returns to a variable factor are demonstrated in Figure 5-2, which shows the levels of total output (units) associated with various levels of the input (crew size).

As described in the introduction to this unit, a *production function* portrays output as a function of inputs and is represented in general as

$$Q = f\,(K, L, E, \ldots)$$

There are a number of specific forms (e.g., linear, multiplicative) that this general relationship can assume. The simplest form is a linear function, such as

$$Q = a + bK + cL + dE + \ldots$$

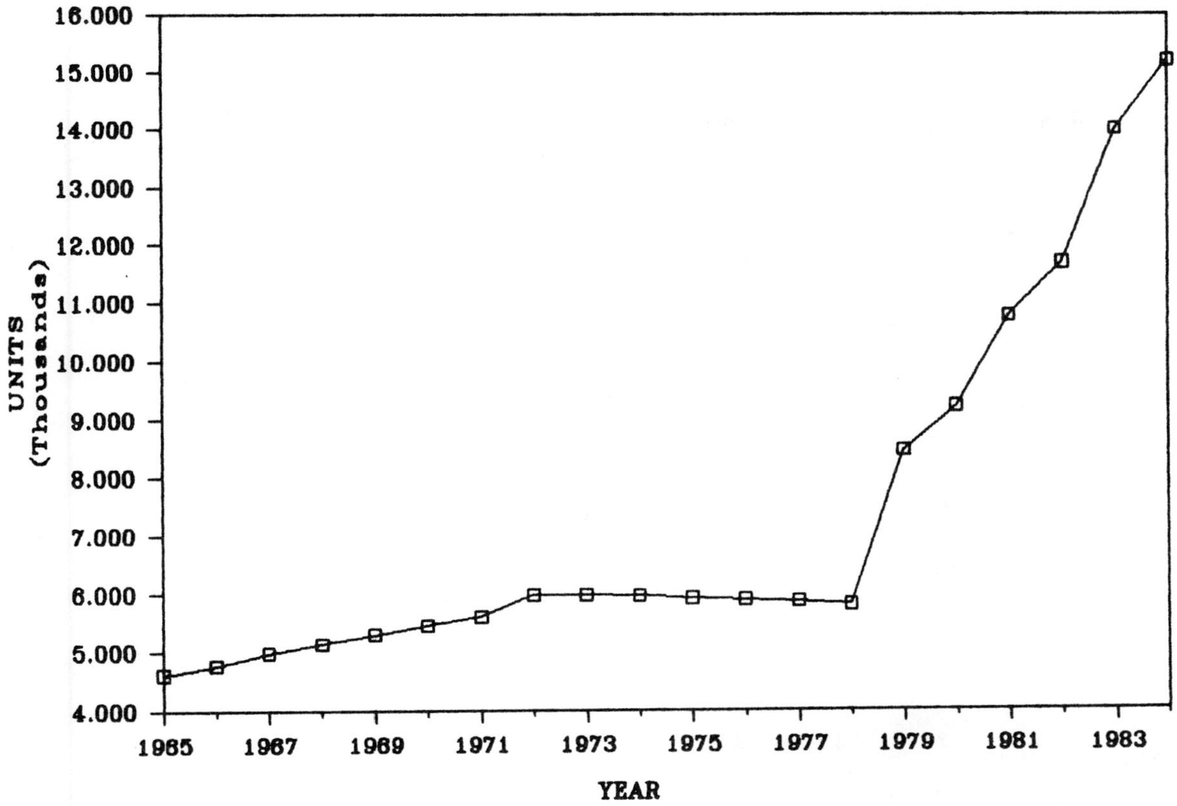

FIGURE 5-1 Production over Time

The production function can not be modeled as a linear one, however, because this linear relationship violates the economic law of diminishing marginal returns to a factor and implies that production can occur even if one input is at level zero. Therefore it is necessary to use a multiplicative form of the production function to describe the relationship among the causal variables. The following is an example of a multiplicative production function:

$$Q = a\, K^b\, L^c$$

Here output Q, is the product of a constant *a*, capital usage K, raised to some power *b*, and labor L, raised to a power *c*; we have dropped energy E, for simplicity in this formulation. This multiplicative specification of the production relationship has the advantage of being linear when transformed into logarithmic form. Thus its parameters can be estimated using linear regression analysis. To do this, it is first necessary to transform the values of output, capital, and labor into logarithmic form. Then the regression is performed to estimate the parameters of the following equation:

$$\ln(Q) = \ln(a) + b \ln(K) + c \ln(L)$$

where ln is the natural log (base *e*) of the respective variable.

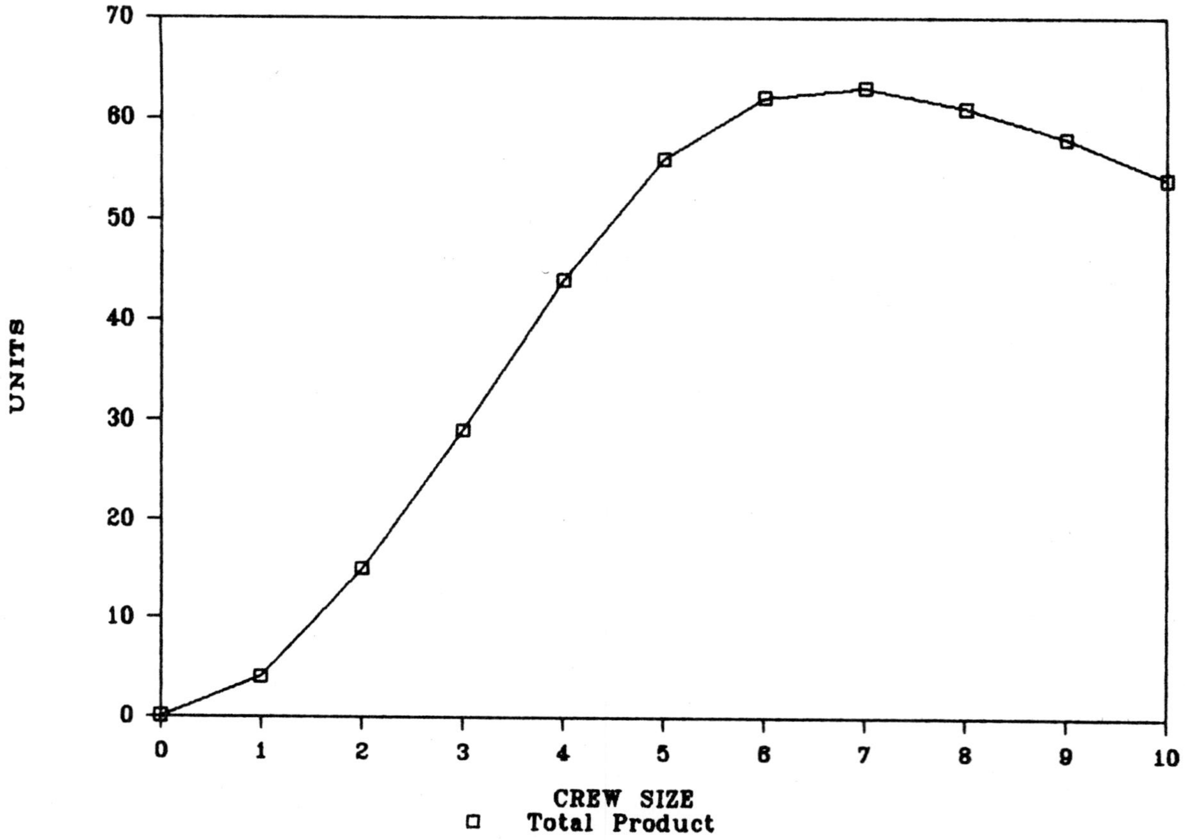

FIGURE 5-2 Total Product Curve

An *input* can consist of capital, labor, energy, raw materials, or any other factor of production. Inputs are typically measured in units, although dollars can be the input measure if they adequately describe the input's usage. Sometimes it is possible to measure capital as the interest rate, that is, the cost of capital. Although in theory, energy is part of the production function, it is seldom included in practice because it is difficult to measure. Consistent with this practice, we limit our focus to labor and capital in this unit.

Outputs are units of the product. Where the firm has a varied product line, it is sometimes possible to construct a variable describing output at an aggregate level, such as output in tons for a steel producer with several types of steel products.

Changes in *scale* are achieved by equal proportional changes in all the inputs. *Returns to scale* is a ratio reflecting the change in output achieved by an increase in all inputs. Returns to scale for manufacturing enterprises normally vary between 0.5 and 1.5. The interpretation for a return to scale of 1.1 is that the firm's output increases 1.1% for a 1% increase in all inputs. (Note that all inputs are increased by the same percentage amount for this analysis, e.g., each is increased by 1%, not one by 2% and another by 0%.) Returns to scale greater than 1 are called *increasing*, those equal to 1 are called *constant*, and those less than 1 are called *decreasing*.

GATHERING THE DATA

Within the Company

Production data are found entirely within the company. Output data consist of the record of units produced. Input data consist of the record of units of input per period. The period of the data can be daily, weekly, monthly, quarterly, or annual and must be the same for all data used. For purposes of statistical analysis, as many observations as possible must be obtained. In some cases, this may necessitate the use of quarterly or monthly data instead of annual data.

Inventory, quality assurance, or production control departments can be the source of output data. Personnel departments can furnish labor input records. For figures on the impacts of capital and energy, operating and accounting reports can be used.

External to the Company

No data external to the company are incorporated directly into production analysis. For purposes of comparison, however, certain industry figures on output and input utilization can be obtained.

THE PROBLEM

As part of its long-range strategic planning functions, you have been asked to analyze the production function of EZRydr and advise on the existence of returns to scale at the current plant. An additional objective is to learn something of the statistical relationship between variations in input usage and the resulting output changes. Management is interested in this latter information in order to assess the impact of a potential labor strike involving a portion of the workforce. Management's questions are these:

1. What would happen to the total output of the firm if the available units of labor decreased by 10%?
2. What would happen to the total output of the firm if the available units of capital increased by 10%?
3. What would happen to the total output of the firm if the company increased its utilization of all inputs by 10%?
4. What would happen to the total output of the firm if the company decreased its utilization of all inputs by 15%?
5. At current production levels, do increasing returns to scale exist?

Departmental Data

The economics department has built up a database from production records and accounting reports. The following data present output together with input usage of capital and labor for the past twenty years.

Year	Output (units)	Capital (index factor)	Labor (1000s of hours)
1965	4597	27850	193
1966	4757	28410	200
1967	4974	29431	207
1968	5135	26681	212
1969	5296	27430	213
1970	5457	32650	215
1971	5610	34891	219
1972	5980	41350	225
1973	5980	43871	222
1974	5963	42540	221
1975	5920	36430	228
1976	5895	39750	222
1977	5868	40120	223
1978	5809	40036	204
1979	8458	57283	233
1980	9226	63446	279
1981	10766	71091	250
1982	11684	98663	237
1983	13995	122208	260
1984	15189	123000	269

Output. This column presents annual output in units from 1965 through 1984.

Capital. This column presents the annual input usage for capital factors, that is, machinery, equipment, and plant. This is an index number based on a formula that includes depreciation charges, net additions to fixed assets, and the amount of charges in a plant repair account that is highly correlated with the intensity of plant operations and thus with capital utilization.

Labor. This column presents units of labor usage in thousands of hours.

Data in the Database

The data listed in the previous section are contained in the data file named PROD_SUM.DBF. The numbers in the database have not been scaled (e.g., rounded to thousands of hours), and are slightly more precise than the values above. The file also includes data for 1985 through 1987, making it more current. You should be able to determine which fields correspond to the columns in the data above.

DEVELOPING THE SPREADSHEET

Before we can address the questions posed by EZRydr's management, we must build a spreadsheet model of the production function. In this section, we discuss the development of such a model. When you save the spreadsheet, call it PRODUCT.

Start with a blank spreadsheet. In cell A1, enter PRODUCTION DATA. Enter labels in row 2, columns A through D, as illustrated in Figure 5-3. Enter the data in columns A through D. Calculate the mean values for output, capital, and labor at the bottom of the appropriate column, (e.g., the formula @AVG(B3..B22) is in B24).

In order to estimate the relationship between output and inputs of capital and labor, it is necessary to take the natural logarithms (logs) of all the data. Set the width of column E to 3 (to provide a visual break) and then compute the logs of the data by using the @LN function in columns F through H. Cell F3, for example, contains the formula for the natural logarithm of B3: @LN(B3). Label each column appropriately. The spreadsheet should look like columns A through H of Figure 5-3.

Before continuing, save the spreadsheet. We use the /**D**ata**R**egression command to perform the regression estimate.[1] The Y-range is F3..F22 because output is the dependent variable. The X-range is G3..H22 because capital and labor are the independent variables. The output range must be set away from the data so that the data are not overwritten. Define the range as J3. Execute the command Go. Move the cursor to the output range area to examine the results, illustrated in the range J3..M11 of Figure 5-3.

As mentioned in the "Basic Concepts" section, the general multiplicative form of a production function is

$$Q = a\, K^{b}\, L^{c}$$

To calculate the value of a we must compute the antilogarithm of the intercept term (Constant) in the Regression Output. This is accomplished by entering the function @EXP(M4) in cell J15. The exponents of capital and labor (b and c) are the coefficients estimated by the regression command. The actual production function derived in EZRydr's case is as follows:

$$Q = (.244448)\, K^{(.642234)}\, L^{(.618463)}$$

CHECKING THE MODEL

To check your spreadsheet, use the production function formula given above, together with the mean values of capital and labor to generate an estimate of Q. In cell L15, enter the formula +J15*(C24)^L10*(D24)^M10. This estimate of Q (7415.432) represents the predicted output when input utilization is at the mean values. Compare your results to Figure 5-3. The value in cell L15 is more than the value of the average output in cell B24. The difference of approximately 1% is caused by the conversion to logarithmic form.

[1] Not all spreadsheet packages include the ability to perform multiple regression. Where the feature is not available, you must use a statistical package to perform the regression and then enter the regression coefficients into a spreadsheet model for further analysis.

	A	B	C	D	E	F	G	H	I	J	K	L	M
1	PRODUCTION DATA												
2	YEAR	OUTPUT	CAPITAL	LABOR		LNOUTPUT	LNCAPITAL	LNLABOR					
3	1965	4597	27850	193		8.433159	10.23458	5.262690			Regression Output:		
4	1966	4757	28410	200		8.467372	10.25449	5.298317		Constant			-1.40874
5	1967	4974	29431	207		8.511979	10.28980	5.332718		Std Err of Y Est			0.063047
6	1968	5135	26681	212		8.543835	10.19170	5.356586		R Squared			0.973534
7	1969	5296	27430	213		8.574707	10.21939	5.361292		No. of Observations			20
8	1970	5457	32650	215		8.604654	10.39360	5.370638		Degrees of Freedom			17
9	1971	5610	34891	219		8.632305	10.45998	5.389071					
10	1972	5980	41350	225		8.696175	10.62982	5.416100		X Coefficient(s)		0.642234	0.618463
11	1973	5980	43871	222		8.696175	10.68900	5.402677		Std Err of Coef.		0.056288	0.280190
12	1974	5963	42540	221		8.693328	10.65820	5.398162					
13	1975	5920	36430	228		8.686091	10.50314	5.429345					
14	1976	5895	39750	222		8.681859	10.59036	5.402677		Constant		Q (predicted)	
15	1977	5868	40120	223		8.677269	10.59963	5.407171		0.244448		7415.432	
16	1978	5809	40036	204		8.667163	10.59753	5.318119					
17	1979	8458	57283	233		9.042868	10.95575	5.451038		OUTPUT SENSITIVITY ANALYSIS			
18	1980	9226	63446	279		9.129780	11.05794	5.631211			PERCENT	PERCENT	
19	1981	10766	71091	250		9.284148	11.17171	5.521460			INPUT	OUTPUT	
20	1982	11684	98663	237		9.365975	11.49946	5.468060		FACTOR	CHANGE	CHANGE	
21	1983	13995	122208	260		9.546455	11.71347	5.560681					
22	1984	15189	123000	269		9.628326	11.71993	5.594711		LABOR	10	6.18	
23										CAPITAL	10	6.42	
24	AVERAGES:	7327.95	51356.55	226.6						BOTH	10	12.61	

FIGURE 5-3 Completed Spreadsheet

USING THE SPREADSHEET

You have been asked a number of questions by the management of EZRydr. We now use our spreadsheet to answer these questions.

1. What would happen to the total output if the units of labor decreased by 10%? The regression output provides us with the information necessary to answer this question. The coefficient estimated for labor, .618463, indicates the output *elasticity* of labor. The interpretation of this coefficient is that as we decrease labor utilization by 1%, holding all other input usage constant, we expect output to decrease by .618463%. Thus, a 10% decrease in labor usage would be expected to cause a 6.18463% decrease in output (ten times the decrease of a 1% change). In other words, losing 10% of the labor force to a strike would result in only a 6% decrease in production.

In order to facilitate your interpretation of the coefficients in this and the following questions, build a table, starting in cell J17. Label this cell OUTPUT SENSITIVITY ANALYSIS. Enter other labels in the range J18..M20 as illustrated in Figure 5-3. Enter 10 in cells K22, K23, and K24. These numbers represent the percentage change in each of the inputs. Cell L22, the output change predicted for a change in labor input usage, is calculated by the formula +K22*M10. The formula for capital in L23 is +K23*L10. For a proportional change in both factors, cell L24, take the hypothetical change in scale in column K times the sum of the estimated coefficients for labor and capital, or +K24*(M10+L10). Set the format for the output change column of this table at two decimal places.

2. What would happen if capital usage went up by 10%? As computed in the output sensitivity table, a 10% increase in capital should cause a 6.42% increase in output, other things equal.

3. What would be the effect of an increase in the scale of operations of 10%? The table indicates that a change in scale of 10% should produce an increase in total output of 12.61%. Remember that a change in scale must be *equiproportional* among the input factors, that is, all inputs are increased equally. The formula in L24 achieves equiproportionality by multiplying the percent increase by the sum of the elasticities.

4. What would be the effect of a decrease in scale of 15%? Change the entry in K24 to 15: a cutback in operations of 15% should produce a reduction in output of 18.91%.

5. Are there increasing returns to scale in this operation? Returns to scale are indicated by the sum of the two output elasticity coefficients, .642234 and .618463, or 1.260697. Since this value exceeds 1.0, the production process is said to exhibit increasing returns to scale. The interpretation is that for a 1% increase in operations, output can be expected to increase by 1.26%.

EXERCISES

With the information derived from the production spreadsheet, it is possible to evaluate the rationality of employment decisions at EZRydr. Economic theory postulates that employers are rational in their employment decisions. This means that an employer does not willingly employ a worker who does not provide an economic benefit in excess of the associated hiring cost. Similarly, in determining the proper number of hours of labor to employ in a given period, an employer compares the expected return from the labor with the expected labor cost in wages. It is possible to calculate the marginal revenue product associated with different units of labor from the equation for total product derived in the production spreadsheet.

1. Consider a hiring decision at a wage of $24,000 per thousand labor hours (i.e., $24 per hour) and a revenue of $666.67 per unit of output. At what point is it not economically beneficial to employ more labor hours, given the current level of capital? Current labor usage is approximately 200,000 hours per year.

   Recall the formula from the multiplicative production function:

   $$Q = (.244448)\ K^{(.642234)}\ L^{(.618463)}$$

	A	B	C	D	E	F
1	PARAMETERS:			Notes:		
2	CAPITAL	123,000		Capital is an index number		
3	WAGE	$24,000		Wage is per 1000 hours		
4	REVENUE	$666.67		Revenue is per unit		
5						
6						
7	LABOR	MRP OF		WAGE		
8	(1000 hours)	LABOR	HIRE?	(1000 hours)		
120	211	24,295	Yes	$24,000		
121	212	24,251	Yes	$24,000		
122	213	24,208	Yes	$24,000		
123	214	24,165	Yes	$24,000		
124	215	24,122	Yes	$24,000		
125	216	24,079	Yes	$24,000		
126	217	24,037	Yes	$24,000		
127	218	23,995	No	$24,000		
128	219	23,953	No	$24,000		
129	220	23,911	No	$24,000		
130	221	23,870	No	$24,000		
131	222	23,829	No	$24,000		
132	223	23,788	No	$24,000		

FIGURE 5-4 The Employment Decision

which gives a method of calculating the predicted output levels for any given level of input. This is a *total product function* and its first derivative with respect to labor is the equation for the *marginal product of labor* (i.e., the incremental output attributable to each additional unit (1000 hours) of labor). Given an equation in the form of $y = cx^n$, the first derivative with respect to x, d(y)/d(x), is $ncx^{(n-1)}$. Therefore, the equation for the marginal product of labor, d(Q)/d(L), is

$$MP_L = c\ a\ K^b\ L^{(c\ -\ 1)}$$

$$= (.618463)\ (.244448)\ K^{(.642234)}\ L^{(.618463\ -\ 1)}$$

$$= (.151182)\ K^{(.642234)}\ L^{(-.381537)}$$

With this equation it is possible to calculate marginal product levels for various levels of labor employment, at a given level of capital.

Begin with a clear spreadsheet (remember to save PRODUCT). Refer to Figure 5-4 for general placement of entries. In rows 1 through 8, enter parameters and labels. In column A, starting in row 9, enter labor usage figures ranging from 100 to 400. In column B, enter the formula for the *marginal revenue product of labor*. This formula is the marginal product of labor times the revenue per unit. The entry for the formula in cell B9

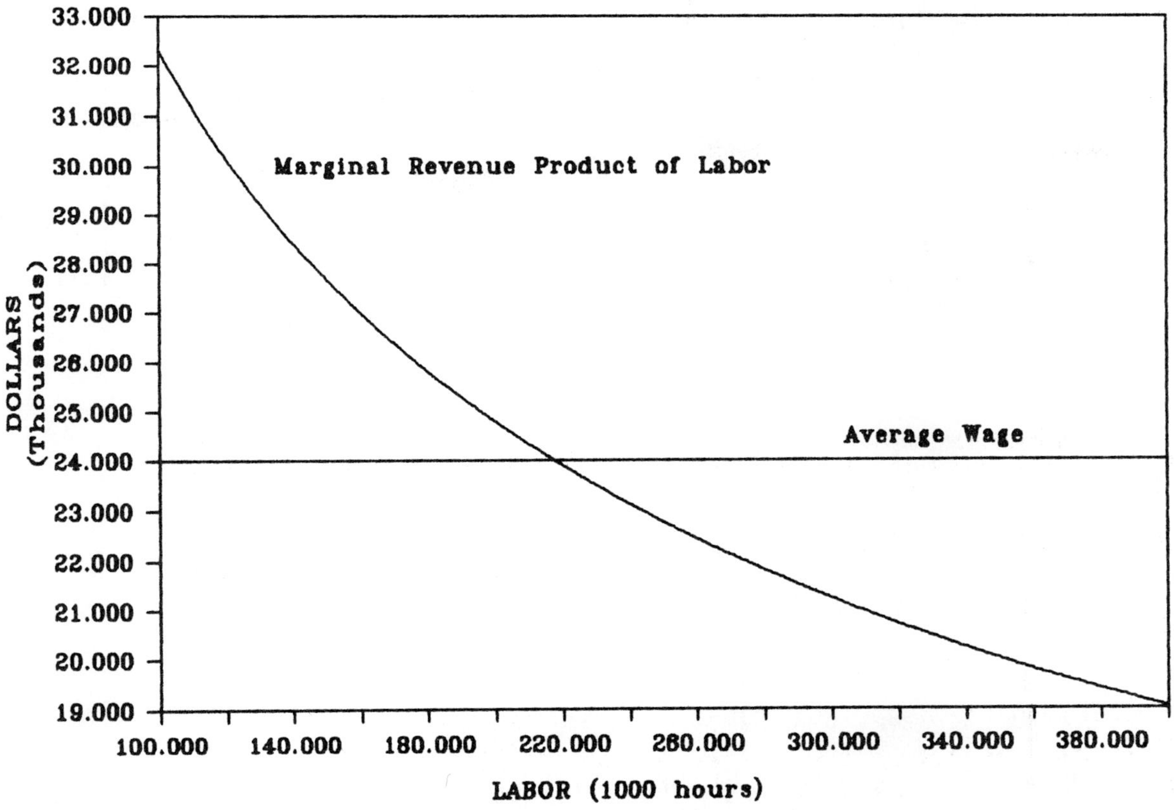

FIGURE 5-5 The Marginal Revenue Product of Labor

is (.151182)*B2^(.642234)*(A9)^(-.381537)*B4. (If your spreadsheet supports absolute cell referencing, use absolute cell references for B2 and B4 in this formula.) Copy the formula to obtain the values for the marginal revenue product of labor at levels of 101 through 400 labor units. For the moment, ignore the entries in columns C and D.

Compare the values in column B with $24,000, the wage rate per thousand hours. The rational employer employs any labor unit for which the marginal revenue product exceeds the wage. According to Figure 5-4, it is rational to employ up to the 217th labor unit. The 218th labor unit has an economic return of only $23,995, so to employ that unit would reduce the profit of the firm. A graph of the marginal revenue product of labor is presented in Figure 5-5.

2. Assume that a union concession has lowered the wage to $23 per hour. Now what is the optimal number of labor units to employ?

3. Create a graph similar to Figure 5-5, illustrating the relationship between marginal revenue product of labor and number of labor units. To obtain the line for Average Wage, make the entries in column D in Figure 5-4. The best way to accomplish this is to refer to cell B3 (as an absolute reference, if possible), so that one change in the parameters section is reflected throughout the spreadsheet.

4. Following the logic in Exercises 1 through 3, determine the equation for the marginal product of capital. Use this equation to determine whether it is rational to purchase additional units of capital in excess of the current 123,000 at $49.00 per unit, given the 1984 level of 269,000 labor hours. At 269,000 labor hours, what is the optimal number of index units of capital?

5. Illustrate the nature of the relationships among average product of labor AP_L, marginal product of labor MP_L, and crew size using the following data for total product and crew size in EZRydr's engine department. (Figure 5-2 contains a graph of the relationship between crew size and total product.)

Crew Size	Total Product
0	0
1	4
2	15
3	29
4	44
5	56
6	62
7	63
8	61
9	58
10	54

The following equations are used to calculate average and marginal product of labor:

$$AP_L = TP_L / L$$

$$MP_L = d(TP_L) / d(L)$$

where TP_L is total product and L is labor, that is, crew size. Thus the calculation for average product at a crew size of 1 is (4/1) (i.e., total product divided by crew size). The calculation for marginal product at crew size of 1, given an increase in crew size from 0 to 1 and an increase in output from 0 to 4, is (4-0)/(1-0) (i.e., change in total product divided by change in crew size). At a crew size of zero, average product is zero and and marginal product is undefined. Create a graph illustrating the relationships among marginal and average products and crew size. Your graph should look like Figure 5-6. Notice that the average product curve begins to fall after the marginal product curve falls below it. Decreasing marginal returns to labor exist after marginal product begins to decline.

ENHANCEMENTS TO THE APPLICATION

There are a few enhancements to the spreadsheet that increase its versatility and usefulness. In this section we point out some changes. You or your instructor may identify additional enhancements beyond those suggested here.

1. Using features such as Lotus's /RangeInput and macro commands, develop a data-entry system for this spreadsheet to facilitate entry of data in years following the current data.

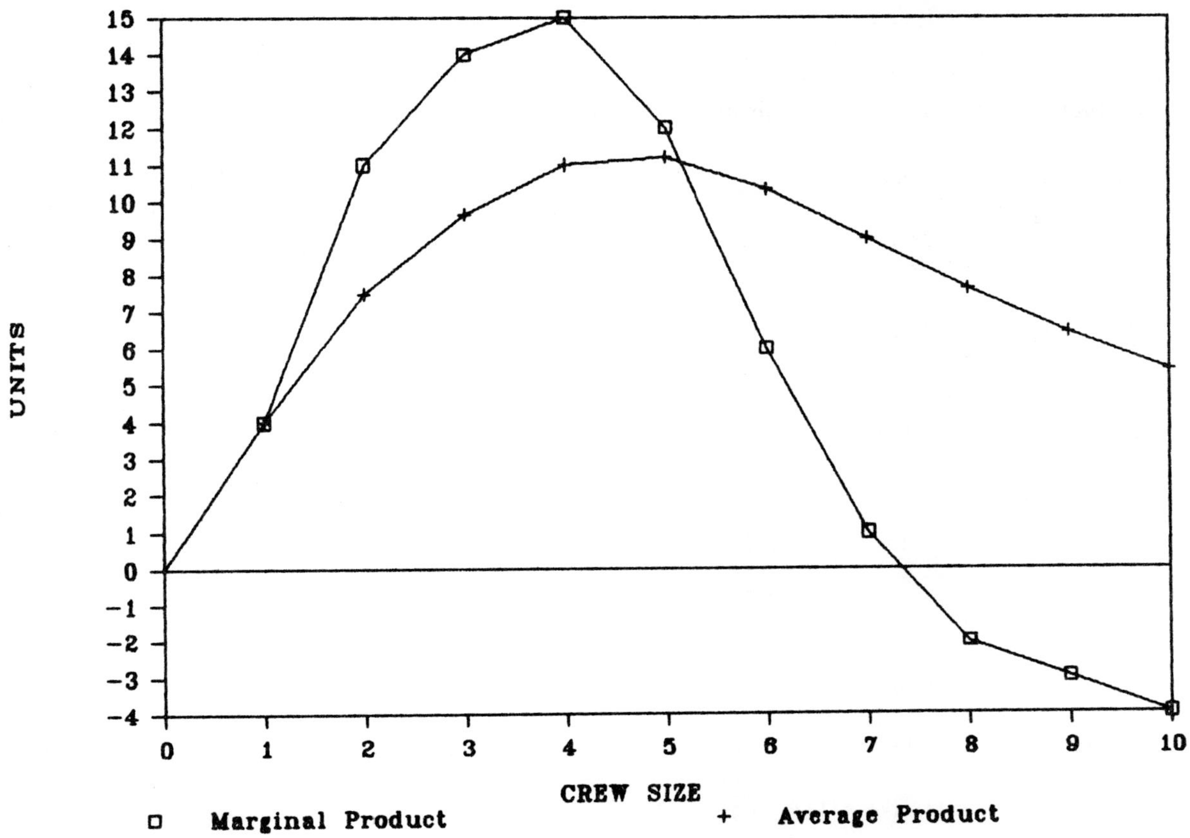

FIGURE 5-6 Marginal and Average Product of Labor Curves

2. Create a database command file that will extract the necessary data and place it in an interim file. Add a feature to your spreadsheet that will import data from that interim file into the proper positions on the spreadsheet. (There are many methods for accomplishing this, depending on the particular software available to you.) This feature is an alternative to Enhancement 1.

3. Write a macro to recompute the regression after additional data have been input or imported.

4. Add a decision statement in the marginal product spreadsheets (e.g., column C in Figure 5-4) that displays "Yes" if the marginal product is greater than the cost of an additional unit of the resource, "No" otherwise. If your spreadsheet package does not support text in conditional clauses, use numeric values such as 1 for yes and 0 for no.

5. Combine the spreadsheets that compute the regression and the marginal products of labor and capital. Develop whatever formulas are necessary to extract coefficients and compute the marginal products so you do not have to transfer the coefficients and manually compute the value of the derivatives.

REVIEW QUESTIONS

1. How can a spreadsheet help a firm analyze its production system?

2. Define the following terms as they are used in this unit.

   a. production function

   b. input

   c. output

   *d. returns to scale

   *e. marginal revenue product

   f. total product

   g. average product

   *h. marginal product

*3. How are historic data used to calculate production relationships?

4. What conditions would make the use of historic data inappropriate?

5. Why is it necessary to use a logarithmic function to model the production relationship?

6. Is it possible to analyze the effect of changes in labor inputs while assuming that capital input usage remains the same?

*7. How can changes in production scale (proportional changes in all inputs) be analyzed?

ADDITIONAL READING

Keating, B., and J. H. Wilson, *Managerial Economics*. Orlando: Academic Press, 1986. Chapter Seven.

Mansfield, E., *Microeconomics*, 5th edition. New York: Norton, 1985. Chapter Seven.

UNIT 6 AGGREGATE PLANNING—MATCHING SUPPLY AND DEMAND

Aggregate planning is the process by which a firm attempts to match its productive capacity with the requirements imposed on it by the demand for all of the items that it produces. Top management of the firm is typically charged with the responsibility of developing the aggregate plan. Though a variety of sophisticated, mathematical techniques have been developed to solve this problem, few of them are actually used because of their complexity. Because trial and error continues to be the technique most frequently used to solve aggregate planning problems, a spreadsheet package is one of the most logical tools to use in developing aggregate planning solutions. In this unit we demonstrate the use of a spreadsheet program in developing an aggregate planning model.

DECISION SUPPORT APPLICATION MATRIX

Accounting & Finance	Economics & Long-Range Planning	Human Resources	Marketing & Logistics	Management Information Systems	Operations Planning & Control	Executive Officers
¤		¤	¤		■¤	¤

■ Departmental area(s) in which the technique is or can be used.

¤ Departmental area(s) that provide input to or are impacted by the technique.

LEARNING OBJECTIVES

1. After completing this unit you should know

   a. the reasons that firms develop aggregate plans,

   b. the basic strategies used in developing an aggregate plan,

   c. the terminology associated with aggregate planning,

Contributed by Richard J. Penlesky

   d. how a spreadsheet package can simplify the aggregate planning process,

   e. how graphs can be used to illustrate aggregate planning solutions.

2. After completing this unit you should be able to

   a. create a spreadsheet for developing and costing aggregate planning solutions,

   b. develop graphic presentations of aggregate planning solutions.

BASIC CONCEPTS

The purpose of aggregate planning is to match a firm's supply with its demand such that total projected production costs are minimized. As you might assume from its name, the focus of aggregate planning is on the aggregate demand and aggregate supply of the firm. As such, the aggregate planning process addresses neither the production of nor the demand for individual products or product lines. Rather, aggregate planning focuses on the total capacity of the productive facility and the total demand for all items produced in that facility.

Top management is typically assigned the responsibility of developing aggregate plans for a firm. Since the purpose of aggregate planning is to match supply and demand, it is essential that the operations function (supply) communicates with the marketing function (demand) in the development of a plan. In addition to these two functional areas, representatives from other areas in the organization that provide productive resources (e.g., capital from finance, labor from personnel) should also be involved in the planning process.

An aggregate plan usually covers a planning horizon of one year on a month-by-month basis. The information required to develop an aggregate plan includes: (1) an aggregate measure of capacity (e.g., direct labor hours per month, or units of production per month, or dollars of production per month); (2) an aggregate demand forecast (remember, this *does not* distinguish between products or product lines); and (3) cost information regarding the variables used in developing the plan (these are discussed in more detail later in this unit).

Aggregate planning is necessary because, while the aggregate demand of a firm is typically seasonal in nature, the most efficient way for most firms to operate is to produce at a constant rate throughout the year (see Figure 6-1).

In developing an aggregate plan, the marketing function should make an initial attempt to dampen demand seasonality by using a combination of demand-influencing variables including product, price, place, and promotion. For example, the dampened demand pattern in Figure 6-2 can be achieved by decreasing the price and increasing advertising in the trough (low point) of the cycle, and by increasing the price and decreasing advertising in the peak of the cycle. Notice that the average demand across the entire planning horizon is the same under the dampened demand pattern as it is under the undampened pattern.

After marketing has dampened demand seasonality as much as possible, the operations function must develop the cost-minimization strategy for providing the products necessary to satisfy that demand. The variables used in developing that strategy include the workforce level, subcontracting, inventory, and backordering.

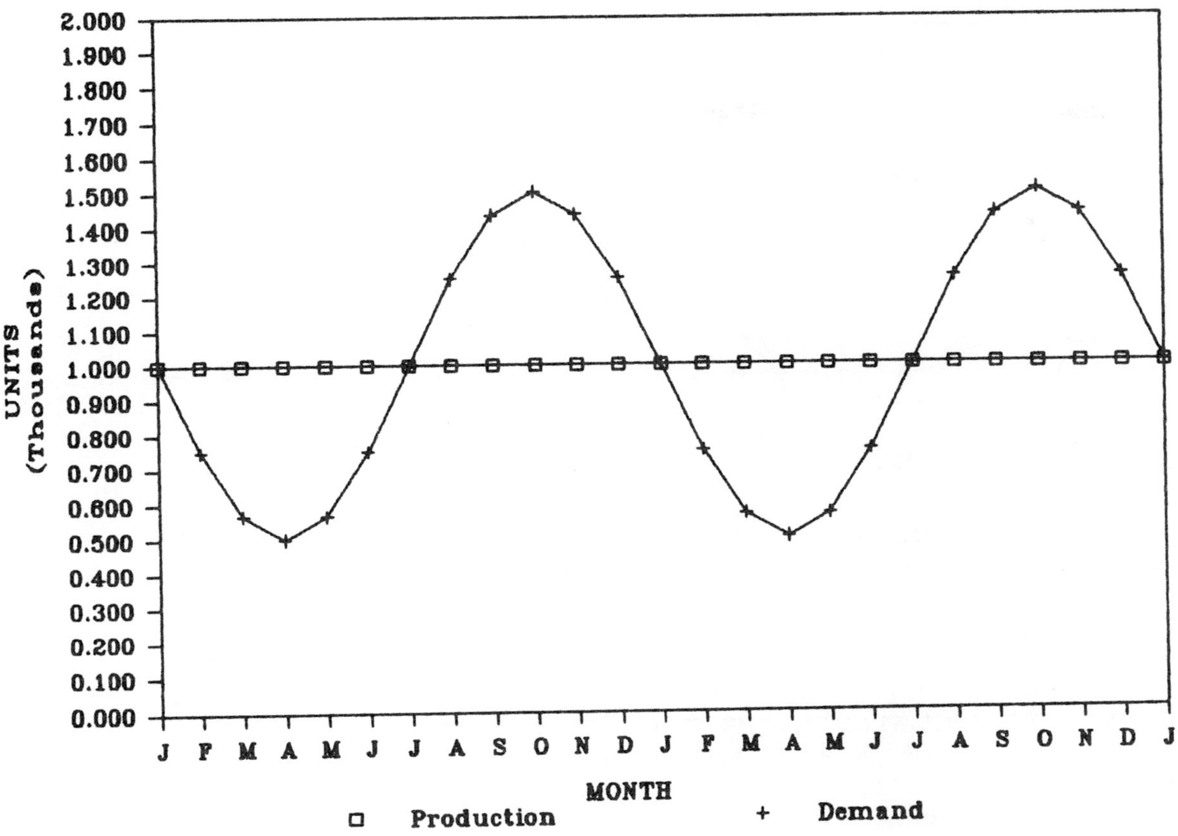

FIGURE 6-1 Seasonal Demand vs. Level Production

In an aggregate planning context, the *workforce* may be categorized as either variable or fixed. In a *variable workforce* situation the employees are usually unskilled and easy to replace. A large pool of such laborers must be available. The workers are typically not unionized. Under these circumstances, it is usually easy and inexpensive to *hire* employees when additional capacity is needed during the peak of the demand cycle and then to *fire* them when less output is required in the trough of the cycle. High school and college students are often used in this manner during the summer months at resorts, farms, beaches, ice cream stands, and so on. The costs of hiring include the paperwork, interviewers' time, and the training-supervisor's time. Firing costs include paperwork and, possibly, severance pay. In a *fixed workforce* situation the employees are usually highly skilled or protected from layoffs by a strong union. Under these circumstances it is quite costly to hire employees when demand is in the peak of its cycle and then to fire them when demand falls into its trough. Thus, *overtime* is used to increase output during the peak of a cycle and *undertime* is used to decrease output in the trough. The cost of using overtime is explicit, since the company typically pays a time-and-a-half premium for any overtime hours worked. The cost of using undertime is implicit, since the company does not incur additional labor cost under this alternative. However, when using undertime, the cost per unit of output increases since the workforce continues to be paid full-day wages but produces only the level of output required to satisfy demand.

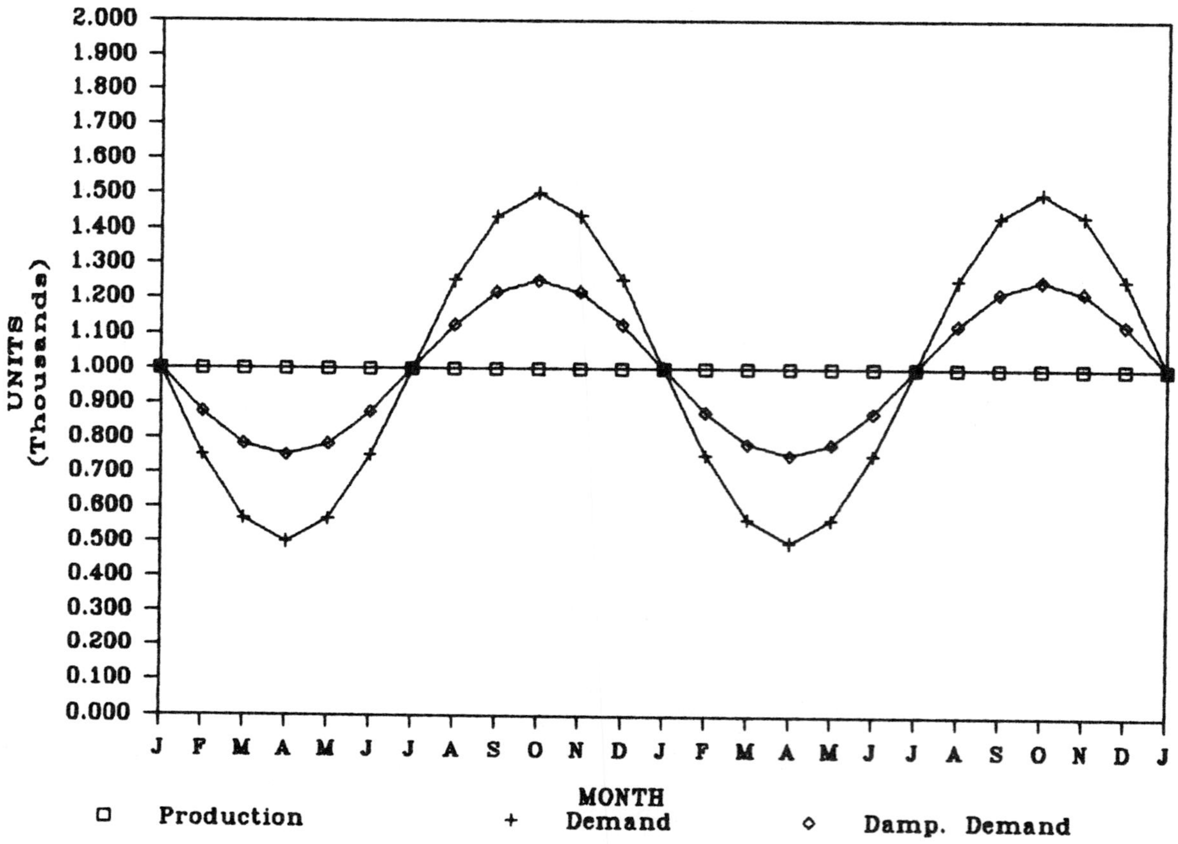

FIGURE 6-2 Marketing's Demand Dampening Effect

Subcontracting is a mechanism for increasing output during the peak of a demand cycle. In a subcontracting situation, firm A purchases productive capacity from its competitor, firm B; that is, firm B produces product and sells it to firm A. Firm A then places its label on the product and sells it to its customers. Both firms benefit because firm B's productive capacity is used more effectively and firm A's customers are satisfied with timely order delivery. However, firm A incurs a variety of costs for using this strategy to increase its level of output. Those costs include less control over quality, increased cost per unit resulting from external rather than internal manufacture, and, possibly, shifting business permanently to competitors.

Inventory is used to shift productive capacity from an earlier to a later period rather than to increase or decrease capacity in any period. The basic idea with inventory is to build product now and sell it later. Thus inventory is built up during the trough of a business cycle when the production rate exceeds the demand rate, and inventory is consumed during the peak of the cycle when demand exceeds production. Inventory is used as an aggregate planning variable when the market for the product is highly competitive. In such a situation, units that are not in inventory at the peak of the demand cycle represent sales that are lost to the competition. The cost of using inventory as an aggregate planning variable is the cost of carrying that inventory. Inventory carrying costs include the costs of capital, obsolescence, insurance, taxes, and the variable costs associated with maintaining the inventory (labor, lights, forklift trucks, etc.)

Backordering is another variable used to shift productive capacity rather than to increase or decrease it. In a backordering situation, a firm sells product now and builds it later. In essence, the firm develops a backlog of orders that are filled at a later date. Backordering is an effective aggregate planning variable only when market conditions are *not* highly competitive. The costs of using backorders in an aggregate plan are a bit more difficult to quantify than those associated with the other variables. They include the costs of lost customer goodwill and, perhaps, loss of contribution to profit and overhead (if the backorder results in a lost sale).

The combination of these variables that a firm uses depends on its particular cost structure, the degree of unionization in the firm, the strength of the firm's market position, and the firm's corporate social policy. After considering each of these variables, the firm establishes its aggregate plan by determining, for each period in the planning horizon, its production rate and workforce size as well as its levels of hiring, firing, overtime, undertime, subcontracting, inventory, and backordering.

Various mathematical techniques have been developed to solve this problem. However, few of them are actually used because of their complexity. Instead, trial-and-error techniques that focus on two pure aggregate planning strategies are most often used. The first of these pure strategies is called the *level workforce strategy*. With the level workforce strategy, the number of employees in a given period remains constant. The number of units produced varies depending on the number of productive days in the period. Using this strategy, the variations in the demand pattern are typically absorbed by variations in inventory or backorder levels (see Figure 6-3). With the second of the pure strategies, called the *chase demand strategy*, production and workforce levels change each period in order to produce exactly what is demanded. The primary trade-off between these two strategies is the cost of carrying inventory or incurring backorders (level) versus the cost of changing production levels (chase).

In practice, few firms use either a pure level strategy or a pure chase strategy. Rather, they combine the best characteristics of each into a mixed strategy that minimizes the aggregate production costs for their firm.

GATHERING THE DATA

Within the Company

Most of the data to support aggregate planning can be found within the company. *Productive days per period* are determined from a calendar (normally called a shop calendar) that lists operational days, holidays, and so on. *Employee productivity* is computed from historical data concerning the number of units produced and number of person-periods (staff-days, manhours, weeks, etc.) worked. At EZRydr, employee productivity is stated in terms of how many hours it takes one employee to build one (average) unit. This may be estimated by the industrial engineering staff based on time and motion studies or obtained from a database containing data about units produced and hours worked. Company records should also contain *current employment level* as well as *current inventory level* and *current backorder level*. Note

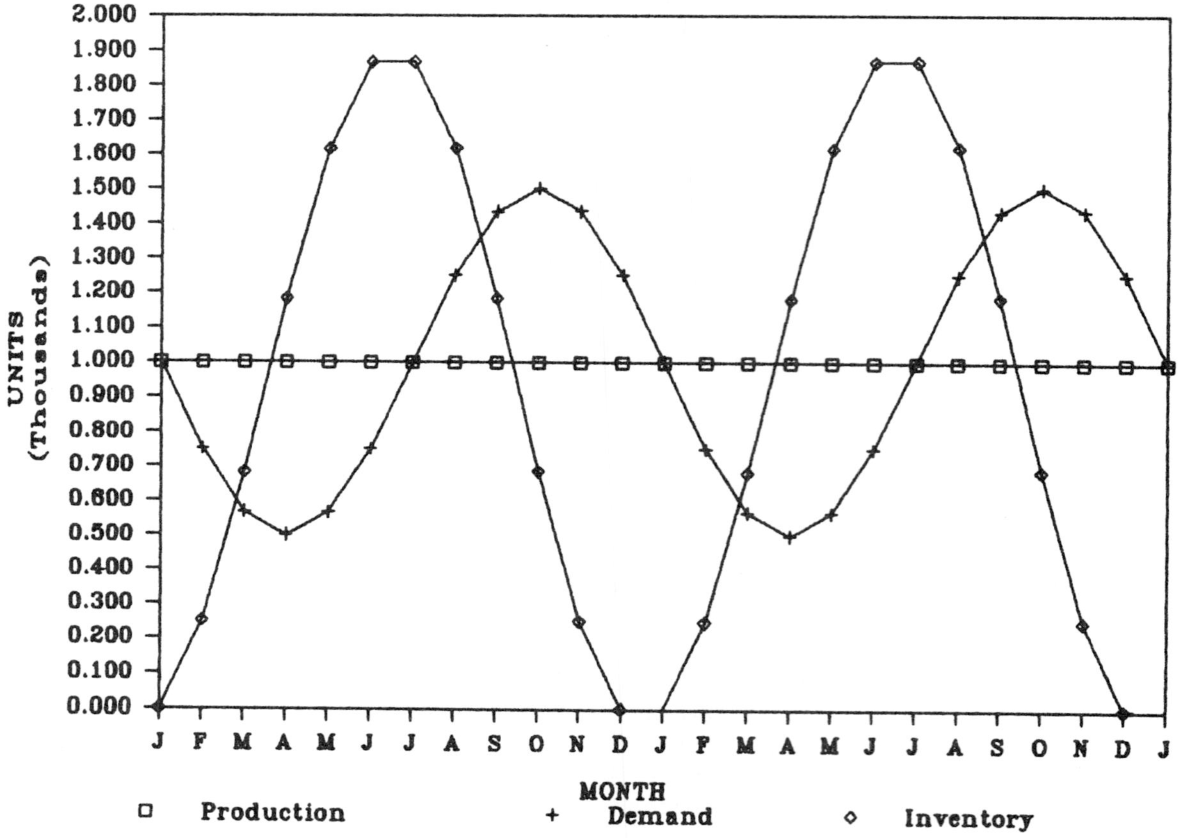

FIGURE 6-3 Inventory Variations under a Level Strategy

that inventory and backorders can exist simultaneously because there is no distinction among product lines. For example, we may have inventory of one model of motorcycle while another model is not available and therefore backordered.

Certain aggregate planning parameters are the result of management decisions. For instance, the *desired ending inventory level* is a management decision based on forecasts, inventory control models, and so on. The process used to make this decision is discussed in Unit 7. *Maximum allowable overtime* is set by personnel regulation or labor agreement. Pay scales, which include *regular wage rate* and *overtime wage rate*, are management or labor relations decisions. *Length of work day* is also a managerial decision.

Some of the data for aggregate planning, especially *cost data*, are estimates developed by the accounting function. These data include hiring and firing cost, additional cost incurred for subcontracting, inventory carrying cost, cost of backordering, and the material cost per unit. A major additional cost that must be determined is *factory overhead* (also called *burden*). Determination and allocation of this cost is discussed in Unit 4. To incorporate overhead costs in aggregate planning, EZRydr adds a certain amount per unit.

Finally, *aggregate demand data* are derived from the annual demand forecast, that is discussed in Unit 8. Using historical patterns, the annual forecast is converted to quarterly or monthly demand levels depending upon the planning needs of the firm.

External to the Company

Although data external to the company are not incorporated directly into the aggregate planning model, external data are important in preparing for aggregate planning. For instance, the demand forecast is based on external data, but forecasting should be done prior to this point in the planning process. The company also considers the experience of other firms when setting wage levels, productivity standards, cost data, and so forth.

THE PROBLEM

Recall that the management of EZRydr has been following a policy of no layoffs for most of the firm's life. They have been following this policy primarily to protect their workers, some of whom are descendants of the first employees of the firm. The management of EZRydr would like to evaluate the cost-effectiveness of this policy, and they have turned to you for some help.

EZRydr's management would like you to answer the following questions:

1. Using a pure level strategy, how many employees should be on the payroll if all work is done on regular time?

2. Using a pure level strategy, how many units should be produced each month?

3. What is the total inventory carrying cost incurred under a pure level strategy?

4. What is the total backorder cost incurred under a pure level strategy?

5. What is the total cost (materials, wages, inventory carrying cost, etc.) of a pure level strategy?

6. How many employees should be on the payroll if a level strategy with the maximum amount of overtime is used?

7. Is a pure level strategy more or less effective than a level strategy with maximum overtime?

8. How many employees are needed in each month using a pure chase strategy?

9. What is the total hiring and firing cost incurred under a pure chase strategy?

10. What is the total cost (materials, wages, inventory carrying cost, etc.) of a pure chase strategy?

11. Does a pure level strategy cost more than a pure chase strategy? If so, by how much? If not, how much money is saved by pursuing a level strategy?

Departmental Data

The following data have been compiled by EZRydr's production control department.

Month	Aggregate Demand (units)	Productive Days	
Jan	200	22	
Feb	250	19	
Mar	700	21	
Apr	1,000	22	
May	1,300	21	
Jun	1,900	21	
Jul	2,500	17	*(vacation)*
Aug	2,100	21	
Sep	1,100	21	
Oct	600	23	
Nov	200	19	
Dec	400	21	

Production Rate	18.00	hours/unit
Regular Wage	$10	/employee/hour
Materials	$850	/unit
Factory Overhead	$90	/unit
Overtime Rate	1.5	x regular wage
Maximum Overtime	20.00	% of regular time
Inv. Carry Rate	1.00	% of item value/unit/month
Backorder Cost	$50	/unit/month
Hire Cost	$250	/person
Fire Cost	$1,000	/person
Subcontract Premium	$70	/unit
Current Inventory	300	units
Desired Ending Inv	50	units
Employment Level	100	employees
Current Backorders	80	units
Length of Workday	8	hours

Data in the Database

The following information can be derived from the database. You must use the departmental data presented above for any figures not discussed below.

Current Inventory Level. This data is found in the production data file (PRODUCTN.DBF) and is the sum of the ON_HAND fields of all of the models for the current month.

Current Employment Level. This figure is found in the summary personnel data file (PERSONNL.DBF) and is the sum of the number of production employees (CATEGORY field = HOURLY) in departments FABRICAT and ASSEMBLE for the past month.

Average Regular Wage Rate. This figure is the average of the hourly rate (RATE) for all current production employees (CATEGORY field = HOURLY in departments FABRICAT and ASSEMBLE). To calculate the figure, you must sum the number of persons and the product of persons and rate, then divide the latter by the former to yield an average rate.

Employee Productivity. At EZRydr, productivity is stated as the number of hours required for one person to build one unit. (At other firms, the productivity might be stated in terms of dollar output per person per year. The following approach assumes that productivity rates have not been altered over the past twelve months as a result of technological or job design changes.) To compute productivity:

1. Determine the number of units produced over the past twelve months; this data is contained in the production data file in the field COMPLETED.

2. Determine the number of hours worked by production employees in the past twelve months; the summary personnel data file contains this data. Sum the R_HOURS and OT_HOURS fields for those whose CATEGORY field is HOURLY in departments FABRICAT and ASSEMBLE.

3. Divide the number obtained in 2 by the number obtained in 1; this is the number of hours required to produce one unit.

Material Cost per Unit. The production data file contains a field named MATERIALS that contains the total material cost per month. To determine average material cost per unit, sum over the past twelve months and divide by units produced during those months.

Direct Labor Cost per Unit. This is the product of average wage rate and productivity, both of which are discussed above.

DEVELOPING THE SPREADSHEET

Before we can address the questions posed by EZRydr's management, we must build a spreadsheet model of the aggregate plan. In this section, we discuss the development of such a model. When you save the spreadsheet, call it AGGPLAN.

Start by entering labels in column A as illustrated in Figure 6-4. Enter planning data numbers in column B. While developing the spreadsheet, use the *Departmental Data* discussed previously. Once all numbers are entered, format cells with dollar, percent, and fixed formats as appropriate. Finally, enter units of measure in column C.

To simplify later calculations, compute the Standard Cost with a formula in cell F5. This is the sum of material cost, factory overhead, and labor cost (hours/unit times wage/hour). Add the explanatory label as illustrated in Figure 6-4. To check the formula, change the Production Rate to 20.00 hours/unit. The Standard Cost should change to $1,140 (because there are two additional labor hours at $10 per hour). You may wish to check the other components of the formula by changing their values and observing the result. After verifying that the formula is correct, remember to restore each planning data item to its original value.

```
A1: [W20] "PLANNING DATA                                                 READY


                A                 B         C        D        E        F        G
1         PLANNING DATA
2
3       Production Rate       18.00 hours/unit                }
4          Regular Wage         $10 /employee/hour            } Standard Cost
5             Materials        $850 /unit                     }   $1,120
6       Factory Overhead        $90 /unit                     }
7         Overtime Rate         1.5 x regular wage
8      Maximum Overtime      20.00% of regular time
9       Inv. Carry Rate       1.00% of item value/unit/month
10       Backorder Cost         $50 /unit/month
11            Hire Cost        $250 /person
12            Fire Cost      $1,000 /person
13  Subcontract Premium         $70 /unit
14    Current Inventory         300 units
15     Desired Ending Inv        50 units
16     Employment Level         100 employees
17    Current Backorders         80 units
18     Length of Workday          8 hours
19
20
12-Jun-86  12:06 PM
```

FIGURE 6-4 The Planning Data Portion of the Spreadsheet

Once the planning data are entered, go to A22 to begin to build the AGGREGATE PLAN section of the spreadsheet. Enter labels in column A as illustrated in Figure 6-5. Next, enter column headings for initial data, months, total, and average across row 24, and monthly demand and productive days data (presented earlier in this unit) across rows 25 and 26.

There are five entries in the Initial column. The values in this column are obtained from the planning data. Three entries in this column are directly available in the planning data section: the number of employees, current inventory level, and current backorder level. For instance, the entry in cell B27 is +$B$16. In Lotus 1-2-3, we use an absolute cell reference because the cell address should not change when we copy this part of the spreadsheet elsewhere. (Some spreadsheet products do not use relative and absolute cell references in formulas, but control cell-address adjustment during the copy or replicate commands.) Other entries in the Initial column are formulas. Initial Regular Production is the initial number of employees times employee productivity per day (the length of the day divided by Production Rate in hours per unit) times the average of the twelve months' productive days. The formula in cell B28 is @INT(B27*($B$18/$B$3)*@AVG(C26..N26)). The @INT (integer) function is used because we wish to determine production in whole units. Any fractional part of the result (even .99) is truncated. Maximum Overtime Production is the maximum overtime rate times regular production. Again, the @INT function should be used to yield an integer value.

	A	B	C	E	F	I	M
1	PLANNING DATA					LEVEL STRATEGY	
2							
3	Production Rate	18.00	hours/unit	}		Number of Employees Required	
4	Regular Wage	$10	/employee/hour	}	Standard Cost	No Overtime	110
5	Materials	$850	/unit	}	$1,120	Maximum Overtime	92
6	Factory Overhead	$90	/unit	}			
7	Overtime Rate	1.5	x regular wage				
8	Maximum Overtime	20.00%	of regular time				
9	Inv. Carry Rate	1.00%	of item value/unit/month				
10	Backorder Cost	$50	/unit/month				
11	Hire Cost	$250	/person				
12	Fire Cost	$1,000	/person				
13	Subcontract Premium	$70	/unit				
14	Current Inventory	300	units				
15	Desired Ending Inv	50	units				
16	Employment Level	100	employees				
17	Current Backorders	80	units				
18	Length of Workday	8	hours				
19							
20							
21							

	A	B	C	D	E	F	G	H	I	J	K	L	M	N	O	P
22	AGGREGATE PLAN		? Strategy												15-May-87	11:40 AM
23																
24	MONTH	Initial	Jan	Feb	Mar	Apr	May	Jun	Jul	Aug	Sep	Oct	Nov	Dec	TOTALS	AVERAGE
25	Demand	---	200	250	700	1000	1300	1900	2500	2100	1100	600	200	400	12250	1021
26	Productive Days	---	22	19	21	22	21	21	17	21	21	23	19	21	248	21
27	# Employees	100	0	0	0	0	0	0	0	0	0	0	0	0	--	
28	Reg. Production	918	0	0	0	0	0	0	0	0	0	0	0	0	0	
29	Max Ovrtime (units)	183	0	0	0	0	0	0	0	0	0	0	0	0	0	
30	Act Ovrtime (units)	---	0	0	0	0	0	0	0	0	0	0	0	0	0	
31	Overtime Check	---	ok	ok	ok	ok	ok	ok	ok	ok	ok	ok	ok	ok	--	
32	Subcontr (units)	---	0	0	0	0	0	0	0	0	0	0	0	0	0	
33	TOTAL PRODUCTION	---	0	0	0	0	0	0	0	0	0	0	0	0	0	
34	Inventory	300	20	0	0	0	0	0	0	0	0	0	0	0	--	
35	Backorders	80	0	230	930	1930	3230	5130	7630	9730	10830	11430	11630	12030	--	
36																
37	Regular Wages	---	0	0	0	0	0	0	0	0	0	0	0	0	0	
38	Overtime Wages	---	0	0	0	0	0	0	0	0	0	0	0	0	0	
39	Hire/Fire Cost	---	100000	0	0	0	0	0	0	0	0	0	0	0	100000	
40	Subcontract Cost	---	0	0	0	0	0	0	0	0	0	0	0	0	0	
41	Material Cost	---	0	0	0	0	0	0	0	0	0	0	0	0	0	
42	Carrying Cost	---	1792	112	0	0	0	0	0	0	0	0	0	0	1904	
43	Backorder Cost	---	0	11500	46500	96500	161500	256500	381500	486500	541500	571500	581500	601500	3736500	
44	Factory Overhead	---	0	0	0	0	0	0	0	0	0	0	0	0	0	
45																
46	TOTAL COST	---	101792	11612	46500	96500	161500	256500	381500	486500	541500	571500	581500	601500	3838404	TOTAL
47	Std. Prod. Cost	---	0	0	0	0	0	0	0	0	0	0	0	0	0	Fixed
48	Incremental Cost	---	101792	11612	46500	96500	161500	256500	381500	486500	541500	571500	581500	601500	3838404	Incre

FIGURE 6-5 The Completed Skeleton Spreadsheet

These last two numbers are provided to the planner so he or she can estimate production capacity given the current employment level. We have entered "---" in all other cells in the Initial column for cosmetic effect.

Once the Initial column is completed, we may begin development of the monthly columns. Each month is similar, so we discuss the development of the formulas for January (column C); you can copy those formulas across the other months. Because the formulas are to be copied, pay close attention to the use of absolute and mixed cell addresses. Any reference to a number in the PLANNING DATA section should be an absolute or mixed address so the formula can be copied across the columns.

The # Employees is determined by the strategy we choose. For the moment, we may set the number of employees at 0 (zero). Later, we develop formulas that tell us how many employees to put in each month of this row.

The formula for Reg. Production is very similar to the formula in the Initial column. However, instead of multiplying by the average number of productive days per month, multiply by the actual number of days in the specific month (row 26).

As above, the Max Ovrtime (units) is the integer portion of the product of the maximum overtime percent allowed and regular production.

Act Ovrtime (units) is also determined by the strategy we choose. For now, enter 0 (zero).

The Overtime Check is included to ensure that we do not exceed the allowable overtime. The formula checks the actual versus the maximum overtime and displays "ERR" if the maximum is exceeded. With some spreadsheet packages (e.g., Lotus 1-2-3 Release 2), we can have the formula display "ok" if the overtime is within bounds; for other packages (e.g., Lotus 1-2-3 Release 1A), the formula displays "0" (zero). The Lotus 1-2-3 formula is one of the following:

```
@IF(C30>C29,@ERR,"      ok")        Release 2
@IF(C30>C29,@ERR,0)                 Release 1A
```

The row entitled Subcontr (units) is another strategy variable; it should contain zeros at this point.

TOTAL PRODUCTION is the sum of regular production (C28), actual overtime (C30), and subcontracted units (C32).

To determine Inventory, we add the previous month's inventory (B34) to the current month's production (C33), then subtract the previous month's backorders (B35) and the current month's demand (C25). This formula by itself is fine when previous inventory plus production (i.e., supply) exceeds previous backorders and current demand (i.e., demand). However, when demand exceeds supply, we obtain a negative figure for inventory, which is not possible (i.e., we cannot have -100 motorcycles in inventory — instead we have 100 on backorder, the next row in the spreadsheet). To prevent the inventory figure from being negative, we use the @MAX (maximum) function:

```
@MAX(0,+B34+C33-C25-B35)
```

When this formula is entered, the number 20 is displayed. Why?

In the formula for Backorders, we use the same logic as in the formula for Inventory, except that the signs of the variables are reversed.

Regular Wages is the product of regular production, production rate in hours per unit, and the regular wage in dollars per hour. Note that, under this formulation, regular wages are based on the number of units produced rather than on the number of hours worked. This implies that the workers are paid on a piece-rate rather than an hourly basis.

Overtime Wages is the product of actual overtime production, production rate, the regular wage rate, and the overtime rate factor.

The Hire/Fire Cost is determined through a logical formula: if the current month's employment (C27) exceeds last month's employment (B27), then we have hired and the Hire/Fire Cost is the difference in the two employment levels times the Hire Cost (B11). If the reverse is true, then the Hire/Fire Cost is the difference times the Fire Cost (B12). The following formula contains the necessary logic:

```
@IF(C27>B27,(C27-B27)*$B$11,(B27-C27)*$B$12)
```

For a modest mental exercise, determine what happens if there are neither hires nor fires. When you enter this formula into the spreadsheet, the number 100000 is displayed. Why?

Subcontract Cost is the number of units subcontracted times the sum of Subcontract Premium per unit and labor cost per unit. In this model, the Subcontract Premium represents the incremental cost per unit incurred by using an external production source. The costs of materials and overhead for all units produced (internal and external) are calculated separately. The following formula yields the residual component of subcontracted units (subcontract premium and labor cost):

```
+C32*($B$13+$B$3*$B$4)
```

Material Cost is the product of total production and the material cost per unit.

Inventory Carrying Cost is the inventory carrying rate (B9) times the standard cost per unit (F5) times the average monthly inventory. Average monthly inventory is estimated as the average of the previous month's (ending) inventory and this month's (ending) inventory. The formula is

```
(B34+C34)/2*($F$5*$B$9)
```

When this formula is entered into the spreadsheet, there is a result other than zero. Why? Do you think the result for the next month is also zero?

Backorder Cost is the product of current month backorders and the backorder cost.

Factory Overhead is the product of total production and the overhead rate.

TOTAL COST is the sum of the costs in rows 37 to 44. This is the total expenditure, including penalty costs for hiring, firing, carrying inventory, and so on.

Std. Prod. Cost is the product of the number of units produced and the standard production cost (F5). This is how much it should cost to produce the items if no penalty costs are incurred (in other words, if we have perfectly level demand and we do not hire, fire, subcontract, carry inventory, or incur backorders).

Finally, Incremental Cost is the difference between total cost and standard cost. Incremental cost is the cost of the strategy, and we wish to minimize incremental cost through judicious use of hiring, firing, overtime, subcontracting, and so on. We should focus on this cost in choosing among the various aggregate planning strategies.

Once you have entered the formulas in column C, your spreadsheet should look like columns A through C in Figure 6-5. If you have different numbers, you may have misentered a formula or value. Check your work carefully against the discussion above. Once you have the a correct spreadsheet, copy the formulas in the range C27..C48 to the other eleven months (D27..N48). (If your spreadsheet package does not use absolute cell references in formulas [e.g., SuperCalc 3], you must specify which cells in the formulas should be adjusted and which should not be adjusted when you use the copy or replicate command.)

At this point, you might use the appropriate command to establish column A as a title column in order to keep the labels in view when you move the cell pointer to the right.

To complete the skeleton spreadsheet, create the TOTALS and AVERAGE columns. Also enter date and time functions, if available, in cells O22 and P22. These provide a *date stamp* whenever the plan is printed, a useful feature that reduces confusion as to which is the most recent printed version.

It is not necessary to complete the LEVEL STRATEGY section at this time. This is done in the "Using the Spreadsheet" section below. Save your spreadsheet before proceeding.

CHECKING THE MODEL

Before using a decision support model, it is *very* important that you check its logic. (When we checked our first model, we found three errors!) To check a model, use sample data and manually compute the result of each formula. In this section, we provide a few simple steps for checking the aggregate planning model, but you should do additional checking.

First, enter 10 (ten) actual overtime units for January. The Overtime Check entry should change to "ERR" because you have exceeded the maximum allowable overtime for that month. (This is because you have, at present, zero employees in January and therefore zero maximum overtime.)

Next, enter 99 employees for January, and 100 employees for February through December. Also enter 10 subcontracted units for the month of January only. Verify each of the following values for the month of January:

Item	Value
Reg. Production	968
Overtime Check	ok *or* 0
Inventory	1008
Hire/Fire Cost	1000

Subcontract Cost	2500
Factory Overhead	88920
Std. Prod. Cost	1106560
Incremental Cost	9925

A final check figure: The TOTAL Incremental Cost is 647046. We leave it to you to check the remainder of the results for January, and throughout the rest of the spreadsheet. If the spreadsheet and the check figures (both those provided here and those you have computed manually) do not agree, you may have misentered a formula or value. Check your work carefully against the discussion in "Developing the Spreadsheet" and make necessary corrections.

USING THE SPREADSHEET

As you recall, EZRydr's management posed a number of questions regarding aggregate planning at their firm. We now use the spreadsheet to answer those questions.

1. Using a pure level strategy, how many employees should be on the payroll if all work is done on regular time? We need to answer this question first to determine what level of employment to use for the level workforce strategy. To answer this question, we must compute the average number of units required per day and the number of units an employee can produce in one day. Dividing the first by the second yields the answer we seek.

   The average number of units required per day is obtained by dividing the total number of units required (total demand plus current backorders plus desired ending inventory minus current inventory) by the number of productive days in the year.

   The number of units per employee per day is length of the workday divided by the production rate (that is the number of hours it takes one employee to produce one unit).

   We wish to build a table that contains the answer to this question and the answer to Question 6 (below). The table, illustrated in Figure 6-6, starts in cell I1. Put the labels shown in that figure in cells I1, I3, J4, and J5. The formula for this particular question is in cell M4. In M4, put the formula

   @ROUND((($O$25+$B$15+$B$17-$B$14)/$O$26)/($B$18/$B$3)+0.49,0)

   Manually check the formula to insure that it yields the proper result. The @ROUND function coupled with the addition of 0.49 is used to "round up" to the next higher whole employee.

2. Using a pure level strategy, how many units should be produced each month? To answer this question, reference cell M4 in the # Employees row for January through December.

   You might take advantage of spreadsheet graphing features at this point to graph the effect of a level workforce. Use the necessary commands to create a graph that is similar to that illustrated in Figure 6-7. This graph illustrates the cycle of inventory build up and backorder increase typical of the level workforce strategy.

```
H1: [W8]                                                        READY


       H       I       J       K       L       M       N       O
1          LEVEL STRATEGY
2
3          Number of Employees Required
4                  No Overtime                   110
5                  Maximum Overtime               92
6
```

FIGURE 6-6 Level Workforce Strategy Computations

3. What is the total inventory carrying cost incurred under a pure level strategy? The answer is in the TOTALS column of the Carrying Cost row.

4. What is the total backorder cost incurred under a pure level strategy? The answer is in the TOTALS column of the Backorder Cost row.

5. What is the total cost (materials, wages, inventory carrying cost, etc.) of a pure level strategy? We leave it to you to find the answer to this question on the spreadsheet.

6. How many employees should be on the payroll if a level strategy with the maximum amount of overtime is used? This question is essentially the same as Question 1, except that the length of the day is increased by the maximum number of overtime hours allowed. Copy the formula from cell M4 to M5, then edit so the formula becomes

   @ROUND((($O$25+$B$15+$B$17-$B$14)/$O$26)/($B$18/$B$3*(1+$B$8))+0.49,0)

   In reality, most companies, including EZRydr, do not work maximum overtime all year. This result yields the minimum number of employees needed if maximum overtime is used.

   Save the spreadsheet at this point to keep a copy of the model as is.

7. Is a pure level strategy more or less effective than a level strategy with maximum overtime? First reference cell M5 across the # Employees row, as you did for Question 2 above. Enter the value displayed in the maximum overtime row in the corresponding month in the actual overtime row. Now compare the total cost under the maximum overtime option with the total cost for the pure level option (see Question 5) to determine the answer to this question.

8. How many employees are needed in each month using a pure chase strategy? To answer this question, we enter formulas, not values, in the # Employees row. The number of employees needed in a month is determined by dividing the number of units that must be produced per day by the number of units an employee can produce in one day.

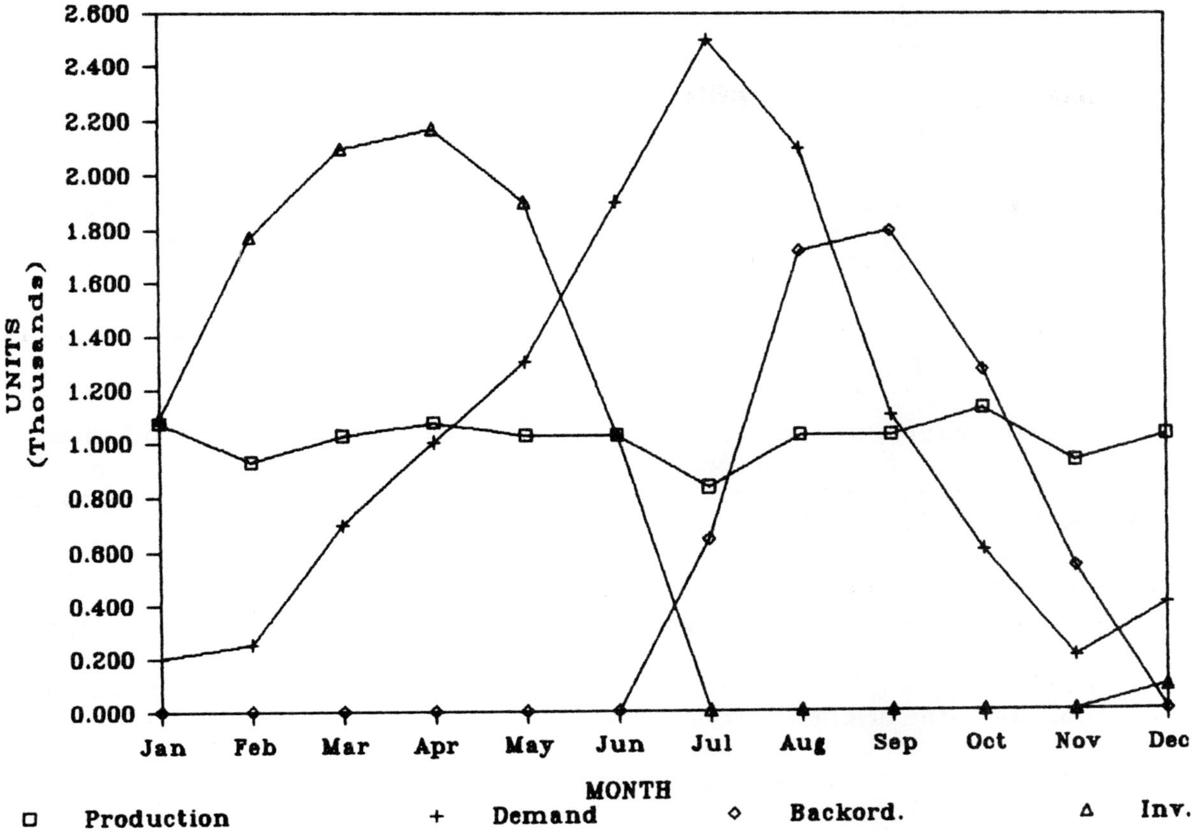

FIGURE 6-7 Effect of EZRydr's Level Workforce Strategy

For all months except the last, the number of units that must be produced in one day is the sum of the month's demand and the prior month's backorder level minus the prior month's inventory level, all divided by the number of productive days in the month. For the last month, the required production must be increased by the desired ending inventory (the assumption is that ending inventory should be zero for all other months under a pure chase strategy).

Employee productivity, as above, is the length of the workday divided by the production rate.

In a pure chase strategy, a situation may arise in which current required production is less than zero because the prior month's inventory exceeds the current month's demand and backorders. This could yield a value less than zero for the number of employees required. To prevent a situation in which there are *negative employees* (in quantity, not attitude), the @MAX function must be used; that is, the formula must be the maximum of zero or the number of employees necessary for the required production level.

We leave it to you to determine the precise formula, which must be copied to each cell of the # Employees row and modified slightly for December.

9. What is the total hiring and firing cost incurred under a pure chase strategy? We leave it to you to find the answer to this question on the spreadsheet.

10. What is the total cost (materials, wages, inventory carrying cost, etc.) of a pure chase strategy? You should be able to find the cell that contains this value.

11. Does a pure level strategy cost more than a pure chase strategy? If so, by how much? If not, how much money is saved by pursuing a level strategy? We leave it to you to determine the answers to these questions.

ENHANCEMENTS TO THE APPLICATION

There are several features of spreadsheet packages that make the aggregate planning spreadsheet easier to use. In this section, we point out some features that you may implement in your model. As you solve the Exercises that follow, you may decide to incorporate enhancements beyond those suggested here.

1. Copy the AGGREGATE PLAN section to another area in the spreadsheet so you can analyze two strategies simultaneously. For rows that contain constants (i.e., Demand and Productive Days), the second copy of the plan should contain references to the cells in the original copy, not the constant values. Then, if forecast demand for a month changes, you need change only the original entry, not both.

   Before continuing, check your second copy, using the method discussed earlier in this unit.

2. Create a summary table somewhere on the spreadsheet that contains the TOTALS column figures for TOTAL COST, Std. Prod. Cost, and Incremental Cost for both strategies. Use the windowing feature of the spreadsheet to insure that this table remains in view as various strategies, cost structures, demand patterns, and so on are tested.

EXERCISES

The Aggregate Planning spreadsheet that we have developed for EZRydr's management is a powerful and versatile decision-making tool. Convince yourself of its usefulness by answering the following questions. As you answer these questions, reset the spreadsheet before every question or subquestion. The easiest way to do this is to save the spreadsheet with the initial values, then change demand or cost data as indicated. Once the question is answered, you may wish to save the spreadsheet with a unique name (e.g., AGGPL1A). When you are ready for the next question or subquestion, load (retrieve) the original spreadsheet.

1. If the decision is based strictly on the incremental cost, would EZRydr prefer a pure level or a pure chase strategy if

   a. demand decreased by 300 units per month in April through September, inclusive?

   b. demand decreased by 300 units per month in April through September, inclusive, and increased by 300 units per month in all other months?

c. the firing cost decreased to $500 per person?

d. the inventory carrying cost increased to 1.5% of item value per unit per month?

e. the backorder cost increased to $100 per unit per month?

2. At what inventory carrying rate would EZRydr be indifferent between a pure level and a pure chase strategy? Assume that all other costs remain constant.

3. As you may recall from the "Using the Spreadsheet" section above, few companies work maximum overtime all year. The formula below is used to calculate the required workforce size if maximum overtime is used for only a portion of the year:

W = RP / {[RT + OT(1 + MO)] x DP}

where, W is required workforce size, RP is required annual production, RT is number of days at regular time (no overtime), OT is number of days of maximum overtime, MO is maximum overtime rate, and DP is daily production rate (units/day/employee). This formula should be placed in cell M6 because it is a variation of the level workforce strategies. Call it Limited Overtime. To use this formula, put the relevant values in nearby cells. For instance, in M7 put the number of overtime days to be worked. In M8 put the number of regular time days, that is the total number of productive days in the year less the number of overtime days. The other values in the formula are similar to the values in the No Overtime and Maximum Overtime formulas in cells above.

a. How many employees are required for maximum overtime during the months of June, July, and August? (In M7, put the formula +H26+I26+J26.)

b. What happens to the incremental cost under this strategy? (Refer to Question 7 under "Using the Spreadsheet" for the steps to follow, and remember to enter overtime only in the three months.)

c. Develop the curve that relates incremental cost to the number of months at maximum overtime. You have already determined three of the thirteen points on the curve: zero months of overtime, overtime for the three months with the highest demand, and overtime for all twelve months. Compute the incremental cost for the other ten points (e.g., overtime for July only [the month with highest demand], overtime for July and August [the two highest-demand months], etc.). Note that both January and November have the same demand. In this situation, work overtime in the month with the greatest demand per productive day. Create a table that contains the number of months of overtime (0, 1, . . ., 12) and the respective incremental cost in a blank area of the spreadsheet. Graph the data in the table. Which number of months at maximum overtime yields the lowest incremental cost?

4. Using any combination of overtime, hiring, firing, and subcontracting, develop the aggregate planning strategy with the lowest possible incremental cost.

You do not need to use the spreadsheet to answer the following questions.

5. When using a pure level strategy, is it more cost effective to use subcontracting or overtime to produce additional units during the peak of the demand cycle?

6. A plot of some of the variables used in EZRydr's Level Workforce Strategy appears in Figure 6-7. One of those variables is Production. Why does production vary from one month to the next, when this is supposed to be a "level" strategy? (As you recall, Figures 6-1 through 6-3 show production as a level line.)

REVIEW QUESTIONS

1. Why do firms develop aggregate plans?

*2. What are the basic strategies used in developing an aggregate plan?

3. Define the following terms as they relate to aggregate planning:

   a. variable workforce

   *b. fixed workforce

   c. undertime

   *d. subcontracting

   e. inventory

   *f. backordering

4. How does a spreadsheet package simplify the aggregate planning process?

*5. Which types of graphs are most useful for illustrating aggregate planning solutions?

ADDITIONAL READING

To understand more about aggregate planning refer to any introductory operations management textbook; see, for example,

Chase, R. B. and N. J. Aquilano. *Production and Operations Management.* Homewood, IL: Irwin, 1985.

Evans, J. R., D. R. Anderson, D. J. Sweeney and T. A. Williams. *Applied Production and Operations Management.* St. Paul: West, 1984.

Fearon, H. E., W. A. Ruch, V. G. Reuter, C. D. Wieters and R. R. Reck. *Fundamentals of Production/Operations Management.* St. Paul: West, 1986.

Harris, R. D., and R. F. Gonzalez. *The Operations Manager: Role, Problems, Techniques.* St. Paul: West, 1981.

Schroeder, R. G.. *Operations Management: Decision Making in the Operations Function.* New York: McGraw-Hill, 1985.

An article entitled "A Heuristic Method for Aggregate Planning: Production Decision Framework" (J. A. Holt, *Journal of Operations Management*, Vol. 2, No. 1, October 1981) presents an aggregate planning technique that could be modeled with a spreadsheet package.

UNIT

7 INVENTORY ANALYSIS—HOW MUCH DO WE ORDER? WHEN?

Inventory is the stock of items or resources held by an organization. There are three general types of inventory: raw materials, work in process, and finished goods. The decision maker is faced with the problem of selecting the appropriate levels of inventory for different items. Several fairly simple models for inventory analysis can be implemented with a spreadsheet package.

DECISION SUPPORT APPLICATION MATRIX

Accounting & Finance	Economics & Long-Range Planning	Human Resources	Marketing & Logistics	Management Information Systems	Operations Planning & Control	Executive Officers
¤			■¤		■¤	¤

■ Departmental area(s) in which the technique is or can be used.

¤ Departmental area(s) that provide input to or are impacted by the technique.

LEARNING OBJECTIVES

1. After completing this unit you should know

    a. the terminology associated with inventory analysis,

    b. the reasons that organizations analyze inventory,

    c. the basic models used to deal with different inventory situations,

    d. which models are most appropriate for a given situation,

    e. how a spreadsheet package can simplify the process of inventory analysis.

Contributed by Rajesh Srivastava

2. After completing this unit you should be able to

   a. create a spreadsheet for solving inventory problems,

   b. develop graphic presentations of inventory problems.

BASIC CONCEPTS

An organization's inventory consists of raw materials that are transformed into products, items that are in the process of completion, and the finished goods that have not yet been sold or shipped. Inventories are one of the major investments made by a firm. They often require significant expenditures to obtain and maintain. There are many reasons why organizations keep inventories. Inventories make it possible for an organization to order larger quantities of goods from suppliers at better prices. They help the organization maintain stable operating levels and workforce levels. Good customer service is maintained by supplying most customer requirements from stock without delay. The purpose of inventory analysis is to determine the quantity and timing of orders for items purchased from suppliers (yielding raw materials) or manufactured internally (yielding work in process and finished goods).

Inventories allow the organization to effectively plan its overall production strategy by decoupling the phases of operations — from acquisition of raw materials through the various stages of production to shipment of finished goods. Raw materials decouple a firm's production process from the operations of its vendors. Work-in-process inventory allows production in each department to proceed independent of that in other departments. Finished goods provide a means for leveling production rates while meeting seasonal product demand. Higher levels of inventory normally provide more flexibility in operations, but higher inventories also cost more to procure and maintain. Therefore the advantages achieved from holding larger inventories must be balanced against the cost of holding inventory. The basic issue to be resolved is what the appropriate level of inventory is for a given item.

Middle and lower levels of management are typically assigned the responsibility of inventory management in a firm. Decision making in inventory management impacts other areas of the organization as well. Customer service level, for instance, is an important consideration for marketing. The level of inventory investment is an important consideration for finance. The decisions made in inventory management must therefore evolve from top management policy. To make this feasible, the focus must be on developing decision systems that take into account the top management policies and also provide consistency in decision making for middle-level management.

In developing an inventory analysis model and a decision system for inventory management, there are various factors to consider. One of the primary factors is the type of demand — independent or dependent. When the demand for a product or component item is established by the market place and therefore is uncertain, the demand for the item is called *independent*. When the demand for an item (usually a component or raw material) is derived from the demand for a final product, the demand is termed *dependent*. Once the demand is known or estimated for independent items, the demand for dependent items can be calculated from the *bill of materials* (a bill of materials for a product is like the ingredient list of a recipe for a cake). In this unit, we discuss independent demand situations. Different techniques, such as *material requirements planning* (MRP), are generally used to plan and control dependent demand inventories.

Different factors influence the choice of technique for controlling the inventory of an independent demand item. Paramount among these is the purpose for which the inventory is maintained. When the intent is to obtain economies of scale in purchase or manufacture, the organization maintains a *cycle stock* of the item. *Safety stock* (sometimes called buffer stock) is carried to protect against normal variation in supply or demand. The organization creates *anticipation stock* when it expects an unusual event, such as a supplier strike or a sales promotion. Inventory that is moving from one place to another (such as motorcycles en route to a dealer) is termed *transit stock*. The inventory planning models discussed in this unit focus on the first two types of stocks.

To establish the appropriate level of inventory for a given item, we must answer two key questions: "How much of the item should we order?" and "When should the order be placed?" There are a variety of models that provide answers to these questions. The choice of model depends on certain assumptions, but all models use a common set of variables. Before discussing the models and their attendant assumptions, we define these variables.

Variables

Order Quantity (Q). This is the size of an order, expressed in units.

Demand (D). This is the rate at which an item (raw material or finished good) is used. Though it can be expressed for any time period, demand is usually expressed as units per year.

Item Cost (C). This is the purchase cost of a raw material or the value of an in-process or finished item. It is expressed in dollars per unit.

Inventory Carrying Rate (i). This is a composite rate that includes the costs of capital, storage, insurance, obsolescence, and handling. It is expressed as a percentage of item cost per unit per period (again, usually per year).

Holding Cost (H). This is the amount that it costs the organization to maintain an item in inventory, calculated as the product of Inventory Carrying Rate and Item Cost: $i \times C$.

Preparation Cost (P). This is the cost incurred when placing an order with a vendor (e.g., paperwork) or when preparing to manufacture an item (e.g., machine setup). Preparation cost is a generic term that encompasses *ordering cost* and *setup cost*. It is expressed in dollars per order or dollars per setup.

Stockout Cost Factor (f). This is a rate that measures the contribution to profit and overhead that is lost by not making a sale. It may be expressed as a percentage of unit cost.

Stockout Cost (S). This is the cost incurred when there is insufficient inventory to satisfy demand. A stockout is a lost sale, and the stockout cost measures the contribution to profit and overhead that is lost by not making the sale of an item. It is the product of Stockout Cost Factor and Item Cost: $f \times C$.

Lead Time (L). This is the time that elapses between placement of an order and the arrival of the item. This may be expressed in days, weeks, months, or years.

Stock Position. This is the sum of items on hand and items on order. The stock position is used in some models as part of the indication of when to place an order, and in other models to determine how much to order.

Models

The answers to the questions "How much?" and "When?" are developed in several models. The focus of most inventory models is on minimizing the total inventory management cost. Simpler models balance the cost of ordering an item against the cost of carrying that item in stock. More advanced inventory control models include additional costs such as stockout costs. In developing a decision system for inventory analysis, the level of detail should be such that the benefits gained from the system outweigh the costs of using the system. The choice of which model to use depends on assumptions about the situation and managerial preferences.

The Basic EOQ Model. The basic *economic order quantity* (EOQ) model relies on several simplifying assumptions:

- Demand is fixed, known, and constant.
- Replenishment lead time is fixed, known, and constant.
- The price per unit is not a function of the order quantity.
- For a given order, all units are delivered at the same time.
- The time value of money is zero.
- Quantity and timing of orders for one item are not affected by those for any other item.

The basic EOQ model produces inventory fluctuations as illustrated in Figure 7-1. In this graph, we illustrate demand of 100 units per month for a period of twenty-four months, orders timed to arrive when the inventory level reaches zero, and three values of order quantity (Q = 200, Q = 400, and Q = 800). The larger the order quantity, the higher the peak and average inventory level (i.e., where Q = 400, the average inventory level is 200) and thus the higher the annual holding cost. But larger order quantities reduce the number of orders that must be placed (i.e., where Q = 400, six orders must be placed over the twenty-four month period), and therefore annual preparation cost is lower. Because the cost per unit does not depend on the number of units ordered, this cost need not be considered in the basic EOQ model. The cost of the units ordered is 1,200 times the unit cost, regardless of the order quantity (200, 400, or 800).

In the basic EOQ model, inventory ranges between zero and the order quantity. Therefore average inventory is one-half the order quantity. Annual holding cost is computed by multiplying the average inventory level by the holding cost per unit:

$$\text{Annual Holding Cost} = (Q/2) \times H$$

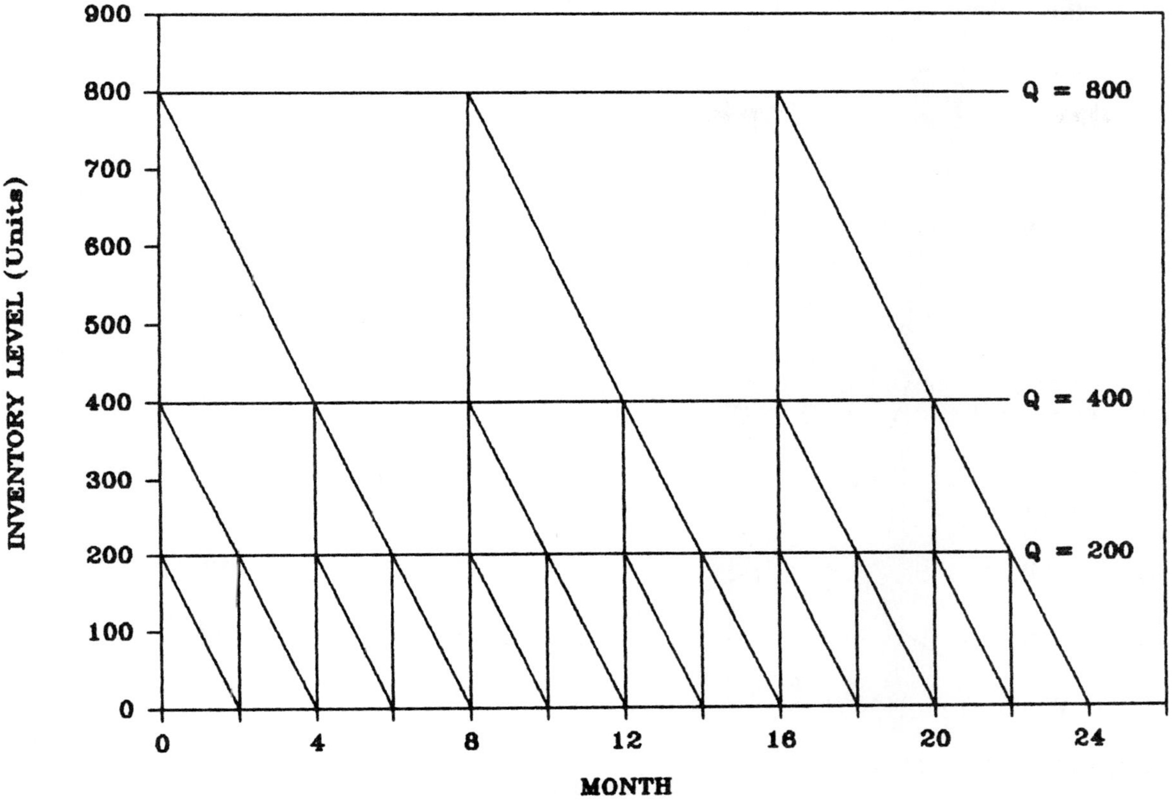

FIGURE 7-1 Inventory Level as a Function of Time and Order Quantity

The number of orders placed in a year is the annual demand divided by the order quantity. Annual preparation cost is the product of the number of orders placed in a year and the cost to place an order:

Annual Preparation Cost = (D/Q) x P

Total annual cost is the sum of the cost of the units ordered, annual holding costs, and annual preparation costs. Because we ignore the cost of the units ordered in the basic EOQ model, we focus on minimizing the sum of the latter two costs, which we call *Total Inventory Management Cost* (TIMC):

TIMC = (Q/2) x H + (D/Q) x P

The relationship between order quantity and annual holding cost, annual ordering cost, and TIMC is illustrated in Figure 7-2. Here we assume that the holding cost is $1.50 per unit per year and ordering cost is $25.00 per order. Note that TIMC is at a minimum where the two other cost lines intersect. This point indicates the economic order quantity. Through calculus, we determine the formula for economic order quantity:

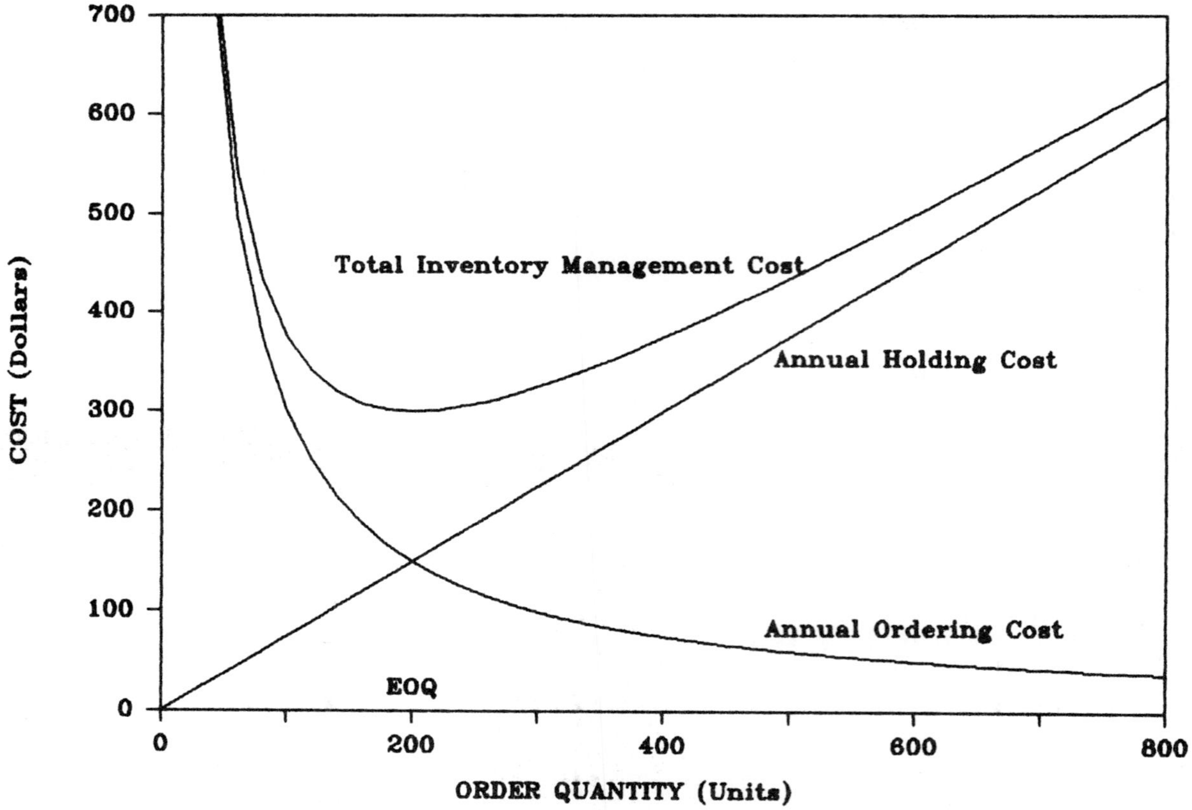

FIGURE 7-2 Costs as a Function of Order Quantity

$$EOQ = \sqrt{(2DP)/H}$$

This formula provides the answer to the question "How much?" For the example discussed here,

$$EOQ = \sqrt{[2(1,200)(25)]/1.5} = 200 \text{ units}$$

The TIMC of this decision rule is

$$TIMC = (200/2)(1.5) + (1,200/200)(25) = \$300$$

The answer to the question "When?" is provided by the *reorder point* (ROP). In the basic EOQ model ROP is the same as the *demand during the lead time* (DDLT) and is calculated by multiplying demand by lead time:

$$ROP = DDLT = D \times L$$

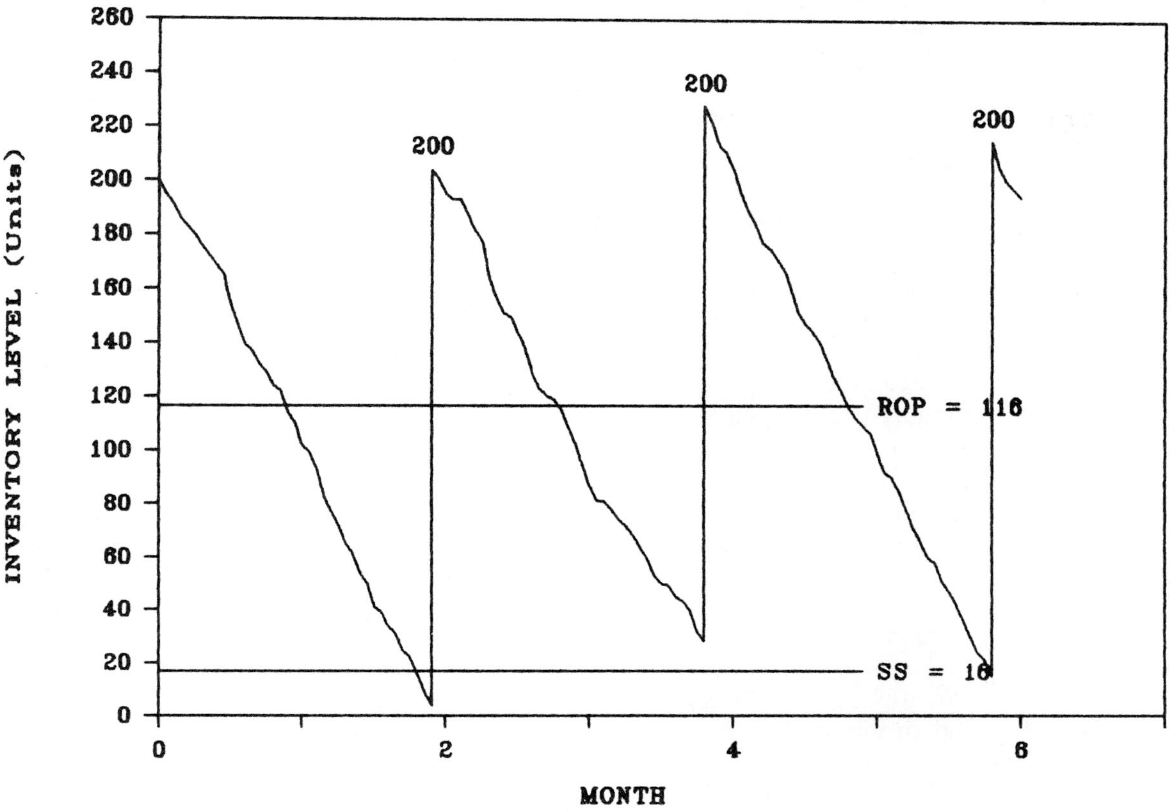

FIGURE 7-3 Inventory Level under a Condition of Uncertain Demand, with Fixed Order Quantity

where D and L are expressed in the same time frame (if L is expressed in days, then D is daily demand, and so on). Here, if the lead time were 1 month (1/12 year), the ROP would be (1/12 year) (1,200 units per year) = 100 units. Thus, the firm should order 200 units whenever the *stock position* (the number of units on hand and on order) is less than or equal to 100 units.

The basic EOQ model is often criticized for its unrealistic assumptions. In the remainder of this section, we relax a number of those assumptions to see how the answers to "How much?" and "When?" change under more realistic conditions. We examine the impact of (1) variable rather than fixed demand; (2) placing orders at fixed time intervals; and (3) quantity discounts.

The Safety Stock Model. With the *safety stock model* the assumption that demand is fixed, known, and constant is relaxed. Although we assume a known *average* demand, the *actual* demand in a given period is uncertain. For instance, in Figure 7-3 we have plotted an actual inventory level, computed daily, over a period of six months. Comparing the downward slope of this figure to Figure 7-1, you see that the slope is not constant but on the average is the same in both figures.

We describe demand in this situation by its mean and standard deviation. The basic EOQ formula is still used to calculate the order quantity in this model; however, the demand term (D) is stated as an average value per period instead of a known value.

In the basic model, the demand during the lead time is invariant and the reorder point is simply the demand during the lead time (DDLT). In this model, calculation of the reorder point changes to account for the uncertain demand which is assumed to be normally distributed during the lead time. The mean of the distribution is the DDLT from above

$$\text{DDLT} = \text{D} \times \text{L}$$

With varying demand, the firm would run out of inventory (stock out) 50% of the time if the ROP was set at DDLT. This is because actual demand is expected to exceed the mean 50% of the time with a normal distribution. To lessen the chances of running out of inventory (therefore providing poor customer service), the firm maintains a *safety stock* — an extra amount of material for times when actual demand exceeds expected demand. The level of safety stock (SS) required to achieve a 95% customer service level is computed by multiplying the standard deviation of the DDLT distribution by 1.645 (the z value associated with a 95% one-tailed probability):

$$\text{SS} = 1.645 \times \text{standard deviation of DDLT distribution}$$

The standard deviation of the DDLT distribution is seldom know directly. Often, the firm will know the standard deviation of demand over a certain period of time (say, a week), and that figure may be converted to the necessary time interval by multiplying it by the square root of the ratio of the lead time to the known time period. That is,

$$\text{SS} = 1.645 \times \text{known standard deviation} \times \sqrt{\text{L / known time interval}}$$

The safety stock is indicated by a horizontal line near the bottom of Figure 7-3. You see that the inventory level falls below the safety stock line twice, once in month two and again in month 6. If the firm did not maintain a safety stock, a stock out would have occurred at these two times.

Maintaining a safety stock increases the TIMC because the firm has a higher average inventory on hand:

$$\text{TIMC} = (\text{SS} + \text{Q}/2) \times \text{H} + (\text{D}/\text{Q}) \times \text{P}$$

Although the TIMC of the safety stock model is higher, carrying a safety stock lessens the probability of a stockout and thus reduces stockout-related cost (which is not explicitly considered in determining EOQ or ROP). When the TIMC and total stockout cost are considered together, the overall cost is generally less with the safety stock model. To calculate the total stockout cost, we estimate the expected number of stockouts per year and multiply that by the stockout cost. The expected number of stockouts per year (SO) at a given customer service level is estimated with the following formula:

$$\text{SO} = (\text{D}/\text{Q}) \times \text{E(z)} \times \text{known standard deviation} \times \sqrt{\text{L / known time interval}}$$

The ratio of D/Q yields the average number of orders placed in a year. The remainder of the formula estimates the expected number of units short per order by multiplying a standardized factor [E(z)] by the standard deviation of the demand during lead time distribution. The standardized factor represents the expected number of units short per order at a given service level for a distribution whose standard deviation is one; the exact value is obtained from a table such as Table 7-1. The total stockout cost is the product of expected number of stockouts and stockout cost per unit.

Total Stockout Cost = SO x S

This is added to the TIMC to determine overall cost in light of stockouts.

The reorder point is the sum of demand during the lead time and safety stock:

ROP = DDLT + SS

The ROP line also appears in Figure 7-3. Again, we know "How much?" and "When?" As with the basic model, we order the quantity of units determined by the EOQ formula when the stock position is less than or equal to the ROP. Because the firm orders at the instant that inventory falls below a certain point, we term this a *continuous review inventory control system.*

TABLE 7-1 Z-values and Expected Number of Units Short per Order

Customer Service Level	Z-value	E(z)
50.0%	0.000	0.39894
80.0%	0.842	0.11177
90.0%	1.282	0.04738
95.0%	1.645	0.02092
97.5%	1.960	0.00945
99.0%	2.326	0.00339
99.9%	3.090	0.00028

The Fixed Order Interval Model. There are times when a continuous review system is not possible. For instance, some suppliers will deliver only on certain days (e.g., the third Friday of the month), or, the firm may consolidate orders on a weekly or monthly basis to reduce shipping costs (as you probably do for your grocery shopping).

Under these circumstances, the time interval between orders is constant but the quantity ordered varies to account for varying demand. (How does this differ from the previous system?) We begin by computing the EOQ as before. To calculate the time between orders (TBO), we divide the EOQ by the average demand:

TBO = EOQ/D

In the example we have been using, where EOQ is 200 units and D is 1200 units per year, the TBO is 1/6 year or two months. This is the time period that the EOQ would last when consumed at the average rate of demand. When the TBO is calculated using this formula, the total inventory management cost is minimized because it is based on the EOQ. However, if a delivery schedule is imposed by the vendor or some other external entity, you may have to adjust the TBO. Here, we assume that the two month TBO is feasible, thus "When?" is answered.

The answer to the question "How much?" varies from order to order and is based on a target ordering value. The target value (T) is designed to provide an adequate inventory level to satisfy demand over a fixed lead time and TBO interval. The target also accounts for uncertainty in demand by providing for safety stock. The necessary safety stock is

$$SS = 1.645 \times \text{known standard deviation} \times \sqrt{(L + TBO) / \text{known time interval}}$$

The target level is a planning variable; the firm may not achieve that level of inventory but determines how much to order based on this target figure. The target value is calculated by

$$T = D \times (TBO + L) + SS$$

The quantity ordered is

$$Q = T - \text{stock position}$$

Figure 7-4 illustrates a plot of inventory level versus month using the fixed time interval model. The target line in that figure is the level the inventory should reach given expected levels of demand during the lead time. This is a *periodic review inventory control system.* Notice that orders are received on the last day of months two, four, and six (while in the continuous review system the orders are received on different days during the month); notice also that the corresponding order quantities are 203, 190, and 212 (whereas in the continuous review system the order quantity was always 200).

The safety stock in the periodic review model is higher than that in the continuous review model because the organization must be protected against stock outs for three months (TBO + L) with the periodic review model, while it needs protection for only one month (L) with the continuous review model. Total inventory management cost under this model is computed by the formula:

$$TIMC = [SS + (D \times TBO)/2)] \times H + (1/TBO) \times P$$

Make sure that D, TBO, and H are expressed in annual terms when computing TIMC with this formula.

We have discussed the two general types of inventory systems, fixed order quantity (continuous review), and fixed order interval (periodic review). Fixed order quantity systems are event-based; the event of reaching a specific inventory level (the reorder point) triggers an order for a fixed quantity. Fixed order interval systems are time-triggered; an order whose quantity varies is placed at the end of a predetermined period of time. The order quantity used in the models can be calculated directly by the EOQ formula, as above, or by the quantity discount model, as discussed in the following section.

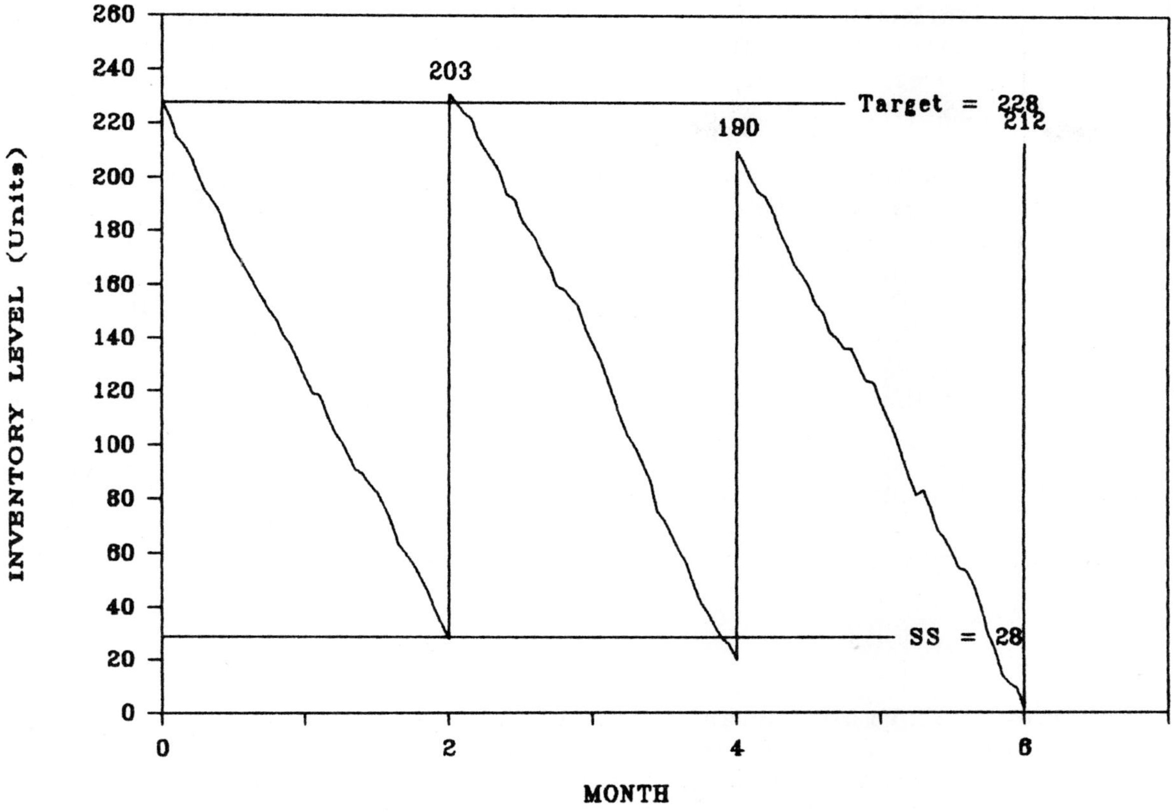

FIGURE 7-4 Inventory Level under a Condition of Uncertain Demand, with Fixed Order Interval

The Quantity Discount Model. The discussion of the above models assumes that the cost per unit ordered does not change based on the quantity ordered. In many situations, however, things are "cheaper by the dozen" and the cost per unit does depend on the quantity ordered. The determination of quantity ordered (Q) is therefore different in this model than in the basic EOQ model. Once Q is determined, it may be used in either the continuous or periodic review inventory control systems discussed above.

Magee and Boodman have developed a five-step method for identifying the minimum-cost order quantity:

1. Calculate the EOQ using the minimum unit cost (i.e., at the highest quantity). The EOQ formula is the same as before, but we explicitly include cost per unit in the formula because that cost varies:

$$EOQ = \sqrt{(2DP)/iC}$$

Compare the quantity computed against the minimum order quantity for the minimum unit cost: if the quantity is greater than or equal to the minimum required, then you have determined the lowest cost order quantity and you may proceed to determine the other parameters (e.g., SS, TBO, T) of whichever model you are using.

2. If the discount structure does not permit ordering the quantity computed in step 1, then the process is more involved. First, calculate EOQ values for all remaining unit costs.

3. Next, calculate the total cost for all EOQ values that fall within the designated range for the associated cost. Total cost includes the cost of the units, holding cost, and preparation cost:

$$TC = CD + (Q/2)iC + (D/Q)P$$

4. Calculate TC for all cost break quantities, that is, use the lower limit quantity for each cost bracket as Q in the total cost formula.

5. The quantity that produces the lowest TC in 3 and 4 is Q.

ABC Analysis

The models discussed above are relevant to individual inventory items. It is probably unrealistic, and overly expensive, to apply this much effort to *every* item in an organization's inventory. A final concept is the ABC classification model for the overall inventory system. The degree of control exercised over any given item in inventory depends on a cost-benefit analysis. A simple way of ensuring that appropriate control is being exercised is to categorize all inventory items according to their total annual dollar volume into three classes — A (highest) to C (lowest) — with A items controlled closely and C items controlled fairly loosely.

To accomplish ABC classification, the total annual dollar volume (usually total purchase cost) is computed for each item. The items are ranked as a percentage of total annual dollar volume from highest to lowest. The top 20% of the items on the list typically account for 80% of the volume and are designated as A items, the next 30% normally account for 15% of the volume and are B items, and the remaining 50% of the items, about 5% of the volume, are C items.

GATHERING THE DATA

Within the Company

Almost all of the data needed to support inventory analysis can be found within the company. Some of the data for inventory analysis, especially cost parameters, are estimates developed by the accounting function of the organization. Inventory carrying rate can be estimated from its various components such as cost of capital, insurance costs for the stored goods, taxes, storage or space costs, and so on. The average cost of ordering can be estimated based on the time and paperwork involved in preparing an order.

Other necessary data, such as lead times, are provided by the purchasing and operations departments. Yet other parameters such as customer service levels are established by top management through the marketing function. Customer service level considerations include both a desired percent availability and a *stockout cost* (an estimate of lost revenue due to nonavailability of a product).

Information related to the inventory level of any specific item can be found in the inventory record. These records also contain other information pertaining to inventory analysis, such as the average lead time needed to procure the item. For some items the inventory record is kept manually, but most organizations with high-cost and large-quantity items maintain at least part of their inventory records on the computer.

Finally, the planning of inventory levels for individual items is done such that the aggregate inventory level (i.e., the total for all items) corresponds to that set in the aggregate plan. Developing the aggregate plan is discussed in Unit 6. The inventory levels for individual items are based on forecasts of demand for these items. Demand forecasting is discussed in Unit 8.

External to the Company

Usually the needed data is internal to the firm. Sometimes, however, external data is used to set inventory analysis parameters. Inventory carrying rate, for example, is a difficult parameter to estimate accurately. Firms with little historical data often use industry figures as guidelines.

THE PROBLEM

Recall that EZRydr makes a set of standardized products (motorcycles). The items it stocks have independent demand, that is, demand from sources external to the firm. In addition, the firm stores components as replacement parts and spares. Even for items whose quantity requirements depend on the quantity needed of the final product (items such as components and subassemblies), the firm may store quantities of these items if it is the least costly approach. The management of EZRydr would like to know whether or not the basic EOQ model they have been using for all items is the most cost-effective and appropriate, especially since the inventory includes both purchased items (raw materials and component parts) as well as finished goods. Management has identified a subset of the total inventory to be analyzed.

1. Using the basic EOQ model, compute EOQ and ROP for each of the items.

2. For each item, what is the total inventory management cost incurred with the basic EOQ model?

3. There is some uncertainty in the demand for all items. Using a 95% target customer service level, how do the EOQ and ROP change?

4. For each item, what is the total inventory management cost incurred with the safety stock model?

5. High customer service levels require high inventory levels. For all end items, calculate the TIMC plus total stockout cost for service levels of 50% (the basic EOQ model with no safety stock), 80%, 90%, 95%, 97.5%, 99%, and 99.9%. What customer service level produces the lowest inventory cost (TIMC plus overall stockout cost)?

6. Using a customer service level of 95%, develop a fixed order interval model for all component parts. Compute TBO, SS, and TIMC.

7. If all components were ordered once every four weeks, the order cost would be halved. Calculate a TBO, SS, and TIMC with this new order cost. How closely does a four-week interval coincide with the ideal TBO for each component? With the four-week order interval, is the TIMC lower or higher than the safety stock model for these items?

8. The vendor has proposed the following quantity discount structure for item CMP002:

Minimum Quantity	Discounted Cost per Unit
1,000	$76
2,000	$72

Use the Magee and Boodman method to determine the minimum-cost order quantity. What is the associated cost?

Departmental Data

The following data have been compiled by EZRydr's inventory control department.

Inventory Carrying Rate	1%	of unit cost/unit/month
Preparation Cost	$500	/order
Stockout Cost Factor	10%	of unit cost/unit stockout
Customer Service Level	95%	

The following data pertaining to individual items were also compiled by the inventory control department. The data is for four models that the company makes and also for four components. These components, which are purchased from outside vendors, are assumed to be typical of all other items for which the firm does inventory analysis. The firm has 50 work weeks in the year.

	End Items				Component Parts			
	BH1500	BS1200	EZ800	EZ500	CMP001	CMP002	CMP003	CMP004
Unit Cost	$1,500	$1,200	$800	$500	$100	$80	$10	$500
Current Inventory Level	100	100	75	100	500	1,000	200	4,000
Average Weekly Demand	100	80	30	35	262	525	118	2,600
Std. Deviation (Weekly Demand)	20	25	10	15	50	45	75	300
Average Lead Time (weeks)	2	2	2	2	1	1	3	2

Data in the Database

Normally inventory management data are contained in at least two files. An inventory master file contains information such as inventory item description, code number, standard cost, lead time, balance on hand and on order, and so on. An inventory transaction file contains information such as orders, receipts, and withdrawals. The MIS department of EZRydr has prepared a data file for your use that contains required information from the inventory master file as well as summarized information from the transaction file. The file, named INV_SMRY.DBF, contains more current figures for the items in the department data listed above, as well as information on other items. Data such as demand, standard deviation of demand, and lead time are expressed in weekly periods. For components, the demand figures include both finished product requirements as well as replacement part demand.[1] You should be able to determine which fields contain which data.

DEVELOPING THE SPREADSHEET

Before we can address the questions posed by EZRydr's management, we must build a spreadsheet to evaluate the alternative inventory control models. In this section we discuss the development of the spreadsheet. When you save the spreadsheet, call it INVPLAN.

Start with a blank spreadsheet. In the upper left corner enter the INVENTORY PLANNING DATA. In rows 1 through 7, enter labels in columns A and C and parameters in column B as illustrated in Figure 7-5. For the moment, enter the value 1.645 in D6 and ') in E6. Later we create a lookup table to extract the appropriate z-value for various customer service levels. Next, enter inventory planning data for individual items as shown in rows 9 through 14.

Once planning data are entered, we can build the various models, beginning with the BASIC EOQ MODEL. As usual, enter labels in column A, build a set of formulas in column B, then copy the formulas across the relevant columns. The examples in this section make use of Lotus 1-2-3's absolute and mixed cell referencing feature. If your spreadsheet package does not support absolute and mixed cell references in formulas, you can normally achieve the same effect when you copy the formulas.

This formula, in B17, computes the EOQ for BH1500:

```
@ROUND(@SQRT(2*B$12*$B$7*$B$4/($B$3*12*B$10)),0)
```

Compare this formula to the formula for the basic EOQ model given earlier in this unit. Weekly demand is multiplied by the number of work weeks per year to yield annual demand; monthly inventory carrying rate is multiplied by 12 to yield annual carrying rate. Note that we round the result to an integer value, assuming that only whole units can be ordered. We round all unit quantities (Q, SS, ROP, and so on) to integer values in this unit.

---

[1] Technically, demand for items used as components is dependent demand and should be treated differently (such as with an MRP model). For ease of analysis, EZRydr and other companies sometimes ignore the distinction and analyze all items using independent demand models.

	A	B	C	D	E	F	G	H	I
1	INVENTORY PLANNING DATA								
2									
3	Inventory Carrying Rate	1.0% of unit cost/unit/month							
4	Preparation Cost	$500 per order							
5	Stockout Cost Factor	10.0% of unit cost/unit stockout							
6	Customer Service Level	95.0%	(z =	1.645)					
7	Length of Year	50 work weeks							
8									
9		BH1500	BS1200	EZ800	EZ500	CMP001	CMP002	CMP003	CMP004
10	Unit Cost	$1,500	$1,200	$800	$500	$100	$80	$10	$500
11	Current Inventory Level	100	100	75	100	500	1000	200	4000
12	Average Weekly Demand	100	80	30	35	262	525	118	2600
13	Std. Dev. of above	20	25	10	15	50	45	75	300
14	Average Lead Time (weeks)	2	2	2	2	1	1	3	2
15									
16	BASIC EOQ MODEL								
17	Order Quantity	167	167	125	171	1045	1654	2217	1472
18	Safety Stock	0	0	0	0	0	0	0	0
19	Reorder Point	200	160	60	70	262	525	354	5200
20	TIMC	$30,000	$24,000	$12,000	$10,247	$12,538	$15,875	$2,661	$88,318
21									
22	SAFETY STOCK MODEL								
23	Order Quantity	167	167	125	171	1045	1654	2217	1472
24	Safety Stock	47	58	23	35	82	74	214	698
25	Reorder Point	247	218	83	105	344	599	568	5898
26	TIMC	$38,460	$32,352	$14,208	$12,347	$13,522	$16,585	$2,918	$130,198
27	Expected No. Stockouts	18	18	4	5				
28	Total Stockout Cost	$2,700	$2,160	$320	$250				
29	TIMC + Tot. SO Cost	$41,160	$34,512	$14,528	$12,597				
30									
31	COST AS A FUNCTION OF CUSTOMER SERVICE LEVEL (End Items Only)								
32									
33	50.00%	$80,700	$64,560	$17,440	$14,597				
34	80.00%	$48,570	$39,720	$14,672	$12,527				
35	90.00%	$42,480	$35,280	$14,368	$12,367				
36	95.00%	$41,160	$34,512	$14,528	$12,597				
37	97.50%	$41,100	$34,896	$14,848	$12,867				
38	99.00%	$42,330	$36,168	$15,248	$13,237				
39	99.90%	$45,660	$39,696	$16,224	$14,207				
40									
41	FIXED ORDER INTERVAL MODEL (Component Parts Only)								
42	Time betw. Orders (yrs.)					0.080	0.063	0.376	0.011
43	Time betw. Orders (wks.)					3.988	3.150	18.791	0.566
44	Safety Stock					184	151	576	791
45	Target Ordering Value					1491	2330	3147	7463
46	TIMC					$14,746	$17,324	$3,352	$135,778
47									
48	ALTERNATIVE FIXED ORDER INTERVAL MODELS (Component Parts Only)								
49	Ideal TBO (yrs.)					0.056	0.045	0.266	0.008
50	Ideal TBO (wks.)					2.820	2.227	13.287	0.400
51	Ideal Safety Stock					161	133	498	765
52	Ideal Target Ordering Value					1162	1827	2420	7006
53	Ideal TIMC					$10,798	$12,502	$2,479	$108,350
54									
55	4-Week TBO (yrs.)					0.080	0.080	0.080	0.080
56	4-Week TBO (wks.)					4.000	4.000	4.000	4.000
57	4-Week Safety Stock					184	166	326	1209
58	4-Week Target Ordering Value					1494	2791	1152	16809
59	4-Week TIMC					$11,621	$14,799	$3,799	$387,665
60									

just load as is

	A	B	C	D	E
61					
62	QUANTITY DISCOUNT MODEL (Item CMP002)				
63		Disc Cost	Quantity	Valid?	Tot Cost
64	EOQ @	$72	1743	no	
65	Break Qty. @	$72	2000	yes	1,905,203
66	EOQ @	$76	1697	yes	2,010,473
67	Break Qty. @	$76	1000	yes	2,012,685
68	EOQ @	$80	1654	no	
69					

Lookup Table	z	E(z)
50.0%	0.000	0.39894
80.0%	0.842	0.11177
90.0%	1.282	0.04738
95.0%	1.645	0.02092
97.5%	1.960	0.00945
99.0%	2.326	0.00339
99.9%	3.090	0.00028

FIGURE 7-5 The Inventory Planning Spreadsheet

This model does not include a Safety Stock, so 0 is entered in B18. The Reorder Point is calculated in B19:

@ROUND(B$12*B$14,0)

Because both demand and lead time are expressed in weeks, conversion to annual data is not required. Finally, TIMC is calculated in B20:

(B18+B17/2)*$B$3*12*B$10+(B$12*$B$7/B17)*$B$4

These formulas can now be copied to columns C through I.

The first four rows of the SAFETY STOCK MODEL are computed with the same logic (which may be copied from A17..I20), except that the following formula is used to compute Safety Stock in row 24:

@ROUND($D$6*B$13*@SQRT(B$14/1),0)

To compute the Expected Number of Stockouts, we create a lookup table that can be used for obtaining z-values and expected number of stockouts at various customer service levels. We place the table in the range G62..I69, using data from Table 7-1. (Actually, we started with the table in a different place and moved it once the final structure of the spreadsheet was determined; we are saving you a few steps.) The Expected Number of Stockouts is calculated in B27 by

@ROUND((B$12*$B$7/B23)*@VLOOKUP($B$6,$G$63..$I$69,2)*B$13*@SQRT(B$14/1),0)

Total Stockout Cost is

$B$5*B$10*B27

and TIMC + Total Stockout Cost is, of course,

+B26+B28

Copy these formulas to end-item columns.

Before proceeding, change the formula in D6 to

@VLOOKUP(B6,G63..H69,1)

which makes the calculation of safety stock dependent on the particular Customer Service Level chosen.

Next, we want to develop a table that can be used to estimate the least-cost customer service level. There are many ways to accomplish this; we used the Lotus /DataTable feature to create the table found in range A31..E39. (If you do not have such a feature in your spreadsheet package, you must use a series of formulas.) The following outlines the general method; we leave it to you to execute the commands.

1. Place customer service level percentages in column A.

2. In row 32, place references to the formulas in row 29 (thus, +B29 is entered in B32; in our illustration, we set hidden format for these cells to remove clutter).

3. Use the /DataTable1 command.

The next task is to develop the analysis of the FIXED ORDER INTERVAL MODEL. Recall that this model is used for component parts only. Enter appropriate labels. In F42, compute Time Between Orders (years) with the following formula:

@SQRT(2*F$12*$B$7*$B$4/($B$3*12*F$10))/(F$12*$B$7)

Because time is a continuous variable, we do not round the order quantity or the result. Time Between Orders (weeks) is the product of the above and number of work weeks in a year (use a reference to cell B7, just in case the company changes the number of work weeks in a year for some future analysis).

To compute Safety Stock in row 44, modify the formula in row 24 to include TBO:

@ROUND($D$6*F$13*@SQRT((F$14+F43)/1),0)

We leave it to you to determine the formulas for Target Ordering Value and TIMC (remember that values in the TIMC formula must all be annual values).

The sector of the spreadsheet entitled ALTERNATIVE FIXED ORDER INTERVAL MODELS is discussed in the "Using the Spreadsheet" section.

The final area of the spreadsheet to be developed is for the QUANTITY DISCOUNT MODEL. Refer to the conceptual discussion of this model for the formulas used to compute EOQ and TC. Enter labels as shown (the "yes" and "no" labels in column D are generated by logical functions; do not enter them now). Enter the Discounted Costs in column B. In column C, compute EOQ in the three rows indicated, and enter the break quantities in the other two rows. There are three different situations that must be included in the validity check column. First, for the rows that contain break quantities, an order of that quantity is always valid. For the rows that contain EOQ quantities, the two additional situations arise: (1) for the lowest discounted cost (top row in this example), an EOQ that is greater than or equal to the break quantity in the row below is valid; (2) for any other discounted cost, an EOQ that is less than the break quantity in the row above and greater than or equal to the break quantity in the row below is valid. Use the capabilities of your spreadsheet to develop formulas that display either text or numeric results for valid and invalid order quantities. Finally, compute Total Cost in column E.

Print original and formulas

CHECKING THE MODEL

Before using the spreadsheet to answer the questions, you should check to ensure that the logic of the model is correct. Compare the results you obtain with those illustrated in Figure 7-5 for the first item, BH1500. Any deviation indicates an error.

Next, determine a set of data for which you can calculate the results manually. Enter those data into the spreadsheet and compare the model's results with your manual calculations. For instance, enter 0 (zero) Preparation Cost and 50% Customer Service Level. All Order Quantities and Safety Stocks should go to 0; Reorder Point for the Safety Stock and Basic EOQ models, and Target Ordering Value for the Fixed Order Interval model should be the same; and Time between Orders should be 0. Several cells will display ERR.

USING THE SPREADSHEET

Recall that EZRydr's management has a number of questions regarding inventory management. We now use the various sections of the spreadsheet to answer those questions.

1. Using the basic EOQ model, compute EOQ and ROP for each of the items. These are computed in rows 17 and 19 of the completed spreadsheet.

2. For each item, what is the total inventory management cost incurred with the basic EOQ model? See row 20.

3. There is some uncertainty in the demand for all items. Using a 95% target customer service level, how do the EOQ and ROP change? Compare row 23 to row 17. The EOQs do not change. Compare rows 25 and 19. The ROP increases by the amount of the safety stock (row 24).

4. For each item, what is the total inventory management cost incurred with the safety stock model? See row 26.

5. High customer service levels require high inventory levels. For all end items, calculate the TIMC plus total stockout cost for service levels of 50% (the basic EOQ model with no safety stock), 80%, 90%, 95%, 97.5%, 99%, and 99.9%. What customer service level produces the lowest inventory cost (TIMC plus overall stockout cost)? The answers are computed in the range A31..E39. Create a graph, such as Figure 7-6, to illustrate. As you can see, the preferred customer service level varies from one item to another, thus there is no one ideal for all items.

6. Using a customer service level of 95%, develop a fixed order interval model for all component parts. Compute TBO, SS, and TIMC. This is computed in rows 41 through 46.

7. If all components were ordered once every four weeks, the order cost would be halved. Calculate a TBO, SS, and TIMC with this new order cost. As illustrated in Figure 7-5, we created a table that first computes the "ideal" TBO and so on, substituting $B$4/2 for $B$4 in the TBO (years) and TIMC formulas. Note that the value of all parameters decreases because it is less expensive to place an order in this scenario.

   The TBOs of this ideal situation cannot be used, however, because the lower order cost applies only when the TBO is exactly four weeks. Therefore, we must force the TBO to be four weeks, which we do in a second part of the table. In row 55, we calculate TBO (years) with the formula 4/$B$7. The remainder of the formulas are the same as the "ideal" set.

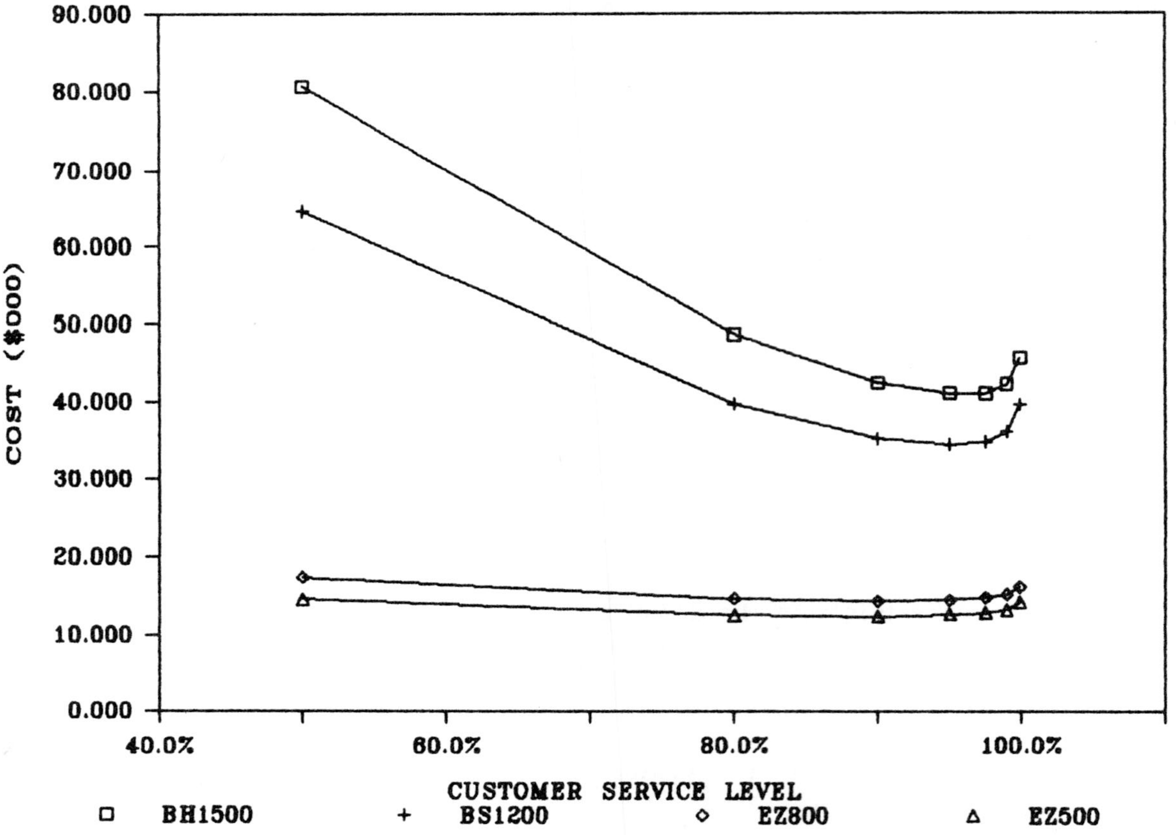

FIGURE 7-6 Cost as a Function of Service Level for Four End Items

How closely does a four-week interval coincide with the ideal TBO for each component? Compare rows 56 and 50. With the four-week order interval, is the TIMC lower or higher than the safety stock model for these items? Compare rows 59 and 26. Why is the cost lower for some components and higher for others?

8. The vendor has proposed the following quantity discount structure for item CMP002:

Minimum Quantity	Discounted Cost per Unit
1,000	$76
2,000	$72

Use the Magee and Boodman method to determine the minimum-cost order quantity. What is the associated cost? The QUANTITY DISCOUNT MODEL section of the spreadsheet contains the answer to this question: order 2000 units at a time, with a total cost of $1,905,203 per annum. Note that these calculations yield the order quantity and associated cost, and do not consider demand uncertainty, customer service level, safety stock, or stockout costs.

EXERCISES

The Inventory Analysis spreadsheet is a useful decision-making tool that allows us to deal with many different situations. The following exercises test the usefulness of this spreadsheet. You may need to reset the spreadsheet before you answer successive questions. The easiest way to do this is to save the spreadsheet and then make modifications.

1. Change a few of the parameters to see their effect on the models. After answering each subquestion, reset all parameters to their original values.

   a. What is the effect of a higher inventory carrying rate on the quantity ordered? Use a carrying rate of 2%. How does this affect the customer service level that the firm should set?

   b. There is some debate in EZRydr as to the accuracy of the Preparation Cost estimate. Considering only the basic EOQ model, how do the decisions of Order Quantity and Reorder Point change if the actual Preparation Cost is 50% of the original estimate? 200% of the original estimate? In each case, by what percent does the TIMC change?

   c. Due to higher than expected demand, EZRydr is considering a 52-week work year. Revise the spreadsheet to accommodate this change. Compare the results to the 50-week model.

   d. If Stockout Cost Factor is 1% instead of 10%, how does the preferred Customer Service Level change for each of the end items?

2. At EZRydr, it is felt that a periodic review system generally results in a lower Preparation Cost than a continuous review system. (See question 7 in "The Problem" section.) Determine how decreases in steps of $25 affect the TIMC of the Fixed Order Interval Model for CMP004. At what Preparation Cost is EZRydr indifferent between Fixed Order Interval and Safety Stock Models (leaving the Preparation Cost for the latter at $500)?

3. The vendor has proposed the following quantity discount structure for item CMP003:

Minimum Quantity	Discounted Cost per Unit
1,000	$9.50
2,000	$9.00
3,000	$8.75

   What is the best order quantity?

4. What is the effect of Current Inventory Level on each of the models? Change the Current Inventory Level of BH1500 to 200 to verify your answer.

5. Conduct an ABC analysis of the inventory items discussed in this unit. Which items would you classify as A items? as C items?

ENHANCEMENTS TO THE APPLICATION

There are a few enhancements that would make this spreadsheet easier to use. In this section we point out some changes. You and your instructor may determine additional enhancements.

1. Use the cell-protection feature to protect the planning data area.

2. Using features such as Lotus's /RangeInput and macro commands, develop a data-entry system for individual item data (rows 9 through 14).

3. Develop a separate data-entry system for the Quantity Discount Model, changing the model from a three-tiered to a five-tiered cost structure.

4. Create database command files that will extract the necessary data and place it in an interim file. Add a feature to your spreadsheet that will import data from that interim file into the proper positions on the spreadsheet. (There are many methods for accomplishing this, depending on the particular software available to you.) This is an alternative to portions of Enhancements 2 and 3.

REVIEW QUESTIONS

1. Why is inventory analysis important to any firm?

2. What are the basic systems for independent demand inventory management?

*3. What is the effect of a 20% error in inventory carrying rate on order quantity? a 50% error?

*4. How does the use of a spreadsheet package such as Lotus 1-2-3 simplify decision making in inventory management?

5. Define the following terms as they are used in inventory analysis:

   *a. inventory carrying rate

   b. lead time

   *c. review period

   d. reorder point

   *e. safety stock

   f. customer service level

   *g. stockout

   h. quantity-price discount

   *i. economic order quantity

ADDITIONAL READING

To understand more about inventory analysis refer to texts such as

Buffa, E. S., and J. Miller. *Production Inventory Systems: Planning and Control.* Homewood, IL: Irwin, 1979.

Chase, R. B., and N. J. Aquilano. *Production and Operations Management.* Homewood, IL: Irwin, 1985.

Krajewski, L. J., and L. P. Ritzman. *Operations Management: Strategy and Analysis.* Reading, MA: Addison-Wesley, 1987.

Magee, J. F., and D. M. Boodman. *Production Planning and Inventory Control.* New York: McGraw-Hill, 1967.

Peterson, R., and E. A. Silver. *Decision Systems for Inventory Management and Production Planning.* New York: Wiley, 1979.

Schroeder, R. G. *Operations Management: Decision Making in the Operations Function.* New York: McGraw-Hill, 1985.

An article entitled "Inventory Analysis: The ABC Technique" (S. L. Nelson, *Lotus*, Vol. 3, No. 6, June 1987) presents a spreadsheet treatment of the ABC analysis technique.

UNIT

8 DEMAND ANALYSIS— HOW MUCH WILL WE SELL?

A business firm seeks to understand its environment by gathering and processing information about the relationship between its own sales and certain other factors, including environmental factors. A *demand model* describes a firm's sales as the result of the relevant and measurable causal variables, such as product price, advertising expenditures, consumer incomes, and the price of competitor products. The *demand function* portrays the general form of a firm's sales as a function of certain causal variables:

$$Q_x = f\,(P_x, \text{Pop}, \text{Int}, P_z, I, \text{Adv}, \ldots)$$

Once postulated, the emphasis in demand analysis is on estimating the precise numerical relationships between firm sales and the independent causal variables in order to forecast demand or to control the variables affecting sales. Today, the firm has at its disposal various software packages, including spreadsheets, capable of estimating the parameters of demand. Since a spreadsheet package is often used for the assembly of data, using the same package for data estimation is convenient. In this unit we demonstrate the use of a spreadsheet model for the compilation, manipulation, and estimation of a demand function for EZRydr. Note that the terms "demand" and "sales" are used interchangeably in this unit. While demand for a product and sales of that product are not necessarily the same, we often use sales as a surrogate for demand because it is easier to measure sales.

DECISION SUPPORT APPLICATION MATRIX

Accounting & Finance	Economics & Long-Range Planning	Human Resources	Marketing & Logistics	Management Information Systems	Operations Planning & Control	Executive Officers
¤	■¤		■¤		¤	¤

■ Departmental area(s) in which the technique is or can be used.

¤ Departmental area(s) that provide input to or are impacted by the technique.

Contributed by Charles H. Breeden

LEARNING OBJECTIVES

1. After completing this unit you should know

   a. the reasons that firms construct and estimate demand models,

   b. the basic approach to building a demand model,

   c. the basic method of estimating demand parameters,

   d. the operational interpretation of demand parameters.

2. After completing this unit you should be able to

   a. use a spreadsheet to estimate simple demand models,

   b. use a spreadsheet to create graphic displays of important demand variables,

   c. use a spreadsheet model to manipulate data relating to demand,

   d. use an estimated demand model to do what-if analysis.

BASIC CONCEPTS

The purpose of demand analysis is to understand the firm's market by understanding the relationship between its sales and the economic factors that affect it. Another purpose for demand analysis is to prepare a foundation for demand forecasts, that is, projections of future sales. Demand analysis is useful when a firm has questions about the impact of environmental influences on sales. It is also useful when a firm seeks to understand the market impact of its internal activities, such as pricing and advertising.

A starting point for the analysis is the examination of the relationship between sales and time. Figure 8-1 depicts sales of small motorcycles over time. Notice that sales of this particular product line are declining over time. This trend is expected as the U.S. market preference for large motorcycles has been increasing steadily for the past twenty-five years.

Law of Demand

The most basic relationship in demand analysis is between quantity demanded and price. The *demand curve* illustrates the different quantities of the product that would be sold at different prices. The demand curve maps price versus quantity sold. A general formula for the demand curve is

$$P = a - bQ$$

where P is price, a is the intercept, b is the slope and Q is quantity demanded.[1] Price is the primary demand-influencing variable because it has a major impact on demand and is easily controlled by the firm. A typical demand curve relationship is

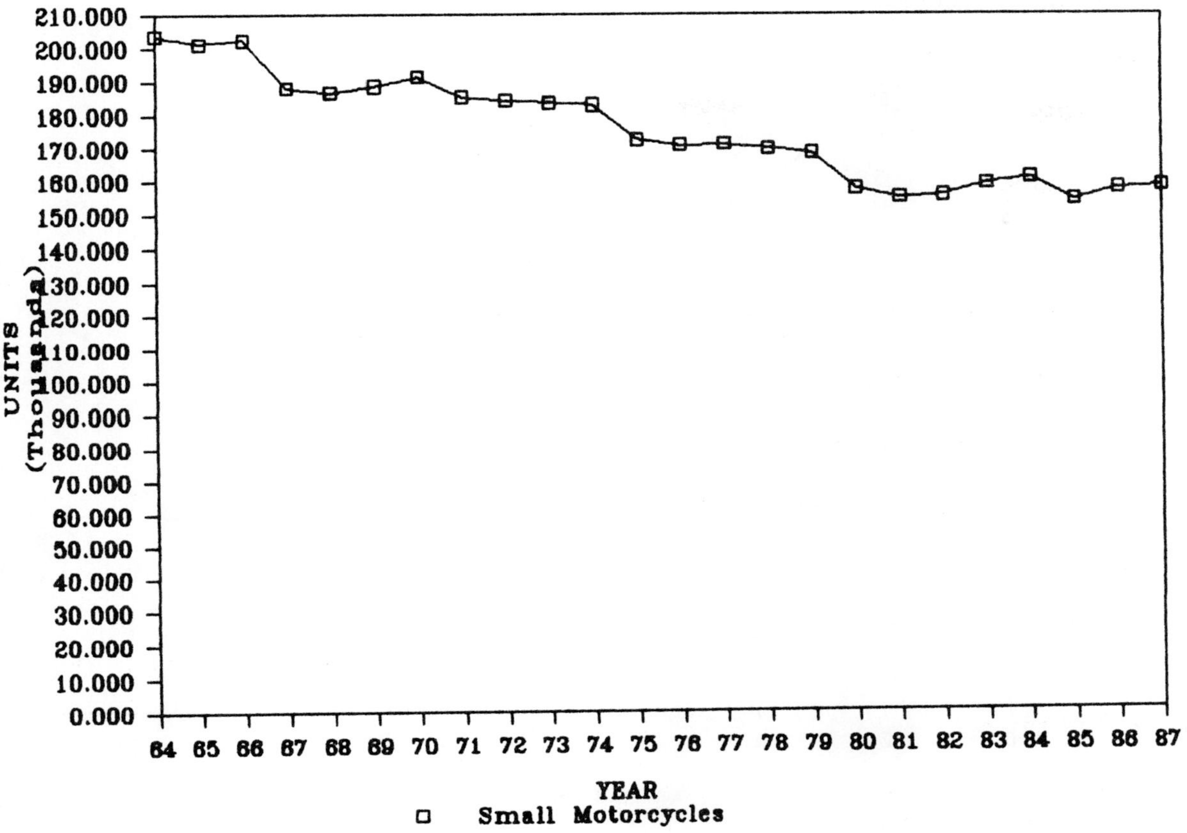

FIGURE 8-1 Sales of Small Motorcycles from 1964 to 1987

$$P = 80 - 5Q$$

Figure 8-2 represents the demand curve generated from this equation. Notice that as price increases, quantity demanded decreases. For purposes of demand analysis, we show Q as a function of P. The inverted relationship is

$$Q = 16 - .2P$$

This is called the *demand function*. In this simplified demand relationship, the intercept term (i.e., 16) represents the residual effect of all other influences on demand. In the next section we identify other variables that influence sales.

---

[1] Historically, demand analysis of markets treats price as the dependent variable and quantity demanded as the independent variable; therefore, quantity demanded is plotted on the horizontal axis of graphs and price is plotted on the vertical axis. For individual firms such as EZRydr, however, it is appropriate to reverse the causality: the quantity of EZRydr's product demanded is a function of the price established by EZRydr.

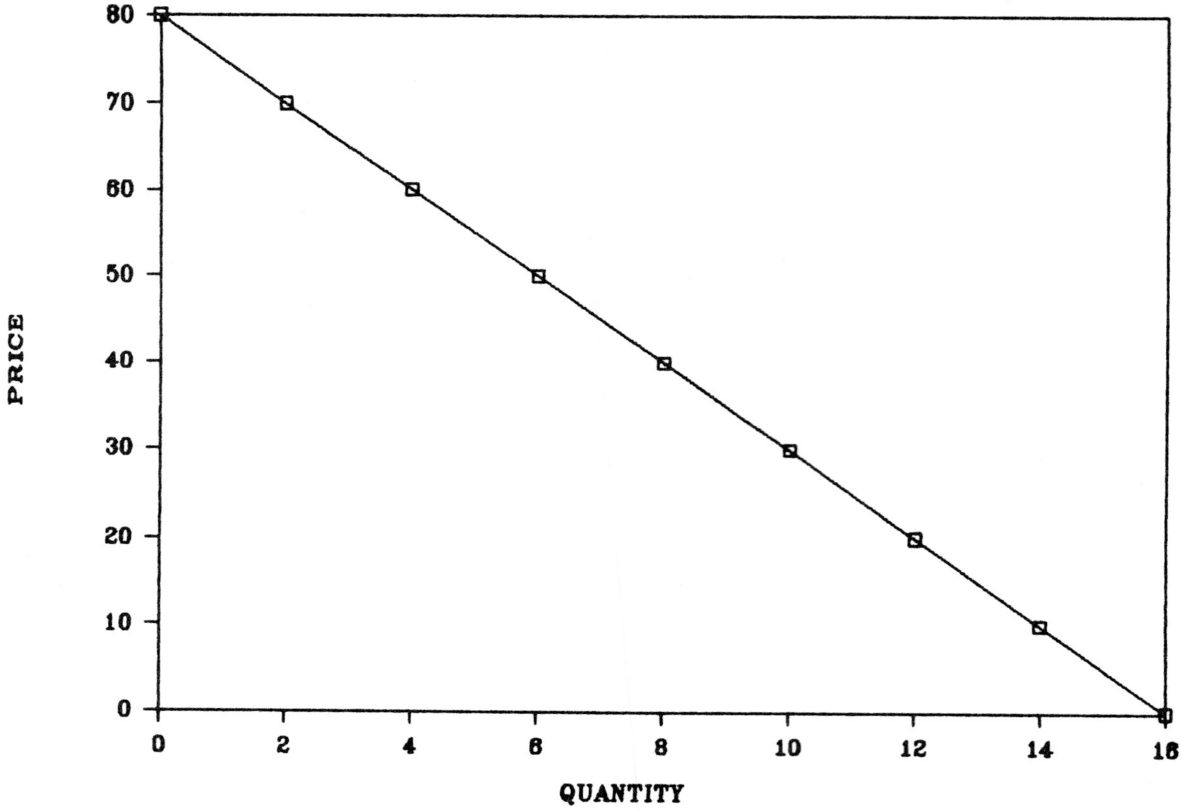

FIGURE 8-2 Demand Curve

Other Demand Variables

The demand relationship portrays sales as a function of many economic variables and is illustrated in general as

$$Q_x = f\,(P_x, \text{Pop}, \text{Int}, P_z, I, \text{Adv}, \ldots)$$

where Q_x is the demand for firm x, P_x is the price charged by firm x for the product, Pop is population, Int is consumer installment interest, P_z is the competitor price, I is consumer income, and Adv is the advertising expenditure. Typically, price increases depress sales, population growth increases sales, high interest rates depress sales, increases in competitor price increase sales, increases in income increase sales, and increases in advertising increase demand. The demand relationship assumes that the influence of each variable on quantity is independent of the other variables.

Linear Demand Model

The demand relationship can be modeled as a linear one:

$$Q_x = a + bP_x + c\text{Pop} + d\text{Int} + eP_z + gI + h\text{Adv} + z$$

where a is the constant, b, c, d, e, g, and h are the slope coefficients for each of the independent variables, and z is the error term. By definition, z represents the residual influence of all other factors not accounted for by the model. Business organizations estimate the values of the coefficients using regression analysis in an effort to predict demand for their product.

GATHERING THE DATA

Within the Company

Data found within the company include sales per period (measured in units or dollars), and advertising expenditures (in dollars). Typically, sales reports indicating quantity sold in either units or dollars can be obtained from the marketing department. Advertising expenditures come from either marketing or accounting.

External to the Company

Data that originate outside the company include consumer incomes, installment loan interest rates, population size and median age, median income, and competitor price. Typically, these data are maintained by marketing research or long-range strategic planning groups. The period of the data can be daily, weekly, monthly, quarterly, or annual. For analysis, always use data with the same period (i.e., all quarterly or all annual).

THE PROBLEM

EZRydr's management would like you to answer the following questions:

1. At current (1987) levels of the independent variables (price, population, income, etc.), what is the expected level of sales (in dollars) of small motorcycles, and how does this compare to the actual sales level for 1987?

2. What would have been the predicted level of sales of small motorcycles in 1987 if the price had been decreased to $3,000?

3. What will the sales of small motorcycles be in 1988?

	A	B	C	D	E	F	G	H
1	DEMAND DATA							
2								
3	Year	Quantity	Price	Pop.	Interest	Price-Z	Income	Advert.
4		($)	($)	(000)	(%)	($)	($)	($ 00,000)
5	64	203,600	450	1,790	6.960	1,150	7,380	4.50
6	65	201,300	450	1,795	7.440	1,150	9,000	4.50
7	66	202,300	480	1,871	7.687	1,400	7,560	4.50
8	67	187,900	720	1,780	7.800	1,400	7,740	4.50
9	68	186,600	720	1,751	7.860	1,400	7,992	5.58
10	69	188,400	720	1,743	7.906	1,660	9,720	5.58
11	70	191,300	720	1,725	9.840	1,750	9,180	6.27
12	71	185,200	890	1,726	10.344	1,750	8,820	7.85
13	72	184,200	920	1,723	10.560	1,750	8,712	7.96
14	73	183,500	920	1,705	11.064	1,840	9,900	5.79
15	74	182,700	920	1,710	11.556	1,860	9,360	5.32
16	75	172,500	1,190	1,702	12.691	1,980	12,600	7.88
17	76	170,700	1,220	1,695	13.596	1,960	11,520	10.73
18	77	170,900	1,220	1,695	13.939	2,300	9,900	7.94
19	78	169,800	1,220	1,692	14.160	2,390	11,700	6.90
20	79	168,200	1,220	1,630	14.196	2,390	12,420	6.77
21	80	157,500	2,240	1,642	15.185	2,390	12,708	8.96
22	81	154,800	2,260	1,635	15.600	2,630	15,336	12.50
23	82	155,500	2,260	1,632	15.871	2,900	13,104	14.88
24	83	158,900	2,260	1,620	16.519	2,990	13,500	19.10
25	84	160,700	2,260	1,615	16.812	3,500	13,896	15.00
26	85	154,000	2,950	1,606	17.366	3,590	14,292	10.79
27	86	157,500	2,950	1,590	18.000	3,820	15,228	9.75
28	87	158,000	3,130	1,597	18.262	4,000	16,200	8.00
29								
30	Mean	175,250	1,429	1,695	12.551	2,248	11,157	8.40
31								
32	Assumed for '88		3,200	1,600	15.000	4,000	16,500	8.50

FIGURE 8-3 Data for Demand Analysis

Departmental Data

The economics department has obtained a database from the marketing and accounting departments. Figure 8-3 presents values for the variables from 1964 to 1987. Note that several of the columns have been scaled (e.g., population is expressed in 1000's).

Data in the Database

The data in Figure 8-3 are contained in the data file named DEMAND.DBF. The numbers in this database have not been scaled, and are slightly more precise than the values that appear in Figure 8-3 because they have not been rounded. You should be able to determine which fields correspond to the columns in the illustration.

DEVELOPING THE SPREADSHEET

Before we can address the questions posed by EZRydr's management, we must build a spreadsheet model of the demand function. In this section we discuss the development of such a model. When you save the spreadsheet, call it DEMAND.

Start with a blank spreadsheet. Set the default numeric format to two decimal places. Starting in cell A1, enter DEMAND DATA. Enter labels in rows 3 and 4, columns A through H, as illustrated in Figure 8-3. Enter the data from Figure 8-3, or from the database, in columns A through H. Calculate the mean values for each column in row 30 using your spreadsheet's average function. Also, add the "Assumed for '88" data illustrated in row 32. Format each column as illustrated.

We use the /**D**ata**R**egression feature of Lotus 1-2-3 Release 2 to perform the regression estimate.[2] The Y-range is B5..B28 because sales is the dependent variable. The X-range is C5..H28 because the independent variables are price, population, interest, competitor price, income, and advertising. (Note that the independent variable set must occupy a series of adjacent columns.) The output range must be set away from the data so that the data are not overwritten: define the range as J3, then execute the regression by selecting Go. Move to the output range to examine the results. You may have to change some column widths. Also, copy the labels in C3..H3 to L1..Q1 to indicate which coefficient corresponds to which variable. Your spreadsheet should look like rows 1 through 11 in Figure 8-4.

In order to interpret the validity of the estimated coefficients, we must calculate t-statistics, a common measure of statistical significance. Label cell J12 T-Statistic. Build a formula in cell L12 that divides the estimated coefficient for each variable by the standard error shown in the cell below that coefficient. Copy that formula across the range M12..Q12.

Recall that the general form of a demand function is

$$Q_x = f\,(P_x, \text{Pop}, \text{Int}, P_z, I, \text{Adv}, \ldots)$$

In our model, Q_x is sales (dollars), P_x is price, Pop is population (thousands), Int is interest, P_z is competitor price, I is income, and Adv is advertising (hundreds of thousands of dollars). The intercept is shown in cell M4 and the estimated coefficients are shown in cells L10 through Q10; with these, the actual demand function is

$$Q_x = 86853.12 - 8.23P_x + 70.30\text{Pop} - 3145.43\text{Int} + 11.51P_z - .27\text{Inc} - 281.12\text{Adv}$$

---

[2] Not all spreadsheet packages include the ability to perform multiple regression. Where the feature is not available, you must use a statistical package to perform the regression and then enter the regression coefficients into a spreadsheet model for further analysis.

	J	K	L	M	N	O	P	Q
1			Price	Pop.	Interest	Price-Z	Income	Advert.
2								
3		Regression Output:						
4	Constant			86853.12				
5	Std Err of Y Est			3973.70				
6	R Squared			0.96				
7	No. of Observations			24.00				
8	Degrees of Freedom			17.00				
9								
10	X Coefficient(s)		-8.23	70.30	-3145.43	11.51	-0.27	-281.12
11	Std Err of Coef.		3.84	34.70	977.35	4.15	0.98	327.97
12	T-Statistic		-2.15	2.03	-3.22	2.77	-0.27	-0.86
13								
14	Mean Value Forecast:							
15	Sales =	86853.12	-11763.04	119137.12	-39476.98	25872.76	-3012.19	-2360.79
16	Sales =	175250.00						
17								
18	87 Forecast:							
19	Sales =	86853.12	-25769.60	112276.56	-57441.85	46038.65	-4373.70	-2248.93
20	Sales =	155334.24						
21	vs. actual	-2665.76						
22								
23	88 Forecast:							
24	Sales =	86853.12	-26345.92	112487.47	-47181.45	46038.65	-4454.70	-2389.49
25	Sales =	165007.68						
26								
27	Elasticities:							
28			-0.16	0.71	-0.36	0.29	-0.03	-0.01

FIGURE 8-4 Regression Output and Forecasts

To interpret this equation, observe the effect of a one-unit increase in each of the variables. A \$1 increase in price implies an \$8.23 decrease in sales; a 1000-person increase in population implies a \$70.30 increase in sales; a 1% increase in the consumer installment interest rate implies a \$3,145 decrease in sales; a \$1 increase in competitor price implies an \$11.51 increase in sales; a \$1 increase in income implies a \$0.27 decrease in sales; and a \$100,000 increase in advertising implies a \$281 decrease in sales.

The implication for advertising is the opposite of what one would anticipate: an increase in advertising *should* yield an increase in sales. Notice, however, that the absolute value of the t-statistic for this variable is less than 2.00 (the rule-of-thumb standard for statistical significance), indicating that the coefficient is not statistically significant.

CHECKING THE MODEL

To check your spreadsheet, use the demand function formula given above, together with the mean values for each independent variable, to generate an estimate of Q. Enter the label Mean Value Forecast in cell J14. Enter Sales = in J15. Enter the cell reference of the constant (M4) in K15. (If your spreadsheet package supports absolute and mixed cell references, use an absolute address for this entry: $M$4.) In L15 enter the product of the coefficient and the mean value for the variable, L10*C30. (Here, the mixed address feature may be used: L$10*C$30.) Copy this formula to cells M15..Q15. Adjust column widths if necessary. Each cell represents the independent variable's marginal effect on total sales. In cell J16, enter Sales =, and in cell K16 use the @SUM (sum) function to compute total sales by combining all of the independent variable marginal effects and the constant. This estimate of Q, $175,250.00, represents the predicted sales when the independent variables are at their mean values. Compare your results to rows 14 through 16 in Figure 8-4.

USING THE SPREADSHEET

You have been asked a number of questions by the management of EZRydr. We now use our spreadsheet to answer these questions.

1. At current (1987) levels of the independent variables (price, populations income, etc.), what is the expected level of sales (in dollars) of small motorcycles and how does this compare to the actual sales level for 1987? To begin answering this question, look at the averages calculated in cells B30..H30 and the sales predictions for this level presented in cell K16. The method of forecasting 1987 sales volume is similar and consists of modifying the formulas to reference the actual 1987 values for each independent variable instead of the averages for those variables. Enter '87 Forecast: in cell J18. Copy J15..Q16 to cells J19..Q20. Note that we copy two rows in this operation because we wish to include both the numeric effect of each independent variable and the summary sales figure, which is the forecast. The formulas in cells L19 to Q19 need to be modified so that the cell references refer to the 1987 values of the independent variables, found in row 28 in the DEMAND DATA section (e.g., the formula in L19 is +L$10*C$28). In cell K20, the new value of Q is $155,334.24. Check your spreadsheet with rows 18 through 20 in Figure 8-4.

   In order to compare the forecasted value of Q with actual sales for 1987, enter the difference between cells K20 and B28 in cell K21. The forecast sales for 1987 are $2,666 less than the actual 1987 sales. This small discrepancy (less than 2%) indicates that the model is relatively accurate.

2. What would have been the predicted level of sales of small motorcycles in 1987 if the price had been decreased to $3,000? This prediction is very similar to the prediction made in Question 1. The only difference is that the price assumption changes from 1987's actual price of $3,130 to $3,000. In order to calculate a new forecast, enter the value 3000 in the cell that contains the 1987 price (C28). The new sales volume, Q, is $156,404.55. An increase in sales volume due to a price decrease is predicted. Once finished with this question, change the content of C28 to the original 3130.

3. What will the sales of small motorcycles be in 1988? In order to forecast sales for 1988, each of the independent variables must be independently forecast for 1988. EZRydr management can provide estimates of the organizationally-determined variables such as price and advertising. A memorandum from management predicts the average 1988 price to be $3,200 and advertising expenditures to be $850,000. Information on population, interest, and income has been obtained from the State Department of Development. Population is expected to increase to 1,600,000, consumer installment interest is expected to decline to 15%, and consumer income is expected to increase to $16,500. Our competitor's price is expected to remain in the neighborhood of $4,000. If you have not already done so, enter these assumptions in row 32, as illustrated in Figure 8-3.

   Calculate the 1988 forecast as you did the 1987 forecast, placing entries in rows 23 to 25 as illustrated in Figure 8-4. For this forecast, multiply the coefficients by the values in row 32. The predicted 1988 sales is $165,007.68. Even though price increased, the decrease in the interest rate and the increase in income and population caused sales to increase from 1987. Compare your spreadsheet with rows 23 through 25 of Figure 8-4.

EXERCISES

1. Management is concerned about rumors of a price decrease by competitors. Compute a new 1988 forecast, decreasing competitor price to $3,500.

2. With the information derived from the DEMAND DATA spreadsheet, it is possible to generate sensitivity analyses of demand using elasticities. The elasticity of an independent variable is the percentage change in demand that is caused by a 1% change in that variable. The elasticity of a variable is

   E = dQ/dX * X/Q

   where E is elasticity, dQ/dX is the coefficient of the independent variable from the regression equation, X is the value of the independent variable being evaluated, and Q is the quantity sold.

   We can construct a table to calculate elasticities using the 1987 actual values of the variables and the coefficients derived from the regression. Enter the label Elasticities: in cell J27. In cell L28 enter the formula for the elasticity of price: +L10*(C28/$B28). Copy this formula to cells L28..Q28. Check your elasticity values with those shown in row 28 of Figure 8-4. The value in cell M28 (.71) is the elasticity of population. The interpretation is that a 1% increase in population will increase output by .71%. These elasticities give management a way of predicting the percentage change in demand associated with a 1% change in an individual independent variable.

3. Reestimate the equation after removing the non-significant variables. Variables can be considered non-significant when the absolute value of the t-statistic is less than 2.0. In the first regression estimate, the variables income and advertising are not significant because the t-statistics are -.27 and -.86, respectively. In order to reestimate the equation, use the /**D**ata**R**egression command to redefine the X-range as C5..F28 and the output range as J30. Move the cursor to the output range to examine the results. Copy the t-statistic label and formulas from J12..O12 to J39..O39. Notice that all the independent variables are significant (t-statistic > 2.0) and have the expected signs, for example, price is negative.

Use the new coefficients to revise the 1988 forecast, as illustrated in Figure 8-5. The new sales volume is $165,240.60, slightly larger than the previous prediction, which included income and advertising. This revised forecast should be considered a better estimate because all the variables are statistically significant.

4. Calculate a new set of elasticities based on the reestimated coefficients in Exercise 3.

5. Economists are projecting a decrease in market interest rates to 12%. Compute a new 1988 forecast based on a 12% interest rate.

ENHANCEMENTS TO THE APPLICATION

There are a few enhancements that would make this spreadsheet easier to use. In this section, we point out some changes. You and your instructor may determine additional enhancements that may be made.

1. Using features such as Lotus's /**R**ange**I**nput and macro commands, develop a data-entry system for adding subsequent year's data to this spreadsheet.

2. Create a database command file that will extract the necessary data and place it in an interim file. Add a feature to your spreadsheet that will import data from that interim file into the proper positions on the spreadsheet. (There are many methods for accomplishing this, depending on the particular software available to you.) This feature is an alternative to Enhancement 1.

3. Combine the various spreadsheets developed in this unit into one. Devise a macro menu that will allow the user to select a particular portion of the analysis to view. For those portions where the user may perform what-if calculations (e.g., any of the Assumed for '88 figures), your menu should allow data input and display of results.

4. Using the variables in the reestimated equation from Exercise 3, draw a graph illustrating the effect of three interest rates — 12%, 15%, and 18% — as illustrated in Figure 8-6. You must compute the relationship between price and quantity demanded to provide the points of the graph. To accommodate the standard practice of plotting price on the vertical axis and quantity on the horizontal axis, you must recompute the regression equations with price as the dependent variable and quantity as one of the independent variables (which requires that you rearrange the data — do so in a separate area of the spreadsheet).

	J	K	L	M	N	O	P	Q
29								
30		Regression Output:						
31	Constant			78839.73				
32	Std Err of Y Est			3843.94				
33	R Squared			0.95				
34	No. of Observations			24.00				
35	Degrees of Freedom			19.00				
36								
37	X Coefficient(s)		-9.12	73.84	-3457.54	12.33		
38	Std Err of Coef.		3.39	32.90	854.43	3.91		
39	T-Statistic		-2.69	2.24	-4.05	3.15		
40								
41	88 Forecast:							
42	Sales =	78839.73	-29182.39	118141.90	-51863.08	49304.43		
43	Sales =	165240.60						
44								
45	Elasticities:							
46			-0.18	0.75	-0.40	0.31		

FIGURE 8-5 Revised Regression Output and 1988 Forecast

REVIEW QUESTIONS

1. How can a spreadsheet help a firm analyze the demand for its product?

2. Define the following terms as they are used in this unit.

   *a. demand function

   b. demand curve

   c. demand variables

   *d. elasticities

*3. How are historic data used to calculate demand relationships?

4. What conditions would make the use of historic data inappropriate?

*5. Is it possible to assess the magnitude of influence of any one demand variable on sales? How?

6. Is it possible to assess the proportional impact of demand variables on sales? How?

*7. Is it possible to "predict" sales for the product for past years? How?

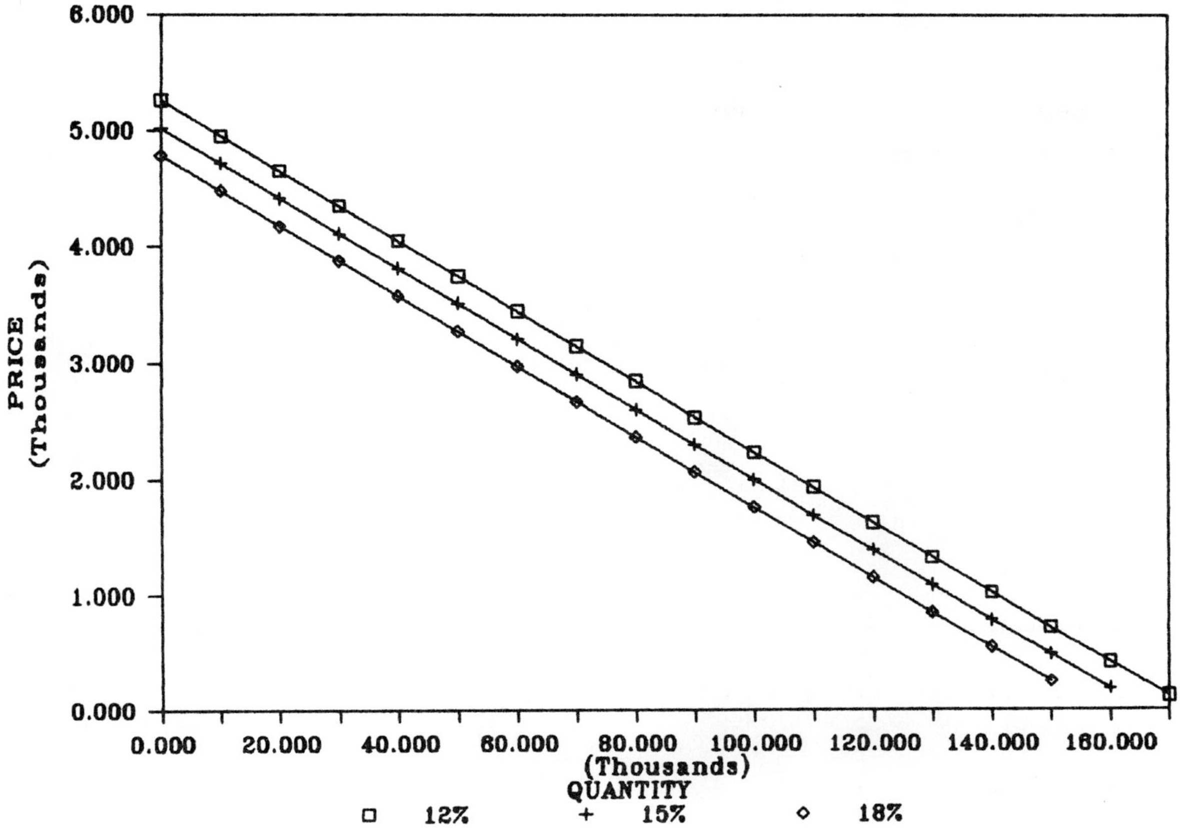

FIGURE 8-6 Demand Curve at Three Levels of Interest

ADDITIONAL READING

For more information about demand forecasting, consult any managerial economics textbook. These textbooks also provide better explanation of the theory on which the demand analysis technique discussed in this unit is based. See, for instance, the following:

Keating, B., and J. H. Wilson, *Managerial Economics*. Orlando: Academic Press, 1986. Chapter Five.

Mansfield, E., *Microeconomics*, 5th edition. New York: Norton, 1985. Chapter Four.

PART

3 ANALYZING AN OPPORTUNITY

In this part, we present three methods that are employed by organizations to decide whether or not to pursue a business opportunity. For EZRydr, the opportunity concerns the expansion of their product line. In Unit 9, a spreadsheet is developed for breakeven analysis, a method for determining minimum necessary sales levels. In Unit 10, decision trees are introduced as a method for dealing with situations in which the outcomes or alternative courses of action are uncertain. Finally, Unit 11 presents simulation analysis as a method for predicting results when precise analytic models are difficult to structure. The tools presented in this part are very general in nature, and may be applied to a broad range of decision situations.

UNIT

9

BREAKEVEN ANALYSIS— ASSESSING THE PROFITABILITY OF A NEW PRODUCT

September 24

The financial analysis appropriate to the decision of whether or not to manufacture and sell a new product involves assembling and analyzing a set of highly tentative estimates. For purposes of analysis, management must gather estimates of selling price, costs, and the number of units likely to be sold. These estimates may then be used to develop a projection of the potential profitability of the proposed new product. Because it is likely that management may wish to examine several different scenarios, each involving different combinations of cost, price, and level of sales, spreadsheets are a most convenient means of formulating the analysis.

DECISION SUPPORT APPLICATION MATRIX

Accounting & Finance	Economics & Long-Range Planning	Human Resources	Marketing & Logistics	Management Information Systems	Operations Planning & Control	Executive Officers
■	¤	■	¤	■	¤	

■ Departmental area(s) in which the technique is or can be used.

¤ Departmental area(s) that provide input to or are impacted by the technique.

LEARNING OBJECTIVES

1. After completing this unit you should know

   a. how to develop a profitability analysis for a proposed new product,

   b. how spreadsheet models can facilitate profit planning,

   c. how variable costs and fixed costs enter into the determination of profitability,

   d. how to prepare a breakeven graph, using spreadsheet graphic capabilities,

Contributed by Lloyd D. Doney

e. how a graphic presentation can provide insights into the new product decision.

2. After completing this unit you should be able to

   a. create a spreadsheet for examining the potential profitability of a proposed new product,

   b. develop a breakeven graph that provides a pictorial representation of the anticipated results of adding the new product.

BASIC CONCEPTS

New-product profitability analysis involves the estimation of the profitability of a proposed new product. Preparing the analysis requires a number of critical estimates which include the level of demand for the new product, the price of the new product, and the costs associated with bringing the new product to market. Once these critical estimates have been formulated, the analysis can be organized in the form of an income statement for the product.

Gathering the estimates involves several areas of expertise within the firm. Developing estimates of the demand and a suitable price for the product is largely the responsibility of the marketing function, although in setting a price, cost considerations must also be taken into account. The task of determining costs of producing the product usually falls to the engineering function within the operations management unit of the firm. Necessary estimates include material costs (including purchased parts and subassemblies), direct labor costs, and any increments in factory overhead costs resulting from producing the new product. Estimates of the additions to marketing costs necessitated by the new product are developed by marketing analysts. Estimates of increments to administrative costs are prepared by the affected administrative units. In most organizations it is quite likely that the accounting function also has a vital role in these estimating efforts, particularly in developing the cost estimates.

To a large extent, information accumulated in the organization pertaining to past operations is irrelevant to this particular decision, with the possible exception of some machine hour and labor rates.

Preparation of the estimates that enter into the analysis is the most critical aspect of the effort to assemble profit projections for the proposed new product. Once these estimates have been finalized, however, they may be combined in an income statement format that emphasizes the potential contribution margin of the proposed new product.

The accounting literature reveals two approaches to income statement preparation. The first, and more familiar of the two, is the *functional approach* which appears as follows:

Revenues	XXXXX
Less: Cost of Goods Sold	XXXXX
Gross Profit	XXXXX
Less: Selling & Administrative Expenses	XXXXX
Net Profit Before Taxes	XXXXX

Of course, the actual form of this income statement shows much greater detail within each of the major categories show above. In a manufacturing firm, for example, the cost of goods sold is often broken down into direct materials, direct labor, and factory overhead. The functional form of the income statement is the format used in the statements published periodically by the firm. It is primarily for external consumption — for use by interested parties external to the reporting organization.

For internal purposes, and particularly for decision-making analysis, a second form of the income statement that emphasizes the *contribution margin* is used. This approach is as follows:

Revenues	XXXXX
Less:	
Variable Manufacturing Costs	XXXXX
Variable Selling and Administrative Costs	XXXXX
Contribution Margin	XXXXX
Less:	
Fixed Manufacturing Costs	XXXXX
Fixed Selling and Administrative Costs	XXXXX
Net Profit Before Taxes	XXXXX

The net profit before taxes in both the functional approach and the contribution margin approach is identical. The difference between the two approaches, then, lies in how costs are classified. In the case of the functional approach, costs are classified as to function, resulting in an emphasis on gross profit, which is the excess of revenues over the cost to manufacture the products. In the contribution-margin approach, costs are classified as variable or fixed in terms of their behavior with respect to the level of activity at which the firm operates. *Variable costs* are those that increase in proportion to the level of activity, whereas *fixed costs* are those that remain at the same level over a range of activity. This approach emphasizes the contribution margin, which is defined as the excess of revenues over the variable costs of producing and selling the product.

For purposes of decision analysis, the contribution margin approach is superior because it emphasizes that a profitable product must sell at a price in excess of its variable cost. The portion of the price greater than the unit variable cost contributes to the fixed costs. When this contribution is sufficient to cover the fixed costs, profits result. For example, if a product sells for $10.00 per unit and variable cost per unit is $7.00, each unit sold contributes $3.00 toward fixed costs and profit. Assuming that total fixed costs are $30,000, 10,000 units, contributing $3.00 each, must be sold in order to break even, that is, to realize zero profit. If the number of units sold exceeds 10,000 units, each unit beyond 10,000 contributes $3.00 to profits.

The contribution margin income statement may be prepared for the entire firm, for product lines, or for individual products. Additionally, it provides a useful framework for organizing an analysis of whether to produce and sell a new product.

GATHERING THE DATA

Within the Company

With the exception of various kinds of economic or market data that can be used to make estimates of the demand for a new product (see Unit 8), the data used in preparing the analysis of a new product's profitability are developed within the organization. Using various kinds of market research methods, analysts in the marketing department develop demand estimates for the product. Marketing is also responsible for determining a specific price or range of selling prices which will result in the demand levels considered feasible, as well as estimates of increments to marketing costs necessitated by the new product. In addition, estimates of selling and administrative expenses need to be made.

The estimates of cost are developed primarily by the engineering function within the operations management area, with inputs from accounting, human resources, purchasing, and management information systems. Generally, cost estimates are derived for the following major cost categories: direct materials, direct labor, variable manufacturing overhead, and fixed manufacturing overhead. Labor and variable overhead costs are calculated by multiplying current rates for each of these categories by engineering estimates of the time necessary to produce the product. Direct material cost is estimated by purchasing and engineering. Fixed overhead cost is estimated by the accounting function (see Unit 4).

External to the Company

Various kinds of aggregate economic, census, and marketing data are used by the marketing department to forecast demand for the product (see Unit 8). This forecast, as well as the estimate of an appropriate price for the product, also entails an examination of competitors and their pricing policies for this or similar products.

THE PROBLEM

For some time the marketing staff at EZRydr has been considering an expansion of the product line. Most recently, a proposal has been submitted suggesting that the company produce and sell a small, two-wheeled trailer as an accessory for the bikes it currently produces. This proposal stems from a belief that a certain number of bikers use their bikes for long-distance travel. Accordingly, it seems that this group of bikers would be interested in adding a small trailer to their bikes for carrying their luggage. Preliminary design drawings have been prepared for the trailer. Before any further action is taken on this new product suggestion, the executive officers of the company would like to see some profit projections for the proposed product. Initially, management would like you to answer the following questions:

1. What is the profit potential of the proposed trailer at the average estimated demand level?

2. What is the profit potential of the proposed trailer if demand is one standard deviation from either side of the mean? Two standard deviations from the mean?

3. How many units of the proposed trailer must be sold in each period to break even?

Departmental Data

The following estimates have been compiled for purposes of the analysis:

Estimated Demand per Period	normally distributed
Mean	700 units
Standard Deviation	120 units
Proposed Price	$349
Estimated Variable Costs (per Unit)	
Direct Materials & Purchased Parts	$120
Direct Labor @ $10.00 per hour	$60
Variable Factory Overhead	$10
Variable Selling & Administrative	$25
Estimated Fixed Costs (per Period)	
Fixed Factory Overhead	$60,000
Fixed Selling & Administrative	$20,000

Data in the Database

Since this is a new product, the data required for the analysis are estimates of what costs and revenues will be rather than what they have been. While past costs and revenues may be somewhat useful in developing the estimates, EZRydr's database does not provide the estimates themselves. In the future, the MIS department will implement a database for proposed projects.

DEVELOPING THE SPREADSHEET

In order to respond to the questions raised by EZRydr's management, we must build a spreadsheet model of the proposed new product's potential profitability using the contribution margin form of the income statement. We also prepare a breakeven graph.

Start with a blank spreadsheet. In the upper left corner of the spreadsheet, enter the estimates given above, with the exception of the estimate of demand, under the heading, ASSUMPTIONS, as shown in Figure 9-1. Use columns A through D to enter the appropriate labels, and column E to enter the costs for each of the cost categories and the proposed price. Notice that some costs are on a per-unit basis, while others are on a per-period basis.

After entering the assumptions, move to line 12 to build the analysis for the situation in which product demand is equal to 700 units, as shown in Figure 9-2. Use columns A through C to enter the labels, structuring the analysis in the format of the contribution margin income statement. Add labels for the unit cost and the profit per unit at the bottom of the statement.

Once the labels have been properly entered, enter the appropriate constants or formulas in column D, which results in a calculation of the potential profitability of the proposed product at the estimated average demand level. Enter the estimated average demand (i.e., 700) in cell D14. Enter the appropriate formula to calculate total revenues in cell D16, that is, demand times price. If your spreadsheet package supports absolute cell addressing, use an absolute cell reference for price to facilitate later expansion of the spreadsheet to include other possible

```
A1: 'NEW PRODUCT PROFITABILITY ANALYSIS                                    READY

        A           B           C           D       E       F       G
1   NEW PRODUCT PROFITABILITY ANALYSIS
2
3   ASSUMPTIONS
4   Direct Materials & Purchase Parts                 120 /unit
5   Direct labor                                       60 /unit
6   Variable Factory Overhead                          10 /unit
7   Variable Selling & Administrative                  25 /unit
8   Fixed Factory Overhead                          60000 /period
9   Fixed Selling & Administrative                  20000 /period
10  Proposed Price                                    349 /unit
11
12
13
14
15
16
17
18
19
20
```

FIGURE 9-1 Assumptions

levels of demand. Enter the appropriate formulas for the variable cost computations in cells D18 through D21. In general, the computation is

Total Cost = Estimated Demand in Units x Cost per Unit

Total Variable Cost is obtained by adding the four items previously calculated in column D, and the Contribution Margin is obtained by subtracting Total Variable Cost from Revenues.

Use cell references to enter the fixed costs for the period in cells D25 and D26. Total Fixed Costs is the sum of these two items. Net Profit (pre-tax) is the difference between Contribution Margin and Total Fixed Costs.

After completing the income statement calculate Unit Cost and Profit per Unit. Unit Cost is obtained by dividing the sum of Total Fixed Costs and Total Variable Costs by the number of units. Profit per Unit is Proposed Price minus Unit Cost. Format numbers and adjust column widths as necessary to achieve the display illustrated in Figure 9-2.

```
A1: 'NEW PRODUCT PROFITABILITY ANALYSIS                                   READY


        A         B           C          D          E          F          G
1   NEW PRODUCT PROFITABILITY ANALYSIS
2
3   ASSUMPTIONS
4   Direct Materials & Purchase Parts            120 /unit
5   Direct labor                                  60 /unit
6   Variable Factory Overhead                     10 /unit
7   Variable Selling & Administrative             25 /unit
8   Fixed Factory Overhead                     60000 /period
9   Fixed Selling & Administrative             20000 /period
10  Proposed Price                               349 /unit
11
12  ANALYSIS
13
14  Units                               700
15
16  Revenues                         244300
17      Less Variable Costs:
18           Materials & Parts        84000
19           Direct Labor             42000
20           Variable Overhead         7000
21           Variable S & A           17500
22           Total Variable Costs    150500
23  Contribution Margin               93800
24      Less Fixed Costs:
25           Fixed Overhead           60000
26           Fixed S & A              20000
27           Total Fixed Costs        80000
28  Net Profit (pre-tax)              13800
29
30  Unit Cost                        329.29
31
32  Profit per Unit                   19.71
```

FIGURE 9-2 Completed Income Statement

After completing the analysis for a demand of 700 units, prepare to expand the number of columns by entering the following potential number of units sold in the spreadsheet:

Cell	Units
E14	580 (Average demand minus one standard deviation)
F14	820 (Average demand plus one standard deviation)
G14	460 (Average demand minus two standard deviations)
H14	940 (Average demand plus two standard deviations)

To complete the expansion of the spreadsheet to include four other possible levels of demand, copy from range D16...D32 to range E16...H32. Execution of the copy command should result in the expansion of the spreadsheet to five columns, showing the potential profitability at five different levels of demand.

Before leaving the spreadsheet, complete two additional tasks. First, include at the bottom of the spreadsheet a Total Cost label and the appropriate formula to calculate Total Cost (Total Variable Costs plus Total Fixed Costs) in column D. Then copy this formula to each of the remaining columns. A spreadsheet row containing the Total Cost will be necessary to produce a breakeven graph. Second, format the Total Cost cells. The completed spreadsheet is illustrated in Figure 9-3. (Do not complete the entry in row 36 at this time; it is discussed in Exercise 1.)

CHECKING THE MODEL

The best method for checking a model such as this is to enter data which will yield easily calculated results. Enter a set of variable costs and purchase price that yields a contribution margin that is equal to $10, and set the sum of fixed costs to be ten times the number of units sold. The net profit (pre-tax) for that number of units sold should be zero. The following set of numbers illustrates the method:

Estimated Demand per Period	
Mean	10 Units
Standard Deviation	n/a
Proposed Price	$20
Estimated Variable Costs (per Unit)	
Direct Materials & Purchased Parts	$3
Direct Labor @ $10.00 per hour	3
Variable Factory Overhead	2
Variable Selling & Administrative	2
Estimated Fixed Costs (per Period)	
Fixed Factory Overhead	$60
Fixed Selling & Administrative	$40

Contribution Margin = ($20 - (3 + 3 + 2 + 2)) x 10 Units = $100

Total Fixed Costs = $60 + 40 = $100

Net Profit = Contribution Margin - Total Fixed Costs = $100 - 100 = $0

Remember to return the spreadsheet to its original state before continuing.

USING THE SPREADSHEET

The NEW PRODUCT PROFITABILITY ANALYSIS spreadsheet was prepared in response to questions raised by EZRydr's management regarding whether or not to market the proposed trailer. It is now possible to use the spreadsheet to respond to each of the questions.

A1: [W6] 'NEW PRODUCT PROFITABILITY ANALYSIS READY

	A B C	D	E	F	G	H
1	NEW PRODUCT PROFITABILITY ANALYSIS					
2						
3	ASSUMPTIONS					
4	Direct Materials & Purchase Parts		$120	/unit		
5	Direct labor		$60	/unit		
6	Variable Factory Overhead		$10	/unit		
7	Variable Selling & Administrative		$25	/unit		
8	Fixed Factory Overhead		$60,000	/period		
9	Fixed Selling & Administrative		$20,000	/period		
10	Proposed Price		$349	/unit		
11						
12	ANALYSIS					
13						
14	Units	700	580	820	460	940
15						
16	Revenues	$244,300	$202,420	$286,180	$160,540	$328,060
17	Less Variable Costs:					
18	Materials & Parts	$84,000	$69,600	$98,400	$55,200	$112,800
19	Direct Labor	$42,000	$34,800	$49,200	$27,600	$56,400
20	Variable Overhead	$7,000	$5,800	$8,200	$4,600	$9,400
21	Variable S & A	$17,500	$14,500	$20,500	$11,500	$23,500
22	Total Variable Costs	$150,500	$124,700	$176,300	$98,900	$202,100
23	Contribution Margin	$93,800	$77,720	$109,880	$61,640	$125,960
24	Less Fixed Costs:					
25	Fixed Overhead	$60,000	$60,000	$60,000	$60,000	$60,000
26	Fixed S & A	$20,000	$20,000	$20,000	$20,000	$20,000
27	Total Fixed Costs	$80,000	$80,000	$80,000	$80,000	$80,000
28	Net Profit (pre-tax)	$13,800	($2,280)	$29,880	($18,360)	$45,960
29						
30	Unit Cost	$329.29	$352.93	$312.56	$388.91	$300.11
31						
32	Profit per unit	$19.71	($3.93)	$36.44	($39.91)	$48.89
33						
34	Total Cost	$230,500	$204,700	$256,300	$178,900	$282,100
35						
36	Breakeven Point	597				

FIGURE 9-3 The Completed Spreadsheet

1. What is the profit potential of the proposed trailer at the average estimated demand level? At sales of 700 units per period, the new product would contribute an additional $13,800 to profits for the period. This can be observed by examining the Net Profit (pre-tax) in cell D28. Further inspection reveals that the average cost per unit at this level of sales is $329.29 and that the average profit per unit is $19.71. If demand is 700 units, the profit implications of the proposed trailer appear to be promising.

2. What is the profit potential of the proposed trailer if demand is one standard deviation on either side of the mean? two standard deviations on either side of the mean? Inspection of the cells containing the Net Profit (pre-tax) for the remaining columns of the spreadsheet present a mixed picture. If demand materializes at levels higher than the average of 700 units predicted, the profit estimates are even more promising. At a demand of 820 units (one standard deviation greater than the mean), estimated profit increases to $29,880; and at a demand of 940 units (two standard deviations greater than the mean), estimated profit rises to $45,960. However, if demand turns out to be only 580 units (one standard deviation lower than the mean), a loss of $2,280 is incurred; at 460 units (two standard deviations lower than the mean), a loss of $18,360 is indicated.

3. How many units of the proposed trailer must be sold in each period to break even? Although in this case it is possible to calculate the breakeven point directly, using an appropriate formula, it is also possible to use the spreadsheet on a trial-and-error basis to obtain the answer. First we use the spreadsheet approach. After we obtain the result using the spreadsheet, we develop a formula solution. The formula solution, then, may serve as a check on the spreadsheet analysis.

   Note that in column D a profit is realized and in column E a loss is indicated. Therefore, the breakeven or zero profit point is somewhere between 580 and 700 units, probably closer to 580 than 700. Using cell E14, systematically increase the number of units until the Net Profit (pre-tax) in cell E28 equals zero. When this occurs, the breakeven number of units has been determined. A possible trial-and-error sequence may be as follows:

   Try 600 units — Net Profit is $400; breakeven point is lower
   Try 595 units — Net Loss is $270; breakeven point is higher
   Try 596 units — Net Loss is $136; breakeven point is higher
   Try 597 units — Net Loss is $2; breakeven point?
   Try 598 units — Net Profit is $132; breakeven point is lower

   Conclusion: The number of units which must be sold to break even is 597. After you complete this analysis, restore the number of units in column E to the original 580 units.

   The breakeven point can also be calculated directly with the following formula:

$$\text{Breakeven Units} = \frac{\text{Total Fixed Costs}}{\text{Unit Selling Price - Unit Variable Cost}}$$

$$= \frac{60{,}000 + 20{,}000}{(349 - (120 + 60 + 10 + 25))}$$

$$= \frac{80{,}000}{134}$$

$$= 597$$

The direct calculation of the breakeven point confirms the result obtained using the trial-and-error approach on the spreadsheet.

As a business student, you have undoubtedly encountered the breakeven graph as a useful analytical device. In fact, a discussion of breakeven analysis and breakeven graphs appears in several business courses — microeconomics, managerial accounting, cost accounting, financial management, and marketing management, to cite a few.

Once the spreadsheet is completed, it is easy to use the graphics capabilities of spreadsheet packages to produce a breakeven graph for the proposed new product. A suitable breakeven graph is illustrated in Figure 9-4. Create a similar graph using your spreadsheet.

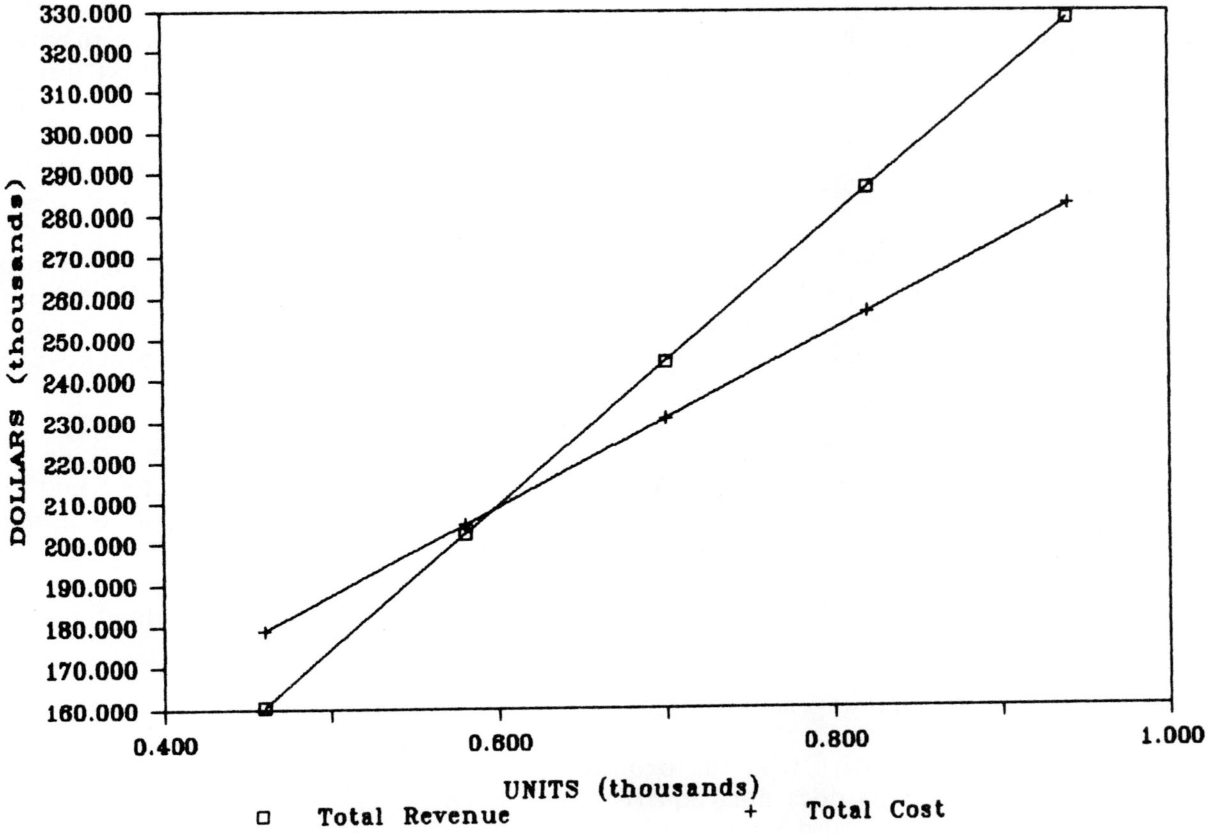

FIGURE 9-4 Breakeven Graph

The breakeven graph confirms the results of the trial-and-error and formula computations. It reveals that the breakeven point is just under 600 units. To the left of the breakeven point, the total contribution margin generated by the number of units sold is less than the total fixed costs, and losses are incurred. The amount of the loss is the vertical distance between the total cost line and the total revenue line on the graph. To the right of the breakeven point, the total contribution margin generated by the number of units sold exceeds the total fixed costs, and profits are realized. The profit at any level of units sold is the vertical difference between the total revenue and the total cost lines. Beyond the breakeven point, each additional unit sold contributes $134 to profits.

EXERCISES

The NEW PRODUCT PROFITABILITY ANALYSIS spreadsheet, developed in response to specific questions raised by EZRydr's management, is a powerful and versatile decision support tool. Unfortunately, the result of the analysis is not entirely conclusive in this case. Although the potential for profits from the new product is greater than 50-50, the undertaking is certainly not without risk. Use the spreadsheet you have created to explore the following questions which may arise as management pursues the decision whether or not to add the trailer to its product line. As you answer these questions, reset the spreadsheet to the original values before every question and subquestion. The easiest way to do this is to save the initial spreadsheet and then make the required changes in the spreadsheet in response to each of the questions. Once a question has been answered, you may either record the answer in your notes or save the spreadsheet with a unique name. When you are ready for the next question or subquestion, load (retrieve) the original spreadsheet.

1. In the lower portion of your spreadsheet, add a direct calculation of the breakeven point using the appropriate variables given in the formula above.

2. EZRydr's marketing analysts feel that there is some opportunity to increase the proposed selling price without impacting negatively on the demand for the trailer. Re-examine the profit potential of the trailer at each of the previously explored levels of demand if the price is increased to $369. What is the new breakeven point? Prepare a breakeven graph to illustrate this analysis.

3. It is believed that, through aggressive purchasing strategies and a simple design change, the estimated unit cost for materials and purchased parts can be reduced by $5.00 and the direct labor cost by another $5.00 per unit. (Note: the price should be the original $349 for this analysis.)

   a. Re-examine the profit potential at each of the previously explored levels of demand in view of these potentially lower costs.

   b. What is the new breakeven point?

   c. What is the probability that the product will be profitable under this set of circumstances? (Note: This does not require a spreadsheet manipulation; rather, it challenges your understanding and ability to use the normal probability table found in your statistics text. Believe it or not, there are uses for statistics in business!)

4. Assuming that the $60,000 of fixed factory overhead represents a one-time expenditure to launch production of the trailer, and that it does not occur in ensuing periods, examine the profitability at all levels of demand previously used in the absence of this particular cost.

5. What is your recommendation to management regarding addition of the trailer to the product line? Why?

ENHANCEMENTS TO THE APPLICATION

Several features of spreadsheet programs can be used to provide a more flexible decision support tool.

1. In the ASSUMPTIONS area, add a place for the entry of Mean Demand and Standard Deviation. In row 14, enter five formulas which automatically compute the demand levels to be analyzed. Instead of the current arrangement, put the formulas in order of ascending demand.

2. Use the cell-protection feature to protect all cells except those in which variable data are entered. Using features such as Lotus's /RangeInput and macro commands, develop a data-entry system for this analysis.

3. Construct a two-way table of numbers computing net pre-tax profit of various selling prices (from Proposed Price minus $50 to Proposed Price plus $50, increment $25) and various levels of sales (from Mean Demand minus three Standard Deviations to Mean Demand plus three Standard Deviations, increment one Standard Deviation). Assume that all costs remain the same. Some spreadsheet packages, such as Lotus 1-2-3, offer the ability to perform this type of what-if analysis using *data tables*. In other cases, you must create the table using formulas.

   If your spreadsheet software allows naming or numbering of graphs, assign a name or number to the first graph. Then create a second graph containing the results of your table.

REVIEW QUESTIONS

*1. What form of the income statement provides a suitable framework in which to examine the profitability of a proposed new product? Why?

2. How does a spreadsheet model facilitate exploration of the potential profitability of a proposed new product?

3. Define the following terms as they are used in new-product analysis:

   *a. variable costs

   *b. fixed costs

   c. contribution margin

d. breakeven point

*e. factory overhead

f. direct labor

*4. What factors other than the potential financial impact of a new product enter into the decision whether or not to introduce the product?

5. Does the breakeven point increase or decrease in each of the following cases?

a. The selling price is increased.

*b. The unit variable cost is reduced.

c. Total fixed costs are reduced.

*d. The selling price is increased and the fixed costs are reduced.

e. The selling price is increased and the fixed costs are increased.

6. What activity in the entire process of new-product profit planning is the most critical?

ADDITIONAL READING

Additional information regarding the financial analysis relevant to the decision of whether or not to add a new product may be found in most managerial accounting and cost accounting texts as well as certain computing manuals. A sample of such references includes:

Gray, P., *Guide to IFPS (Interactive Financial Planning System)*, 2nd edition. New York: McGraw-Hill, 1987.

Horngren, C. T., and G. Foster, *Cost Accounting: A Managerial Emphasis*, 6th edition. Englewood Cliffs, NJ: Prentice-Hall, 1987.

Horngren, C. T., and G. L. Sundem, *Introduction to Management Accounting*, 7th edition. Englewood Cliffs, NJ: Prentice-Hall, 1987.

Killough, L. N., and W. E. Leininger, *Cost Accounting Concepts and Techniques for Management*, 2nd edition. St. Paul: West, 1987.

Rayburn, G. R., *Principles of Cost Accounting: Managerial Applications*, revised edition. Homewood, IL: Irwin, 1983.

UNIT

10 DECISION TREES—ANALYZING ALTERNATIVES

Managers must routinely make decisions in the face of uncertainty. They must make decisions *today* without fully knowing what the consequences of those decisions will be *tomorrow*. Retail managers must decide which products to stock on their shelves, financial managers must decide which stocks to include in a portfolio and when to buy and sell those stocks, marketing managers must decide which new products warrant development and which do not, and so on. In each of these instances, the managers must choose a course of action based on the *expected* outcome of their decisions. One technique that can be used under these circumstances to systematically organize, evaluate, and integrate both information and intuition is decision tree analysis. Given the costs (or revenues or profits) of competing alternatives and a probabilistic statement of the outcomes proceeding from each of those alternatives, decision trees can assist in identifying the best alternative to pursue (i.e., the one with the lowest expected cost or the highest expected revenue or profit). Spreadsheet software packages provide a powerful modeling tool for developing and analyzing decision trees.

DECISION SUPPORT APPLICATION MATRIX

Accounting & Finance	Economics & Long-Range Planning	Human Resources	Marketing & Logistics	Management Information Systems	Operations Planning & Control	Executive Officers
■¤	■¤	■¤	■¤	■¤	■¤	■¤

■ Departmental area(s) in which the technique is or can be used.

¤ Departmental area(s) that provide input to or are impacted by the technique.

Contributed by Richard J. Penlesky

LEARNING OBJECTIVES

1. After completing this unit you should know

   a. the terminology associated with decision tree analysis,

   b. how to construct and analyze decision trees,

   c. how decision tree analysis can be applied to a variety of probabilistic business decisions,

   d. why the time value of money can be important in decision tree analysis,

   e. how a spreadsheet package can be used to develop and analyze decision trees.

2. After completing this unit you should be able to

   a. create a spreadsheet model of a decision tree,

   b. use a decision tree spreadsheet to solve a product-line diversification problem,

   c. incorporate the time value of money in a decision tree analysis.

BASIC CONCEPTS

We all make decisions on a routine basis. Some of those decisions deal with fairly mundane matters, such as deciding what clothes to wear, what to have for breakfast, or which way to drive to school or work. Other decisions focus on momentous occasions in our lives, such as which college to attend, what major to pursue in school, what job to accept after graduation, or whether or not to marry. From the mundane to the momentous, all decisions can be modeled with three primary building blocks: (1) the list of alternatives from which we must select in making the decision, (2) the anticipated outcome(s) of selecting each alternative, and (3) an estimate of the likelihood of each outcome occurring. When we make a decision, we typically combine these building blocks in the following fashion (though not necessarily in the order listed, and not necessarily at a conscious level):

1. Identify the list of alternatives.

2. Establish the criteria to be used in making the decision.

3. Identify the possible outcome of each alternative (note that the outcomes should be defined in terms of the criteria established in step 2).

4. Estimate the likelihood of each of the possible outcomes occurring.

5. Combine the likelihood estimates with the benefit or cost of each of the possible outcomes to determine the *expected* benefit or cost of each alternative.

6. Select the alternative that provides the highest *expected* benefit or lowest expected cost.

When using decision trees to select among alternatives, only *one criterion* (such as cost or location or time) is used to make the decision. Decisions that require consideration of *multiple criteria* (such as cost and location and time) must be made using a different decision-making technique, such as the weighted factor approach (see Unit 12).

Decision trees are a fairly generic decision-making tool; they can be used to make decisions in the marketing function just as easily as they can in the finance function, the operations function, and so on. In this regard, decision trees are similar to the weighted factor approach (Unit 12) and different from aggregate planning (Unit 6) and inventory control (Unit 7); the latter two techniques are used to solve fairly specific problems.

Single Stage Decisions

Decision trees are most often used in stochastic decision-making situations. In a *stochastic* decision-making situation there are many possible outcomes associated with each alternative, and the decision maker assigns probabilities to each of those outcomes occurring. For example, an investor may be faced with the task of deciding which of two stocks to purchase, as in Table 10-1.

TABLE 10-1 Comparison of Two Investment Alternatives

Alternatives	Anticipated Rates of Return (Outcomes)		Estimated Outcome Probabilities
Stock I	High	35%	.25
	Medium	20%	.30
	Low	5%	.45
Stock II	High	25%	.50
	Medium	15%	.30
	Low	5%	.20

Stock I has a probability of .25 of yielding a high return of 35%, a probability of .30 of yielding a medium return of 20%, and a probability of .45 of yielding only a 5% return. Stock II's figures should be interpreted in a similar fashion. Note that the sum of the outcome probabilities for each stock is equal to 1.00. To reflect that all possible outcomes are being considered, the sum of the outcome probabilities must be equal to 1 for each alternative.

If the investor focuses only on the rates of return, it appears that Stock I is preferable to Stock II, because the rates of return for Stock I are all greater than or equal to those for Stock II. However, because the probability of a high rate of return for Stock I is much lower than that for Stock II (.25 vs. .50) and the probability of a low rate of return for Stock I is much higher than that for Stock II (.45 vs. .20), Stock I is a riskier investment than Stock II. Thus, in this instance, the investor must consider both the return and the risk when choosing between the alternative investments. These two considerations can be combined by calculating the *expected rate of return* (Expected ROR) for each of the alternatives by summing the product of each anticipated rate of return and its associated probability across all of the possible outcomes for each alternative:

Expected ROR (I) = (.25 x 35) + (.30 x 20) + (.45 x 5) = 17%

Expected ROR (II) = (.50 x 25) + (.30 x 15) + (.20 x 5) = 18%

Based on this analysis, the investor should purchase Stock II, since its 18% Expected ROR exceeds the 17% Expected ROR for Stock I.

To structure this decision in decision tree format, we must introduce a few terms and symbols. Decision trees are constructed by connecting *decision nodes* [ ] with *probabilistic outcome nodes* ( ) in a network that gives the appearance of a tree. The decision maker has control over what happens at a decision node but does not have control over what happens at a probabilistic outcome node. In the investment example above, the investor has control over which stock to choose but does not have control over the rate of return that is ultimately realized from the investment. The tree for the investment decision is illustrated in Figure 10-1.

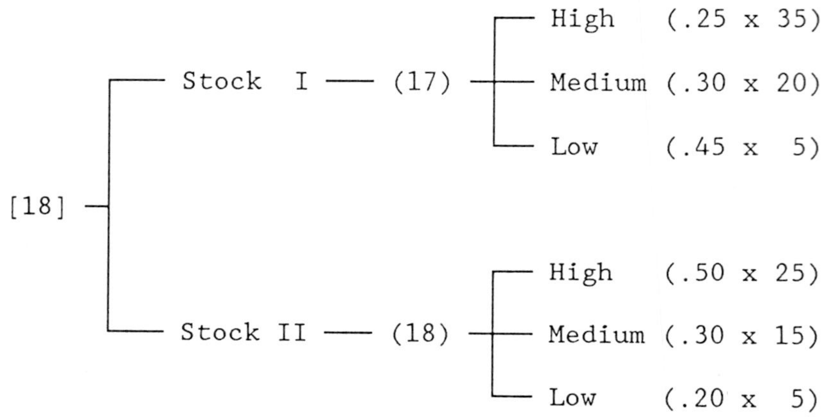

FIGURE 10-1 Decision Tree for Two Investment Alternatives

The expected return is calculated and entered at each of the probabilistic outcome nodes, and the best of the returns is then entered at the decision node. In this example, the decision tree indicates that Stock II should be purchased: the 18% entered at the decision node matches the 18% expected return entered at the probabilistic outcome node for that alternative.

Multistage Decisions

In addition to single-stage decision-making problems (such as the investment example described above), decision trees can be used to solve multistage decision-making problems. Consider Chris, for example, a bright student who is about to graduate from high school. Chris has identified three career alternatives. These alternatives are described below.

Alternative	Description
1 [WF]	Enter the workforce.
2 [AD]	Enroll in a two-year technical program, earn an Associate Degree, and then
	a. [WF] enter the workforce.
	b. [BS] enroll in a university program, earn a Bachelor of Science degree, and enter the workforce.
3 [BS]	Enroll in a four-year university program, earn a Bachelor of Science degree and then enter the workforce.

This is a multistage decision-making problem because the decision that Chris makes right now (Stage I) is influenced by a second decision that will be made if the Associate Degree alternative is pursued (i.e., whether to enter the workforce or to go on to earn a Bachelor's Degree).

TABLE 10-2 Career Alternative Financial Data

Alternative	Time Period (years)	Annual Expenses	Annual Income	Income Probability
1	1 - 20	\$8,000	\$10,000 L \$15,000 H	.40 .60
2	1 - 2	\$10,000	\$3,000 L \$5,000 H	.70 .30
2a	3 - 20	\$9,000	\$12,000 L \$16,000 H	.30 .70
2b	3 - 5	\$14,000	\$8,000 L \$10,000 H	.50 .50
	6 - 20	\$10,000	\$18,000 L \$22,000 H	.40 .60
3	1 - 4	\$14,000	\$3,000 L \$5,000 H	.40 .60
	5 - 20	\$10,000	\$17,000 L \$22,000 H	.50 .50

Assume that Chris will choose the alternative that maximizes "profit" (i.e., income - expenses) over the next twenty years. Also assume that Chris and the high school guidance counselor have compiled the information in Table 10-2 regarding the alternatives identified above (note that the figures in the table are probably quite different from those that might apply in your particular situation). In this situation, the decision tree might appear as illustrated in Figure 10-2. The numbers in braces { } next to the low (L) and high (H) income possibilities represent the time in years that that income level will be in effect.

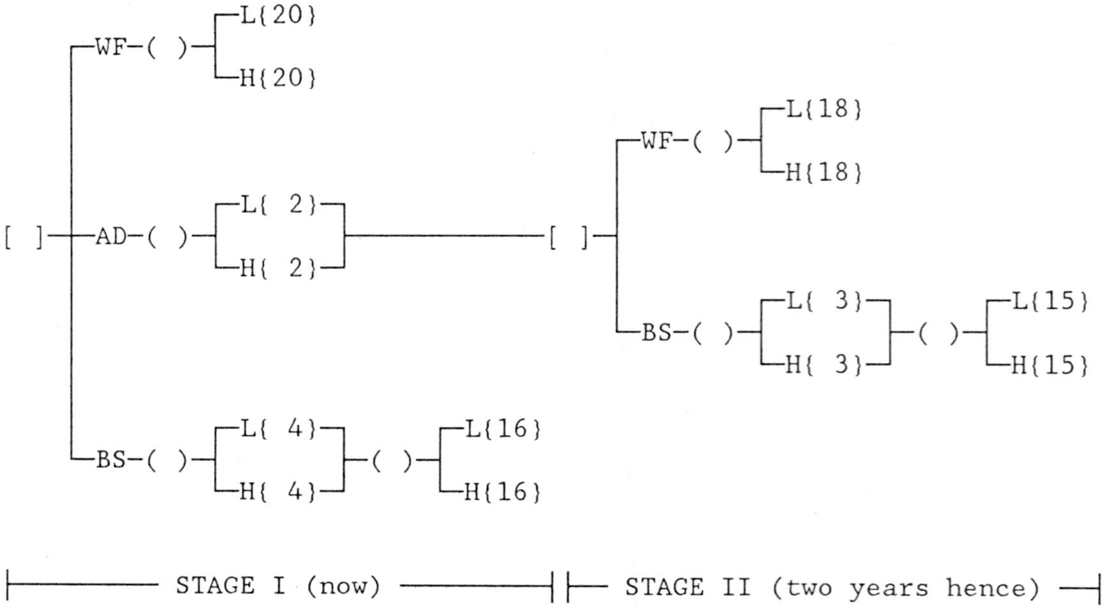

FIGURE 10-2 Career Alternative Decision Tree

We analyze the decision tree by "working backwards" from its "leaves and branches" to its "trunk." The expected profit (EP) of the workforce (WF) alternative is calculated as follows:

$$EP_{WF} = \text{Expected Income - Expense}$$

$$= 20 \times [(.4)(10{,}000) + (.6)(15{,}000)] - 20 \times 8{,}000$$

$$= 260{,}000 - 160{,}000$$

$$= 100{,}000$$

As indicated by the complexity of the decision tree, the EP of the Associate Degree (AD) alternative is a bit more complicated to calculate. We begin by calculating the EP of entering the workforce immediately after receiving the Associate Degree (i.e., working for eighteen years):

$$EP_{AD18} = 18 \times [(.3)(12{,}000) + (.7)(16{,}000)] - 18 \times 9{,}000$$

$$= 104{,}400$$

Next we calculate the EP of entering the workforce *after having completed* the requirements for a Bachelor's Degree (BS) (i.e., working for fifteen years after completing an additional three years of schooling):

$$EP_{AD15/3} = 15 \times [(.4)(18{,}000) + (.6)(22{,}000)] - 15 \times 10{,}000 +$$

$$3 \times [(.5)(8{,}000) + (.5)(10{,}000)] - 3 \times 14{,}000$$

$$= 141{,}000$$

Since the EP of entering the workforce after completing the requirements for the BS degree ($141,000) is greater than that of entering the workforce immediately after receiving the Associate Degree ($104,400), we assume that Chris will get a BS after completing the Associate Degree. Then, in order to calculate the EP of the Stage I AD alternative, we add the $141,000 EP of the BS degree to the EP of the two-year Associate Degree program as follows:

$$EP_{AD} = 2 \times [(.7)(3{,}000) + (.3)(5{,}000)] - 2 \times 10{,}000 + 141{,}000$$

$$= 128{,}200$$

Finally, the EP of the BS alternative is calculated by combining the EP of the sixteen working years with that of the four schooling years for that alternative:

$$EP_{BS} = 16 \times [(.5)(17{,}000) + (.5)(22{,}000)] - 16 \times 10{,}000 +$$

$$4 \times [(.4)(3{,}000) + (.6)(5{,}000)] - 4 \times 14{,}000$$

$$= 112{,}800$$

Based upon this analysis, Chris should enroll in the two-year technical program and earn an Associate Degree — the expected profit of this alternative ($128,200) is greater than that of the four-year university program ($112,800) and the workforce option ($100,000).

The Time Value of Money

The foregoing analysis is based on the assumption that the time value of money is equal to zero; that is, the analysis assumes that a dollar earned today has exactly the same value as a dollar earned twenty years from now. In situations where the time frame of the decision is relatively short (i.e., one to two years), this assumption does not have a significant impact on the decision. However, when the time frame of the decision is quite long, as it is in the example above, the time value of money can have a significant impact on the decision. A positive time value of money implies that a dollar earned today is worth more than a dollar earned tomorrow because the dollar earned today can be invested and thus be worth more than a dollar tomorrow.

Conversely, a dollar earned tomorrow is worth less than a dollar earned today; that is, the *present value* of a dollar earned tomorrow is actually less than a dollar. For example, if the time value of money is 2% per month, a rational investor would be indifferent between receiving $100 now and $102 one month from now. The investor would be indifferent because the present value of receiving $100 today is $100 and the present value of receiving $102 in one month at a *discount rate* of 2% is \$102/1.02 = \$100. The discount rate is the interest rate used to discount the value of future dollar amounts and thus to convert them to present value amounts.

In order to include the time value of money in Chris's career decision, let us assume that the time value of money is 10% per year and that, rather than being spread evenly throughout the year, all of Chris's income and expenses occur on the first day of each year (the latter assumption is made for the sake of simplicity). What we must do is discount the cash flow streams for each of Chris's three alternatives using the 10% discount rate. A cash flow stream can be discounted to time zero by using the following formula:

$$PV = FV/(1 + DR)^n$$

where PV is the present value of the amount, FV is the future value of the amount, DR is the discount rate per period (expressed as a decimal), and n is the number of periods in the future that the transaction occurs.

Table 10-3 shows the simple cash flow and discounted cash flow streams for each of Chris's three career alternatives.

TABLE 10-3 Simple and Discounted Cash Flows for Career Alternatives

	Alternative 1 [WF]		Alternative 2 [AD]		Alternative 3 [BS]	
Year	Simple Cash Flow	Discounted Cash Flow	Simple Cash Flow	Discounted Cash Flow	Simple Cash Flow	Discounted Cash Flow
1	5000	5000	-6400	-6400	-9800	-9800
2	5000	4545	-6400	-5818	-9800	-8909
3	5000	4132	-5000	-4132	-9800	-8099
4	5000	3757	-5000	-3757	-9800	-7363
5	5000	3415	-5000	-3415	9500	6489
6	5000	3105	10400	6458	9500	5899
7	5000	2822	10400	5871	9500	5363
8	5000	2566	10400	5337	9500	4875
9	5000	2333	10400	4852	9500	4432
10	5000	2120	10400	4411	9500	4029
11	5000	1928	10400	4010	9500	3663
12	5000	1752	10400	3645	9500	3330
13	5000	1593	10400	3314	9500	3027
14	5000	1448	10400	3013	9500	2752
15	5000	1317	10400	2739	9500	2502
16	5000	1197	10400	2490	9500	2274
17	5000	1088	10400	2263	9500	2067
18	5000	989	10400	2058	9500	1880
19	5000	899	10400	1871	9500	1709
20	5000	818	10400	1700	9500	1553
Total	100000	46825	128200	30507	112800	21670

Notice that the total of the Simple Cash Flow column matches the value we calculated earlier for each of the alternatives. Then notice that the totals in the Discounted Cash Flow columns are significantly less than those in the Simple Cash Flow columns. The discounted totals represent the present value of the simple cash flow stream. For example, under Alternative 1, year 20 shows a simple cash flow amount of $5,000 and a discounted cash flow amount of $818. The $818 in the Discounted column indicates that Chris should be indifferent between receiving $818 now or $5,000 in twenty years, given that the time value of money is 10% per year. If Chris received $818 now and invested it at a rate of 10% per year, that investment would grow to $5,000 in twenty years.

Comparison of the discounted cash flow totals for the three alternatives indicates that the present value of entering the workforce immediately after graduation ($46,825 — Alternative 1) is greater than that of enrolling in a two-year technical program ($30,507 — Alternative 2), which, in turn, is greater than that of enrolling in a four-year university program ($21,670 — Alternative 3). The reason for this ranking can be traced primarily to the increasingly negative cash flows that occur in the early years of the planning horizon as you look first at Alternative 1, then 2, and finally 3. Thus, according to this analysis, Chris should get a job right after graduating from high school. (We leave it to you, as both a mental and a computational exercise, to identify the psychic and monetary considerations that were ignored in arriving at this conclusion.)

GATHERING THE DATA

As mentioned earlier, decision trees are a fairly generic decision-making tool and thus can be used to study a broad range of decision-making problems. The source of the data for such problems varies with the scope of the problem. In general, short-term, tactical decisions are based on more data from internal sources, and long-term, strategic decisions require the collection of more external data. For example, the costs, benefits, and outcome probabilities associated with a quality-improvement program at a particular machine center can usually be obtained from internal records and from estimates supplied by operating personnel. On the other hand, the costs, benefits, and outcome probabilities associated with a company-wide quality-improvement program are usually obtained from company sources, industry sources, association publications, educational literature, consultants, and so on.

THE PROBLEM

In the past, EZRydr has followed a policy of no layoffs in order to stabilize employment and to protect the workers. Because of the seasonal nature of the motorcycle business and the six-month lead time in motorcycle manufacturing, this policy has led to excess capacity during the summer months. EZRydr works at capacity during the winter months to produce the motorcycles that will be sold the following summer. When summer arrives, capacity utilization declines drastically because few motorcycles are sold in the winter months. To use the excess summer capacity more effectively, management at the firm is considering expansion of its operation.

EZRydr has identified two product lines that have production requirements similar to those of motorcycles. The first product line, snowmobiles, has a demand cycle that is counter-cyclic relative to that of motorcycles. When the demand for motorcycles is high (in the summer), the demand for snowmobiles is low, and vice versa. This counter-cyclic demand cycle would generate a counter-cyclic production cycle for EZRydr and thus tend to level the firm's capacity utilization. The second product line, all-terrain vehicles (ATVs), has a demand cycle that is more level than those of motorcycles and snowmobiles, since ATVs can be used in both summer and winter. Management at EZRydr suspects that the firm can use the excess capacity that occurs in the summer months more effectively (when the production requirement for motorcycles is low) if it expands its operation to include one or both of these product lines. They would like you to help them decide which, if any, of these alternatives to pursue by using decision tree analysis to answer the following questions:

1. Should EZRydr expand its operation?

2. If EZRydr expands its operation,

   a. which product line(s) should be added now?

   b. which product line(s) should be added later?

3. How sensitive is the expansion decision relative to changes in

   a. the time value of money?

   b. outcome probabilities?

   c. revenue estimates?

   d. expense estimates?

   e. expansion cost estimates?

Departmental Data

The expansion decision data were compiled by various personnel in EZRydr's economics, marketing, and operations planning and control departments. Significant input regarding outcome probabilities and demand estimates was also provided by the firm's executive officers.

Management would like to use an overall time frame of five years to evaluate the expansion decision. However, they have identified two stages in their decision-making process. In Stage I (the current decision) management is considering four alternatives: (1) do nothing (i.e., continue making motorcycles, but do not expand into either of the target markets); (2) enter the all-terrain vehicle (ATV) market only; (3) enter the snowmobile (SM) market only; and (4) enter both the all-terrain vehicle and the snowmobile (ATV&SM) markets. If EZRydr enters either or both of the new markets now, the firm will remain committed to that decision for the entire five-year planning horizon.

Stage II of the decision-making process will occur at the end of the third year of the planning horizon. At that time, management expects that the market for these two product lines will begin to mature and, consequently, that the demand for the products will increase. Thus the Stage II decision faced by management is whether or not to enter the new product market(s) that was (were) not entered at the time of the Stage I decision. If, for example, the Stage I decision was to enter the ATV market, then the Stage II decision would be whether or not to enter the SM market.

The data shown in Table 10-4 reflect the two-stage timing scheme for the expansion decision as well as the outcome probabilities, annual revenues, annual expenses, and expansion costs for the two product lines under consideration. EZRydr estimates that the cost of capital is 9% per year.

TABLE 10-4 Product Line Financial Data

Years	Demand Level	Probability	Annual Revenues ($ million)	Annual Expenses ($ million)	Expansion Cost ($ million)
All-Terrain Vehicles (ATV)					
1,2,3	high	.30	4.00	3.00	1.50
	medium	.30	3.00	2.50	
	low	.40	2.00	2.25	
4,5	high	.40	6.00	3.50	2.00
	medium	.30	5.00	3.00	
	low	.30	3.00	2.50	
Snowmobiles (SM)					
1,2,3	high	.20	5.00	3.50	3.00
	medium	.50	4.00	3.00	
	low	.30	1.00	2.00	
4,5	high	.30	6.00	4.25	3.50
	medium	.50	5.00	3.50	
	low	.20	3.50	2.75	

Data in the Database

Since these are new products, the data required for the analysis are estimates of what costs and revenues will be rather than what they have been. While past costs and revenues may be somewhat useful in developing the estimates, EZRydr's database does not provide the estimates themselves. In the future, the MIS department will implement a database for proposed projects.

```
A1: [W7] '* * * ALL-TERRAIN VEHICLES * * *                                 READY

       A     B        C             D           E           F           G
1    * * * ALL-TERRAIN VEHICLES * * *                                  Annual
2                                 Annual      Annual   Expansion    Interest
3     Years        Probability   Revenue     Expense        Cost        Rate
4     =====        ===========   =======     =======   =========    ========
5     1,2,3  H           30.0%      4.00        3.00
6            M           30.0%      3.00        2.50        1.50        9.0%
7            L           40.0%      2.00        2.25
8
9       4,5  H           40.0%      6.00        3.50
10           M           30.0%      5.00        3.00        2.00
11           L           30.0%      3.00        2.50
12
13   * * * SNOWMOBILES * * *
14    1,2,3  H           20.0%      5.00        3.50
15           M           50.0%      4.00        3.00        3.00
16           L           30.0%      1.00        2.00
17
18      4,5  H           30.0%      6.00        4.25
19           M           50.0%      5.00        3.50        3.50
20           L           20.0%      3.50        2.75
19-May-87  04:30 PM
```

FIGURE 10-3 Decision Tree Spreadsheet: Decision Data

DEVELOPING THE SPREADSHEET

While the first two questions posed by EZRydr's management can be answered quite easily and effectively using pencil and paper, the third question (How sensitive is the decision relative to changes in the data values?) could be quite burdensome to address without the use of a spreadsheet model. In this section, we discuss the development of such a model. When you save the spreadsheet, call it DTREE.

Start with a blank spreadsheet. In the upper left corner, enter the decision data and appropriate labels as illustrated in Figure 10-3. When you enter the outcome probabilities in column C, enter fixed values for the high (H) and low (L) values, and enter a formula to calculate the middle (M) value. For example, enter .3 in C5, enter .4 in C7, and enter 1-(C5+C7) in C6. This approach assures that the sum of the outcome probabilities is equal to 1 (one) for each alternative, and it also simplifies adjustment of the outcome probability values when you use the spreadsheet for what-if analysis. Adjust column widths, value formats, and text justification as necessary to match the display illustrated in Figure 10-3.

A21: [W7] READY

	A	B	C	D	E	F	G
21							
22					CASH FLOWS		
23							
24			Year	Neither	ATV	SM	ATV&SM
25			0	0.000	-1.500	-3.000	-4.500
26			1	0.000	0.350	0.500	0.850
27	Stage I		2	0.000	0.350	0.500	0.850
28	Decision		3	0.000	0.350	0.500	0.850
29			4	0.000	1.750	1.425	3.175
30			5	0.000	1.750	1.425	3.175
31							
32			Year	Neither	ATV	SM	ATV&SM
33			0	0.000	0.000	0.000	0.000
34			1	0.000	0.000	0.000	0.000
35	Stage II		2	0.000	0.000	0.000	0.000
36	Decision		3	0.000	-2.000	-3.500	-5.500
37			4	0.000	1.750	1.425	3.175
38			5	0.000	1.750	1.425	3.175
39							
40							

19-May-87 04:31 PM

FIGURE 10-4 Decision Tree Spreadsheet: Cash Flows

While in A1, strike the PgDn key. The cursor will move to A21 and a clear screen will appear. On this screen we develop the expected cash flow streams for the four primary alternatives of the Stage I and Stage II decisions. Enter the labels in columns A and C and in rows 24 and 32 on the CASH FLOWS screen (illustrated in Figure 10-4). Note that the year labels begin with year 0 rather than year 1. The present value library function used by most spreadsheet software packages assumes that all transactions occur at the end of the period. Thus period 0 must be added to the beginning of the planning horizon to accommodate EZRydr's expansion cost, which occurs at the beginning of period 1 (or, equivalently, at the end of period 0).

Enter zeros for both cash flow streams of the Neither alternative (column D); then calculate the expected cash flow streams for the other Stage I alternatives. For the ATV alternative, transfer the expansion cost from the decision data section of the spreadsheet by entering -1*F6 in cell E25. The expansion cost is multiplied by -1 because it is a cash outflow. The values for the remaining years represent the expected cash flow amounts calculated from the probabilities, revenues, and expenses in the decision data section of the spreadsheet. For example, the following is the entry for cell E26 (we have used Lotus 1-2-3 absolute addresses in this entry because it is later copied to other cells):

```
+$C$5*($D$5-$E$5)+$C$6*($D$6-$E$6)+$C$7*($D$7-$E$7)
```

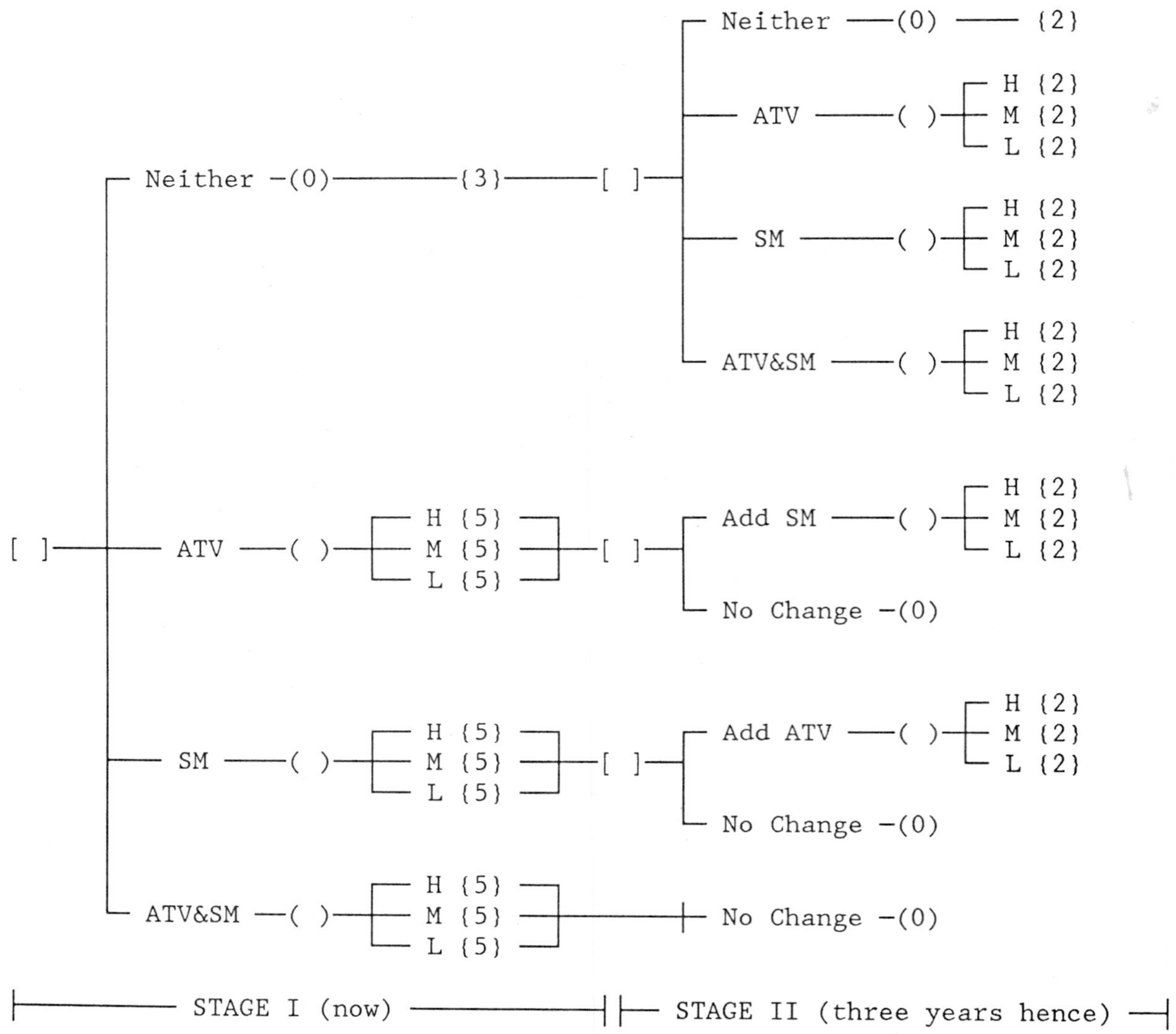

FIGURE 10-5 Decision Tree for Product Expansion Problem

This entry can be copied into cells E27 and E28 since the cash flow in years 2 and 3 is the same as in year 1. A similar formula based on the data in the C9..E11 range should appear in cells E29 and E30. We leave it to you to develop the exact formula.

The expected cash flows for the SM alternative at Stage I are developed in a manner similar to those for the ATV alternative. The cash flows for the ATV&SM alternative are obtained simply by adding those of the ATV and SM alternatives (e.g., the entry in cell G25 is +E25+F25). Once again, the specifics are left to you.

To calculate the cash flows for the Stage II alternatives, we begin by entering zeros in the E33..G35 range. The appropriate expansion costs are entered in cells E36..G36 in a manner similar to those for the Stage I entries. Remember that the expansion costs for the Stage II alternatives correspond to year 3 because we have assumed that all cash flows occur at the end of the period and that the end of year 3 is the *same as* the beginning of year 4. The remaining cash flow entries can be obtained by copying the E29..G30 range to E37. At this point save the spreadsheet to protect against losing your work.

Having entered the decision data and calculated the expected cash flows from that data, we can now begin constructing the decision tree. The first step in that process is to draw the decision tree for this problem on a sheet of paper. By first using pencil and paper to draw the tree, you get an idea of how to structure the tree on your spreadsheet. Your hand-drawn tree should resemble Figure 10-5. Remember that [ ] represents a decision node, ( ) represents a probabilistic outcome node, and { } indicates the number of years over which the alternative is evaluated.

Because we have already calculated the expected cash flows for the various alternatives in another section of the spreadsheet, the tree can be collapsed as illustrated in Figure 10-6.

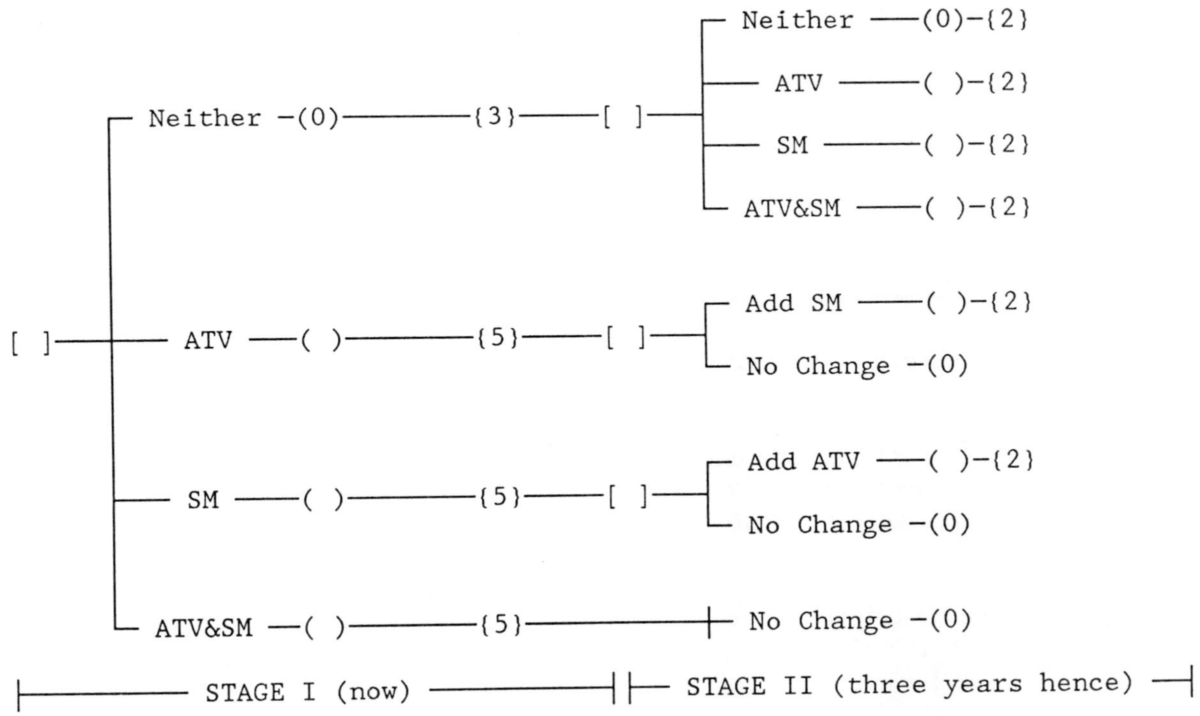

FIGURE 10-6 Revised Decision Tree for Product Expansion Problem

We now construct the spreadsheet model of this collapsed tree in another blank section of the work area. Type Home and then <TAB>, and the cursor should move to cell H1. Set the widths of columns H through P as follows:

Column	H	I	J	K	L	M	N	O	P
Width	9	4	9	9	9	9	4	9	9

```
H1: [W9] 'DECISION TREE - PRODUCT LINE EXPANSION                              READY


       H     I      J         K        L        M     N       O         P
1   DECISION TREE - PRODUCT LINE EXPANSION
2
3               Stage I
4               plus     --- Stage  I ---|  -------- Stage II --------|
5     Best      Best
6    Overall    Stage II  Alt.     Value     Best        Alt.      Value
7    =======    ========  ====     =====     ====        ====      =====
8                                                  {  Neither     0.000
9            {     0.833  Neither   0.000    0.833 --{   ATV       0.833
10           {                                     {    SM      -0.767
11           {                                     {  ATV&SM     0.066
12           {
13    1.964 --{    1.763     ATV     1.763    0.000 --{  Add SM    -0.767
14           {
15           {     1.034     SM      0.201    0.833 --{  Add ATV    0.833
16           {
17           {     1.964  ATV&SM    1.964    0.000 --{ No Change   0.000
18
19  Interest Rate      9.0%
20
19-May-87  04:32 PM
```

FIGURE 10-7 Decision Tree Worksheet: Expansion

Enter the screen label in H1 and the column headings as shown in Figure 10-7. The labels in columns I, K, N, and O can also be entered at this time. We have entered the label Interest Rate in cell H19 and the formula +G6 in cell J19 to remind the user of the current value of the interest rate.

After entering the descriptive information on the spreadsheet, we can begin entering the formulas. Remember that decision trees are analyzed "backwards"; that is, we begin the analysis at the "leaves" (the far right side of the tree) and conclude the analysis at the "trunk" (the far left side of the tree). Consequently, the first formulas we enter on the spreadsheet are those that determine the value of the Stage II alternatives (in column P). Because we are incorporating the time value of money in our analysis, we use the net present value function provided by the spreadsheet package to determine the values of the alternatives. For example, using Lotus 1-2-3, the formula in P8 appears as follows:

@NPV($G$6,D$34..D$38)+D$33

The @NPV function assumes that the interest rate per period is found in cell G6 and that the cash flow stream (with all payments occurring at the *end of the period*) can be found in the range D34..D38. The function discounts the expected cash flow stream to the beginning of period 1. We then add the expansion cost (+D$33) to the discounted cash flow stream to obtain the overall value of the Neither Stage II alternative. Enter similar formulas in cells P9, P10, and P11. Because P13 and P15 are the same as P10 and P9, respectively, enter +P10 in P13 and +P9 in P15. Enter a zero for the No Change alternative in P17.

Next we determine the best of the Stage II alternatives for each of the four major branches that enter that stage. For instance, to determine the best Stage II alternative following the Neither alternative in Stage I, we compute the maximum of the values that appear in P8..P11 [using Lotus 1-2-3, enter @MAX(P8..P11)] in cell M9. We enter @MAX(0,P13) in cell M13 to determine whether it is better to add snowmobiles (Value = -0.767) or do nothing (Value = 0.000) following a Stage I decision to produce ATVs. Enter a similar formula in M15 for the Add ATV alternative. Because no product lines can be added at Stage II if we have decided to produce both ATVs and snowmobiles at Stage I, simply enter +P17 in M17.

The values of the Stage I alternatives are calculated in the same fashion as those of the Stage II alternatives. Use the Stage I expected cash flows and enter the appropriate formulas in cells L9, L13, L15, and L17.

In column J we calculate the sum of the value of each Stage I alternative and its corresponding best Stage II value. In this fashion, each figure in column J represents the total value of the current (Stage I) decision and the best of all possible subsequent decisions (Stage II) that emanate from each alternative. The formula in J9 is +L9+M9. Copy this formula into cells J13, J15, and J17.

To complete the tree we need to determine the best of the Stage I plus Best Stage II values. This can be done by entering @MAX(J9,J13,J15,J17) in cell H13.

Remember to save your completed spreadsheet.

CHECKING THE MODEL

You can do a quick check of your model by striking the Home key and comparing what appears on your screen to the content of Figure 10-3. Then strike the PgDn key and compare what you see to Figure 10-4. Finally strike Home and then <TAB> and compare your screen to Figure 10-7.

As a further check, change the interest rate (cell G6) to 0%. When the interest rate is 0%, the future and present values of money are the same. Therefore, the Value of any Stage II alternative is simply the sum of the expected cash flows for that alternative. For instance, the Value of Add SM to ATV (cell P13) should be -0.650 (i.e., -3.500 + 1.425 + 1.425) when the interest rate is 0%. Manually check other results on the PRODUCT LINE EXPANSION screen. Remember to change the interest rate to 9% before continuing.

USING THE SPREADSHEET

As you recall, EZRydr's management posed a number of questions regarding the potential expansion of their operation. We now use our spreadsheet to answer those questions.

1. Should EZRydr expand its operation? The answer to this question is provided in cell H13 of the spreadsheet. Given the decision data provided by EZRydr's management, the Best Overall decision provides an expected net present value that is positive (i.e., $1,964,000). This indicates that the firm can increase its profit picture by expanding its operation. Thus they should expand.

2. If EZRydr expands its operation,

   a. which product line(s) should be added now?

   b. which product line(s) should be added later?

   The answers to both parts of this question can be obtained by "tracking" the source of the Best Overall through the decision tree. Hit Home and then <TAB> so that the DECISION TREE - PRODUCT LINE EXPANSION portion of the spreadsheet is showing on your screen. Notice that the 1.964 shown in the Best Overall column matches the value shown in the Stage I plus Best Stage II column that appears next to the ATV&SM Stage I alternative. This indicates that both the ATV and the snowmobile product lines should be added now. Since both product lines should be added now, it is clear that no additional lines will be added later.

3. How sensitive is the expansion decision relative to changes in

   a. the time value of money?

   b. outcome probabilities?

   c. revenue estimates?

   d. expense estimates?

   e. expansion cost estimates?

   The effort expended in developing a spreadsheet model for the expansion decision becomes worthwhile only when we use the model to answer what-if questions of the type posed here. Beyond knowing the right course of action to pursue based on the *given* decision data, management often would like to know how robust their decision is in regard to *changes* in the decision data. For example, management assumed that the time value of money was 9% per year in arriving at the decision to expand into both the ATV and the snowmobile lines at the current time. Use the spreadsheet to confirm that the expansion decision will change as a function of the time value of money as illustrated in Table 10-5.

   It is clear that the "correct" decision might also change as a function of changes in the other data used to arrive at the decision. A number of what-if questions regarding changes in the outcome probabilities, annual revenues, annual expenses, and expansion costs are posed as exercise questions in the next section of this chapter.

TABLE 10-5 Expansion Decision as a Function of the Time Value of Money

Time Value of Money (%)	Value of Best Overall Alternative ($ million)	Best Decision Stage I	Best Decision Stage II
0	4.400	ATV&SM	No Change
3	3.464	ATV&SM	No Change
6	2.660	ATV&SM	No Change
9	1.964	ATV&SM	No Change
12	1.446	ATV	No Change
15	1.170	ATV	No Change
18	.929	ATV	No Change
21	.717	ATV	No Change
24	.531	ATV	No Change
27	.366	ATV	No Change
30	.220	ATV	No Change
33	.130	Neither	ATV
36	.093	Neither	ATV
39	.061	Neither	ATV
42	.035	Neither	ATV
45	.013	Neither	ATV
48	.000	Neither	Neither
51	.000	Neither	Neither

EXERCISES

The decision tree spreadsheet we have developed for EZRydr's management is a powerful and versatile decision-making tool. Convince yourself of its usefulness by answering the following questions. As you answer these questions, reset the spreadsheet before every question or subquestion. The easiest way to do this is to save the spreadsheet with the initial values, then change the decision data as indicated. Once the question is answered, you may wish to save the spreadsheet with a unique name (e.g., DTREE1A). When you are ready for the next question or subquestion, load (retrieve) the original spreadsheet.

1. Would EZRydr's expansion decision change as a result of

   a. a 10% increase in the annual revenue projections for snowmobiles?

   b. a 20% increase in the annual revenue projections for snowmobiles?

   c. a 10% increase in the annual expense projections for ATVs?

   d. a 20% increase in the annual expense projections for ATVs?

   e. a 10% increase in the expansion costs for the ATVs?

f. a 20% increase in the expansion costs for the ATVs?

g. exchanging the outcome probabilities of the ATVs and the snowmobiles?

h. using the ATV outcome probabilities for both the ATVs and the snowmobiles?

i. using the snowmobile outcome probabilities for both the snowmobiles and the ATVs?

j. making any number of other interesting changes to the decision data?

2. Recent history has indicated that the time value of money can change dramatically over relatively short periods of time. In the decision tree model that we have just developed, we assume that the time value of money remains constant over the entire five-year planning horizon. How would you modify the model to accommodate different interest rates for the first and second stages of the decision-making process (keep in mind that the expected cash flows that occur in years 4 and 5 must first be discounted to the beginning of year 4 using the Stage II interest rate and that those values must then be discounted to the beginning of year 1 using the Stage I rate)? Would EZRydr's decision change if they used a 9% interest rate for the Stage I decision and

   a. a 6% interest rate for the Stage II decision?

   b. a 12% interest rate for the Stage II decision?

   c. a 15% interest rate for the Stage II decision?

   d. an 18% interest rate for the Stage II decision?

   e. a 21% interest rate for the Stage II decision?

3. The expansion costs provided in the decision data assume the existence of no economies or diseconomies of scale regarding the magnitude of the expansion; that is, at each stage of the decision-making process the cost of expanding into both the ATV and the snowmobile markets at the same time is assumed to be the sum of the costs of expanding into each of those markets individually (e.g., at Stage I, 1.50 + 3.00 = 4.50; at Stage II, 2.00 + 3.50 = 5.50). Would EZRydr's decision change if

   a. economies of scale existed in regard to the expansion costs such that the costs of expanding into both markets simultaneously were 4.00 at Stage I and 4.75 at Stage II?

   b. diseconomies of scale existed in regard to the expansion costs such that the costs of expanding into both markets simultaneously were 5.00 at Stage I and 6.25 at Stage II?

   c. diseconomies of scale existed at Stage I (5.00) and economies of scale existed at Stage II (4.75)?

ENHANCEMENTS TO THE APPLICATION

By performing the EXERCISES above you should have developed an appreciation for the power and versatility of the decision tree spreadsheet as a decision-making tool. However, you may also have developed a feeling that "there must be a better way" to enter the many repetitive key strokes necessary to answer the exercise questions. In order to minimize some of that repetition and to improve the "user-friendliness" of your spreadsheet, you may wish to incorporate any or all of the following enhancements.

1. Develop macros that can be used to modify the annual revenues, annual expenses, and expansion costs in the decision data section of the spreadsheet. Set up the macros so that they make it easier to develop the answers for Exercise 1.

2. Use windowing to eliminate the necessity of moving to the DECISION TREE section to see the result of changing values in the decision data section.

3. Set up a data table to summarize the results of Exercise 2.

REVIEW QUESTIONS

1. Define the following terms as they relate to decision tree analysis:

   *a. expected cost

   b. stochastic

   c. alternative

   *d. present value

2. What are the basic building blocks of decision tree construction?

*3. How does single-stage decision making differ from multistage decision making?

4. Identify the types of business decisions for which decision tree analysis is appropriate.

*5. Why can the time value of money be important in decision tree analysis?

6. How does a spreadsheet package simplify the analysis of decision trees?

ADDITIONAL READING

To understand more about decision trees, refer to textbooks such as:

Chase, R. B., and N. J. Aquilano, *Production and Operations Management.* Homewood, IL: Irwin, 1985.

Turban, E., and N. P. Loomba, *Cases and Readings in Management Science.* Dallas: Business Publications, 1982.

An article entitled "Risk Analysis with 1-2-3" (E. Jones, *Lotus*, Vol. 1, No. 3, July 1985, pp. 65-67) illustrates the application of decision tree analysis in the legal environment with a litigation risk-analysis model.

APPLICATION-SPECIFIC SOFTWARE PACKAGES

A number of PC-based software packages have been developed specifically for building and analyzing decision trees, including the following:

Decision 1-2-Tree. FAST Decision Systems, Inc. P. O. Box 264, Cambridge, MA 02238. (617) 324-4901

SMLTREE. Dr. James Hollenberg. 445 East 68th Street, Box 20, New York, NY 10021. (212) 472-5252

SUPERTREE 5.0. SDG Decision Systems. Dept. 703-i, 3000 Sand Hill Road, Menlo Park, CA 94025. (415) 854-9000

UNIT

11 SIMULATION—EXPERIENCE IS THE BEST TEACHER

"Experience is the best teacher." You have heard that expression many times, but have you ever thought about it or questioned it? Do you learn from experience? Do you think it is the best way to learn? Sometimes, obtaining that experience can be expensive, may be painful, or may take a long time. An alternative to learning from real-life experience is to learn from a simulated experience. With a *simulation* of the real world we compress the time and reduce the pain and the cost. In this unit we illustrate how to construct different types of simulation models and demonstrate how to use spreadsheet software to structure a simulation and evaluate various measures of effectiveness.

DECISION SUPPORT APPLICATION MATRIX

Accounting & Finance	Economics & Long-Range Planning	Human Resources	Marketing & Logistics	Management Information Systems	Operations Planning & Control	Executive Officers
■¤	■¤	■¤	■¤	■¤	■¤	■¤

■ Departmental area(s) in which the technique is or can be used.

¤ Departmental area(s) that provide input to or are impacted by the technique.

LEARNING OBJECTIVES

1. After completing this unit you should know

   a. the reasons that firms develop simulation models,

   b. the different types of simulation models,

   c. the general structure of simulation models,

   d. the difference between simulation models and optimization models,

Contributed by Robert L. Armacost

e. how a spreadsheet package can be used for simulation.

2. After completing this unit you should be able to

a. identify problems for which simulation is a good approach,

b. formulate decision problems as simulations,

c. create a simulation spreadsheet and evaluate simulation results.

BASIC CONCEPTS

The Wright brothers attempted to fly many times before they had enough experience to make the right design changes and finally get off the ground. Now, we do not build a plane and see if it flies. First we build a model and simulate its flight in a wind tunnel. Then, based on the simulation results, we make design changes and test again until we get the results we want.

In the same way, an organization should not make a major change in its production line to see if productivity or throughput will improve. The better course of action is to create some sort of model of the production process and then modify the model to see what happens to productivity. The (mathematical) model is an abstraction of reality; it is a *simulation.* Every spreadsheet is such a simulation, and every time you change a value in a cell to ask a *what-if* question, you are simulating a change in policy or procedure. Clearly, testing modifications with a model is much less costly than testing the same changes in the real world.

Deterministic Simulation

In a *deterministic simulation* the coefficients or parameters are known. Typical spreadsheet models are deterministic simulations. A good example is the aggregate planning model in Unit 6. In that model the cost coefficients, the demands, and all of the other parameters are known. When a specific set of data and policy variables are entered, the model determines fixed values for the output measures. Some of these output measures are *measures of effectiveness* that are used to evaluate that policy in light of the data set. When using the spreadsheet to ask what-if questions, you see the effect of policy or data set changes on the measures of effectiveness. This process simulates the real production system.

Stochastic (Monte Carlo) Simulation

In the real world, you do not always know the values of the coefficients or parameters of a model with certainty. In the aggregate planning problem, point (single-value) estimates of demand based on previous demand patterns and demand forecasts are provided, but the exact demand in a particular month may vary from this estimate. In the model in Unit 6, all coefficients and parameters are treated as fixed rather than variable values. In many cases, however, you are able to establish point estimates and probability distributions that describe the random behavior of the variables. When you use probability distributions for some of the parameters, the simulation is called a *stochastic* (based on probability) *simulation.* Those parameters that vary according to a probability distribution are called *stochastic variables*, those that do not are called *deterministic variables.*

Working with a stochastic simulation is similar to working with a deterministic simulation, except that the output measures are calculated more times to capture the effect of the stochastic variables. In order to include a stochastic component in the aggregate planning model, for example, you would select a demand value for a given month from a monthly demand probability distribution. Do the same thing for the other months, and then solve the deterministic simulation using that set of demands. The output (measures of effectiveness) from this model represents one trial of an experiment. In simulation analysis you would like to know what the average behavior of the system is, so you must repeat the experiment several times, each time picking another set of random demands (according to the monthly demand probability distribution), solving the deterministic simulation model, and recording the associated outputs. You repeat this process until you have "enough" trials and then calculate the average result. This type of simulation is called a *Monte Carlo simulation* after the famous gambling casino and its games of chance.

Because you must estimate the average demand for each month to define its probability distribution, you might think that simply using the average monthly demand in the deterministic simulation would give you the average results. If that were true, you would not have to run the simulation more than once to estimate the average behavior of the system. However, in general, you do not obtain proper estimates by using the average values of the coefficients or parameters in the simulation. The exception is when all of the relationships among the random coefficients and the output variables are linear. But even in that case, there is another advantage to using a Monte Carlo simulation. In addition to calculating an average, you can also calculate the variance and estimate the probability distribution that describes the random output. This can be an important factor in decision making. If the expected profit is $100,000, it makes a difference whether the standard deviation is $1,000 or $50,000. Risk is a critical element in decision making, and the variance calculation in a Monte Carlo simulation helps to quantify that risk.

Random Numbers

The basic building block in a Monte Carlo simulation is the *random number*. A number is said to be random if its chance of occurring is the same as that of any other number. If you were selecting numbers between 1 and 100, you would expect as many to be between 1 and 10 as are between 21 and 30, or 44 and 53, for example. We say that random numbers are equally likely, or that they come from a *uniform probability distribution.*

The question, of course, is Where are random numbers obtained? Over the years, various tables of random numbers have been generated and one of these could be included in a spreadsheet application. Many computer programs, including spreadsheets, contain a random number function that generates random numbers ranging from zero to one, with as many decimal places as the program can support. In most computer applications, however, the random number generating function actually produces a pseudo-random number; that is, it generates a number that acts like a random number but is actually determined by a formula that depends on a particular *seed* or starting point. With pseudo-random number generators you get the same series of random numbers when you start with the same seed. An advantage of this characteristic is that you can run a simulation using two different policies and the same random-number seed in order to be sure that any differences in outcomes are due to the different policies and are not due to a different set of random numbers.

It is important to realize that the random number generator in many spreadsheet packages, such as Lotus 1-2-3, does not use a user-controlled seed. Each time you load and run Lotus 1-2-3 (Release 1A), you start with the same random-number seed and you obtain the same first random number from the @RAND function (0.1475065968). The sequence of "random" numbers generated within a particular spreadsheet will be the same. In Lotus 1-2-3 (Release 2), you get a different random number each time you load and run Lotus 1-2-3. Therefore, it is impossible to generate the same sequence of random numbers using the @RAND function in Release 2. Appendix C of this book provides a program that generates a table of random numbers that can be imported into an application program in order to provide repeatability without restarting Lotus. (Appendix C also contains a method for you to test your particular spreadsheet package to determine whether the initial seed is constant, user-controlled, or random.)

As noted above, truly random numbers must each be equally likely. In probability terms, they must come from a uniform probability distribution. In order to test whether a set of random numbers could have come from a uniform distribution, a statistical test, the *Chi-square goodness-of-fit test*, is used. This is the same test that is used to determine whether a set of data could have come from any other specific distribution. The basic idea is to compare the number of observations that occur in a particular interval with the number expected to occur in that interval based on the chosen distribution. Appendix C also illustrates the use of the goodness-of-fit test.

Probability Distributions

Parameters like the demand for a product and the service time in a bank are more likely to be random variables than fixed values. Often you can estimate the probability distribution that describes the behavior of a random variable and then use values obtained from that distribution in a simulation model. Probability distributions may be continuous or discrete. A *continuous distribution* is used to describe variables that can be measured to any degree of divisibility, such as waiting time (e.g., 5 minutes, 5.20 minutes, 5.2023 minutes). Two important continuous probability distributions used in simulation problems are the *exponential distribution* and the *normal distribution*. Both of these continuous distributions are described in Appendix C. A *discrete distribution* is used to describe variables that are typically measured in whole units, such as the monthly demand for cars (e.g., 30 cars, 40 cars, or 52 cars). The following is the discrete probability distribution that has been estimated at EZRydr for first-quarter aggregate demand.

Demand, x	Probability, p(x)
950	.05
1050	.15
1100	.40
1250	.30
1300	.10

The average demand is 1150 units (950 x .05 + 1050 x .15 + . . . + 1300 x .10). You can plot the probability distribution in the familiar histogram style, but the values on the X axis are actually points rather than ranges. The probability distribution is depicted in Figure 11-1.

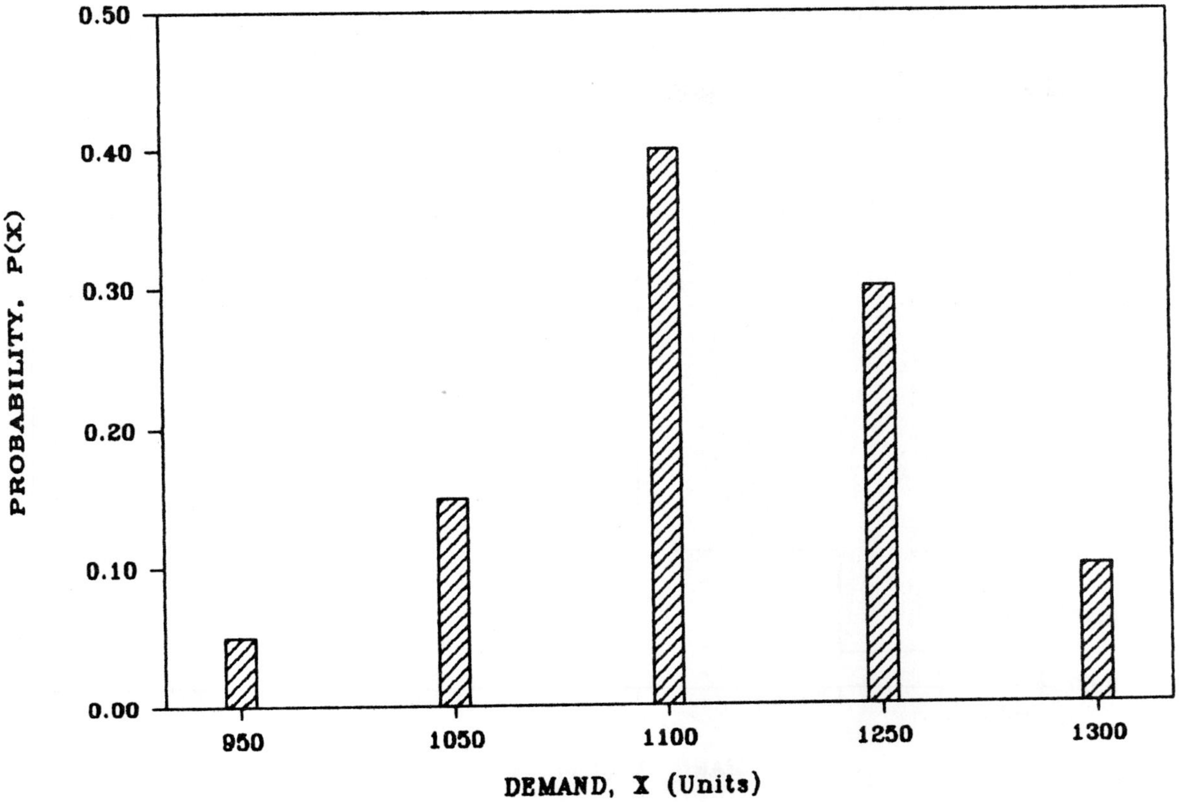

FIGURE 11-1 Discrete Probability Distribution

Obtaining the values of stochastic variables from a probability distribution is accomplished using the *cumulative distribution function* (CDF). A CDF is a function with a range from zero to one that accumulates the probabilities of all possible outcomes. The CDF for EZRydr's first quarter demand probability distribution is shown below:

Demand, x	Cumulative Probability, F(x)
950	.05
1050	.20
1100	.60
1250	.90
1300	1.00

F(x) is the probability that demand is at or below the specified value x. Because this is a discrete distribution, F(1050) = p(950) + p(1050). This CDF is plotted in Figure 11-2.

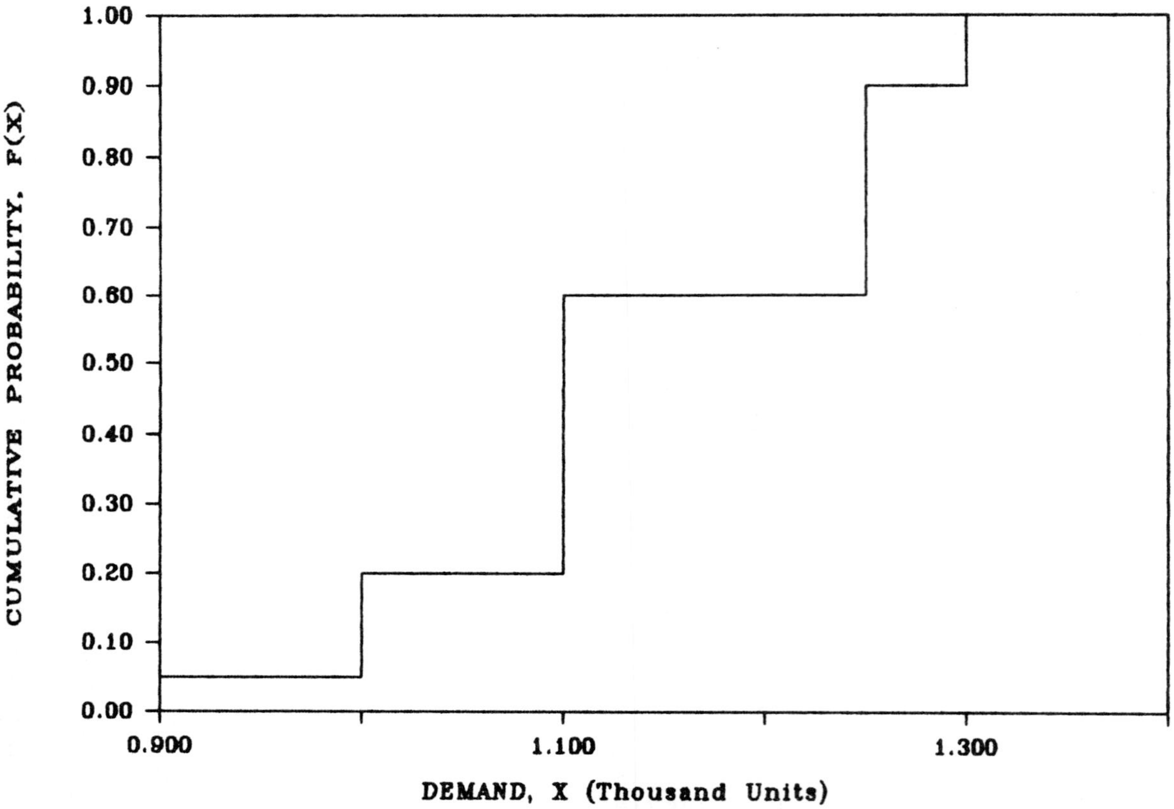

FIGURE 11-2 Cumulative Probability Distribution

A cumulative distribution function divides the probability distribution of a stochastic variable into partitions so that random numbers (ranging from zero to one) can be used to generate values for that variable (regardless of the range of the variable). For EZRydr's problem, the demand values and the partitions (intervals) are shown below:

Demand, x	Partition
950	$0.00 \leq F(x) \leq .05$
1050	$0.05 < F(x) \leq .20$
1100	$0.20 < F(x) \leq .60$
1250	$0.60 < F(x) \leq .90$
1300	$0.90 < F(x) \leq 1.00$

To obtain a demand value from these partitions, generate a random number, assign it to F(x), and select the demand associated with the partition in which the assigned value of F(x) falls. For example, suppose you generate a random number equal to 0.4376. Then F(x) = 0.4376 and demand is 1100 units because F(x) is in the interval 0.2 to 0.6. This procedure, called the *method of inversion*, can be applied to any CDF that can be described, as long as the random numbers are uniformly distributed.

Measures of Effectiveness

In building a simulation model, it is important to identify and properly define the measures of effectiveness — those output measures used to evaluate the policy or procedure under consideration. Although this seems obvious, it is often overlooked or treated superficially in practice. The types of measures selected depend on the type of problem being analyzed. Typical measures of effectiveness in a queueing problem include waiting time, service time, number of people waiting, and cost of service. In a production problem, measures of effectiveness may include the production rate, delays, backorders, inventory, and cost of production. Care must be taken, however, not to overdo it. Probably only a few measures will be used in making a decision, so the important task is to identify those measures that are most relevant and concentrate on them. The ability to analyze decisions using multiple criteria distinguishes simulation models from optimization models, which typically concentrate on one criterion or measure of effectiveness (see Unit 14).

Execution of the Simulation

There are two issues that affect the execution of a simulation: whether or not steady-state conditions exist and the number of replications required to achieve statistically meaningful results.

A system operating within its normal range of activities is said to be in *steady-state* mode. If the conditions under which the simulation is started do not reflect the steady-state conditions under which we would like to measure the system, we must eliminate their effect. While there are a number of ways to eliminate the effect of start-up conditions on the results of a simulation, the easiest is to ignore the results of early periods. How many to ignore depends on the particular problem. For instance, in the aggregate planning problem, EZRydr starts with 100 employees, a current inventory of 300 units, and current backorders of 80 units. These reflect current conditions, and the system is operating at approximately the level of activity to be simulated. In this case, we do not need to ignore the results of early periods. On the other hand, if we were starting with zero employees, we would not be starting within the range of normal operations and we would ignore the results of one or more periods to allow the system to achieve steady state.

The second issue concerns sample size, the number of observations required to achieve statistically meaningful results. (In the model we develop in this unit, each observation is derived from a run of ten iterations, i.e., ten calculations of the aggregate plan with a different set of random demand values for each calculation.) In general, the more observations you obtain, the lower the variance of the results. The lower the variance, the greater the confidence we have in our estimate of the average. Unfortunately, it costs something to obtain each observation, so there is a trade off between the cost of running the simulation and the level of confidence desired in the result. Sampling theory can be used to determine the number of observations necessary to achieve a desired level of confidence with a given level of precision (e.g., you wish to be 95% sure that your estimate is within 15 units of the true value). The standard deviation of the primary output measure must be estimated, either from historical data, expert knowledge, or a pilot run of the simulation. The number of observations (N) is determined by the values of the desired confidence level (z, from the normal distribution), the desired precision level (p), and the preliminary estimate of the standard deviation (s) in the following formula:

$$N = [\ (z \times s)\ /\ p\ ]^2$$

For instance, assume we wish to be 95% sure (z = 1.96) that our estimate is within 15 units of the true value and we estimate that the standard deviation is 30 units. The required number of observations is thus

$$N = [\ (z \times s)\ /\ p\ ]^2 = [\ 1.96 \times 30\ /\ 15\ ]^2 = 35$$

In this case the desired precision level is 50% of the standard deviation (15/30). Regardless of the specific values of the precision level and standard deviation, fifteen observations will always create a 95% confidence interval with a level of precision that is 50% of the standard deviation. At the 95% confidence level, a precision level that is 10% of the standard deviation requires 384 observations.

Several methods can be used for gathering observations to estimate the variance of the results. Here we look at a simple approach called the *replication method* that typically requires a large number of passes through the simulation. The length of each run (the number of iterations) is established considering the number of periods, if any, to ignore to account for start-up conditions. The simulation is executed for the desired number of iterations and an average result is obtained for that run. This average result is considered a single observation. Next the simulation is repeated with a different set of random numbers to yield a second observation. Each run is called a *replication*, and each yields an observation. Repeat for the appropriate number of replications (e.g., N = 35 from above), and then find the mean of the observed means as well as the standard error of the mean. These statistics can be used for a variety of further analyses, such as determining confidence intervals for the true mean and analysis of variance.

KISS: A Rule of Thumb

A general principle for simulation is "Keep It Simple, Stupid" (KISS). There is a tendency to include more and more factors in a simulation because it appears to be easy to do so. But each time you add another factor, you increase the level of complexity of the model and thus make the results provided by the model more difficult to collect, analyze, and interpret. The basic idea behind using a simulation model is to provide an abstraction of the real world that permits you to obtain meaningful information for use in decision making. You should keep the model as simple as possible while still generating meaningful information.

When to Simulate

This book presents many different models and approaches to support decision making. When should you use a simulation model? In general, simulation should be used as a method of last resort. If an analytical model, such as breakeven analysis or demand analysis, does not exist, or the relations among the variables are difficult to specify under the assumptions of a particular model, or if you just do not know what else to do, simulation may be the best or the only choice. For instance, when you want to see what will happen to a number of factors, simulation may be the only way to generate data for the analysis. Remember that a simulation can never guarantee the optimal answer. It simply describes the outcome from a particular process and is limited to comparative evaluations.

GATHERING THE DATA

Two things must be considered when collecting data for simulation models: identify the data that must be collected and estimate the distributions of stochastic variables. The specific model to be simulated indicates the nature and the source of the data. The details concerning data collection for various models are discussed in the other units of this book. See, for instance, Unit 6 for the data needed for aggregate planning. The estimation of stochastic variable distributions can be based on data found within the company or external to the company.

Within the Company

Sometimes data necessary to estimate the distribution is contained in the company as historical data or expert opinion. For example, if you are trying to determine the demand distribution for an existing product, and you do not expect a significant change from the past, the basic data should be available in company records. Plot the past demand values in a histogram, with demand level on the X axis and frequency of occurrence on the Y axis. The relative frequencies in the histogram constitute a discrete distribution of the demand variable. Alternatively, guess a particular continuous distribution based on your interpretation of the histogram, and test your hypothesis using the goodness-of-fit test described in Appendix C.

External to the Company

Often a simulation includes an operation that is new to the company. In this case, it is essential to go outside of the company to get the data necessary to model the new operation. You may have to rely on general industry data, or hire consultants with expertise in that area to provide reasonable estimates for your model.

THE PROBLEM

The management of EZRydr is considering the production of snowmobiles and all-terrain vehicles (ATVs) in addition to their line of motorcycles. Before making a commitment to production, however, top management would like to have an idea of what the possible outcomes might be if they decide to produce one or both of these new vehicles. Because they have no experience with these vehicles, they commissioned a consultant to provide them with quarterly demand forecasts for snowmobiles and ATVs.

For planning purposes, management is willing to assume that the production rate and material cost per unit for snowmobiles and ATVs are the same as for motorcycles. Management is comfortable with the aggregate planning model they are currently using (see Unit 6) but sees a need to incorporate probabilistic demand into the model. Therefore they would like you to develop a simulation model based on the aggregate planning model to evaluate whether to produce snowmobiles, or ATVs, or both. Management realizes that a reduction in the average cost per unit would be a strong indicator supporting an addition. Consequently, you should consider the average cost per unit as one of the measures of effectiveness.

Departmental Data

The data used in the aggregate planning model remains valid. It is necessary, however, to change the model from a monthly to a quarterly basis to accommodate the demand forecasts for the new vehicles. In reviewing the aggregate demand forecasts, the production control department realized that the data are average demands based on historical records. From this data, they were able to describe the probability distributions for the quarterly aggregate demand for the motorcycles they now produce. The consultant developed separate demand distributions for both ATVs and snowmobiles. The probability distributions for all three types of vehicles are shown in Table 11-1.

TABLE 11-1 Demand Distributions for Each Vehicle Type

Aggregate Motorcycle Demand

	Q1 Demand, x	Q1 p(x)	Q2 Demand, x	Q2 p(x)	Q3 Demand, x	Q3 p(x)	Q4 Demand, x	Q4 p(x)
	950	.05	3700	.10	5400	.20	1100	.20
	1050	.15	3950	.10	5600	.30	1150	.40
	1100	.40	4150	.30	5800	.20	1300	.30
	1250	.30	4300	.30	5900	.20	1400	.10
	1300	.10	4500	.20	6000	.10		
Avg	1150		4200		5700		1200	

Forecasted Snowmobile Demand

	Q1 Demand, x	Q1 p(x)	Q2 Demand, x	Q2 p(x)	Q3 Demand, x	Q3 p(x)	Q4 Demand, x	Q4 p(x)
	250	.25	50	.20	20	.20	300	.20
	300	.30	75	.40	40	.30	400	.30
	350	.25	100	.30	60	.30	500	.40
	400	.20	120	.10	80	.20	550	.10
Avg	320		82		50		435	

Forecasted All-Terrain Vehicle Demand

	Q1 Demand, x	Q1 p(x)	Q2 Demand, x	Q2 p(x)	Q3 Demand, x	Q3 p(x)	Q4 Demand, x	Q4 p(x)
	200	.10	400	.10	500	.20	100	.10
	300	.15	450	.20	550	.40	150	.40
	350	.50	500	.40	600	.20	250	.30
	400	.25	550	.30	650	.20	350	.20
Avg	340		495		570		215	

Data in the Database

As noted in Unit 6, many of the aggregate planning parameters can be derived from data in the database. Also, the data in Table 11-1 can be found in the data file named FORE_DEM.DBF. This data file contains fields named VEH_TYPE, QUARTER, DEMAND_X, and P_X. Note that there is more than one entry per vehicle per quarter; there are as many entries per vehicle per quarter as there are forecast levels of demand (e.g., five entries for Motorcycle, Q1; four entries for Snowmobile, Q1). The averages are not entered in the database because they can be calculated by summing the products of x·p(x) for a given product in a given quarter.

DEVELOPING THE SPREADSHEET

Because management wants to continue to use the aggregate planning model developed in Unit 6, the first adjustment necessary is to convert the monthly model to a quarterly one. Copy the aggregate planning spreadsheet you developed earlier and use that new file for the quarterly model. Set the recalculation mode to automatic. Because we need to convert the monthly data to quarterly data, go to cell C25. Edit the cell contents so it is the sum of demands for the first quarter (January, February, and March): 200+250+700. You must use the actual values, not cell references. Repeat this procedure in cells D25 through F25 until you have captured each quarter's demand. The same steps must be taken to capture each quarter's productive days. Next, modify the model by erasing the range containing the May through December entries, and relabel the remaining four columns Q1, Q2, Q3, and Q4 in cells C24..F24. Move the Total and Average columns to columns G and H, and edit these formulas as necessary.

The spreadsheet must also be modified to include the alternatives of producing snowmobiles and all-terrain vehicles in addition to motorcycles. Insert three new rows following row 25. Move the information in C25..F25 to C26..F26. Change the label in A25 to Total Demand, and place the labels Motorcycle Demand, Snowmobile Demand, and ATV Demand in cells A26..A28. The value in the total demand row should be the sum of the demands in the motorcycle, snowmobile, and ATV rows. The Lotus formula in C25 is @SUM(C26..C28). Copy the formula to columns D, E, and F. You may have to adjust some of the other functions in the spreadsheet due to circular references or ERR inputs. Because we use the unit production cost as a measure of effectiveness, place the label Cost per Unit in E53 and enter the formula +G49/G36 in cell G53. (If Total Production [G36] is currently zero, then ERR will display in G53.)

We are using quarterly data, so adjust the inventory carry rate and the backorder cost to quarterly rates. Change the inventory carry rate to 3% of item value/unit/quarter and the backorder cost to $150/unit/quarter.

For the pure level strategy, you find, as before, that an average of 110 employees per quarter is required to meet the expected annual demand. Placing this average number of employees in your spreadsheet results in the spreadsheet illustrated in Figure 11-3. (Demand for snowmobiles and ATVs is entered as zero; also, the sample worksheet was developed using Lotus 1-2-3 Release 1A, and the Overtime Check returns values [0 indicates "ok"] rather than text.) For this quarterly model of motorcycle-only production, the total production is 12,123 units at a total cost of $13,960,080. This compares with a total production of 12,117 units at a total cost of $13,986,308 for the monthly aggregate planning model with a pure level strategy. Although the total production is nearly the same for the quarterly and monthly approaches,

A22: "AGGREGATE PLAN READY

	A	B	C	D	E	F	G
22	AGGREGATE PLAN		Level Strategy				02-Nov-86
23							
24	QUARTER	Initial	Q1	Q2	Q3	Q4	TOTALS
25	Total Demand	---	1150	4200	5700	1200	12250
26	Motorcycle Demand	---	1150	4200	5700	1200	12250
27	Snowmobile Demand	---	0	0	0	0	0
28	ATV Demand	---	0	0	0	0	0
29	Productive Days	---	62	64	59	63	248
30	# Employees	100	110	110	110	110	--
31	Reg. Production	2755	3031	3128	2884	3080	12123
32	Max Ovrtime (units)	551	606	625	576	616	2423
33	Act Ovrtime (units)	---	0	0	0	0	0
34	Overtime Check	---	0	0	0	0	--
35	Subcontr (units)	---	0	0	0	0	0
36	TOTAL PRODUCTION	---	3031	3128	2884	3080	12123
37	Inventory	300	2101	1029	0	93	--
38	Backorders	80	0	0	1787	0	--
39							
40	Regular Wages	---	545580	563040	519120	554400	2182140
41	Overtime Wages	---	0	0	0	0	0
42	Hire/Fire Cost	---	2500	0	0	0	2500
43	Subcontract Cost	---	0	0	0	0	0
44	Material Cost	---	2576350	2658800	2451400	2618000	10304550
45	Carrying Cost	---	40337	52584	17287	1562	111770
46	Backorder Cost	---	0	0	268050	0	268050
47	Factory Overhead	---	272790	281520	259560	277200	1091070
48							
49	TOTAL COST	---	3437557	3555944	3515417	3451162	13960080
50	Std. Prod. Cost	---	3394720	3503360	3230080	3449600	13577760
51	Incremental Cost	---	42837	52584	285337	1562	382320
52							
53					Cost per Unit		1152
54							

FIGURE 11-3 Quarterly Aggregate Planning Spreadsheet: Level Strategy

the total cost for the quarterly model is lower. Most of the difference is explained by the fact that both the inventory carrying cost and the backorder costs are reduced in the quarterly model because a model with fewer periods has fewer period to period fluctuations in variables such as these. The cost per unit under the quarterly model is $1,152, whereas the cost per unit under the monthly model is $1,154.

F26: (F0) 1200 READY

	A	B	C	D	E	F	G
22	AGGREGATE PLAN		Chase Strategy				03-Nov-86
23							
24	QUARTER	Initial	Q1	Q2	Q3	Q4	TOTALS
25	Total Demand	---	1150	4200	5700	1200	12250
26	Motorcycle Demand	---	1150	4200	5700	1200	12250
27	Snowmobile Demand	---	0	0	0	0	0
28	ATV Demand	---	0	0	0	0	0
29	Productive Days	---	62	64	59	63	248
30	# Employees	100	34	148	217	45	--
31	Reg. Production	2755	930	4200	5700	1250	12080
32	Max Ovrtime (units)	551	186	840	1140	250	2416
33	Act Ovrtime (units)	---	0	0	0	0	0
34	Overtime Check	---	0	0	0	0	--
35	Subcontr (units)	---	0	0	0	0	0
36	TOTAL PRODUCTION	---	930	4200	5700	1250	12080
37	Inventory	300	0	0	0	50	--
38	Backorders	80	0	0	0	0	--
39							
40	Regular Wages	---	167400	756000	1026000	225000	2174400
41	Overtime Wages	---	0	0	0	0	0
42	Hire/Fire Cost	---	66250	28477	17429	172730	284886
43	Subcontract Cost	---	0	0	0	0	0
44	Material Cost	---	790500	3570000	4845000	1062500	10268000
45	Carrying Cost	---	5040	0	0	840	5880
46	Backorder Cost	---	0	0	0	0	0
47	Factory Overhead	---	83700	378000	513000	112500	1087200
48							
49	TOTAL COST	---	1112890	4732477	6401429	1573570	13820366
50	Std. Prod. Cost	---	1041600	4704000	6384000	1400000	13529600
51	Incremental Cost	---	71290	28477	17429	173570	290766
52							
53					Cost per Unit		1144
54							

FIGURE 11-4 Quarterly Aggregate Planning Spreadsheet: Chase Strategy

After you save this model, you can modify it to evaluate a chase strategy. The necessary modification requires inserting a formula to calculate the number of employees required each quarter. The number of employees is the sum of the quarterly demand and backorders less the inventory, all divided by the production rate (units per quarter). The Lotus 1-2-3 formula for cell C30 is @ROUND(@MAX(((C25+B38-B37)*$B$3/$B$18)/C29,0)+0.49,0). The formulas for D30 and E30 are similar, but the formula in F30 must account for the desired ending inventory. These modifications result in the output shown in Figure 11-4. The total production is 12,095 units at a total cost of $13,832,485. This compares with a total production of 12,080 and total cost of $14,029,254 for the monthly aggregate planning model using a chase strategy. The major difference is due to a much larger hire/fire cost for the monthly model which has three times as many periods in which hiring and firing decisions are made. The cost per unit under the monthly model is $1,161 whereas the cost per unit under the quarterly model is $1,144 for the chase strategy.

In the comparisons between the monthly and quarterly models above, cost per unit is used as the single measure of effectiveness. In Unit 6 the basic measure of effectiveness used to compare the pure level strategy with the chase strategy is the incremental cost. This measure indicates that a pure level strategy is preferred to a chase strategy ($415,268 vs. $499,654). However, this comparison overlooks the fact that the two strategies produce at different levels, 12,117 units for the level strategy and 12,080 for the chase strategy (the chase strategy results in a smaller inventory at the end of the last month; because of the requirement to employ whole, not fractional, employees, neither strategy guarantees to hit the desired ending inventory level of exactly 50 units). This suggests that a better measure for this comparison might be the cost per unit produced. Notice that with the monthly model both the incremental cost and the cost per unit indicate that the level strategy is preferred. Using the quarterly model, however, both the incremental cost and the cost per unit indicate that the chase strategy is preferred. Note that the different measures of effectiveness yield the same conclusions, even though the conclusions are opposite for the monthly and quarterly models. While your initial reaction to these contrary conclusions may be one of confusion, the opposite conclusions are easily explained by the differences in hiring/firing and have to be considered by management when deciding which strategy to use.[1]

Each of the models discussed above uses the average (expected) demand for motorcycles. In building a simulation model, we must develop a means of introducing and using the probability distribution of demand for each quarter. We illustrate how to do this with motorcycle demand. The demand data and cumulative probability values are entered in a table and a random number is used to select a specific demand level, as we have already discussed. Here, we modify our spreadsheet to incorporate a cumulative probability distribution in a lookup table and select the appropriate demand using a random number. First, we build the table. Enter the label Motorcycle Demand in J11. Then, in cell J12, enter the label Q1 (for the first quarter data). In cells K13..K17 enter the various demand levels for the first quarter (950, 1050, . . .). The last demand level (1300) must be repeated in K18 due to a peculiarity of spreadsheet lookup functions. Before proceeding, determine partitions for this demand data from the probability distribution presented in Table 11-1, using the method discussed in the "Probability Distributions" section of this unit. In J13 enter 0, the lower limit of the first partition. In J14..J17 enter the lower limits of each of the remaining partitions, and in J18 enter 1.00, the upper limit of the CDF. Finally, place the label Avg in J19, and in K19 calculate the expected (average) demand using the following formula:

(J14-J13)*K13+(J15-J14)*K14+(J16-J15)*K15+(J17-J16)*K16+(J18-J17)*K17

Do the same for subsequent quarters, using the data in Table 11-1. The result is shown in Figure 11-5.

---

[1] In effect, a quarterly chase model is a *hybrid model* because it includes characteristics of both the monthly level and the monthly chase models. That is, a quarterly chase model is actually a chase model *between* quarters and a level model on a month-to-month basis *within* a quarter. Hybrid models often produce better results than pure models, as is the case here.

J11: 'Motorcycle Demand READY

	I	J	K	L	M	N	O	P	Q	R
11		Motorcycle Demand								
12		Q1		Q2		Q3		Q4		
13		0.00	950	0.00	3700	0.00	5400	0.00	1100	
14		0.05	1050	0.10	3950	0.20	5600	0.20	1150	
15		0.20	1100	0.20	4150	0.50	5800	0.60	1300	
16		0.60	1250	0.50	4300	0.70	5900	0.90	1400	
17		0.90	1300	0.80	4500	0.90	6000	1.00	1400	
18		1.00	1300	1.00	4500	1.00	6000			
19		Avg	1150	Avg	4200	Avg	5700	Avg	1210	
20										

FIGURE 11-5 Cumulative Probability Distributions, Quarterly Motorcycle Demand

Now that you have the motorcycle probability distributions in the spreadsheet, use a table lookup procedure to extract demand values. The @VLOOKUP (vertical lookup) function requires that you define the table as a range. (If you are not using Lotus 1-2-3, carefully read the description of the equivalent function in your software.) In this case, you actually have four tables, one for each quarter of motorcycle demand. Name the four ranges PQ1M, PQ2M, PQ3M, and PQ4M (**P**robability distribution for **Q**uarter **1** for **M**otorcycles, etc.). Range PQ1M includes cells J13..K18. Note that the row containing the averages is *not* in the range. The syntax of the table lookup command is @VLOOKUP(x,range,offset). The ranges are named, and because you have only the index and one additional column, the offset is 1 (one). The next step is to determine the entering argument. You could generate a table of random numbers and systematically go through that table as the entering arguments. Here, we simply generate a random number using the @RAND function. Move the pointer to cell C26 (motorcycle demand in the first quarter). Enter the formula @VLOOKUP(@RAND,PQ1M,1).[2] Copy this formula to cells D26..F26 and then edit those entries to put in the correct range names for each quarter. The result should be a spreadsheet similar to Figure 11-6. Notice that new random demands are produced each time you make an entry or edit a cell because the spreadsheet is in an automatic recalculation mode. When working with random numbers, it is often preferable to have the spreadsheet in a manual recalculation mode. Set this mode with the appropriate command. New random numbers (and random demands) are generated every time the spreadsheet is recalculated (in Lotus, when you hit the F9 {calc} key). Now you are in a position to check the spreadsheet.

---

[2] The effect of @VLOOKUP varies slightly from the theoretical statement of a cumulative distribution function. While the theoretical statement for each partition of a CDF excludes the value of the lower limit (<) and includes the value of the upper limit ($\leq$), lookup functions typically include the lower limit ($\leq$) and exclude the upper limit (<). Thus, although the second partition of the CDF in this unit is expressed as $0.05 < F(x) \leq .20$, the lookup function evaluates this partition as $0.05 \leq F(x) < .20$. The two approaches yield different answers only when the random number is *exactly* on a limit, which should occur only once in approximately 10^{14} calculations and may be ignored in most practical situations.

C22: 'Level Strategy READY

	A	B	C	D	E	F	G
22	AGGREGATE PLAN		Level Strategy				03-Nov-86
23							
24	QUARTER	Initial	Q1	Q2	Q3	Q4	TOTALS
25	Total Demand	---	950	4150	5800	1100	12000
26	Motorcycle Demand	---	950	4150	5800	1100	12000
27	Snowmobile Demand	---	0	0	0	0	0
28	ATV Demand	---	0	0	0	0	0
29	Productive Days	---	62	64	59	63	248
30	# Employees	100	110	110	110	110	--
31	Reg. Production	2755	3031	3128	2884	3080	12123
32	Max Ovrtime (units)	551	606	625	576	616	2423
33	Act Ovrtime (units)	---	0	0	0	0	0
34	Overtime Check	---	0	0	0	0	--
35	Subcontr (units)	---	0	0	0	0	0
36	TOTAL PRODUCTION	---	3031	3128	2884	3080	12123
37	Inventory	300	2301	1279	0	343	--
38	Backorders	80	0	0	1637	0	--
39							
40	Regular Wages	---	545580	563040	519120	554400	2182140
41	Overtime Wages	---	0	0	0	0	0
42	Hire/Fire Cost	---	2500	0	0	0	2500
43	Subcontract Cost	---	0	0	0	0	0
44	Material Cost	---	2576350	2658800	2451400	2618000	10304550
45	Carrying Cost	---	43697	60144	21487	5762	131090
46	Backorder Cost	---	0	0	245550	0	245550
47	Factory Overhead	---	272790	281520	259560	277200	1091070
48							
49	TOTAL COST	---	3440917	3563504	3497117	3455362	13956900
50	Std. Prod. Cost	---	3394720	3503360	3230080	3449600	13577760
51	Incremental Cost	---	46197	60144	267037	5762	379140
52							
53					Cost per Unit		1151
54							

FIGURE 11-6 Aggregate Plan with Random Demand: Level Strategy

CHECKING THE MODEL

Before proceeding, check the logic of the basic aggregate planning portion of the model using the procedures discussed in Unit 6. Also, check the operation of each of the four lookup functions by replacing the random function with numbers in the sequence .00, .20, .40, . . . , 1.00 and observing the value returned. Remember to replace the random function when you have finished checking the functions.

USING THE SPREADSHEET

The spreadsheet must be structured so that important output measures are captured as the simulation runs. Remember that each observation obtained with this model is derived from a run of a specified number of iterations. In this example, ten iterations are used for each run, that is, the aggregate plan is calculated ten times with a different set of random demand levels for each calculation. The data we accumulate from the iterations are summarized into one observation, which may include the values of several variables. A key question is, For which variables should we record data? Each iteration yields data about a large number of variables, for example, regular production level, actual overtime, inventory level, material cost, total cost, and so on. But we must limit our data collection to our measures of effectiveness. Initially, keep track of the total demand, total production, and total cost. These are located in cells G25, G36, and G49. Edit the formulas in these three cells, changing the cell addresses to absolute references, because these cells are to be copied elsewhere on the spreadsheet.

An observation is the mean and standard deviation of each output measure obtained from a set of ten iterations. We could accumulate summary values in designated cells and calculate the statistics after the required number of iterations is completed. Or, we could record the results of each iteration in a table and then calculate the statistics from that table. We employ the latter approach here. Many spreadsheet packages provide the facility for the kind of programming necessary to accomplish this task. Here, we describe the logic behind a Lotus 1-2-3 macro command that causes the model to cycle through a number of iterations and build a table of results by capturing values of measures of effectiveness from each iteration of the model.

There are several issues involved in building the table of results. The contents of cells containing the measures of effectiveness, G25, G36, and G49, must be copied to another section of the spreadsheet. Because these cells are defined by formulas that ultimately depend on the @RAND function, every time the spreadsheet is recalculated the values copied from those cells are also recalculated. To save the values, they must be converted from formulas to constants. With some versions of Lotus 1-2-3, this is accomplished by moving the cell pointer to the appropriate cell and pressing the {edit} then the {calc} function keys: F2 then F9.[3] But if that is done to the original cells you lose the formulas in those cells. The trick is to copy from the original cells to some intermediate cells, {edit} {calc} those intermediate cells to convert their contents to constants, and then copy the constants to the table.

Another issue concerns the placement of data in the table. The values from the intermediate cells are copied to a line at the top of the table. (By always copying to the same row, at the top of the table, we eliminate the need to keep track of how many iterations have been completed.) Then a row is inserted in the spreadsheet, moving the table down one row. After all of the iterations are completed, the table will have data from each of the iterations. The average and standard deviation functions are then used to calculate the sample mean and sample standard deviation for each column in the table.

---

[3] Lotus 1-2-3 Release 2 and some other spreadsheet software packages offer a command that copies the value of a formula instead of the formula itself. That feature, if available, is a better approach than the {edit} {calc} method. The Lotus command is /RangeValue.

```
U1: '/rncTD~G25~/rncSTD~C57~/rncTTD~C65~                                READY


       U       V       W       X       Y       Z      AA      AB      AC      AD
1    /rncTD~G25~/rncSTD~C57~/rncTTD~C65~                  } name data ranges
2    /rncTP~G36~/rncSTP~E57~/rncTTP~E65~                  } name data ranges
3    /rncTC~G49~/rncSTC~G57~/rncTTC~G65~                  } name data ranges
4    /rncDATA~C57..G57~                                   } name data ranges
5    /rncLIMIT~B61~/rncCOUNT~C56~{goto}LIMIT~             } set iteration limit
6    /xnENTER NUMBER OF ITERATIONS  ~LIMIT~               } set iteration limit
7    /rncLOOP~U10~                                        } name LOOP
8    /wgrm~/reA66..G150~                                  } clear data area
9    {goto}COUNT~0~+COUNT+1~                              } initialize counter
10   {calc}~                                              } LOOP starts here
11   {goto}STD~/c$TD~~{edit}{calc}~                       } convert formula
12   {goto}STP~/c$TP~~{edit}{calc}~                       } convert formula
13   {goto}STC~/c$TC~~{edit}{calc}~                       } convert formula
14   {goto}C64~{down}~                                    } move to table area
15   /c$DATA~~/wir~~                                      } copy results
16   /xiCOUNT<=LIMIT~/xgLOOP~                             } end of LOOP
17   {goto}TTD~/rncTTD~.{end}{up}~                        } rename TTD range
18   {down}~@avg(TTD)~/c~{right}{right}.~/c~{right}{right}{right}{right}.~
19   {down}~@sqrt(@count(TTD)/(@count(TTD)-1))*@std(TTD)~
20   /c~{right}{right}.~/c~{right}{right}{right}{right}.~
21   /rff2~.{end}{right}~                                 } summary statistics
22   {left}~'St. Dev.~{up}~'Average~                      } summary statistics
```

FIGURE 11-7 Simulation Macro

The operations discussed above must be performed repeatedly (for the desired number of iterations) and a loop can be used to automate the process. The final issue concerns the technique for controlling the number times the loop is executed. Three things are required: a counter, a limit, and a test to see if the limit has been exceeded. In developing a counter, the easiest approach is to place a formula in a cell that increments the cell value by one on each recalculation. (For example, place the formula 1+C56 in cell C56.) An if command (/**XI** in Lotus 1-2-3) can then be used to test the counter against the limit.

Many spreadsheet packages allow the user to assign names to cells and ranges of cells. In this application, we have used that capability. The alternative is to use cell addresses.

The series of macro commands shown in Figure 11-7 implements the logic we have just described. The macro is located in cells U1..U22. Comments explaining the operation of the macro are contained in column AB. The macro defines the necessary ranges (in cells U1..U5), inputs the number of iterations desired (U6), defines the internal loop (U7), sets the spreadsheet to manual recalculation and erases the old table (U8), and initializes the counter (U9). The calculation and iterative copying is carried out in cells U10..U15, and cell U16 uses the /**XI** command to test the counter against the specified limit. Cells U17..U22 calculate the statistics. Because the @STD (standard deviation) function calculates the population standard deviation, it is necessary to modify the result so that it represents a sample standard deviation. Study the macro and verify that it performs the functions indicated. As a general practice with macros, you should manually test the keystrokes to see what happens, before entering the macro.

A macro must have a name before it can be invoked. The allowable names are \A through \Z. Name the upper left cell in the macro (U1), with an appropriate name (e.g., \S for *simulation*). The macro can now be invoked by simultaneously pressing the Alt key and the letter of the macro name (e.g., Alt-S).

At this point, *before testing the macro*, save the spreadsheet under a unique name, for example SIMTEST. Invoke the macro. If the macro fails to function, do the following:

1. Attempt to determine where the problem is. A malfunctioning macro normally stops in the middle of a command. Make a screen print of what is displayed, then press <CR> and move to the macro range on the spreadsheet. Locate the text displayed on your screen print. *The error is in the macro logic before the point that the macro stopped.* Compare your screen with Figure 11-7. The problem is usually a missing ~ character or typographical error in range name or cell address.

2. Once you have determined the problem and how to fix it, load SIMTEST and make the necessary changes. Do not make the changes on the spreadsheet after you have executed the macro, because the range name commands may fail to function properly.

3. Save SIMTEST before retesting the macro.

Once the macro functions properly, you can use the simulation to compare the pure level strategy with the pure chase strategy under several randomly-estimated levels of demand. For the level strategy, you still estimate the number of employees using the expected (i.e., average) demand. The formula in M4 must be altered slightly to use total expected demand (cells K19+M19+O19+Q19) instead of total actual demand (G25).[4] The entries in cells C30..F30 should refer to M4. Execute the simulation by invoking the macro. Your results range should be similar to the top half of Figure 11-8. The Total Demand column may be different than illustrated because of different random numbers. Print your results range to obtain a copy for comparison with the chase strategy.

Next, alter the spreadsheet for analysis of the chase strategy. The formula used to compute the number of employees is similar to the formula used earlier in this unit. However, instead of referring to the actual demand (e.g., C25 in quarter 1), the formula must refer to the expected demand for that quarter (e.g., K19). Execute the simulation by invoking the macro. Your results range should be similar to the bottom half of Figure 11-8. The Total Demand column may be different than illustrated because of different random numbers. Print your results range to obtain a copy for comparison with the level strategy.

---

[4] If the formula used to compute the number of employees uses total actual demand, then the organization would be making its decision under a condition of perfect information. Instead, the organization must decide how many employees to hire based on *expected* demand. Because the sum of the expected demand across the four quarters is the same as the total demand in the problem in Unit 6, the formula still yields 110 as the required number of employees.

	A	B	C	D	E	F	G
61	No. of Iterations	10					
62			Total		Total		Total
63			Demand		Prod		Cost
64	Level Strategy						
65							
66			12050		12123		13951800
67			12050		12123		13921800
68			12100		12123		13955100
69			12300		12123		13951740
70			12600		12123		14046988
71			12500		12123		14004568
72			12100		12123		13941660
73			12100		12123		13920060
74			12250		12123		13965000
75			12250		12123		13965000
76		Average	12230		12123		13962372
77		St. Dev.	191.78		0.00		38148
78							

	A	B	C	D	E	F	G
61	No. of Iterations	10					
62			Total		Total		Total
63			Demand		Prod		Cost
64	Chase Strategy						
65							
66			12050		12001		13765427
67			12050		11805		13560504
68			12100		12059		13825020
69			12300		12059		13825162
70			12600		12508		14354800
71			12500		12255		14049372
72			12100		12063		13863005
73			12100		11847		13598528
74			12250		12200		13998945
75			12250		12200		13998945
76		Average	12230		12100		13883971
77		St. Dev.	191.78		204.41		231663
78							

FIGURE 11-8 Simulation Results: Level and Chase Strategies

Notice that the demands for the two results are the same in Figure 11-8. This occurred because Lotus 1-2-3 (Release 1A) was restarted for each model. Because the same set of demands is used to evaluate each strategy, differences in performance are due to the differences in the strategy and not due to random variation.

Even though the demand levels are the same, the two strategies produce results that appear to be different. The chase strategy yields a lower average Total Cost, but the standard deviation is higher. Recall that when we used the expected demand for motorcycles (see Figures 11-3 and 11-4), we compared the level and chase strategies by using the expected values of the chosen measures of effectiveness. Now we have a whole set of results (one run of ten iterations) for which we have calculated the average value and the sample standard deviation. Let us use the Total Cost for discussion purposes. According to the Central Limit Theorem, the distribution of sample means is always normal and therefore the exact distribution of the underlying data need not be known, even though here we could assume a reasonably normal distribution based on the pattern of the quarterly demand levels. Note that the number of iterations is ten, which is considered a statistically small sample. In this case, therefore, we must use the t-distribution in computing confidence intervals (if the number of iterations were thirty or more, the z-distribution could be used). Because of the robustness of the t-distribution, we can use it to calculate a confidence interval on the true mean total production cost. Table 11-2 contains the total expected cost for both strategies (from Figures 11-3 and 11-4) and the lower and upper limits for a 95% confidence interval on total production cost that were derived from the data in Figure 11-8. To compute the confidence interval, the standard deviation is multiplied by the appropriate value from the t-distribution ($t_{.05,9} = 2.262$) and added to or subtracted from the mean.

TABLE 11-2 Total Expected Costs For Level and Chase Strategies

	Strategy	
	Level	Chase
True Expected TC	$13,960,080	$13,820,366
Lower Limit	$13,876,081	$13,359,949
Sample Average	$13,962,372	$13,883,971
Upper Limit	$14,048,663	$14,407,993

Note that the sample averages are reasonably close to the true expected total costs, and that the confidence intervals do include the true expected total costs. When we compared the level and chase strategies using the expected demands, we noted that the two aggregate plans produced different numbers of total units. The same result is obtained for the simulation. The level strategy produced 12,123 units while the chase strategy produced an average of 12,100 units. For purposes of comparison then, we reduce the level strategy costs by the cost of those 23 units (at $1,120 per unit). This reduction amounts to $25,760. Comparing the two strategies on the basis of average cost, the chase strategy is preferable even with the reduction in level-strategy cost.

Note also that there is a much larger variability in total cost with the chase strategy than with the level strategy. The confidence interval for the chase strategy extends more than $500,000 below the lower limit for the level strategy and nearly $360,000 above the upper limit for the level strategy. If we think of those intervals as probabilities, we might interpret the results as saying that the chase strategy is more likely to have a lower total cost. On the other hand, the wide range of variability indicates much less certainty about the production and profit levels with the chase strategy. This variability can be reduced, thus yielding a higher level of precision, by increasing the number of replications. Recall the formula for how many runs are necessary to yield a desired level of precision:

$$N = [(z \times s) / p]^2$$

We can use the standard deviation from our first run as an estimate of the value of s. To achieve a level of precision of $140,000 (approximately 1% of total cost) at a 95% confidence level, the calculation for the level strategy is

$$N = [(1.96 \times 38{,}148) / 140{,}000]^2 = 0.29$$

which means that we have already achieved the desired level of precision for this strategy. (You could have determined that without a calculator, the standard deviation times the z-value at 95% confidence level is much less than the desired level of precision.) Performing the same calculation for the chase strategy:

$$N = [(1.96 \times 231{,}663) / 140{,}000]^2 = 10.52$$

Here, result indicates that we need eleven runs of ten iterations each to achieve the desired level of precision. Sample statistics can then be computed from the average results from these eleven runs.

Monte Carlo simulation is a very useful tool when you cannot obtain explicit analytical results. In those cases where certain aspects of the model involve probability distributions, simulation provides a means to obtain not only the expected or average results, but also good estimates of the variability of the results.

ENHANCEMENTS TO THE APPLICATION

The Monte Carlo simulation of the aggregate planning model gave you a chance to look at simulation in the context of a familiar model and also to compare the results obtained using stochastic variables with results obtained using deterministic variables. Three enhancements can be implemented to make the spreadsheet a more powerful tool.

1. To achieve exact repeatability of the random numbers without having to restart 1-2-3, use the program in Appendix C to generate a table of random numbers, name them as a range, and copy them into your spreadsheet. Then use the iteration counter and table lookup to obtain the random number used to generate the random demand. Of course, this technique is required to achieve repeatability if you are using Lotus 1-2-3 Release 2 or any other spreadsheet which does not always provide the same first random number.

2. Modify the spreadsheet to allow multiple runs, recording the result from each set of iterations in a second table. Modify the macro to ask for both number of runs and number of iterations per run. You must implement a second counter to track number of runs. The index for the random number lookup (if implemented in Enhancement 1) is now a combination of the two counters, specifically

   [(run number - 1) x (number of iterations per run)] + (iteration number)

3. Either in conjunction with the above, or separately, modify the spreadsheet to include both strategies. The same demand values should be used in both strategies. Do not have two sets of @VLOOKUP and @RAND statements. Demand values for one of the strategies should reference cells in which the values of the stochastic variables are computed for the other.

Monte Carlo simulation can be used on many different types of problems. You can simulate a simple one-equation break-even analysis with random demand, or a complex waiting-line problem with different types of customers and servers, such as a machine shop scheduling problem. These problems may use other probability distributions, examples of which are included in Appendix C. In any type of simulation problem, the principles illustrated in this unit continue to apply.

EXERCISES

The spreadsheet presented in this unit illustrates the fundamental concepts involved in developing and analyzing a simulation model, but it is incomplete as far as EZRydr's problem is concerned. Your task is to modify this model as necessary to address EZRydr's basic question of whether to add snowmobiles or ATVs to their production line.

1. Because the level and chase strategies result in different production levels, cost per unit is an important measure of effectiveness. Top management is also interested in looking at employee levels. Modify the spreadsheet to include calculation of both the average number of employees and the cost per unit produced.

2. Because they are important measures, modify the simulation macro to record the average number of employees and the cost per unit produced in the output table. Include the provision to calculate the average and sample standard deviation of these two additional entries to the output table.

3. Because we are interested in evaluating snowmobiles and ATVs for production, add the quarterly demand probability distributions for snowmobiles and ATVs to the spreadsheet and modify the spreadsheet entries to calculate the quarterly random demand for snowmobiles and ATVs.

4. Use the modified spreadsheet to evaluate whether EZRydr should produce snowmobiles, ATVs, or both, in addition to their existing motorcycle line.

REVIEW QUESTIONS

1. When should simulation models be used?

2. What are some of the advantages and disadvantages of simulation models?

*3. How can sequences of random numbers be repeated with a spreadsheet package?

4. How are random numbers used with probability distributions to generate values of random variables?

*5. How can the effect of a random number be preserved in a spreadsheet model?

6. How are probability distributions generated and used?

*7. How are repeated loops programmed?

ADDITIONAL READING

Anderson, D. R., D. J. Sweeney, and T. A. Williams, *An Introduction to Management Science.* St. Paul: West, 1985.

Pritsker, A. A. B., and C. D. Pegden, *Introduction to Simulation and SLAM.* New York: Wiley, 1979.

Taha, H. A., *Operations Research.* New York: Macmillan, 1982.

APPLICATION-SPECIFIC SOFTWARE PACKAGES

Spreadsheet models provide a relatively easy method for conducting Monte Carlo simulations, but some clever programming is required. For complex problems with more measures of effectiveness and many random variables, consider one of the specialized simulation languages such as the following:

GPSS/PC. Mainstream Software, P. O. Box 171, Stow, MA, 01775. (800) 223-1430.

PC SIMSCRIPT II.5. CACI, 3344 N. Torrey Pines Court, LaJolla, CA 92037. (619) 457-9681.

SLAM II/PC. Pritsker & Associates, Inc. 1305 Cumberland Ave., P. O. Box 2413, West Lafayette, IN 47906. (317) 463-5557. (SLAM II includes the GASP simulation program.)

PART

4 PLANNING FOR NEW OPERATIONS

In this part we present three methods that can be used to support decisions necessary to implement new operations. These techniques are also appropriate for support of current operations (Part 2) or analyzing an opportunity (Part 3). The models developed in this part are fairly complex, both because of the underlying theories as well as the mechanics of implementing the models in a spreadsheet. For EZRydr, the new operations revolve around the decision to add snowmobiles and all-terrain vehicles to their product line. In Unit 12, a spreadsheet is developed to facilitate decision making when multiple criteria are to be considered. In Unit 13, the economic benefit of a capital investment is determined. Finally, Unit 14 is devoted to discussion of techniques for the allocation of limited resources to maximize profit. As in Part 3, the tools presented in this part are very general in nature, and may be applied to a broad range of decision situations.

UNIT 12 WEIGHTED FACTOR APPROACH—DECISION ANALYSIS USING MULTIPLE CRITERIA

The weighted factor approach is used to analyze decisions in which there are several criteria to be considered. In this unit we demonstrate this technique using a facility location decision. The number of factors that influence management in making a facility-location decision is virtually unlimited. Rather than focusing exclusively on one criterion in making a location decision, management usually considers such things as the cost of the land, the cost of the building, the availability of labor, the accessibility to land, water, or air transportation, the potential for expansion of the facility, and so on. There are few optimizing algorithms for solving multiple-criterion problems such as this, but the weighted factor approach allows the decision maker to systematically evaluate an unlimited number of alternative locations using an unlimited number of criteria. A spreadsheet is an excellent tool for performing the what-if analyses associated with weighted factor models.

DECISION SUPPORT APPLICATION MATRIX

Accounting & Finance	Economics & Long-Range Planning	Human Resources	Marketing & Logistics	Management Information Systems	Operations Planning & Control	Executive Officers
■¤	■¤	■¤	■¤	■¤	■¤	■¤

■ Departmental area(s) in which the technique is or can be used.

¤ Departmental area(s) that provide input to or are impacted by the technique.

LEARNING OBJECTIVES

1. After completing this unit you should know

   a. the terminology associated with facility location,

   b. some of the criteria used to solve different types of facility-location problems,

Contributed by Richard J. Penlesky

c. the names and underlying principles of a variety of optimizing and satisficing facility-location techniques,

d. how the weighted factor approach can be used to solve the facility-location problem and other problems with multiple-criterion objective functions,

e. how spreadsheet software can be used to develop and use weighted factor approach models.

2. After completing this unit you should be able to

a. create a spreadsheet for developing weighted factor approach models,

b. use a weighted factor approach spreadsheet to solve a facility-location problem,

c. use a weighted factor approach spreadsheet to solve a variety of problems characterized by a multiple-criterion objective function.

BASIC CONCEPTS

Before discussing the weighted factor approach, we examine the problem of facility location. Facility location is a long-term, capacity-acquisition decision. Because of its strategic nature, the facility-location decision is typically made by top management. In making a facility-location decision, top management typically assesses the capacity needs of the firm over a three- to five-year planning horizon. If those needs are not covered by capacity available in existing facilities, additional capacity must be acquired. If the additional capacity is not to be added to the existing facility, then determining the location of the new facility becomes an important step in the capacity-acquisition decision.

The criteria used to evaluate the merits of competing location alternatives vary depending on the nature of the business activity in which the firm is involved. In some cases a single criterion is sufficient, but in other cases multiple criteria are required. Manufacturing, warehousing, and distribution firms typically focus on cost minimization in locating their plants, warehouses, and distribution centers. They attempt to minimize the costs of transporting materials to and from their facilities. Retail firms tend to view the world differently, focusing on revenue maximization in locating their facilities. To maximize revenues, retail firms attempt to locate their shops near centers of high population or places with high levels of pedestrian or automobile traffic. Emergency service facilities, such as fire departments, police departments, and paramedic units, are located primarily with the objective of minimizing response time and only secondarily in regard to cost. The general considerations for each of these types of location problems may contain several subordinate criteria. For instance, cost criteria include land cost, transportation cost, building cost, taxes, and so on.

Single Criterion Techniques

A number of techniques can be used to solve single-criterion problems. Linear programming (in particular, the transportation method) is well suited to solving single-criterion facility-location problems since it involves optimizing an objective function (e.g., minimize response time) subject to a set of constraints (e.g., cost cannot exceed X dollars, the facility must be located within the city limits). Refer to Unit 14 for a more detailed discussion of linear programming.

A technique called the *center of gravity method* is often used to locate a single warehouse facility. The center of gravity method is a satisficing rather than an optimizing technique. Whereas the transportation method of linear programming guarantees the best possible solution under the stated constraints (i.e., an optimum solution), the center of gravity method guarantees only a satisfactory solution. The center of gravity method can be implemented either mathematically using a number of formulas or physically using strings, weights, and pulleys. When the method is implemented physically, the supply and demand sites to be serviced by the warehouse are identified as point estimates on a map. The map is fastened (glued) to a piece of plywood and a hole is drilled through the map and board at each of the identified sites. A piece of string is then dropped through each of the holes and laid over a pulley in order to reduce the friction of the string on the edge of the hole. After all of the pieces of string are knotted together on top of the map, weights are hung on the strings dangling below the piece of plywood. The amount of weight hung on each string is directly proportional to the volume of product moved to or from each of the sites (i.e., considerable weight on high-volume sites and less weight on low-volume sites). After the weights are hung, the system is allowed to pull and tug at the knot until the knot is positioned over the center of gravity of the system. The location beneath the knot represents the minimum-cost location for the warehouse. While this method guarantees neither optimality nor feasibility (the knot might stabilize over a river!), it does provide a good approximation for the facility location.

Ardalan (1984) developed a heuristic technique for locating service facilities such as banks, restaurants, and similar service institutions. The heuristic uses a population-distance matrix to identify service locations that are near population centers and thus minimize the number of people who must travel long distances to obtain the service. The technique can be used to determine the timing sequence for opening multiple facilities that serve the same community. For example, a new fast food chain may wish to open one new outlet per year for the next four years in a given city. If outlets are to be located on the north, south, east, and west sides of the city, the heuristic can be used to determine the sequence in which those four restaurants should be opened.

A Multiple Criterion Technique: The Weighted Factor Approach

Each of the techniques mentioned above focuses on one and only one criterion for establishing the location of a facility (e.g., cost, revenue, population, distance). In many instances, however, it is difficult to measure the adequacy of a facility location by a single criterion. For example, though response-time minimization is normally the primary criterion for locating a fire department, it is also important to consider the cost of building the fire house, the availability of fire fighters, and the viability of the community (i.e., is the community growing or shrinking?). In those instances in which multiple criteria must be considered in selecting a facility location, a heuristic method called the *weighted factor approach* can be used.

The weighted factor approach is a satisficing technique that allows the decision maker to consider both quantitative and qualitative criteria simultaneously in arriving at a decision. Although we discuss the technique in the context of solving facility-location problems, it can be used in virtually any decision-making situation. It could be used, for example, by a recent college graduate for choosing among competing job offers on the bases of salary, location, potential for promotion, fringe benefit package, and collegiality in the work environment (an exercise along these lines is suggested at the end of this unit).

When using the weighted factor approach to solve a facility-location problem, the first step is to identify both the factors (*criteria*) to be used to evaluate each of the potential locations and the relative importance (*weight*) of each of the factors. The three factors identified in Table 12-1 might all be considered crucial in selecting the location of a new manufacturing facility. The level of importance of each of the factors is identified by its corresponding percentage weight. Notice that the sum of the weights is (and must always be) 100%.

TABLE 12-1 Manufacturing Facility-Location Factors and Weights

Factor	Weight (%)
Cost of the Land (CL)	30
Cost of the Building (CB)	50
Potential for Expansion (PE)	20
TOTAL	100

The second step is to identify the potential site locations and to evaluate each according to each of the factors. Table 12-2 illustrates the *factor rating scores* developed for two potential sites for the manufacturing facility-location example.

TABLE 12-2 Factor Rating Scores

		Rating Score	
Factor	Weight (%)	Site 1	Site 2
CL	30	$1,000,000	$ 900,000
CB	50	2,600,000	2,800,000
PE	20	fair	excellent
TOTAL	100		

The third step is to develop a *normalized rating score* for each of the factors at each of the potential sites. Whereas the non-normalized rating scores have various units of measure associated with them (e.g., dollars, tons, miles), the normalized scores are unitless numbers. The reason for developing the normalized rating scores is to allow them to be combined to develop a composite score for each site. The non-normalized scores cannot be added together since one cannot add apples and oranges or, in this case, dollars and "fair" or dollars and "excellent." Under the assumption that the site with the highest composite score is the preferred location, the procedure necessary to develop normalized rating scores is stated below.

1. Assign a numerical score to each subjective factor (those factors evaluated as poor, fair, good, etc.). Though the scale used to assign the numerical scores may be arbitrary, a scale of 0 to 10 is often used (0 = worst; 10 = best).

2. For each factor, determine whether it is preferable to have a high or a low factor score.

3. For factors for which it is preferable to have a high score, such as the potential for expansion (PE) factor in Table 12-2, divide the factor score for each site by the sum of the factor scores for all sites. The sum of the scores for a factor across all sites equals 1.

$$NS_i = S_i / (S_1 + S_2 + \ldots + S_n)$$

where NS_i is the normalized score for site i, S_i is the factor score for site i, and n is the number of alternative sites.

4. For factors for which a low score is preferable, such as the land and building costs, divide the factor score for each site by the sum of the factor scores for all sites and subtract this quotient from 1 to yield an intermediate result. The effect of subtracting the quotient from 1 is to assign high normalized ratings to factors for which a low non-normalized rating is preferred. One further calculation is necessary to yield a normalized factor score. Because we are taking the *complement* of the ratio of the score of one site to the sum of the scores of all sites, the sum of these normalized scores will always be 1 less than the number of alternatives. However, to make these scores comparable with those calculated above, the sum of the normalized scores for each factor *must always be equal to 1*. Thus, the intermediate result must be divided by the number of alternatives minus 1, yielding the normalized score.

$$NS_i = \{1 - [S_i / (S_1 + S_2 + \ldots + S_n)]\} / [n - 1]$$

where the variables are as defined above.

The result of applying this procedure to the manufacturing facility-location example is shown in Table 12-3.

TABLE 12-3 Normalized Factor Rating Scores

		Rating Score		Normalized Score	
Factor	Weight (%)	Site 1	Site 2	Site 1	Site 2
CL	30	$1,000,000	$ 900,000	.47	.53
CB	50	2,600,000	2,800,000	.52	.48
PE	20	fair	excellent	.29	.71
TOTAL	100				

Note that the sum of the normalized rating scores for each factor across all sites must always be equal to 1.

The fourth and final step in using the weighted factor approach is to multiply each normalized rating score by its corresponding weight in order to develop a *weighted, normalized rating score* for each factor at each site. Add the weighted, normalized rating scores for all factors at a given site to determine the overall score for that site. The result of applying this step to the example is shown in Table 12-4.

TABLE 12-4 Weighted, Normalized Factor Rating Scores

		Rating Score		Normalized Score		Weighted Normalized Score	
Factor	Weight (%)	Site 1	Site 2	Site 1	Site 2	Site 1	Site 2
CL	30	$1,000,000	$ 900,000	.47	.53	14.1	15.9
CB	50	2,600,000	2,800,000	.52	.48	26.0	24.0
PE	20	fair	excellent	.29	.71	5.8	14.2
TOTALS	100					45.9	54.1

In this example, Site 2 is the preferred location since its overall weighted, normalized rating score (54.1) is greater than that for Site 1 (45.9). Notice that the sum of these two scores is 100 (representing 100% of the decision) and thus the average is 50. If there had been three sites in the example, the sum of the scores would once again be 100, but the average would be 33.3. The degree to which an individual site score differs from the average is a measure of the strength of the preference for a particular site; if the overall scores for Sites 1 and 2 were 49 and 51, respectively, Site 2 would still be preferred over Site 1, but the strength of that preference would not be as great as it is in the original example.

GATHERING THE DATA

Within the Company

The facility-location decision requires that some planning be done and data be developed within the company before data collection begins at the potential site locations. Top management, perhaps in conjunction with a facility-location project team, must first identify the factors (criteria) that will be used to evaluate the alternative locations. These factors are used as a basis for collecting data at the various sites. The weights associated with the various factors must also be established by someone within the firm.

External to the Company

Both the identification of the potential site locations and the individual factor scores for a given site are normally based on data obtained outside of the company.

THE PROBLEM

The management at EZRydr has decided to expand the firm's operation. In addition to motorcycles, they intend to begin producing all-terrain vehicles (ATVs) and snowmobiles (SM). This expansion decision requires that the firm obtain additional productive capacity. Because zoning laws prohibit expansion of the existing manufacturing plant, management must find a location to build a new plant. They would like you to help them choose among the three potential site locations they have identified. Use the weighted factor approach to answer the following questions:

1. At which of the three potential site locations should the new manufacturing plant be located?

2. How strong is your recommendation to locate at the site chosen in question 1?

3. How would your location recommendation change, if at all, as a result of

   a. a 20% decrease in the construction cost at Site 2?

   b. a 50% increase in the cost of the land at Site 3?

   c. improvements in the rail and interstate access conditions at Site 1 such that both of those factor rating scores increase to "excellent"?

   d. a shift in focus from one-time expenditures to ongoing expenses such that the weight for the land cost is reduced to 10% and the weight for the construction cost is reduced to 15% while the weight for the taxes is increased to 25%?

Departmental Data

The following data regarding the site-location problem have been compiled by the facility-location project team at EZRydr.

		Rating Scores		
Factor	Weight	Site 1	Site 2	Site 3
Skilled Labor Availability	10%	very good	fair	excellent
Unskilled Labor Availability	15%	excellent	excellent	good
Corporate Income Taxes ($)	5%	500,000	300,000	750,000
Access to Rail Transportation	5%	good	very good	very good
Access to Interstate Transportation	15%	fair	good	excellent
Cost of the Land ($)	20%	1,000,000	600,000	1,200,000
Construction Cost ($)	25%	5,000,000	6,000,000	4,000,000
Room for Potential Expansion	5%	excellent	very good	good

Data in the Database

For most manufacturing firms, facility-location decisions occur infrequently. When they do occur, they are usually handled on a project basis. Thus data to support a decision of this sort can seldom be found in an existing database in the firm. As the location decision is being made and while the expansion is underway, a database may be developed to support these activities. However, once the construction project is completed and the new plant is up and running, this project database is no longer of any value to the firm and thus is normally discarded. The staff of EZRydr has compiled the data listed above, as well as other factors and sites, into a database file named FAC_PLAN.

DEVELOPING THE SPREADSHEET

Before we can address EZRydr management's questions, we must build a weighted factor approach spreadsheet model. In this section we discuss the development of such a model. When you save the spreadsheet, call it LOCATION.

Start with a blank spreadsheet. In the upper left corner, enter the site location data that is presented in the departmental data section of this chapter. Use the following scale to convert the qualitative data to a quantitative format: excellent = 10, very good = 8, good = 6, fair = 4, poor = 2, and unacceptable = 0. After entering the data, your spreadsheet should be similar to that in Figure 12-1. Note that the column widths have been adjusted. Also note that the TOTAL of the weights is calculated and, as always, equals 100%.

Strike Home and then <TAB> to position the cursor in F1. Both the normalized factor scores and the weighted, normalized factor scores will be calculated in this area. Enter the column headings as shown in Figure 12-2, and set the width of the blank columns (F and J) to five characters.

Recall that there are two different procedures for normalizing scores, depending on whether it is preferable to have a high value or a low value. Thus, the formulas for normalizing Skilled Labor Availability, Unskilled Labor Availability, Access to Rail, Access to Interstate, and Room to Expand are different from those for the cost-oriented factors (i.e., Taxes, Land Cost, and Construction Cost). In G7 enter the following formula for normalizing the Skilled Labor Availability factor at Site 1:

+C7/@SUM($C7..$E7)

In this Lotus 1-2-3 formula, we have used mixed cell references to facilitate copying the formula for Sites 2 and 3. The normalized scores for the remaining high-value factors can be calculated by copying the G7..I7 range to G8, G10, G11, and G14.

The formula for normalizing EZRydr's cost-oriented factors is a bit more complicated. Following the procedure described earlier in this unit, the formula in G9 is

(1-C9/@SUM($C9..$E9))/(@COUNT($C9..$E9)-1)

In order to complete the table of normalized scores on the spreadsheet, copy this formula to H9 and I9, and then copy the G9..I9 range to G12 and G13. Save the spreadsheet to protect yourself against losing your work.

To complete the spreadsheet, the weighted, normalized scores must be calculated for each factor and then added together for each site. To calculate the weighted, normalized scores, enter

100*$B7*G7

in cell K7, then copy that formula throughout the K7..M14 range. Multiplying the weights by 100 (100*$B7) converts the decimal weights to their percentage equivalent and displays the weighted, normalized scores at a "comfortable" order of magnitude. Add the scores for each site. Remember to save the completed spreadsheet.

A1: [W25]   READY

	A	B	C	D	E
1		EZRYDR'S FACILITY-LOCATION PROBLEM			
2			PLANNING DATA		
3					
4				Rating Scores	
5	Factor	Weight	Site 1	Site 2	Site 3
6	======	======	======	======	======
7	Skilled Labor Avail.	10%	8	4	10
8	Unskilled Labor Avail.	15%	10	10	6
9	Taxes	5%	$500,000	$300,000	$750,000
10	Access to Rail	5%	6	8	8
11	Access to Interstate	15%	4	6	10
12	Land Cost	20%	$1,000,000	$600,000	$1,200,000
13	Construction Cost	25%	$5,000,000	$6,000,000	$4,000,000
14	Room to Expand	5%	10	8	6
15					
16	TOTAL	100%			
17					
18					
19					
20					

FIGURE 12-1 Facility-Location Spreadsheet: Planning Data

CHECKING THE MODEL

You can do a quick check of your model by striking the Home key and comparing what appears on your screen to the content of Figure 12-1. Then strike the <TAB> key and compare what you see to Figure 12-2. For a more general check, insure that

- the sum of the weights is 100%.
- the sum of the normalized scores across all sites for each factor is 1.0.
- the sum of the weighted, normalized scores across all sites for each factor is equal to the percentage weight assigned to that factor.

To further test the logic of the model, change any of the weights to 0. The sum of the weights should change to a number less than 100%, and the weighted, normalized scores in the corresponding row should all be 0. Remember to set the weight to its original value before proceeding.

```
F1: [W5]                                                              READY

      F     G       H       I      J     K       L       M
1                          EZRYDR'S FACILITY-LOCATION PROBLEM
2                                 CALCULATION SCREEN
3
4              Normalized Scores            Weighted, Normalized Scores
5            Site 1  Site 2  Site 3          Site 1  Site 2  Site 3
6            ======  ======  ======          ======  ======  ======
7             0.364   0.182   0.455             3.6     1.8     4.5
8             0.385   0.385   0.231             5.8     5.8     3.5
9             0.339   0.403   0.258             1.7     2.0     1.3
10            0.273   0.364   0.364             1.4     1.8     1.8
11            0.200   0.300   0.500             3.0     4.5     7.5
12            0.321   0.393   0.286             6.4     7.9     5.7
13            0.333   0.300   0.367             8.3     7.5     9.2
14            0.417   0.333   0.250             2.1     1.7     1.3
15
16                                             32.3    32.9    34.7
17
18
19
20
```

FIGURE 12-2 Facility-Location Spreadsheet: Calculations

USING THE SPREADSHEET

As you recall, EZRydr's management posed a number of questions about the location of their new manufacturing operation. We now use our spreadsheet to answer those questions.

1. At which of the three potential site locations should the new manufacturing plant be located? The new manufacturing plant should be located at the site with the highest weighted, normalized factor score. The score for Site 1 is 32.3, for Site 2 it is 32.9, and for Site 3 it is 34.7. Thus the plant should be located at Site 3.

2. How strong is your recommendation to locate at the site chosen in question 1? If the three potential sites were equally desirable, each of them would have a weighted, normalized score of 100/3 = 33.3. Since the actual scores for Sites 1 and 2 are only slightly below that value, and the score for Site 3 is only slightly above that value, the recommendation to locate at Site 3 is relatively weak. Slight changes in the factor weights or rating scores could cause the recommendation to shift from Site 3 to either of the other two sites. In this case, an analysis to establish the robustness of the decision to locate at Site 3 is clearly indicated.

3. How would your location recommendation differ, if at all, as a result of the following modified assumptions? After analyzing each change, remember to enter the original value in any changed cell.

   a. The construction cost at Site 2 decreases by 20%. Multiply the Construction Cost in D13 by 0.8. The new scores for Sites 1 through 3, respectively, become 31.9, 33.6, and 34.5. Thus Site 3 is still the preferred site, though it is preferred by a smaller margin over Site 2 than it was under the original conditions.

   b. The cost of the land at Site 3 increases by 50%. Multiply the Land Cost in E12 by 1.5. The new scores for Sites 1 through 3, respectively, become 32.9, 33.3, and 33.7. Thus Site 3 is still the preferred site, though the margin of preference over Site 2 is considerably less than under the original conditions.

   c. There are improvements in the rail and interstate access conditions at Site 1 such that both of those factor rating scores at that site increase to "excellent." Change the rail and interstate rating scores in C10 and C11 to 10. The new scores for Sites 1 through 3, respectively, become 35.6, 31.6, and 32.7. Thus, under these revised circumstances, Site 1 is clearly superior to the other sites. Note that the margin of preference here is greater than the margin in any of the prior scenarios.

   d. A shift in focus from one-time expenditures to ongoing expenses occurs such that the weight for the land cost is reduced to 10% and the weight for the construction cost is reduced to 15%, while the weight for the taxes is increased to 25%. Change the affected weights. The new scores for Sites 1 through 3, respectively, become 32.5, 34.1, and 33.4. Thus, under these revised circumstances, Site 2 is preferred to the other sites.

EXERCISES

The facility-location spreadsheet we have developed for EZRydr's management is a powerful and versatile decision-making tool. Convince yourself of its usefulness by answering the following questions. As you answer these questions, reset the spreadsheet before every question or subquestion. The easiest way to do this is save the spreadsheet with the initial values, then change the decision data as indicated. Once the question is answered, you may wish to save the spreadsheet with a unique name (e.g., FACLOC1A). When you are ready for the next question or subquestion, load (retrieve) the original spreadsheet.

1. The management at EZRydr has just been informed of a fourth potential plant location site. The rating scores for that site are as follows:

Factor	Rating Scores Site 4
Skilled Labor Availability	excellent
Unskilled Labor Availability	very good
Corporate Income Taxes ($)	600,000
Access to Rail Transportation	very good
Access to Interstate Transportation	excellent
Cost of the Land ($)	900,000
Construction Cost ($)	3,500,000
Room for Potential Expansion	very good

Modify your weighted factor approach spreadsheet model to accommodate this fourth potential site. Where should the new manufacturing plant be located? How strong is your recommendation to locate at that site?

2. In your original spreadsheet you used the following linear scale to convert the qualitative data to a quantitative format: excellent = 10, very good = 8, good = 6, fair = 4, poor = 2, and unacceptable = 0. How would your location recommendation change, if at all, if that linear conversion scale was changed to the nonlinear scale shown below?

Qualitative Score	Quantitative Equivalent
Excellent	25
Very Good	16
Good	9
Fair	4
Poor	1
Unacceptable	0

3. In an attempt to identify a plant location site for which a strong preference exists, the management at EZRydr has decided to add three factors and to alter the weights of the original factors as shown below:

Factor	Weight	Rating Scores Site 1	Site 2	Site 3
Skilled Labor Availability	5%	very good	fair	excellent
Unskilled Labor Availability	15%	excellent	excellent	good
Corporate Income Taxes ($)	5%	500,000	300,000	750,000
Access to Rail Transportation	5%	good	very good	very good
Access to Interstate Transportation	5%	fair	good	excellent
Cost of the Land ($)	15%	1,000,000	600,000	1,200,000
Construction Cost ($)	20%	5,000,000	6,000,000	4,000,000
Room for Potential Expansion	5%	excellent	very good	good
Skilled Labor Wage Rates ($/hr)	10%	15.00	20.00	15.00
Unskilled Labor Wage Rates ($/hr)	10%	8.00	9.50	15.00
Quality of the Business Climate	5%	excellent	fair	good

Modify your model to include the three additional factors and the new factor weights. Based on your new spreadsheet: (a) Where should the new manufacturing plant be located? (b) How strong is your recommendation to locate at that site? (c) Did the changes that you made strengthen or weaken your recommendation?

4. Develop a weighted factor approach spreadsheet model that could be used by a recent college graduate to choose among three competing job offers on the bases of salary, location, potential for promotion, fringe benefits package, and collegiality in the work environment.

5. Develop a weighted factor approach spreadsheet model either for a decision that you have made in the recent past or for one that is plaguing you right now.

ENHANCEMENTS TO THE APPLICATION

By performing the Exercises you should have developed an appreciation for the power and versatility of the weighted factor spreadsheet as a decision-making tool. However, you may also have developed a feeling that "there must be a better way" to enter the many repetitive keystrokes necessary to answer the Exercise questions. In order to minimize some of that repetition and to improve the user-friendliness of your spreadsheet, you may wish to incorporate the following enhancements.

1. Display the overall site scores on the PLANNING DATA screen so that you do not have to change screens to see the effect of changing any of the planning information. This enhancement is illustrated in Figure 12-3, on row 16.

2. On the PLANNING DATA screen display the maximum of the overall site scores and a conditional expression that indicates which of the sites is the preferred location. The label in C19 (using Lotus 1-2-3, Release 2) is generated by the following formula:

```
@IF(C18=C16,"      Site 1",@IF(C18=D16,"      Site 2","      Site 3"))
```

In each string there are six blank spaces preceding the word "Site."

A1: [W25] READY

	A	B	C	D	E
1		EZRYDR'S FACILITY-LOCATION PROBLEM			
2			PLANNING DATA		
3					
4				Rating Scores	
5	Factor	Weight	Site 1	Site 2	Site 3
6	======	======	======	======	======
7	Skilled Labor Avail.	10%	8	4	10
8	Unskilled Labor Avail.	15%	10	10	6
9	Taxes	5%	$500,000	$300,000	$750,000
10	Access to Rail	5%	6	8	8
11	Access to Interstate	15%	4	6	10
12	Land Cost	20%	$1,000,000	$600,000	$1,200,000
13	Construction Cost	25%	$5,000,000	$6,000,000	$4,000,000
14	Room to Expand	5%	10	8	6
15					
16	TOTAL	100%	32.3	32.9	34.7
17					
18	Maximum Weighted Scaled Score:		34.7		
19	LOCATE THE FACTORY AT:		Site 3		
20					

FIGURE 12-3 Facility-Location Spreadsheet: Enhanced Planning Data Section

Figure 12-3 illustrates how the PLANNING DATA screen might appear if Enhancements 1 and 2 were added to the spreadsheet.

3. Develop a bar graph of the overall site scores. This graph would provide the decision maker with a visual indication of the degree to which individual site scores differ from each other and thus provide a measure of the strength of the preference for a particular site. This graph is illustrated in Figure 12-4.

4. Develop a macro or if statements to convert the qualitative factor scores (excellent, very good, etc.) to their numeric equivalents (10, 8, etc.). This enhancement allows you to enter the factor scores as labels into the PLANNING DATA portion of the spreadsheet. This enhancement expedites evaluation of the impact of alternative conversion scales or changes in a specific qualitative factor score.

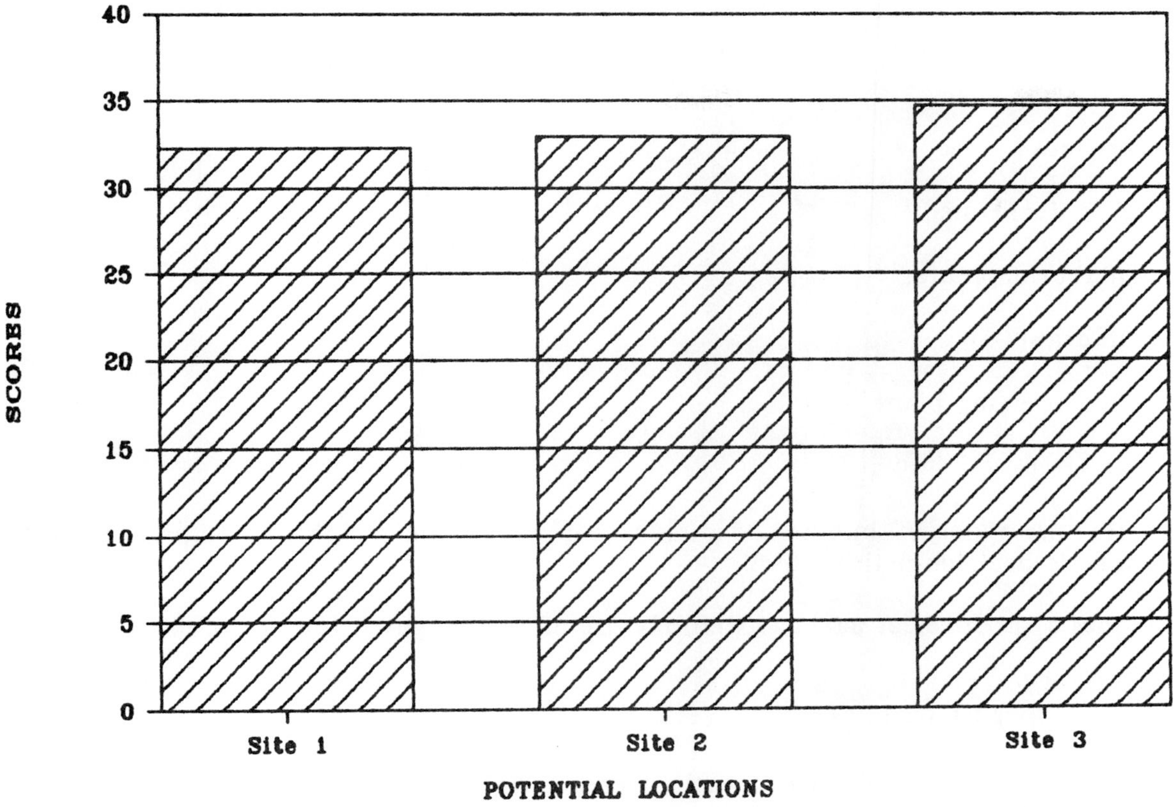

FIGURE 12-4 Comparison of the Three Sites

REVIEW QUESTIONS

1. Define the following terms as they relate to the facility-location problem:

    a. optimizing

    *b. satisficing

    c. linear programming

    *d. center of gravity method

    *e. population-distance matrix

    f. multiple-criterion technique

    *g. weighted factor approach

    h. factor weights

*i. normalized factor score

2. Identify the primary criterion that is typically used to solve the following facility-location problems:

   *a. warehouse

   b. police department

   *c. distribution center

   d. restaurant

   *e. manufacturing plant

   f. hair salon

3. Identify the types of business decisions for which the weighted factor approach is an appropriate decision-making tool.

*4. How does a spreadsheet package simplify use of the weighted factor approach model?

ADDITIONAL READING

To understand more about facility location refer to introductory operations management textbooks such as:

Chase, R. B., and N. J. Aquilano. *Production and Operations Management.* Homewood, IL: Irwin, 1985.

Evans, J. R., D. R. Anderson, D. J. Sweeney, and T. A. Williams. *Applied Production and Operations Management.* St. Paul: West, 1984.

Fearon, H. E., W. A. Ruch, V. G. Reuter, C. D. Wieters, and R. R. Reck. *Fundamentals of Production/Operations Management.* St. Paul: West, 1986.

Harris, R. D., and R. F. Gonzalez. *The Operations Manager: Role, Problems, Techniques.* St. Paul: West, 1981.

Schroeder, R. G. *Operations Management: Decision Making in the Operations Function.* New York: McGraw-Hill, 1985. This book provides an excellent overview of the weighted factor approach.

An advanced, comprehensive treatment of the facility-location problem is provided by R. L. Francis and J. A. White. *Facility Layout and Location: An Analytical Approach.* Englewood, NJ: Prentice-Hall, 1974.

A. Ardalan published an article entitled "An Efficient Heuristic for Service Facility Location" in the *Proceedings* of the Northeast American Institute for Decision Sciences 1984 Meeting, pp. 181-82. In this article Ardalan develops a population-distance matrix for locating service facilities. This technique is summarized in the Chase and Aquilano book listed above.

An article entitled "Analyzing Subjective Decisions with a Spreadsheet" (E. S. Gardner, Jr., *Lotus*, Vol. 3, No. 1, January 1987, pp. 68-71) illustrates an alternative formulation of the weighted factor approach using a spreadsheet format.

UNIT

13 FINANCIAL ANALYSIS—ANALYZING THE RETURN ON AN INVESTMENT

Financial analysis of an equipment replacement decision involves assembling and analyzing information about the potential savings and costs resulting from the replacement. For purposes of analysis, management must gather estimates of the cost to acquire the new piece of equipment, any additional expenditures that the new machine will require during its life, savings to be realized over the life of the new machine, and any costs or benefits associated with the disposition of the machine currently in use. The analysis must also consider tax implications. These difficulties, plus the fact that management may wish to explore several scenarios involving key estimates used in the analysis, make spreadsheets a convenient and useful vehicle for organizing and evaluating the data.

DECISION SUPPORT APPLICATION MATRIX

Accounting & Finance	Economics & Long-Range Planning	Human Resources	Marketing & Logistics	Management Information Systems	Operations Planning & Control	Executive Officers
■		¤			■	¤

■ Departmental area(s) in which the technique is or can be used.

¤ Departmental area(s) that provide input to or are impacted by the technique.

LEARNING OBJECTIVES

1. After completing this unit you should know

   a. the difference between costs that are relevant and irrelevant to the equipment replacement decision,

   b. how to use net present value and internal rate of return as criteria for evaluating equipment replacement,

Contributed by Lloyd D. Doney

   c. how taxes impact capital equipment investment decisions.

2. After completing this unit you should be able to

   a. create a spreadsheet for analyzing the equipment replacement decision,

   b. use windows to observe selected portions of the spreadsheet simultaneously.

BASIC CONCEPTS

One of the major reasons for replacing equipment is to increase productivity, which is defined as the ratio of units of output per unit of input. If current demand is unmet, the new piece of equipment may generate more units of output with no increase in input, thereby increasing productivity. If current demand is being satisfied, the new machine may produce the same number of units of output as the old machine, but with fewer units of input, and thus increase productivity. In either case, if the improvement in productivity is sufficient, purchase of the new machine is indicated.

Some of the costs, benefits, and other considerations that enter into the financial analysis of the equipment replacement decision are as follows:

- purchase cost of the new machine
- estimated life of the new machine
- estimated salvage value, if any, of the new machine at the end of its useful life
- estimated periodic costs, if any, that will be incurred for maintaining or overhauling the new machine during its useful life
- estimated savings that will result from acquiring the new machine
- depreciation method to be used on the new machine
- estimated cash inflow or trade-in value of the old machine
- estimated tax consequences resulting from disposal of the old machine
- current tax rate

Each of these items has a role in evaluating the economic consequences of the decision. Relevant costs and relevant cash inflows are those costs and revenues that matter in making a particular decision. Other items, particularly costs associated with the old machine, are irrelevant in that they play no role in the replacement decision. The following items, though important in the financial accounting system of the firm, play no part in the replacement decision.

- The purchase cost of the old machine. In terms of the decision to replace, this item is often referred to as a *sunk cost*, a cost incurred in the past that does not change between the decision alternatives currently under consideration. Whether the old machine is kept or replaced, this item is unchanged. As such, the purchase cost of the old machine is irrelevant to the replacement decision.

- The book value of the old machine (original cost less accumulated depreciation to date) is also irrelevant except for the tax consequences attached to any gain or loss on disposition. If the old machine is disposed of for an amount in excess of book value, there may be a taxable gain; if the old machine is disposed of for an amount less than book value, there may be a tax loss.

There are simple methods of analysis that may be used in this situation such as payback period and accounting rate of return. In this unit, however, we use the more sophisticated measures of net present value and internal rate of return. These methods are viewed by many to be more appropriate than either payback period or accounting rate of return in that they take into account the time value of money.

THE PROBLEM

Managers in the operations planning and control department have been considering replacing a painting machine in the finishing division of the assembly department. The new machine offers considerable cost savings over the equipment currently in use. The new machine is a quasi-robotic system that requires substantially less human attention, resulting in labor cost savings. Even though the old machine is still performing adequately and is expected to last for a couple of years more, the managers believe that this may be the proper time to acquire the new machine. Specifically, management would like you to answer the following questions. The impact of taxes is to be taken into account.

1. Using a 10% discount rate, what is the estimated net present value of acquiring the new machine?

2. What internal rate of return is the new machine expected to generate?

3. If the minimum acceptable rate of return on new investments at EZRydr is 10%, is replacement of the old machine justified at this time?

4. What is the impact on the net present value and the internal rate of return if the original estimates of cost savings over the life of the new machine were 15% higher than they should have been?

Departmental Data

The following items and estimates have been assembled by the accounting department and by staff specialists in the operations planning and control department regarding the disposition of the old machine and acquisition and use of the new machine:

Purchase Cost of New Machine	$190,000
Estimated Life of New Machine	4 years
Salvage Value of New Machine	$20,000
Tax Rate	30%
Depreciation Method	Straight-Line
Cash Savings Before Tax	
Year 1	$62,000
Year 2	$65,000
Year 3	$65,000
Year 4	$60,000

The old machine had an original cost of $75,000. Its current book value, original cost less accumulated depreciation, is $5,000. It is expected that the old machine will bring in $5,000 from a metal salvaging company. It is assumed that at the end of the four years, the new machine will sell for $20,000, its book value at that time, in the used machine market.

Data in the Database

The original cost of the old machine and its current book value are available in the accounting records of EZRydr. The database can also provide current operating cost data for the old machine. To forecast the cost savings achieved with the new machine, the staff must estimate the cost of operating the new machine and subtract this from the current operating cost. (Other savings, such as more efficient use of raw material are also included in these calculations.) The purchase cost of the new machine is known with some certainty, and other factors such as estimated life and salvage value are often set by management. In the future, the MIS department is expected to implement a database for proposed capital expenditures.

DEVELOPING THE SPREADSHEET

In order to answer the questions raised by EZRydr's management regarding the possibility of replacing the painting machine, we must build a spreadsheet that encompasses the relevant costs and benefits estimated for the replacement. The analysis is arrayed in the form of a spreadsheet. Time periods where the costs and benefits associated with acquiring the new machine are entered in columns. There is usually one column for the present time (period 0) and one column for each of the time periods over the life of the proposed new machine. Row labels identify the various costs and benefits. The spreadsheet is completed by entering the net inflows or outflows in the body of the table and using the proper functions for financial calculations. When you save your spreadsheet, name it MACHINE.

Start with a blank spreadsheet. In cell A1 enter EQUIPMENT REPLACEMENT DECISION. Enter the estimates that have been gathered in connection with this analysis as illustrated in Figure 13-1. Estimates of expected relevant costs and cash inflows, as well as the method of depreciation, tax rate, and the minimum acceptable rate of return required by management are entered.

```
A1: [W25] 'EQUIPMENT REPLACEMENT DECISION                                   READY


              A                     B          C         D         E         F
1   EQUIPMENT REPLACEMENT DECISION
2
3   ASSUMPTIONS:
4   Cost of New Machine       $190,000
5   Life of New Machine              4
6   Salvage Value-New Mach.    $20,000
7   Depreciation Method:     Straight-Line
8   Interest Rate                  10%
9   Tax Rate                       30%
10  Disposal Value-Old Mach.    $5,000
11                                                   Period
12                                             1         2         3         4
13  Cash Savings Before Tax              $62,000   $65,000   $65,000   $60,000
14
15
16  TAX CALCULATIONS
17
18  Cash Savings Before Tax              $62,000   $65,000   $65,000   $60,000
19  Taxes                                $18,600   $19,500   $19,500   $18,000
20  After-tax Cash Savings               $43,400   $45,500   $45,500   $42,000
21  Tax Savings: Depreciation            $12,750   $12,750   $12,750   $12,750
22  Disposal of New Machine                                            $20,000
23  Net Cash Inflows                     $56,150   $58,250   $58,250   $74,750
24
25  NPV AND IRR ANALYSIS
26                                                 Period
27                                   0         1         2         3         4
28  Cost of New Machine       $190,000
29  Disposal Value-Old Mach.    $5,000
30  Net Cash Flow           ($185,000)   $56,150   $58,250   $58,250   $74,750
31
32  Net Present Value           $9,005
33
34
35  Internal Rate of Return        12%
36
```

FIGURE 13-1 Equipment Replacement Decision Spreadsheet

In the next section of the spreadsheet, the necessary tax calculations are made. Use columns C through F to represent the four periods of the machine's life. First, in row 18 enter formulas that refer to the cells in the ASSUMPTIONS sections that contain the Cash Savings Before Tax (e.g., in C18 enter +C13). Next, in row 19 enter the amount of taxes that must be paid on the savings for each period. The rationale here is that the expected cash savings increase net income, other things being equal, and that this additional income is subject to tax at the assumed rate. In cell C19 multiply Cash Savings Before Tax by the Tax Rate (B9). Copy this formula to D19..F19.

Compute the After-tax Cash Savings in C20..F20 by subtracting Taxes from Cash Savings Before Tax. In C21 enter formulas to compute the Tax Savings: Depreciation. Because depreciation reduces net income (and taxable income), the depreciation in any period results in tax savings as follows:

$$\text{Tax Savings: Depreciation} = \text{Depreciation for Period} \times \text{Tax Rate}$$

In this case, straight-line depreciation is used, so enter the appropriate cell references to effect the following computation:

$$\text{Tax Savings: Depreciation} = \frac{\text{Cost - Salvage Value}}{\text{Life}} \times \text{Tax Rate}$$

The computation for straight-line depreciation is the same for each period, so copy C21 to D21..F21. In F22 enter +B6, the $20,000 cash inflow that is expected to be realized in period 4 from the disposal of the new machine. There are no tax consequences on this disposal. In period 4, the book value equals the assumed salvage value received, and there is no taxable gain or loss. Finally, calculate the Net Cash Inflows in C23..F23 as shown in Figure 13-1.

After completing these entries, we develop the analysis for evaluating the financial implications of the proposed machine. Enter the labels shown in rows 25 and below in Figure 13-1; then enter +B4 in cell B28 to show the cost (outflow) of the new machine in period 0. In cell B29, enter +B10 to record the amount received on disposal of the old machine. In cell B30, compute the net of the new machine cost and the old machine disposal revenue, -B28+B29. In cells C30 through F30 enter formulas that refer to the cells in the TAX CALCULATIONS section that show the amount of Net Cash Inflows.

To compute the net present value of the replacement investment, enter the formula +B30+@NPV(B8,C30..F30) in cell B32. Cell B30 is the net cash outflow in Period 0, cell B8 is the discount rate set by management for this decision, and the range C30..F30 includes the net (after-tax) cash flows over the four periods to be discounted to period 0. Because the Lotus @NPV function assumes that the first cash flow in the range occurs at the end of period 0 (beginning of period 1) and cell B30 contains a value that occurs at the beginning of period 0, that cell is not included in the range of cash flows that are discounted by the net present value function.

To complete the spreadsheet, calculate the internal rate of return of the investment by entering the formula @IRR(0.05,B30..F30) in cell B35. In this instance, the 0.05 is a user-supplied estimate of the internal rate of return. You may enter any rate that is reasonable. The closer the user-supplied estimate is to the actual rate however, the more quickly the result is returned to the spreadsheet. The range B30..F30 is the range of values over which the internal rate of return is to be computed. Note that, in this case, the range is expanded to include cell B30, which contains the initial net cost of acquiring the new machine. In the net present value calculation, the inclusion of this net cost is accomplished by adding the initial cash outlay to the net present value of the savings over the four subsequent periods.

Compare your spreadsheet to Figure 13-1. Format all dollar amounts and percentages as in the figure. Remember to save the spreadsheet before continuing.

CHECKING THE MODEL

To check your model, change both the Interest Rate and the Tax Rate to 0%. The Taxes in row 19 and the Tax Savings: Depreciation should change to zero. The Net Cash Inflows should be the same as the Cash Savings Before Tax except for column F, where the amounts differ by the $20,000 disposal value of the new machine.

Manually add the Net Cash Flows in row 30. The present value of these cash flows is the same as the future value, so the Net Present Value in B32 should be the sum of B30..F30. The Internal Rate of Return in this case is 17%.

USING THE SPREADSHEET

The EQUIPMENT REPLACEMENT DECISION spreadsheet was prepared in response to questions raised by EZRydr's management. It is now possible to use the spreadsheet to answer each of the questions.

1. Using a 10% discount rate, what is the estimated net present value of acquiring the new machine? The estimated net present value is $9,005, as revealed in the spreadsheet.

2. What internal rate of return is the new machine expected to generate? The internal rate of return expected to be generated by acquiring the new machine is 12% as revealed in the spreadsheet. There is, of course, a relationship between the net present value and the internal rate of return computations. If the net present value were exactly zero, then the internal rate of return would be exactly 10% (the discount rate used in the net present value computation). Since the net present value is positive, the internal rate of return is greater than 10%. If the net present value were negative, the internal rate of return would be less than 10%.

3. If the minimum acceptable rate of return on new investments at EZRydr is 10%, is replacement of the old machine justified at this time? Using net present value with a desired interest rate of 10% as the criterion, the answer is yes. The estimated or expected net present value is positive. Calculation of the internal rate of return also supports this conclusion. On the basis of the financial expectations surrounding this decision, it is a "go" choice. Of course, in connection with any decision, there are often other considerations that cannot be captured in financial terms. In some cases subjective disadvantages may lead management to a different conclusion despite the promising results of the financial evaluation.

4. What is the impact on the net present value and the internal rate of return if our original estimates of cost savings over the life of the new machine were 15% higher than they should have been? Using the completed spreadsheet, create a horizontal window as shown in Figure 13-2 that allows us to see the period savings in the ASSUMPTIONS section of the spreadsheet and the net present value and internal rate of return simultaneously. Edit

```
A1: [W25] 'EQUIPMENT REPLACEMENT DECISION                                READY

                A                  B          C          D          E          F
1   EQUIPMENT REPLACEMENT DECISION
2
3   ASSUMPTIONS:
4   Cost of New Machine        $190,000
5   Life of New Machine               4
6   Salvage Value-New Mach.     $20,000
7   Depreciation Method:      Straight-Line
8   Interest Rate                   10%
9   Tax Rate                        30%
10  Disposal Value-Old Mach.     $5,000
11                                                   Period
12                                            1          2          3          4
13  Cash Savings Before Tax             $53,913    $56,522    $56,522    $52,174
                A                  B          C          D          E          F
31
32  Net Present Value           ($9,246)
33
34
35  Internal Rate of Return          8%
36
```

FIGURE 13-2 Spreadsheet with Revised Assumptions

the savings amounts in cells C13 through F13, dividing each by 1.15. This reduces the estimates to the lower amounts required by the question. These changes result in a Net Present Value of -$9,246 and an Internal Rate of Return of 8%. Note that using these less optimistic estimates of savings leads to the opposite decision. In view of the 10% desired rate, the investment in the new machine is not indicated.

EXERCISES

Our initial analyses are inconclusive. Under the first set of assumptions, replacement is indicated; however, under the less-optimistic set of savings assumptions, replacement is not indicated. Use the spreadsheet you have built to answer each of the following. As you answer these questions, reset the spreadsheet to the original values before every question or subquestion.

1. Assume the cost of the new machine rises to $200,000. What is the impact on the net present value and the internal rate of return?

two spreadsheets

2. New tax laws may increase or decrease corporate tax rates. Assuming that a tax rate of 35% is likely in the near future, what decision is suggested with respect to replacement? Explore the same question for a tax rate of 25%. whether a new machine is needed to replace the old one

3. Accelerated methods of depreciation are said to be advantageous to companies in that they delay tax payments to later periods, reducing the tax impact in terms of the time value of money. One such method is the sum-of-the-years-digits method. Using your basic financial accounting text, refresh your memory of the sum-of-the-years-digits method of depreciation. Then make the appropriate changes in the spreadsheet using this method. What advantage, if any, do you observe using this accelerated method of depreciation?

4. ~~Create a window so that the spreadsheet on the screen simultaneously shows the assumptions section and the NPV and IRR analysis section.~~ Find the savings required in period 1 that reduces the net present value to 0 (a trial-and-error approach is required). What is the internal rate of return when the net present value is 0? – email

5. On a new spreadsheet (save MACHINE one last time!), enter the following stream of cash flows. Using the IRR and NPV functions, find the internal rate of return and net present value at a discount rate of 15% for this cash flow stream. To determine whether or not the formulas you have entered in the spreadsheet are working properly, make each of the calculations manually using a printed table of interest factors.

Period 0	-50,000
Period 1	20,000
Period 2	20,000
Period 3	20,000
Period 4	20,000

ENHANCEMENTS TO THE APPLICATION

There are a few enhancements that would make this spreadsheet easier to use. In this section, we point out some potential improvements. You and your instructor may determine additional enhancements that may be made.

1. Use the cell-protection feature to protect all cells except those in which the ASSUMPTIONS data are entered.

2. Using features such as Lotus's /**R**ange**I**nput and macro commands, develop a data-entry system for this spreadsheet.

3. Using your database management system, create a database command file that will extract the necessary data from database files and place it in an interim file. Add a feature to your spreadsheet that will import data from that interim file into the proper positions on the spreadsheet. (There are many methods for accomplishing this, depending on the particular software available to you.) This feature is an alternative to Enhancement 2.

4. Revise the model to allow the comparative analysis of several (up to 5) competing projects. This should include a table summarizing the results of the five alternatives.

REVIEW QUESTIONS

*1. Define "relevant" and "irrelevant costs" as they relate to the equipment replacement decision and give an example of each.

2. How do taxes impact investments in capital equipment?

*3. How does the use of the sum-of-the-years-digits method of depreciation impact the net present value of machine replacement?

4. What is meant by "the time value of money"?

*5. Why would a firm use an assumed or target rate of return in the analysis, such as the 10% used by EZRydr. Where does the 10% come from?

6. What factors other than potential financial benefits might affect the decision whether to replace a machine?

*7. What specific cost savings might be included in the estimate of savings generated by the new machine for each period. Who might provide these estimates?

ADDITIONAL READING

Additional information on decision making involving long-term investments can be found in most managerial accounting, cost accounting, and financial management texts, such as:

Horngren, C. T., and G. Foster, *Cost Accounting: A Managerial Emphasis*, 6th edition. Englewood Cliffs, NJ: Prentice-Hall, 1987.

Horngren, C. T., and G. L. Sundem, *Introduction to Management Accounting*, 7th edition. Englewood Cliffs, NJ: Prentice-Hall, 1987.

Killough, L. N., and W. E. Leininger, *Cost Accounting Concepts and Techniques for Management*, 2nd edition. St. Paul: West, 1987.

Matz, A., and M. Usry, *Cost Accounting Planning and Control*, 8th edition. Cincinnati: South-Western, 1984.

Rayburn G. R., *Principles of Cost Accounting Managerial Applications*, revised edition, Homewood, IL: Irwin, 1983.

UNIT 14 RESOURCE ALLOCATION—MAKING THE RIGHT CHOICES

Resource allocation decisions are made every day in the normal course of business. One such decision may involve maximizing profit by determining the number of units of different products to produce in the face of constraints on production capacity. Another decision might entail maximizing the rate of return by deciding what capital projects to pursue given a limited capital budget and a policy limit on the internal rate of return. These examples hint at the scope and diversity of business resource allocation decisions. In this unit you learn how to recognize a resource allocation situation, how to structure it in a mathematical format, and how to use spreadsheet software to develop "good" resource allocation information for use in decision making.

DECISION SUPPORT APPLICATION MATRIX

Accounting & Finance	Economics & Long-Range Planning	Human Resources	Marketing & Logistics	Management Information Systems	Operations Planning & Control	Executive Officers
■¤	■¤	■¤	■¤	■¤	■¤	■¤

■ Departmental area(s) in which the technique is or can be used.

¤ Departmental area(s) that provide input to or are impacted by the technique.

LEARNING OBJECTIVES

1. After completing this unit you should know

   a. the reasons that firms develop resource allocation models,

   b. the different types of resource allocation models that can be used,

   c. the general structure of linear programming models,

Contributed by Robert L. Armacost

d. the difference between optimizing and satisficing,

e. how a spreadsheet package can be used to make better resource allocation decisions.

2. After completing this unit you should be able to

a. identify resource allocation problems,

b. formulate resource allocation problems as linear programs,

c. create spreadsheets to obtain good decision information from linear programs.

BASIC CONCEPTS

Most decisions made within a firm are resource allocation decisions. There are three types of approaches that can be used to make these kinds of decisions using spreadsheets. One approach involves describing the various problem relationships in a spreadsheet and asking *what-if* questions. The spreadsheet model is able to display the consequences of changes in various elements of the model. A second approach is on a higher level. It shows not only what happens if you make a change, but also *how to* achieve a specified goal. This requires that you set a goal and work backwards through the model to find the appropriate values of the decision variables. The third approach, on a still higher level, answers the question *what is best?* Here the model must find the values of the decision variables that yield the best value for the criterion, not just some specified level that was set as a goal.

This book is filled with many different approaches and spreadsheet applications for making routine but critical decisions. For instance, you have learned that the purpose of aggregate planning is to match a firm's supply with its demand for product such that the total production costs are minimized. The spreadsheet model developed in Unit 6, however, can only represent relationships and help us compare alternatives — not find the plan that actually minimizes the costs. Similarly, with decision trees (Unit 10), you learned how to incorporate uncertainty in evaluating alternative courses of action. In these cases, as well as other applications, the firm must decide among alternatives in order to achieve something "good" while being mindful of the limited resources (people, money, equipment) available. The spreadsheet models address the what-if and how-to questions. It seems logical, however, that in these resource allocation models, there should be some set of alternatives that is *best.* The kinds of models that permit selecting the best option are called *optimization models.*

Optimization

There is normally some sort of criterion used in making a decision in a particular business situation. It may be that you wish to maximize the profit or minimize the cost associated with a particular production process, or you may wish to minimize the travel time to deliver a number of orders to customers. The criterion that you wish to maximize or minimize (i.e., optimize) is described by the *objective function.* This function includes the level of the various activities (things you do) performed by the business and the individual contribution of each activity to the profit or cost.

You seldom have a free hand in determining the "best" activity levels. There are usually certain restrictions on what you can do, and there are other requirements, such as specifying minimum levels of activities, which you *must* pursue. These restrictions and requirements are generally called *constraints*.

When you can describe the objective function and the constraints in a suitable mathematical form, the resulting mathematical programming problem of maximizing (or minimizing) the objective function, subject to satisfying the constraints, can be solved to yield the *optimal solution*. It is essential to remember that this solution is only optimal for the particular model. Because the model is an abstraction of the real world, the solution can probably be considered only "very good" in the real world.

Optimizing versus Satisficing

We obviously want to make the best decision possible in any business situation. There are many different algorithms and software packages that solve these complicated problems and give "optimal" solutions. These packages may or may not always be available. Sometimes, it helps just to know what to do to make a particular situation better.

Finding solutions that are "close enough" or "good enough" rather than optimal solutions is called *satisficing*. Although it is very difficult to use a spreadsheet package to obtain the optimal solution of even the simplest models, such software may be used quite easily in a satisficing mode to find a good solution or to improve an existing solution.

Linear Programming

Linear programming, which should not be confused with computer programming, is a mathematical technique used to select the optimal or best *program* (decision, course of action) from a set of alternative actions. It is *linear* because the relationships among the variables in the objective function and the constraints are linear or first-power relationships.

Properties. There are several properties that must be satisfied in the decision problem before it can be modeled as a linear program (LP). The first property is *proportionality*. This means that an increase in an activity level is accompanied by a proportional increase in the resources consumed and the output produced by that activity. If we increase the production level of Product X by 10%, the revenue associated with that product increases by 10% as does the hours of labor required to make Product X. The second property is *additivity*. This means that the results of two activities are added together. If it takes 10 hours of machine department labor to make one unit of Product X and 14 hours of machine department labor to make one unit of Product Y, then it will take 10 times the number of units of Product X plus 14 times the number of units of Product Y hours of machine department labor for that production level. As you can see, both proportionality and additivity are the basic ingredients for linearity. The third property is *divisibility* or *continuity*. This means that activity levels are continuous variables, and fractional amounts (e.g., 1.35 units of Product X) are possible. The fourth property is called *deterministic coefficients*. This means that all of the coefficients in the problem are determined, or known exactly (e.g., it is known that it takes exactly 10 hours of machine department labor to make one unit of Product X).

It is easy to see that these properties can be violated in practice. You may not know the coefficients exactly, or more often, you can only make integer numbers of a particular product. Sometimes there are price breaks, consequently returns to scale are not constant and proportionality is violated. At other times, there are interactions among products such that they use different total resources when made together than when they are made separately. When the properties are not satisfied, an LP model is an approximation and the results may be a good solution, but they are not necessarily optimal.

Formulation Requirements. In order to formulate a decision problem as an LP, several requirements have to be met. First you have to be able to identify the activities in your situation. Activities are the things you do. They are the controllable variables. Typically you want to know what activities you should do and at what level they should be done to achieve the best result. Next you have to identify the limited resources that are consumed (e.g., time, material) and any minimum and maximum levels of activity imposed by management policy or market conditions (e.g., maximum quantity of a product that can be sold in a period, or minimum staffing level). In addition to knowing the levels of the limited resources that are available, you must also know how much of each resource is consumed in performing a given activity at the unit level (e.g., 10 hours of machine department labor for each unit of Product X). With these factors identified, you must state a single criterion or objective that the firm wishes to maximize (e.g., profit, revenue) or minimize (e.g., cost). You must then be able to express this objective and the various requirements and restrictions as mathematical equations or inequalities.

Linear Programming Example

As you know, EZRydr has decided to produce snowmobiles and ATVs. Suppose that they are considering production of the ATVs at the plant that now produces only the Boss Hog motorcycle. In the example that follows, we analyze the level of operations at that plant for a hypothetical month. Both ATVs and Boss Hogs require machine department and assembly department work. Each Boss Hog requires 10 hours of machine department labor and 17 hours of assembly department labor. Each ATV requires 14 hours of machine department labor and 12 hours of assembly department labor. The marketing department has projected maximum sales of 30 Boss Hogs in the month, while requiring that at least 14 units be produced. Market research also indicates maximum sales of 25 ATVs for the month. Given the current labor conditions at the plant, there are 450 hours of machine department labor and 600 hours of assembly department labor available during the month. The finance department has provided expected profit figures of $400 for each Boss Hog and $300 for each ATV produced and sold. It is also assumed that each unit produced will be sold. Your task is to develop a production plan that maximizes the profit to EZRydr.

Problem Formulation. The activities are to produce Boss Hogs and ATVs. We must determine how many of each to produce. The machine and assembly departments labor hours are the limited resource restrictions; the marketing department has provided production requirements. To see what is happening, we look at each constraint algebraically and graphically.

To start, specify variables for each activity. Let HOG represent the number of Boss Hogs produced and let ATV represent the number of ATVs produced. The problem is to determine the optimal value of these variables, that is, the number of motorcycles and ATVs to produce in order to maximize profit. Assume that all of the properties of a linear program are satisfied, and that EZRydr can (at least for planning purposes) produce fractional numbers of these vehicles.

The total machine department labor used is the sum of the hours of labor used in making the motorcycles and ATVs, namely

Machine Department Labor = 10 HOG + 14 ATV

Because machine department labor is restricted to 450 hours or less, the total labor used cannot exceed that amount; this is the first constraint:

10 HOG + 14 ATV $\leq$ 450

To get an idea of what is taking place in LP, it is helpful to look at this kind of simple problem graphically. The first task is to graph the machine department labor constraint. Note that the constraint is an inequality. An inequality always divides an area into two parts. The first part includes all points that satisfy the inequality and the second part includes all points that do not satisfy it. To plot the inequality, first plot the equation. Then use a test point to see if it satisfies the inequality. (A common test point is the origin, where all of the variables equal zero, e.g., HOG = 0, ATV = 0.) If the test point satisfies the inequality, then the inequality represents the area that includes the point; otherwise, it is the other part. Figure 14-1 illustrates the plot of the machine department inequality. Arrows in the figure point to the area satisfying the inequality.

The available assembly department labor of 600 hours also restricts the number of vehicles that can be produced. As with the machine department, this represents another less-than inequality constraint:

17 HOG + 12 ATV $\leq$ 600

If you add the assembly department constraint to the problem, you further restrict the possible solutions. Now two inequalities must be satisfied, as illustrated in Figure 14-2.

The marketing department has placed some requirements and restrictions on the numbers of vehicles that can be produced: at least 14 and no more than 30 HOGs, and no more than 25 ATVs. Algebraically, these inequalities are

HOG $\leq$ 30
HOG $\geq$ 14
ATV $\leq$ 25

We have now identified the constraints imposed by the organization. In LP, the decision variables (i.e., HOG and ATV) must have non-negative values (i.e., $\geq$ 0). When these last constraints are added to the graph, the set of points that satisfies all of the constraints simultaneously is called the *feasible region*: the shaded area in Figure 14-3.

One of the common difficulties in formulating LP problems is inclusion of constraints that cannot all be satisfied simultaneously. Suppose, for example, that the marketing department requires production of at least 25 ATVs. Instead of being below the line ATV = 25, the area that satisfies this new constraint would be above that line in Figure 14-3. A look at Figure 14-3 shows that you cannot satisfy this new marketing department constraint if you are

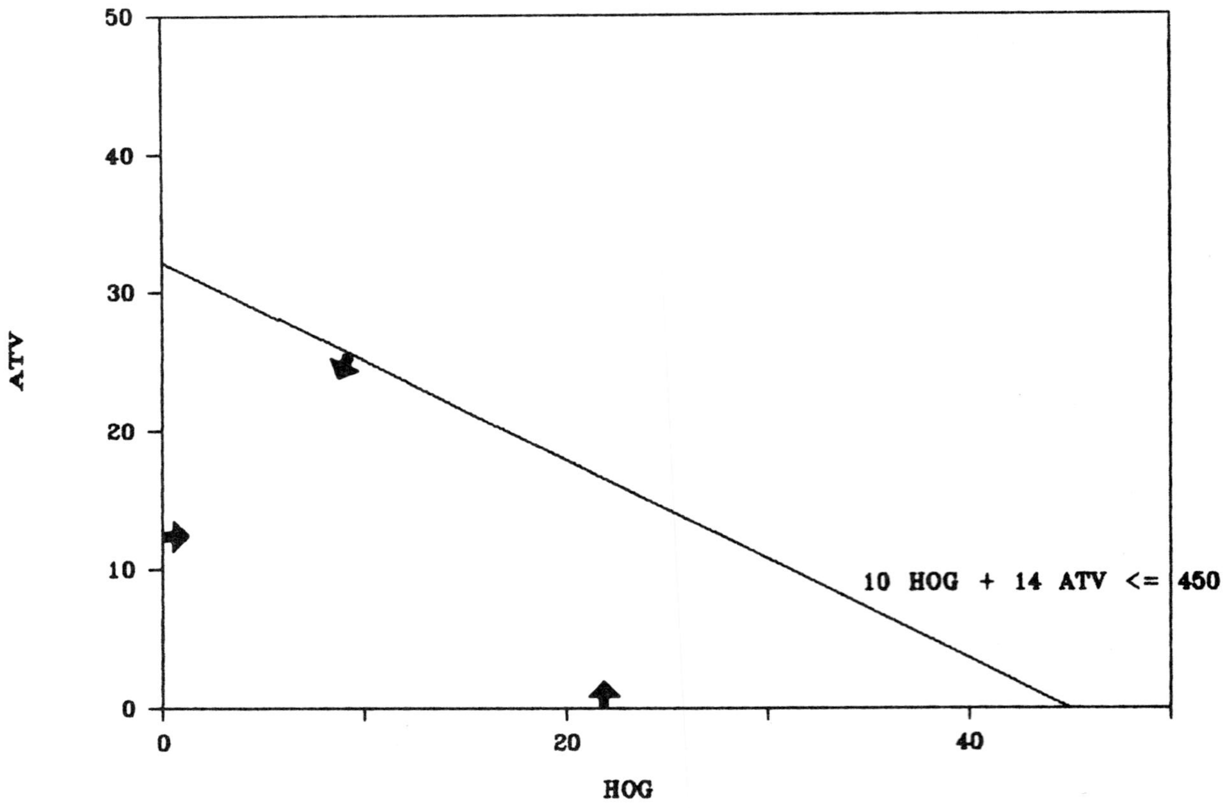

FIGURE 14-1 Machine Department Constraint

satisfying all of the others. This set of constraints is said to be *infeasible*, which usually occurs when an inappropriate constraint is included or when there is bad data for one or more of the coefficients.

With the constraints and feasible region specified, we next look at the *criterion function* (objective function). We want to maximize profit, so we must define an objective function that represents the total profit and depends on the decision variables. Recall that the expected profit for the sale of a Boss Hog is $400 and for the sale of an ATV is $300. Multiplying by the number of units produced and adding the results, the total profit is

PROFIT = 400 HOG + 300 ATV

You can plot this profit function for different values of total profit. These *iso-profit contours* are illustrated in Figure 14-4 for total profits of $4,000, $8,000, and $12,000.

We have looked at all parts of the decision problem both algebraically and graphically. Now we state the entire LP. We wish to find the values of HOG and ATV that

Maximize PROFIT = 400 HOG + 300 ATV

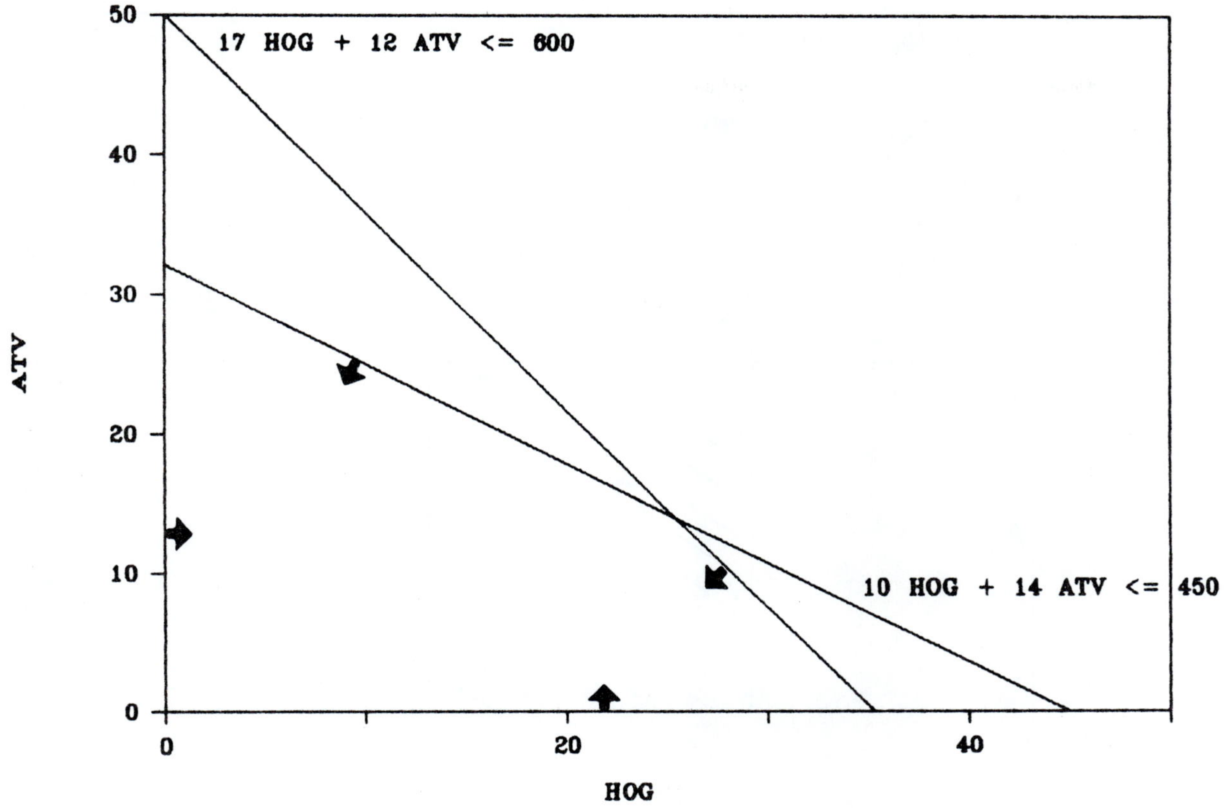

FIGURE 14-2 Assembly and Machine Department Constraints

Subject to

10	HOG	+	14	ATV	$\leq$	450		machine department labor
17	HOG	+	12	ATV	$\leq$	600		assembly department labor
1	HOG				$\leq$	30	}	
			1	ATV	$\leq$	25	}	marketing department requirements
1	HOG				$\geq$	14	}	
1	HOG				$\geq$	0	}	non-negativity requirements
			1	ATV	$\geq$	0	}	

Now that we have defined the problem, the next task is to solve it for the optimal values of HOG and ATV.

Graphical Solution. A simple problem in two variables like this one can be solved easily using graphical methods. If you superimpose the iso-profit contours of Figure 14-4 over the feasible region in Figure 14-3, you see that the objective function keeps increasing until it gets to a point on the edge of the feasible region where the objective function cannot increase further without violating the constraints. It is apparent that this must occur at a corner of the feasible region. Corner points are called *basic feasible solutions.* (Note that if the objective function is parallel to a constraint, the optimal solution includes both corner points and

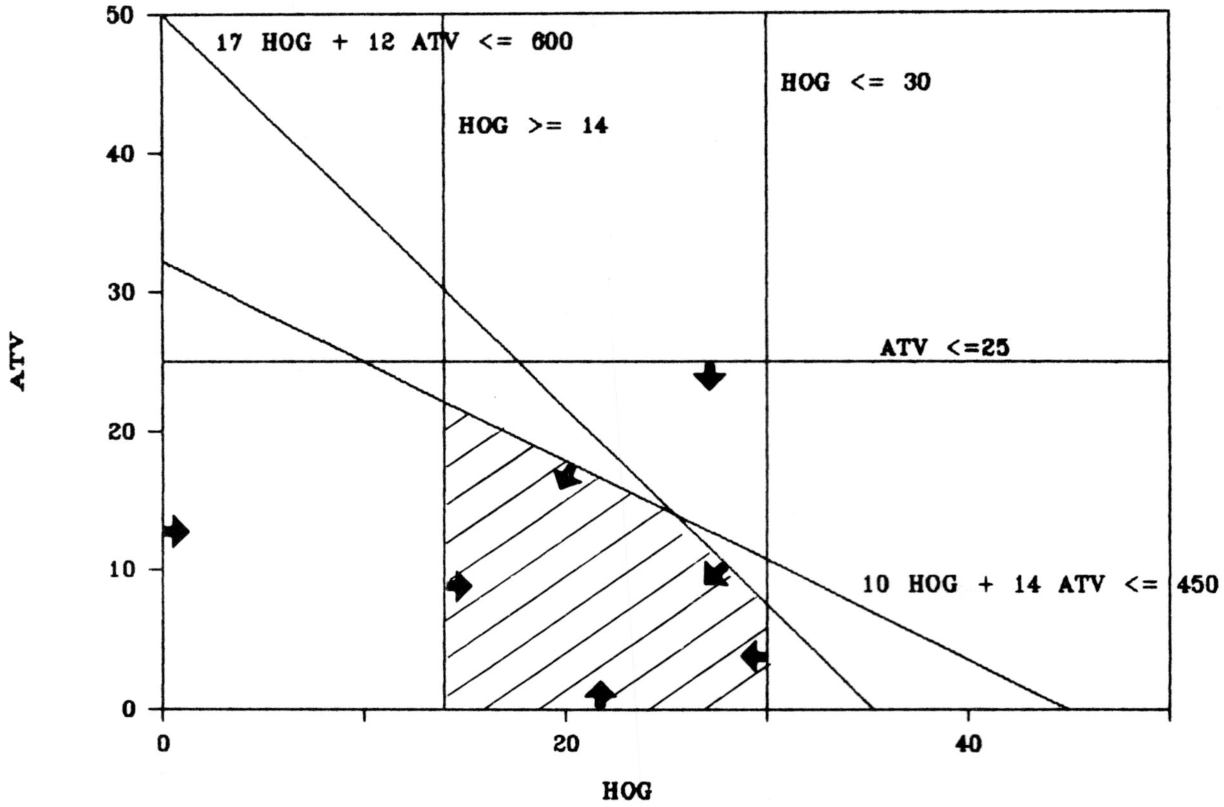

FIGURE 14-3 Constraints and the Feasible Region

all points on the line in between. These are called *alternative optima.*) The graphical solution is illustrated in Figure 14-5. The optimal solution occurs at the intersection of the machine department and assembly department labor constraints.

If you are very careful in constructing the graph, you can read the optimal solution from the coordinates of the solution point. Usually, though, the graph tells you which constraints are satisfied exactly (i.e., are equalities rather than inequalities at the solution point), and you then solve those equations for the optimal solution. These are called *active*, or *binding*, constraints. In this case, they are

10 HOG + 14 ATV	= 450	machine department labor
17 HOG + 12 ATV	= 600	assembly department labor

Solving these two equations simultaneously, you find that the optimal solution (denoted by asterisks after the variable names) is

HOG* = 25.424 and ATV* = 13.983

Substituting in the objective function, the maximum (or optimal) profit associated with this production plan is

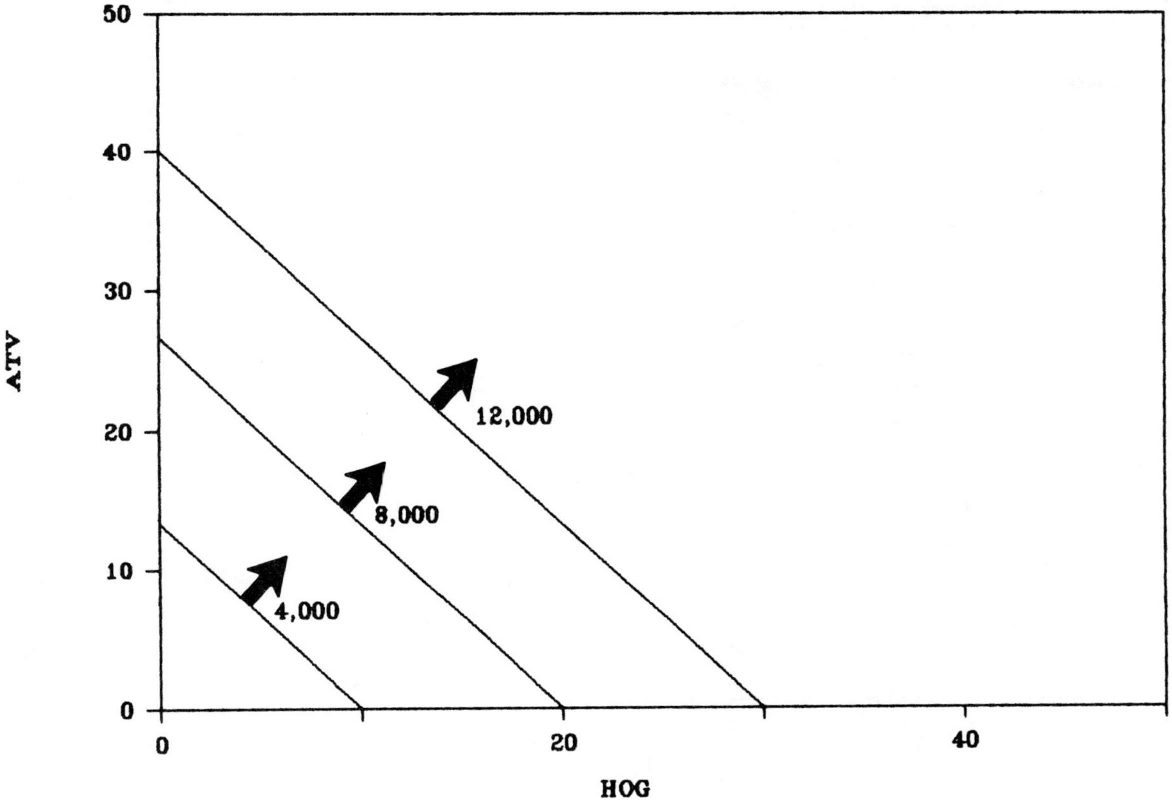

FIGURE 14-4 Iso-profit Contours

PROFIT* = $14,364.50

If you were to make a third product at this plant, such as snowmobiles, you would obviously have a much more difficult time determining the solution graphically. Nonetheless, the ideas developed here for a two-dimensional problem apply to all linear programming problems.

Simplex Method Solution. Until the late 1940s, there was no general way to solve an LP. Then George Dantzig developed a procedure, the *simplex method*, that efficiently examines the solutions at successive corner points until there can be no further improvement in the value of the objective function. Again, in Figure 14-5, you see that if you start at the point where HOG = 14 and ATV = 0, you can move to one of two adjacent corner points and the objective function increases. Once there, you move to the next one, and so on, until you reach a point where the next move would result in a decrease in the objective function. You have reached the optimal solution.

The simplex method performs this kind of search efficiently. The procedure can be used by hand for small problems, but computer assistance is usually needed for larger problems. The results for the example EZRydr problem using a microcomputer package are shown in Figure 14-6 (in this example, a package by Erikson and Hall was used: see "Application-Specific Software Packages" at the end of this unit).

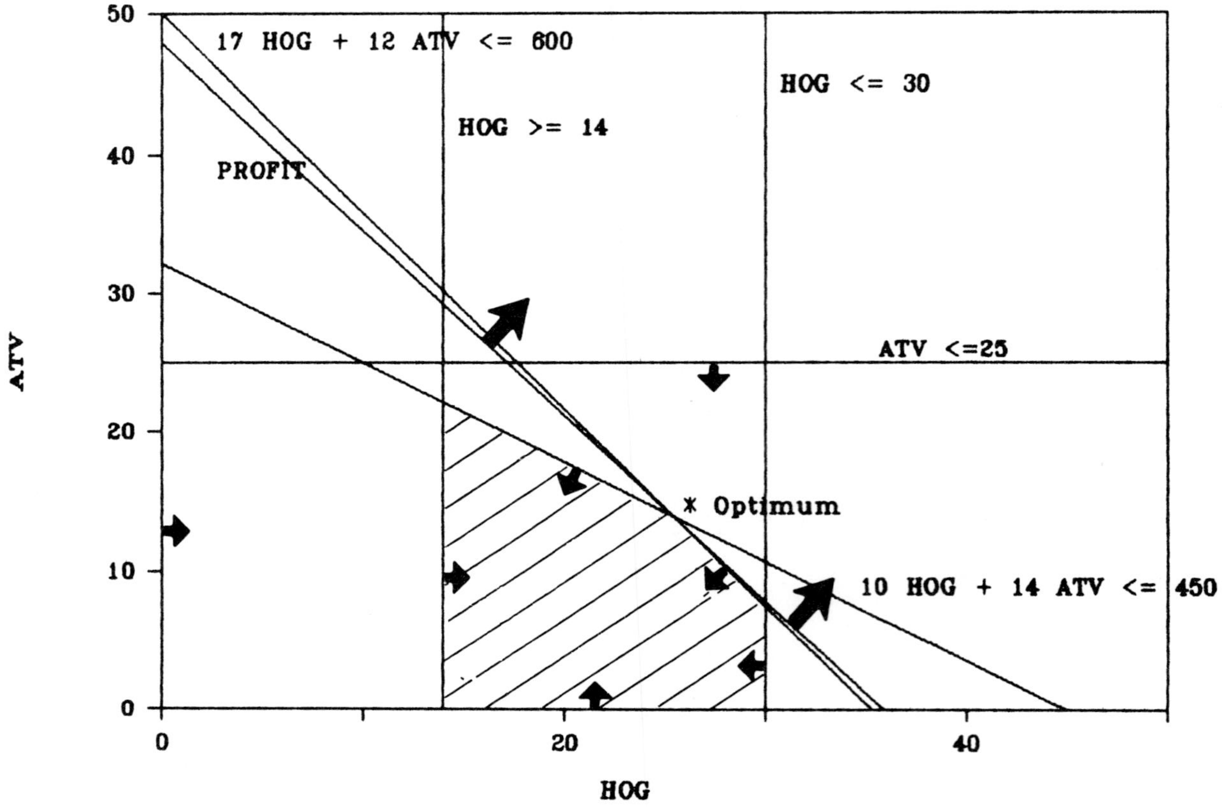

FIGURE 14-5 Graphical Solution

One of the nice features of the simplex method is that it provides data at the solution point that lets you conduct certain kinds of sensitivity analyses. In particular, you can see the effect on the objective function if you change one of the objective function coefficients or one of the right-hand side values (the limit values of the constraints). The solution also tells you how large the change can be without altering the original optimal solution. Sensitivity analysis data is also included in Figure 14-6. It tells you how much it would be worth to have another hour of machine department labor available, or how much your profit margins can increase or decrease before your production plan is affected. Spreadsheet software provides the ability to do sensitivity analysis by changing certain coefficients, including the coefficients of the constraints.

Solution by Inspection. The graphical approach is useful only for simple two-dimensional problems. The simplex method requires that we learn another algorithm. As an alternative, for problems that are not too complicated, we can use an *inspection approach* to arrive at a near-optimal solution. (This is the approach we use with a spreadsheet in this unit.) The solution-by-inspection approach does the same kind of thing as the simplex method, moving from corner to corner while improving the objective function.

-=*=- RESULTS -=*=-

VARIABLE	VARIABLE VALUE	ORIGINAL COEFFICIENT	COEFFICIENT SENSITIVITY
HOG	25.424	400	0
ATV	13.983	300	0

CONSTRAINT NUMBER	ORIGINAL RIGHT-HAND VALUE	SLACK OR SURPLUS	SHADOW PRICE
1	450	0	2.542
2	600	0	22.034
3	30	4.576	0
4	25	11.017	0
5	14	11.424	0

OBJECTIVE FUNCTION VALUE: 14364.407

-- SENSITIVITY ANALYSIS --

OBJECTIVE FUNCTION COEFFICIENTS

VARIABLE	LOWER LIMIT	ORIGINAL COEFFICIENT	UPPER LIMIT
HOG	214.286	400	425
ATV	282.353	300	560

RIGHT-HAND-SIDE VALUES

CONSTRAINT NUMBER	LOWER LIMIT	ORIGINAL VALUE	UPPER LIMIT
1	405	450	526.471
2	503.714	600	638.571
3	25.424	30	NO LIMIT
4	13.983	25	NO LIMIT
5	NO LIMIT	14	25.424

FIGURE 14-6 Simplex Method Solution and Sensitivity Analysis

Solution by inspection proceeds as follows:

1. Start with an initial feasible solution, at the intersection of two constraints. Compute the value of the objective function. Compute the contribution ratios (as described below).

2. Compute slack and surplus values, and allowable changes (these terms are defined below).

3. Determine which variables to change:

   a. Among those variables that have allowable changes, pick the variable that has the greatest desired effect on the objective function (e.g., the variable with the largest positive coefficient in a function that you are attempting to maximize). This is the *increase variable.*

b. Next, among those variables that have a positive value, pick the variable that has the least desired effect on the objective function (e.g., the variable with the smallest positive coefficient in a function that you are attempting to maximize). This is the *decrease variable*. If no other variable has a positive value, then there is no decrease variable.

4. Change the increase variable by the amount of its minimum allowable change.

5. Check the new solution for feasibility:

   a. For "less than" constraints, if the slack is less than zero then the solution is *not* feasible.

   b. For "greater than" constraints, if the surplus is less than zero then the solution is *not* feasible.

   c. For "equal" constraints, if the equality is not satisfied then the solution is *not* feasible.

6. If the solution is feasible, then proceed to step 7. If the solution is *not* feasible, obtain a feasible solution by alternately changing the decrease and increase variables by the amount of their allowable changes (which should eventually converge on zero). A feasible solution can also be obtained by solving the affected equations simultaneously.

7. Determine if further changes can be made to improve the objective function value. If no further changes that improve the objective function are possible, an optimal or near-optimal solution has been reached.

   a. If there is no constraint with slack or surplus, then no further change can be made (this is almost never the case).

   b. Look at the allowable changes. Determine if there are one or more allowable changes that would increase the value of the objective function. Identify increase and decrease variables following the logic in step 3.

   c. Consider the changes identified in step 7b vis-a-vis variables currently in the solution. First, any change that would exactly reverse the previous change will not improve the objective function (i.e., if the previous change was to increase variable X and decrease variable Y, then any change that would increase Y and decrease X is not indicated.)

      Second, for any constraint that has no slack or surplus (allowable changes for all variables are zero — a *binding constraint*), you must determine whether a change in the increase variable would yield greater benefit than the corresponding change in the decrease variable. This is determined by comparing the contribution ratios of the two variables for this constraint. If the contribution ratio of the increase variable is greater than the contribution ratio of the decrease variable, then the change is indicated and you should proceed from step 4, above. Otherwise, the change is not appropriate.

   d. If steps 7b and 7c fail to identify an acceptable change, then stop, an optimal or near-optimal solution has been reached.

This procedure is best illustrated by example, using the previous maximization problem:

Maximize PROFIT = 400 HOG + 300 ATV

Subject to

(1)	10 HOG	+	14 ATV	$\leq$	450	machine department labor
(2)	17 HOG	+	12 ATV	$\leq$	600	assembly department labor
(3)	1 HOG			$\leq$	30 }	
(4)			1 ATV	$\leq$	25 }	marketing department requirements
(5)	1 HOG			$\geq$	14 }	
(6)	1 HOG			$\geq$	0 }	non-negativity requirements
(7)			1 ATV	$\geq$	0 }	

Because the profit coefficients are positive in the objective function, the easiest starting point is at the lower limit of each variable since that point does not violate any of the other constraints and is feasible.[1] This gives the lowest possible value for PROFIT and also starts us at a corner point. Constraint (5) requires that HOG $\geq$ 14 and non-negativity condition (7) requires that ATV $\geq$ 0. Substituting into the objective function

PROFIT = \$400 x 14 + \$300 x 0 = \$5600

Variable	HOG	ATV	PROFIT
	14.000	0.000	\$5,600.00

The *contribution ratio* for each variable and constraint combination is calculated by dividing the objective function coefficient for a variable by the constraint coefficient for that variable. Where the variable does not appear in a constraint, there is no contribution ratio (indicated by ***).

Constraint	(1)	(2)	(3)	(4)	(5)	(6)	(7)
HOG Contribution Ratio	40.0	23.5	400	***	400	400	***
ATV Contribution Ratio	21.4	25.0	***	300	***	***	300

We next determine if there are any limited resources left that allow an increase in production (and profit). Here we introduce two new terms: slack and surplus. For a "less-than" inequality constraint, the difference between the resources available (the right-hand side value) and the resources used (the left side of the inequality) is called the *slack* [e.g., for constraint (1), 10 x 14 + 14 x 0 = 140; thus slack is 450 - 140 = 310 hours]. This is the amount of resources still available to be used. For a "greater-than" inequality constraint, the difference between the expression on the left side and the right-hand side value is called the *surplus*. This represents the excess produced above the minimum requirement. Where the slack or surplus equals zero, the constraint is said to be a *binding constraint*. The slack and surplus values for the seven constraints at the starting solution are shown in the following table. Binding constraint numbers are enclosed in [brackets].

---

[1] Suppose you had another policy constraint, one that required a combined output of at least 15 vehicles. Mathematically, the constraint would be HOG + ATV $\geq$ 15. In this case, the initial solution using the lower limits would not be feasible, and you would have to increase one or more of the variables until a feasible solution was found.

Constraint	(1)	(2)	(3)	(4)	[5]	(6)	[7]
Slack	310	362	16	25			
Surplus					0	14	0

The slacks on constraints (1)-(4) mean that there are unused resources. Each objective function coefficient represents the *marginal return* for one unit increase in the corresponding variable (i.e., increasing HOG production by one unit increases PROFIT by $400). Clearly, increasing HOG by one unit has the greater marginal return. We divide the slacks and the negative of the surpluses by the constraint coefficients for a variable to yield *allowable changes*. These indicate the number of units by which we can increase that variable without violating ≤ constraints and the number of units by which we can decrease that variable without violating ≥ constraints.

Constraint	(1)	(2)	(3)	(4)	[5]	(6)	[7]
Slack	310	362	16	25			
Surplus					0	14	0
HOG Coefficients	10.0	17.0	1.0	0.0	1.0	1.0	0.0
HOG Allowable Changes	31.0	21.3	16.0	***	0.0	-14.0	***
HOG Contribution Ratio	40.0	23.5	400	***	400	400	***
ATV Coefficients	14.0	12.0	0.0	1.0	0.0	0.0	1.0
ATV Allowable Changes	22.1	30.2	***	25.0	***	***	0.0
ATV Contribution Ratio	21.4	25.0	***	300	***	***	300

Positive entries in the allowable changes rows indicate allowable increases due to slack resources; negative entries indicate allowable decreases due to surplus conditions. The *** entries indicate that the constraint does not include the variable.

Because we have slack, we wish to increase the value of one of our variables. HOG has the greater desired effect on the objective function, so we designate HOG as the *increase variable*. In this case, there is no *decrease variable*. The minimum allowable change for HOG is 16.00 [constraint (3)]; therefore, we increase the value of HOG by that amount:

Variable	HOG	ATV	PROFIT
	30.000	0.000	$12,000.00

We check each constraint to see if these variable values are feasible (they are). This solution is better than the previous solution (by $6,400). We now calculate new slacks, surpluses, and allowable changes.

Constraint	(1)	(2)	[3]	(4)	(5)	(6)	[7]
Slack	150	90	0	25			
Surplus					16	30	0
HOG Coefficients	10.0	17.0	1.0	0.0	1.0	1.0	0.0
HOG Allowable Changes	15.0	5.3	0.0	***	-16.0	-30.0	***
HOG Contribution Ratio	40.0	23.5	400	***	400	400	***
ATV Coefficients	14.0	12.0	0.0	1.0	0.0	0.0	1.0
ATV Allowable Changes	10.7	7.5	***	25.0	***	***	0
ATV Contribution Ratio	21.4	25.0	***	300	***	***	300

Slack still exists, but we can no longer increase HOG because of the zero allowable change in constraint (3). Therefore ATV is the increase variable and HOG is the decrease variable. The lowest allowable change for ATV is 7.5, which we implement:

Variable	HOG	ATV	PROFIT
	30.000	7.500	$14,250.00

Upon checking, we note that this solution is feasible and the objective function value has improved. Recompute slack, etc.

Constraint	(1)	[2]	[3]	(4)	(5)	(6)	(7)
Slack	45	0	0	17.5			
Surplus					16	30	7.5
HOG Coefficients	10.0	17.0	1.0	0.0	1.0	1.0	0.0
HOG Allowable Changes	4.5	0.0	0.0	***	-16.0	-30.0	***
HOG Contribution Ratio	40.0	23.5	400	***	400	400	***
ATV Coefficients	14.0	12.0	0.0	1.0	0.0	0.0	1.0
ATV Allowable Changes	3.2	0.0	***	17.5	***	***	-7.5
ATV Contribution Ratio	21.4	25.0	***	300	***	***	300

There is still slack in the machine department. Constraint (3) prohibits the increase of HOG, but we can increase ATV and remain within the limit imposed by constraint (4). We note that constraint (2) is a binding constraint, however, and therefore we must analyze any further change in our increase variable (ATV) versus the decrease variable (HOG). Note that the contribution ratio for ATV on constraint (2) is higher than that for HOG (25.0 versus 23.5) and thus, any change that decreases HOG and increases ATV along this constraint is profitable. We increase ATV by its minimum allowable change:

Variable	HOG	ATV	PROFIT	
	30.000	10.714	$15,214.20	*infeasible*

Constraint	[1]	(2)	[3]	(4)	(5)	(6)	(7)
Slack	0	-38.6	0	14.3			
Surplus					16	30	10.7
HOG Coefficients	10.0	17.0	1.0	0.0	1.0	1.0	0.0
HOG Allowable Changes	0.0	-2.3	0.0	***	-16.0	-30.0	***
HOG Contribution Ratio	40.0	23.5	400	***	400	400	***
ATV Coefficients	14.0	12.0	0.0	1.0	0.0	0.0	1.0
ATV Allowable Changes	0.0	-3.2	***	14.3	***	***	-10.7
ATV Contribution Ratio	21.4	25.0	***	300	***	***	300

We note that this solution is not feasible because it violates the assembly department constraint (slack is -38.6 hours). We must determine values for HOG and ATV that satisfy constraints (1) and (2) simultaneously. One method of accomplishing this is to alternatively reduce the decrease variable and increase the increase variable by minimum allowable change values until the slack for the two constraints is reduced to zero. Here, the next step is to reduce HOG by 2.3 units. That will create slack that can be consumed by increasing ATV. Eventually the slack for constraints (1) and (2) will be zero. (We can achieve this result more quickly by solving the two binding constraints simultaneously. See "Enhancements to the

Application" for suggestions.) The solution is

Variable	HOG	ATV	PROFIT	
	25.424	13.983	$14,364.50	*feasible*

Constraint	[1]	[2]	(3)	(4)	(5)	(6)	(7)
Slack	0	0	4.6	11.0			
Surplus					11.4	25.4	14.0
HOG Coefficients	10.0	17.0	1.0	0.0	1.0	1.0	0.0
HOG Allowable Changes	0.0	0.0	4.6	***	-11.4	-25.4	***
HOG Contribution Ratio	40.0	23.5	400	***	400	400	***
ATV Coefficients	14.0	12.0	0.0	1.0	0.0	0.0	1.0
ATV Allowable Changes	0.0	0.0	***	11.0	***	***	-14.0
ATV Contribution Ratio	21.4	25.0	***	300	***	***	300

The next possible change is to further increase ATV while decreasing HOG, moving along constraint (1). (Recall that we do not reverse the direction of the previous change.) This change is not indicated, however, because the contribution ratio is in favor of HOG (40.0 versus 21.4). Therefore, we have reached a final solution:

Variable	HOG*	ATV*	PROFIT*
	25.424	13.983	$14,364.50

Solution by inspection is not as efficient as the simplex method if you have simplex software available. But, unlike the graphical procedure, it can be used when there are more than two decision variables. The approach illustrated above can be used to determine whether a proposed solution is feasible, and to guide the search for an improved solution to a linear program.

Extensions. There are two variations from the above example that you may encounter. The first is that the objective function may be one that you wish to minimize. In such cases, the solution-by-inspection procedure is adjusted to pick changes allowed by surplus constraints that result in the greatest decrease in the objective function value. (Another way to handle a minimization problem is to maximize the negative of the objective function.) A second variation may be the inclusion of equality constraints as well as inequality constraints. Here, you are limited to variable values that satisfy the equalities.

GATHERING THE DATA

Within the Company

Data requirements for resource allocation models depend on the degree of refinement of the model and the intended application. A very complex model requires a larger amount of detailed data. A large portion of that data should be available within company records. Other data must be obtained using some sort of sampling procedure.

When unit profit margins are of interest, unit revenue (selling price) and unit cost must be known. The unit revenue may be a management decision, but more often it is based on some sort of market analysis, which in turn may depend on external factors. For existing products, the unit cost is typically known from past experience; for new products, engineering projections are required.

Company records usually include data on the production volume of the various product lines and the total labor used in the relevant departments. However, those records may not include the labor breakdown by department for each type of unit. In the example above, the average machine department labor hours required to produce a HOG is needed. There may be specific job-labor accounting sheets that have this data. On the other hand, it may be necessary to collect this data by sampling. For a new product, such labor estimates may have to be based on engineering computations or derived experimentally in a prototype operation.

External to the Company

In this example, the major data for resource allocation obtained external to the company concerns the demand forecast. Although part of that data is based on the company's experience (and internal data), a reasonable part of it depends on evaluations of external factors, competitors, and market research, particularly with regard to new products (see Unit 8). In other situations, external consultants may be asked to determine various parameters of the problem.

THE PROBLEM

EZRydr has decided to diversify its production to include snowmobiles and ATVs. Initially only one model of each type of new vehicle will be produced. This production will be integrated with the existing production of motorcycles. EZRydr manufactures five models of motorcycles. The Boss Hog is the heavy, cruising motorcycle. The Buffalo Scout is the heavy-duty dirt bike. The Super Sport is the 2000 cc racing motorcycle. The Easy Rider is the 750 cc touring motorcycle. The Rough Kid is the lightweight dirt bike. The actual production plan is developed on a monthly basis.

The production process involves four major departments: machining, major assembly, finish assembly, and test and inspection. The marketing department has provided a forecast of the demand for each type of product for the next month, and the sales department has provided the required deliveries for each product for the next month based on current contracts. All sales are to wholesale dealers at a fixed price. The finance department has determined the actual manufacturing cost of each product, so the unit profit margins are known. The president of EZRydr has determined that no more than 40% of the motorcycle production (in units) can be in the dirt bike category and no more than 20% of the total production can be in snowmobiles and ATVs.

EZRydr's management would like you to develop a production plan to determine how many snowmobiles, ATVs, and motorcycles of each type they should produce in the coming month. What would be the resulting profit? In addition to determining the production plan, there are several other questions for which management wants answers. The sales department has recommended that the wholesale price of every unit be reduced by $100. How would that affect the production plan and the profit? The company feels that they can hire two part-time employees. Assuming that all costs remain unchanged and that each employee can contribute 35 hours per month, to which departments should they be assigned?

Departmental Data

The following data have been assembled from the various departments.

	Boss Hog	Super Sport	Easy Rider	Buffalo Scout	Rough Kid	Snow-mobile	ATV
Unit Profit($)	500	450	300	375	200	375	400
Demand Forecast	50	190	400	150	250	40	120
Minimum Sales	30	75	200	80	100	0	0
Machining/Unit (hrs)	10.0	8.0	6.0	7.5	4.0	8.0	14.0
Major Assembly/Unit (hrs)	17.0	14.0	12.0	13.0	9.0	11.0	12.0
Finish Assembly/Unit (hrs)	4.0	3.5	3.5	3.0	2.5	3.5	4.5
Test & Insp/Unit (hrs)	2.5	2.5	2.0	2.5	1.5	2.0	3.0

With the vacation schedules set, the shop foremen project the following labor hour availability in the next month: machining — 5000 hours; major assembly — 7000 hours; finish assembly — 2000 hours; and test & inspection — 2000 hours.

Data in the Database

The following information can be derived from the database file named TIMELOG.DBF. The hours per unit data derived from the database are more accurate than the estimates presented above. Data for unit profit, demand forecast, and minimum sales are not contained in the database; you must use the figures in the previous section.

TIMELOG contains the following fields (as well as other fields not relevant to the problem at hand):

DEPARTMENT	the name of the department in which the work is done
MODEL	model name
YEAR_MONTH	the year and month (e.g., 8708) in which the work is performed; character-type data
HOURS	the hours spent in the department working on the model during the month
COMPLETED	number of units completed during the month

With dBASE III, you can index the file on DEPARTMENT+MODEL, then use the following command to create a database file of yearly totals (for more information, see S. C. Ross, *Understanding and Using dBASE III*, Unit 17):

```
total on department+model to sum_time
```

Numeric fields (i.e., HOURS and COMPLETED) in the output file (SUM_TIME.DBF) then contain totals for each department/model combination. The required statistics may be readily extracted from the data file with a command such as

list all department, model, completed/hours

DEVELOPING THE SPREADSHEET

In developing the spreadsheet that will help answer EZRydr management's questions, we use the example problem that we solved graphically, with simplex method software, and by inspection. As a reminder, the problem was to

Maximize PROFIT = 400 HOG + 300 ATV

Subject to

(1)	10 HOG	+	14 ATV	$\leq$	450	machine department labor
(2)	17 HOG	+	12 ATV	$\leq$	600	assembly department labor
(3)	1 HOG			$\leq$	30 }	
(4)			1 ATV	$\leq$	25 }	marketing department requirements
(5)	1 HOG			$\geq$	14 }	
(6)	1 HOG			$\geq$	0 }	non-negativity requirements
(7)			1 ATV	$\geq$	0 }	

First we create a spreadsheet that will determine objective function, slack, surplus, allowable change, and contribution ratio values and provide a feasibility check. Start with a blank spreadsheet and set the default numeric format to integer. Enter RESOURCE ALLOCATION PROBLEM in the upper left corner. Enter labels in column A as illustrated in Figure 14-7. Next enter the coefficients and variable names (B3..C13, leaving B4, C4, and B5 blank at this time).

We need symbols in column D to indicate the type of constraint. These are used in if functions to indicate whether slack, surplus, or error should be calculated. Some software, such as Lotus 1-2-3 Release 1A, does not allow us to use symbols such as =, $\leq$, and $\geq$, or labels such as EQ, LE, and GE, as the operands of a relation. (Even though the particular problem does not include an equality constraint, we discuss equality constraints to make the approach more general.) So, like a baseball catcher, we must use other signals. If your software requires numeric operands, let 1 represent $\leq$, let 2 represent $\geq$, and let 3 represent =. (You could also use -1, 0, 1 or any other three numbers.) If your software does allow labels as operands of a relation, then you may enter LE and so forth in this column. The illustrations in this unit contain labels, but formulas for both situations are provided in the text. Put the relational symbols in column D.

Put the right-hand side constants in column E. Enter the values HOG = 14 (cell B4) and ATV = 0 (cell C4). This corresponds to the initial feasible solution used in the "Solution by Inspection" section. To calculate the value of the objective function, enter the formula +B3*B4+C3*C4 in cell B5. The resulting spreadsheet is shown in Figure 14-7. (You must specifically format cells B4, C4, and B5.)

```
A1: PR [W18] 'RESOURCE ALLOCATION PROBLEM                                  READY


            A                B          C       D    E       F       G       H
1   RESOURCE ALLOCATION PROBLEM
2   Variable Name          HOG        ATV
3   Coefficient            400        300
4   Variable Value      14.000      0.000
5   Objective Fn Value 5,600.00
6
7
8   Constraints:           HOG        ATV          RHS
9    Machine Dept           10         14     LE   450
10   Assembly Dept          17         12     LE   600
11   HOG Demand              1          0     LE    30
12   ATV Demand              0          1     LE    25
13   HOG Requirement         1          0     GE    14
14
15
16
17
18
19
20
```

FIGURE 14-7 Initial Spreadsheet

Put the labels Slack, Surplus, and Error in F8..H8. Next we develop a function that calculates the slack value if the constraint is a ≤ constraint, and makes some other entry if it is not. This can be done with an @IF logical function. The following are Lotus 1-2-3 functions for cell F9:

Lotus 1-2-3 Release 1A:
@IF($D9=1,$E9-($B9*$B$4)-($C9*$C$4),$Z$1)
Lotus 1-2-3 Release 2:
@IF($D9="LE",$E9-($B9*$B$4)-($C9*$C$4),$Z$1)

This expression tests for a ≤ constraint. If there is one and the constraint is not violated the function calculates the slack; if the constraint is violated, a negative number is displayed; if the constraint is not a ≤ constraint, it places the value of cell Z1 in the cell. Enter the value -10^32 in Z1. This is a large negative number and will display as **** across the column when the constraint is not a ≤ constraint. Analyze this function carefully to ensure that you understand how it works. Copy it to the other rows in this column.

Calculate the surplus in a similar way using the following formula in G9 and copying it to the other rows in that column.

Lotus 1-2-3 Release 1A:

@IF($D9=2,($B9*$B$4)+($C9*$C$4)-$E9,$Z$1)

Lotus 1-2-3 Release 2:

@IF($D9="GE",($B9*$B$4)+($C9*$C$4)-$E9,$Z$1)

The formula for surplus shows a positive value when there is surplus, a negative value when there is an error, a zero value when the constraint is binding, and **** where no value is applicable.

Calculate the error for equality constraints using the following formula in H9 and copying it to the other rows in that column.

Lotus 1-2-3 Release 1A:

@IF($D9=3,($E9-($B9*$B$4)-($C9*$C$4)),$Z$1)

Lotus 1-2-3 Release 2:

@IF($D9="EQ",($E9-($B9*$B$4)-($C9*$C$4)),$Z$1)

This formula shows zero when the equality is satisfied and a positive or negative number when it is not. As above, **** are displayed when the constraint is not applicable.

As we work through the solution-by-inspection procedure, we must remember the variable and objective function values of the previous feasible solution. We can retain these on the spreadsheet as well as calculate the difference between the currently-proposed solution and the previous solution. Refer to Figure 14-8. Enter the labels illustrated in D6, G2, and H2. In G4 and H4, enter 0. In G5, enter +B3*G4+C3*H4. In F6 enter +B5-G5, the difference between the currently-proposed solution and the previous solution. At this point, your spreadsheet should look like the top 13 rows of Figure 14-8.

The next task is to compute Allowable Changes. Enter labels in the range A15..C20. Recall that the Allowable Change is the slack or negative surplus divided by the coefficient. Therefore, we may use the following formula in B16.

@IF(B9,@MAX($F9,-$G9,$H9)/B9,$Z$1)

We leave it to you to determine what this formula accomplishes. Copy it to the other cells in the Allowable Changes section.

The Contribution Ratio section includes labels in row 15 and formulas such as this in G16:

@IF(B9,B$3/B9,$Z$1)

The resulting spreadsheet is illustrated in Figure 14-8. With this spreadsheet, for any values of HOG and ATV, we can find the value of the objective function and be able to tell if that point is a feasible solution.

```
A1: PR [W18] 'RESOURCE ALLOCATION PROBLEM                                     READY


            A               B         C       D    E       F       G       H
1   RESOURCE ALLOCATION PROBLEM
2   Variable Name         HOG       ATV                            HOG      ATV
3   Coefficient           400       300
4   Variable Value     14.000     0.000                          0.000    0.000
5   Objective Fn Value 5,600.00                                      0
6                                     Difference     5600
7
8   Constraints:          HOG       ATV        RHS    Slack Surplus   Error
9    Machine Dept          10        14   LE   450    310.0 ***************
10   Assembly Dept         17        12   LE   600    362.0 ***************
11   HOG Demand             1         0   LE    30     16.0 ***************
12   ATV Demand             0         1   LE    25     25.0 ***************
13   HOG Requirement        1         0   GE    14 ********     0.0 ********
14
15  Allowable Changes:    HOG       ATV     Contr. Ratio:      HOG      ATV
16   Machine Dept      31.000    22.143                      40.00    21.43
17   Assembly Dept     21.294    30.167                      23.53    25.00
18   HOG Demand        16.000 ********                      400.00 ********
19   ATV Demand   *********** 25.000                      ******* 300.00
20   HOG Requirement    0.000 ********                      400.00 ********
```

FIGURE 14-8 Completed Spreadsheet

CHECKING THE MODEL

The first step in checking your model is to compare it to Figure 14-8. If your model does not yield the same results, check all formulas carefully. To further test the logic, make entries for HOG and ATV (cells B4 and C4) and manually calculate the expected results. For instance, to test constraint (1), enter HOG = 20 and ATV = 20. The slack for this constraint (cell F9) should be -30 (20 x 10 + 20 x 14 = 480, which is 30 more than 450). For constraint (2), the slack should be 20; for constraint (3), 10; for constraint (4), 5; and for constraint (5), the surplus should be 6. F6 should show 14,000. HOG Allowable Changes for constraint (1) should be -3, and ATV Allowable Changes for that constraint should be -2.1, indicating that we are producing 3.0 more HOGs *or* 2.1 more ATVs than allowed. If you obtain an incorrect value for one slack or surplus, check the coefficients for that constraint (columns B and C). If you obtain incorrect values for more than one slack or surplus, check the formulas used to calculate slack or surplus values (columns F and G). (With Lotus 1-2-3, the problem may be caused by incorrect use of relative, mixed, and absolute addresses; with other software packages the problem may be caused by improper execution of the copy command.)

```
B4: (F3) U [W11] 14+16                                                    READY


              A                  B          C       D     E       F        G        H
1   RESOURCE ALLOCATION PROBLEM
2   Variable Name               HOG        ATV                               HOG      ATV
3   Coefficient                 400        300
4   Variable Value           30.000      0.000                            14.000    0.000
5   Objective Fn Value    12,000.00                                         5600
6                                                 Difference      6400
7
8   Constraints:                HOG        ATV           RHS    Slack  Surplus    Error
9    Machine Dept                10         14     LE    450    150.0 ****************
10   Assembly Dept               17         12     LE    600     90.0 ****************
11   HOG Demand                   1          0     LE     30      0.0 ****************
12   ATV Demand                   0          1     LE     25     25.0 ****************
13   HOG Requirement              1          0     GE     14 ********     16.0 ********
14
15  Allowable Changes:          HOG        ATV       Contr. Ratio:       HOG      ATV
16   Machine Dept            15.000     10.714                         40.00    21.43
17   Assembly Dept            5.294      7.500                         23.53    25.00
18   HOG Demand               0.000  ********                         400.00 ********
19   ATV Demand         ***********     25.000                       ******* 300.00
20   HOG Requirement        -16.000  ********                         400.00 ********
```

FIGURE 14-9 Spreadsheet with Second Solution

USING THE SPREADSHEET

At this point, we have set up the spreadsheet to identify feasible solutions. Now we must use the spreadsheet to identify the optimal solution or one close to it.

To solve the problem, we begin with some feasible solution, our initial best solution. Then we try another set of variable values. If feasible and if the objective function value is better than the previous solution, this new set becomes the best solution. To use this approach, we must compare the current solution with the previous best solution. We keep a record of the previous best solution in the area G2..H5 and compute the difference in F6.

We place zero values in G4 and H4 and let HOG = 14 and ATV = 0 in B4 and C4 (the initial feasible solution in the solution-by-inspection approach). We have the spreadsheet results shown in Figure 14-8. Notice that there are no negative entries for slacks or surpluses, which means that the solution is feasible.

```
C4: (F3) U [W8] 0+7.5                                                   READY


              A                 B         C      D    E      F        G       H
1    RESOURCE ALLOCATION PROBLEM
2    Variable Name            HOG       ATV                          HOG      ATV
3    Coefficient              400       300
4    Variable Value        30.000     7.500                       30.000    0.000
5    Objective Fn Value 14,250.00                                  12000
6                                           Difference      2250
7
8    Constraints:             HOG       ATV          RHS    Slack Surplus  Error
9     Machine Dept             10        14     LE   450     45.0 ***************
10    Assembly Dept            17        12     LE   600      0.0 ***************
11    HOG Demand                1         0     LE    30      0.0 ***************
12    ATV Demand                0         1     LE    25     17.5 ***************
13    HOG Requirement           1         0     GE    14 ********    16.0 ********
14
15   Allowable Changes:       HOG       ATV        Contr. Ratio:     HOG      ATV
16    Machine Dept          4.500     3.214                         40.00    21.43
17    Assembly Dept         0.000     0.000                         23.53    25.00
18    HOG Demand            0.000  ********                        400.00 ********
19    ATV Demand       ***********  17.500                       ******* 300.00
20    HOG Requirement     -16.000  ********                        400.00 ********
```

FIGURE 14-10 Spreadsheet with Third Solution

Now that we have an initial feasible solution, we attempt to improve the value of the objective function. There are unused resources (slacks greater than zero). The Allowable Changes indicate that both HOG and ATV can be increased. Because it has the larger objective function coefficient, we consider HOG first. The Allowable Changes section of the spreadsheet tells us that HOG cannot be decreased, but can be increased by as much as 16 units (minimum of the allowable increases). We copy B4..C4 to G4..H4, then add 16 to the previous value of 14, yielding 30. The spreadsheet at this point should look like Figure 14-9.

The new solution is feasible and the objective function value has improved. Is further improvement possible? There are still unused resources. Following the procedure outlined earlier, we look in the Allowable Changes section and note that HOG cannot be increased further. Therefore we next attempt to increase ATV. Noting that there is an Allowable Change of 7.5 units of ATV (see C17 in Figure 14-9), we copy the previous values from B4..C4 to G4..H4, then enter 7.5 into C4. Check F6 for improvement. The spreadsheet at this point should look like Figure 14-10.

```
C4: (F3) U [W8] 0+7.5+3.214                                           READY


              A                B        C      D   E        F        G        H
1  RESOURCE ALLOCATION PROBLEM
2  Variable Name              HOG      ATV                          HOG      ATV
3  Coefficient                400      300
4  Variable Value          30.000   10.714                       30.000    7.500
5  Objective Fn Value 15,214.20                                   14250
6                                          Difference      964
7
8  Constraints:               HOG      ATV         RHS    Slack  Surplus   Error
9   Machine Dept               10       14    LE   450      0.0 ****************
10  Assembly Dept              17       12    LE   600    -38.6 ****************
11  HOG Demand                  1        0    LE    30      0.0 ****************
12  ATV Demand                  0        1    LE    25     14.3 ****************
13  HOG Requirement             1        0    GE    14 ********   16.0 ********
14
15 Allowable Changes:         HOG      ATV       Contr. Ratio:      HOG      ATV
16  Machine Dept            0.000    0.000                        40.00    21.43
17  Assembly Dept          -2.269   -3.214                        23.53    25.00
18  HOG Demand              0.000 ********                       400.00 ********
19  ATV Demand        *********** 14.286                        ******* 300.00
20  HOG Requirement       -16.000 ********                       400.00 ********
```

FIGURE 14-11 Spreadsheet with Infeasible Solution

Next we determine if any further improvement is possible. There are still unused resources. We look in the Allowable Changes section and note that the Assembly Department constraint is binding since the Allowable Change for all variables (both HOG and ATV) is zero. The HOG Demand constraint indicates that HOG cannot be increased further. Since the Contribution Ratios associated with the Assembly Department constraint indicate that it is profitable to increase ATVs and decrease HOGs, we next attempt to increase ATV. We copy the current solution to G4..H4 and then add 3.214 to the ATV value (see Figure 14-11). Note that this solution is not feasible: there is a negative value in the Slack column. At this point we may either work toward a solution by alternately changing HOG and ATV values or we may solve the affected equations simultaneously. See "Enhancements to the Application" for an illustration of how we accomplished the latter in this case. The solution is illustrated in Figure 14-12.

Is further improvement possible? The only alternative here is to continue to increase ATV and decrease HOG. However, if we check the Contribution Ratios for the Machine Department constraint, we see that it is not profitable to continue to decrease HOG and increase ATV. Therefore, the solution in Figure 14-12 is close to an optimal solution. Unlike the simplex method for linear programming, there is no exact test to determine when you have arrived at an optimal solution using the spreadsheet/inspection approach. However, if you follow the procedure outlined you will achieve an optimum or a solution close to it.

A1: PR [W18] 'RESOURCE ALLOCATION PROBLEM READY

	A	B	C	D	E	F	G	H
1	RESOURCE ALLOCATION PROBLEM							
2	Variable Name	HOG	ATV				HOG	ATV
3	Coefficient	400	300					
4	Variable Value	25.424	13.983				30.000	7.500
5	Objective Fn Value	14,364.50					14250	
6				Difference		115		
7								
8	Constraints:	HOG	ATV		RHS	Slack	Surplus	Error
9	Machine Dept	10	14	LE	450	0.0	***************	
10	Assembly Dept	17	12	LE	600	0.0	***************	
11	HOG Demand	1	0	LE	30	4.6	***************	
12	ATV Demand	0	1	LE	25	11.0	***************	
13	HOG Requirement	1	0	GE	14	********	11.4	********
14								
15	Allowable Changes:	HOG	ATV		Contr. Ratio:		HOG	ATV
16	Machine Dept	0.000	0.000				40.00	21.43
17	Assembly Dept	0.000	0.000				23.53	25.00
18	HOG Demand	4.576	********				400.00	********
19	ATV Demand	***********	11.017				*******	300.00
20	HOG Requirement	-11.424	********				400.00	********

FIGURE 14-12 Spreadsheet with Final Solution

The above spreadsheet technique uses the solution-by-inspection procedure. An initial feasible solution is found and changes are made in the decision variables until a near-optimal solution is reached. One of the advantages of a spreadsheet model is that once a near-optimal solution is reached, the spreadsheet can be used to examine some important practical considerations. Suppose, for instance, that only integer numbers of vehicles can be made (a fractional vehicle would be one that is partially completed). The spreadsheet solution is HOG = 25.423 and ATV = 13.983. We could simply enter the integer values for HOG and ATV looking at all of the combinations, rounded up and down. In this case, since there are two variables, there are only four points: (26,14), (26,13), (25,14), and (25,13). Substituting these values in the spreadsheet, you find that the first point is infeasible, and that the point HOG = 26, ATV = 13 yields the highest profit — $14,300. This method is easy when there are only two decision variables. In general, if there are n variables, then there are 2^n points and the process is more difficult.

Sensitivity analysis is used to examine the effects of changes in a problem coefficient on a solution such as the one we have just reached. It is the typical what-if question that spreadsheets are very good at. You can use the solution-by-inspection approach to obtain a new near-optimal solution after changes in the problem coefficients are made.

```
C3: [W8] 200                                                      READY


              A                B        C      D    E        F        G       H
1  RESOURCE ALLOCATION PROBLEM
2  Variable Name              HOG      ATV                           HOG      ATV
3  Coefficient                300      200
4  Variable Value          25.424   13.983                        30.000    7.500
5  Objective Fn Value   10,423.80                                  10500
6                                          Difference       -76
7
8  Constraints:               HOG      ATV        RHS    Slack  Surplus   Error
9   Machine Dept               10       14   LE   450      0.0 ****************
10  Assembly Dept              17       12   LE   600      0.0 ****************
11  HOG Demand                  1        0   LE    30      4.6 ****************
12  ATV Demand                  0        1   LE    25     11.0 ****************
13  HOG Requirement             1        0   GE    14 ********   11.4 ********
14
15 Allowable Changes:         HOG      ATV      Contr. Ratio:      HOG      ATV
16  Machine Dept            0.000    0.000                       30.00    14.29
17  Assembly Dept           0.000    0.000                       17.65    16.67
18  HOG Demand              4.576 ********                      300.00 ********
19  ATV Demand        *********** 11.017                       ******* 200.00
20  HOG Requirement       -11.424 ********                      300.00 ********
```

FIGURE 14-13 Spreadsheet with New Objective Function Coefficients

Suppose that EZRydr cuts the price of every unit by $100. The effect of this change, using the old production plan, is illustrated in Figure 14-13. You see that the old production plan is still feasible. The available resources are nearly used up and there appears to be little room to change the production plan and still increase profits. Because the objective function coefficients have changed, however, the current solution may no longer be the optimal solution. We can check the optimality of the current solution by reanalyzing the non-binding constraints. Following the earlier procedure, we determine the new optimal solution at HOG = 30 and ATV = 7.5 with an objective function value of $10,500, up from the $10,424 using the old production plan with the new profit coefficients.

If you use the spreadsheet to explore the integer points around this solution, you find that the point HOG = 30, ATV = 7 has the objective function value of $10,400. If you explore further, you find two other points (HOG = 28, ATV = 10; HOG = 26, ATV = 13) that also have the same objective function value. These points are called *alternative optima.*

Based on this example, it should be clear that using a spreadsheet to solve a linear programming problem is more complex than most of the other applications in this book. However, the spreadsheet does lend itself to modeling a moderate-sized problem and exploring incremental changes to a given solution. The spreadsheet also provides the capability of computing the effect of changing any of the problem parameters.

The limitations associated with using the solution-by-inspection approach can be overcome in several ways. Ho (1987) has developed *OptiMacros* that use the capability of Lotus 1-2-3 Release 2 to actually solve a linear programming problem. Other programs, such as *VINO* and *What's Best* interact with spreadsheet models of LP problems and solve the LP using an add-on program. Both programs read Lotus 1-2-3 and Symphony worksheets and work in conjunction with the spreadsheet software to determine the optimal solution. This approach seems to marry the best of both worlds.

Extension to Other Types of Problems

The resource allocation problems illustrated in this chapter are linear. These types of problems occur frequently in a business environment. In addition, linear models are often used as an approximation of nonlinear models because it is more difficult to solve nonlinear models. The spreadsheet approach gives you the capability to model many nonlinear problems. You are only limited by what you can put in a cell formula and the functions available. Although modeling a nonlinear problem may be straightforward and the spreadsheet useful for asking what-if questions, solving for an optimal solution can be extremely difficult. Nonetheless, you may be able to identify feasible solutions and use the spreadsheet to search for better solutions.

The restriction that integer numbers of items be produced can be a further complicating factor. This unit illustrated an approach for dealing with the integer requirement, but this too is difficult as the problem size increases.

ENHANCEMENTS TO THE APPLICATION

The screen size is a limitation when working with a larger problem. You may therefore, find it useful to use windows when working with larger problems to ensure that the Allowable Changes and Contribution Ratio sections and the Objective Function Value are visible at the same time.

Use graphing capabilities to illustrate the constraints and current objective function value. Your graph should look like Figure 14-5.

Manually entering the variable values in the previous best solution section allows for error. You can write a macro that will copy variable values from B4 and C4 to G4 and H4. Such a macro would be of even greater value as more variables are included in the problem. Also, you should develop a second macro that will reinstate the previous best solution, that is, copying from G4..H4 to B4..C4. Finally, develop a "start-fresh" macro that enters the initial feasible solution in B4..C4 and zeros in G4..H4.

The check for feasibility can be automated. Recall that an infeasible solution is one in which there is slack or surplus less than zero or an equality is not satisfied. You need to develop a function that returns ERR if any of these is true, and **** otherwise. To accomplish that within the structure of the current worksheet requires knowledge of Lotus database statistical functions (or the equivalent for different software) and several entries. The general concept is as follows:

- Establish criterion ranges that check each of Slack, Surplus, and Error entries for a value greater than Z1.

- Enter the value .005 in Z2 (or any other convenient cell). This establishes a level of precision that accommodates rounding to three decimal places.

- Create a function that returns **** (Z1) when

  - the minimum Slack (that passes the criterion) is greater than or equal to -Z2, *and*

  - the minimum Surplus (that passes the criterion) is greater than or equal to -Z2, *and*

  - the absolute value of the sum of all Error values (that pass the criterion) is less than or equal to Z2;

  and returns ERR otherwise.

Finally, you can set up an area in the spreadsheet for solving two-variable simultaneous equations such as those in the example problem. The *cancellation method* can be adapted to this purpose. We illustrate by solving the intersection of the machine department and assembly department constraints. First, write the equations:

(1)	10	HOG	+	14	ATV	=	450	machine department labor
(2)	17	HOG	+	12	ATV	=	600	assembly department labor

Multiply (2) by the ratio of the HOG coefficients, that is 10/17, yielding (2a):

(1)	10.000	HOG	+	14.000	ATV	=	450.000	machine department labor
(2a)	10.000	HOG	+	7.059	ATV	=	352.941	assembly department labor

Subtract (2a) from (1), yielding an equation with one unknown:

0.000 HOG + 6.941 ATV = 97.059

Solve for ATV:

ATV = 97.059/6.941 = 13.983

Substitute this value into either of the original equations, solve for HOG: 25.424. A portion of the spreadsheet that accomplishes this is illustrated in Figure 14-14. You should be able to develop the relevant formulas for rows 25 through 28 based on the discussion above. This technique can be extended to solve the values of two variables in two equations when the values of all other variables are held constant.

The /**D**ata**M**atrix command of Lotus 1-2-3 Release 2 can also be used to solve simultaneous equations. The process requires that you copy the coefficients and right-hand side values for the two equations to an empty part of the worksheet, then multiply the right-hand side vector by the inverse of the coefficient matrix. Refer to Ho (see "Additional Reading") for details.

```
A21: [W18]                                                             READY


              A                B          C      D    E       F      G      H
21
22  Simultaneous Equation Solver:
23   Machine Dept              10         14     LE   450
24   Assembly Dept             17         12     LE   600
25  Scale 2nd Equation       10.0        7.1        352.9
26  Difference                0.0        6.9         97.1
27  Solve for 2nd Var                 13.983
28  Solve for 1st Var      25.424
29
```

FIGURE 14-14 Simultaneous Equation Solver

EXERCISES

The linear programming spreadsheet model is a useful tool for assisting EZRydr's management in making production planning decisions. Your task is to use a spreadsheet to model the linear programming production function and make recommendations to management about the production plan for the coming month using the data given in "The Problem" section.

1. Identify the activities and limited resources, define the decision variables, and formulate the linear programming model for EZRydr's production problem.

2. Develop a spreadsheet model for the linear program.

3. Use the spreadsheet model to develop a good production plan for EZRydr. What production levels should be planned for the seven different vehicles? What is the expected profit level?

4. What will be the impact on the production plan and the profit if the sales department's recommendation to reduce the wholesale price (and company net profit) by $100 per vehicle is adopted?

5. Management is considering hiring two part-time employees. Assume that all costs remain unchanged and that each employee can effectively contribute 35 hours per month. Should any employees be hired? If so, how many, and to which departments should they be assigned?

REVIEW QUESTIONS

*1. What are the basic criteria that must be satisfied in order to use a linear programming model?

2. When an LP model is solved, is the solution really optimal?

3. How can a spreadsheet model assist in solving a linear programming problem?

*4. What are the limitations in using a spreadsheet in solving a linear programming problem?

ADDITIONAL READING

To understand more about linear programming, refer to any introductory management science textbook; see, for example,

Anderson, D. R., D. J. Sweeney, and T. A. Williams. *Quantitative Methods for Business.* St. Paul: West, 1986.

Eppen, G. D., F. J. Gould, and C. P. Schmidt. *Introductory Management Science*, 2nd edition. Englewood Cliffs, NJ: Prentice-Hall, 1987.

These books discuss software programs that have been developed to work in conjunction with spreadsheet software to solve linear programming problems:

Ho, J. K. *Linear and Dynamic Programming with Lotus 1-2-3 Release 2.* Portland, OR: Management Information Source, 1987.

Cunningham, K., and L. Schrage. *Optimization in Spreadsheets with VINO.* Redwood City, CA: Scientific Press, 1987.

APPLICATION-SPECIFIC SOFTWARE PACKAGES

A number of PC-based software packages have been developed specifically for solving linear programming problems in conjunction with spreadsheet software, including the following:

VINO. The Scientific Press, 507 Seaport Court, Redwood City, CA 94063-2731. (415) 366-2577.

What's Best!. General Optimization, 2251 North Geneva Terrace., Chicago, IL 60614. (800) 441-BEST.

There are a number of textbooks with accompanying menu-driven software packages that include a linear programming capability for small (less than 40 variables and constraints) such as:

Chang, Y., and R. S. Sullivan. *Quantitative Systems for Business.* Englewood Cliffs, NJ: Prentice-Hall, 1986.

Dennis, T. L., and L. B. Dennis. *Microcomputer Models for Management Decision-Making.* St. Paul: West, 1986.

Erikson, W. J., and O. P. Hall, Jr. *Computer Models for Management Science.* Reading, MA: Addison-Wesley, 1986.

For larger problems, one of the more popular LP packages is

LINDO. The Scientific Press, 507 Seaport Court, Redwood City, CA 94063-2731. (415) 366-2577.

APPENDIX

A GLOSSARY OF LOTUS 1-2-3 COMMANDS, FUNCTIONS, FEATURES

This appendix[1] presents lists of Lotus 1-2-3 commands and functions as well as a brief discussion of some of the features of the program. It is intended to be a quick reference for persons who are using Lotus in conjunction with this book, and as a cross-reference for those who are using a different spreadsheet product. For persons in the latter category, we have provided a space where you can enter equivalent commands and functions for your particular product.

LOTUS 1-2-3 COMMANDS

Following is an outline of the various command hierarchies of Lotus 1-2-3, Release 2. For more information, consult *Understanding and Using Lotus 1-2-3 Release 2.*

________ /Worksheet *commands in this series generally affect the entire workspace.*

________ Global *used to set default values.*

________ Format *establishes the format of all numeric entries not specifically formatted by /RangeFormat; allowable formats are Fixed, Scientific, Currency, , (comma), General, +/-, Percent, Date, Text, and Hidden.*

________ Label-Prefix *establishes default alignment of subsequently-entered labels (text); choices are Left, Right, and Center.*

________ Column-Width *establishes width of all columns not specifically set by /WorksheetColumnSet-width.*

________ Recalculation *determines automatic or manual recalculation, row- or columnwise or natural order, and number of iterations.*

________ Protection *sets protection on or off for the entire worksheet, when enabled changes can be made to only those cells that have been unprotected by /RangeUnprotect.*

---

[1] The material in this appendix is excerpted from: S. C. Ross, *Understanding and Using Lotus 1-2-3 Release 2* published in 1987 by West Publishing Company.

/Worksheet
Global, continued

________ Default *establishes operating system defaults for Printer, Directory, and Other features.*
________ Zero *suppresses the display of any cell that evaluates to 0 (zero).*
________ Insert *adds a blank column or row to the worksheet, adjusting all formulas that refer to displaced cells.*
________ Delete *removes a column or row from the worksheet, adjusting all formulas that refer to displaced cells.*
________ Column *allows the width of a specific column to be changed, also allows an entire column to be hidden from display.*
________ Erase *clears the worksheet and all settings.*
________ Titles *freezes rows or columns so they remain on the screen when text is scrolled right or down.*
________ Window *allows display of two different portions of the worksheet at once.*
________ Status *displays information concerning memory usage, current settings of default settings, and location of circular logic.*
________ Page *inserts a page break when the worksheet is printed.*

________ /Range *commands in this series generally affect only a portion of the worksheet.*
________ Format *establishes the format for all numeric values in the range; choices are the same as /WorksheetGlobalFormat.*
________ Label *changes alignment of labels already entered into the worksheet.*
________ Erase *blanks an area of the worksheet.*
________ Name *allows the assignment of a name to an area of the worksheet, the name can be entered by the user or drawn from adjacent cells.*
________ Justify *changes arrangement of label (text) entries in a series of vertically contiguous cells.*
________ Protect *re-establishes protection of cells that have been /RangeUnprotected.*
________ Unprotect *designates cells that can be changed when /WorksheetGlobalProtection is enabled.*
________ Input *restricts user data entry to a specified range of unprotected cells.*
________ Value *copies the values of a range of formulas.*
________ Transpose *transposes a range of numbers (not recommended for use with formulas).*

________ /Copy *duplicates cell entries (see discussion of relative, absolute, and fixed cell reference in the "Features" section of this appendix).*

________ /Move *relocates cell entries; in Lotus, this command does not insert blank space for the cells moved, any previously existing data is overwritten.*

________ /File *commands in this series are used to move data to and from disk storage.*
________ Retrieve *loads a worksheet file, anything currently in the worksheet is lost.*
________ Save *places the current worksheet on a disk.*
________ Combine *incorporates all or part of one worksheet into the current worksheet; contents of incoming worksheet overwrite current data, or are added to or subtracted from current data.*
________ Xtract *places a portion of the current worksheet on a disk; either formulas or the current values of the formulas can be saved.*
________ Erase *removes a file name from the disk directory.*
________ List *displays directory entries for specified types of files.*
________ Import *incorporates a file in ASCII-text format into the current worksheet.*
________ Directory *displays and changes the current (sub)directory used by Lotus for file storage and retrieval.*

________ /Print *commands in this series prepare a paper or disk file image of the worksheet display or its underlying formulas.*
to Printer *or* File *the destination of the output must be specified.*
followed by
________ Range *identifies the area to be printed.*
________ Line *advances one line.*
________ Page *advances one page.*
________ Options *a series of features that alter the output.*
________ Header *specifies text to be printed at the top of each output page.*
________ Footer *specifies text to be printed at the bottom of each output page.*
________ Margins *allows changing of Left, Right, Top, and Bottom margins.*
________ Borders *designates Columns and Rows to be printed on all pages.*
________ Setup *allows entry of a printer initialization code.*
________ Pg-Length *specifies number of lines per page.*
________ Other *allows printing of worksheet As-Displayed or the Cell-Formulas, allows Formatted or Unformatted page output.*
________ Quit *exits /Print . . . Options menu.*
________ Clear *erases all or some print settings; choices are All, Range, Borders, and Format.*
________ Align *informs Lotus that current printer position is top-of-page.*
________ Go *executes printing to paper or output to disk.*
________ Quit *exits /Print menu.*

________ /Graph *commands in this series are used to prepare and view graphs on the screen and prepare them for printed output.*
________ Type *specifies the form of the graph from one of Line, Bar, XY, Stacked-Bar, and Pie.*
________ X A B C D E F *specify the ranges of data to be graphed.*
________ Reset *allows removal of all settings or a specific range.*
________ View *displays the graph on the screen.*
________ Save *places the current graph image in a disk file for later printing by the PrintGraph program.*
Options *a series of features that control the appearance of the graph.*
________ Legend *specifies the text for each range for a legend.*
________ Format *designates whether data in XY and Line graphs are plotted by Lines, Symbols, Both or Neither*

/Graph
Options, continued

________ Titles *allows entry of two lines of text at top of graph and one on each axis.*
________ Grid *specifies whether or not grid lines appear in the body of the graph.*
________ Scale *allows control over range and format of Y Scale and X Scale information.*
________ Color *displays the graph in color (on the proper equipment); bars are solid.*
________ B&W *displays the graph in a single color; bars are cross-hatched.*
________ Data-Labels *allows entry of points to be plotted in the body of the graph.*
________ Quit *exits the /GraphOptions menu.*
________ Name *specifies a label for the current graph to permit maintenance of several graphs in the same worksheet.*
________ Quit *exits the /Graph menu.*

________ /Data *commands in this series are used for data computation and data selection operations.*
________ Fill *computes a series of numbers, placing them in contiguous cells.*
________ Table *computes the values of one or more formulas with one or two variables.*
________ Sort *arranges a range of data according to one or two key columns.*
________ Query *selects data from a range according to a criterion for editing, writing to an output area, or deleting.*
________ Distribution *determines the distribution of a range of data values.*
________ Matrix *inverts one matrix or multiplies two matrices.*
________ Regression *performs multiple regression of one range on others.*
________ Parse *interprets a column of label data for division into multiple columns.*

________ /System *allows execution of some DOS commands while the worksheet remains in memory.*

________ /Quit *exits the worksheet mode (***note:** *does not automatically save latest version of worksheet).*

LOTUS ACCESS SYSTEM COMMANDS

The commands in the previous section are available when the user is in Lotus 1-2-3 *worksheet mode*. There are two additional program features that are available from the *Lotus Access System*:

________ PrintGraph *prints graphs that have been created and saved in worksheet mode with the /Graph and /GraphSave commands.*

________ Translate *converts the data format of files; see Appendix B of this book for more information.*

LOTUS 1-2-3 FUNCTIONS

Functions are used to form all or part of a formula. Lotus functions always begin with the @ (*at* or *apiece*) sign. The terms in parentheses that follow a function are called *arguments* of the function. In the examples below, *x* can be a cell, a constant value, a formula, or another function. For instance, @ABS(x) could be either **@ABS(A10)**, **@ABS(5029)**, **@ABS(A10-B12)**, or **@ABS(@MIN(G9,H9))**. Some functions accept a range of cells as an argument (the concept of a range of cells is discussed in the next section).

Mathematical Functions

________ @ABS(x) *absolute value of x.*

________ @ACOS(x) *arc cosine of x*, the angle in radians whose cosine is *x*. If *x* is not between -1 and +1, the value is ERR. To convert radians to degrees, multiply [radians]*180/@PI: for example, if cell H8 contains a cosine, then the angle in degrees is determined by the function **@ACOS(H8)*180/@PI**

________ @ASIN(x) *arc sine of x*, the angle in radians whose sine is *x*. If *x* is not between -1 and +1, the value is ERR. To convert radians to degrees, multiply [radians]*180/@PI: see @ACOS(x) above for an example.

________ @ATAN(x) *arc tangent of x*, the angle in radians whose tangent is *x*. To convert radians to degrees, multiply [radians]*180/@PI: see @ACOS(x) above for an example.

________ @ATAN2(x,y) *arc tangent of y/x*, the angle in radians whose tangent is *y/x*. See the manual for the distinction between this and @ATAN(x). To convert radians to degrees, multiply [radians]*180/@PI: see @ACOS(x) above for an example.

________ @COS(x) *cosine of x in radians.* To convert degrees to radians, multiply [degrees]*@PI/180: for example, if cell G12 has a number in degrees, then the function is **@COS(G12*@PI/180)**

________ @EXP(x) *exponential*: e^x.

________ @INT(x) *integer part of x.* The cell entry **@INT(2.95)** yields the value 2. The cell entry **@INT(-2.95)** yields the value −2.

________ @LN(x) log_e *of x.*

________ @LOG(x) log_{10} *of x.*

________ @MOD(x,y) *x mod y: modular part* (remainder) of *x/y*. The cell entry **@MOD(6,4)** yields the value 2.

________ @PI *pi* is 3.141592653589794

________ @RAND *random number* between 0 and 1.

________ @ROUND(x,n) *Round number x to n decimal places.* The cell entry **@ROUND(2.85,1)** yields the result 2.9.

________ @SIN(x) *sine of x in radians.* To convert degrees to radians, multiply [degrees]*@PI/180: see @COS(x) above for an example.

________ @SQRT(x) *square root of x.*

________ @TAN(x) *tangent of x in radians.* To convert degrees to radians, multiply [degrees]*@PI/180: see @COS(x) above for an example.

Special Functions

________ @CHOOSE(x,v0,v1, . . . vn) *select value*: if *x* = 0, then the cell containing this function will have value *v0*; if *x* = 1, then the cell will have value *v1*; and so forth. *x* and *v0 . . . vn* can be constants, other cell addresses, or functions.

________ @HLOOKUP(x,range,offset) *table lookup with index row*: this function is used to select a value from a table based on the value of *x*.

________ @VLOOKUP(x,range,offset) *table lookup with index column.*

________ @INDEX(range,row,col) *value of cell at intersection*: this yields the value of the cell in *range*, *row* rows from the top and *col* columns from the left. For instance, @INDEX(A1..C9,0,0) returns the value of A1, while the result of @INDEX(A1..C9,K3,J9) will depend on the values of K3 and J9 as well as the values in the range A1..C9.

Logical Functions

1-2-3 considers any non-zero value to be TRUE. Only zero is FALSE.

________ @NA *not available*; sets the value of the cell to **NA**.

________ @ERR *error*; sets the value of the cell to **ERR**. Any cell that depends on this cell via a formula will also have the value **ERR**.

________ @FALSE *false*, 0 (zero).

________ @TRUE *true*, 1 (one).

________ @IF(cond,x,y) *if the condition is true or non-zero, then x; if the condition is false or zero, then y.*

________ @ISNUMBER(x) *1 (TRUE) if contents of x is a value.* Values are generated by numeric entries, formulas, most functions (including @NA and @ERR), and blank cells which are considered a numeric 0 (zero).

________ @ISSTRING(x) *1 (TRUE) if contents of x is a string (label).* Strings are generated by label entries and the string functions discussed below.

________ @ISNA(x) *1 (TRUE) if contents of x is NA.*

________ @ISERR(x) *1 (TRUE) if contents of x is ERR.*

Financial Functions

Cash Flows

________ @IRR(guess,range) *Internal rate of return* of the series of cash flows in the *range*. The *guess* is necessary because some income streams have more than one IRR. It is generally safe to use 0.10 as the guess.

________ @NPV(x,range) *Net present value* of the series of cash flows in the *range*, discounted at per-period interest rate of *x*.

Annuities

________ @FV(pmt,int,term) *Future value of an ordinary annuity* with payments of *pmt* at the end of each period, at a per-period interest rate of *int*, for *term* periods. The cell entry **@FV(100,12%/12,5*12)** would be used to determine how much would accumulate with monthly payments of $100, invested at 12% interest, over a period of five years. (The result is 8166.97.)

________ @PV(pmt,int,term) *Present value of an ordinary annuity* with payments of *pmt* at the end of each period, at a per-period interest rate of *int*, for *term* periods. The cell entry **@PV(100,12%/12,5*12)** would be used to determine the current dollar equivalent of monthly receipts of $100, invested at 12% interest, over a period of five years. (The result is 4495.50.)

________ @TERM(pmt,int,fv) *Number of periods*, the number of end-of-period payments necessary to achieve the future value *fv*, given the payment *pmt* and interest *int*. The cell entry **@TERM(200,11.5%/12,20000)** would be used to determine the number of months necessary for a $200 monthly payment to grow into $20,000 at 11.5% annual interest. (The result is 70.5 months.)

________ @PMT(prn,int,term) *Payment* on a loan of principal *prn* at a per-period interest rate of *int*, for *term* periods. The cell entry **@PMT(20000,11.5%/12,5*12)** would be used to determine the monthly payment on a $20,000 loan at 11.5% annual interest. (The result is 439.85.)

Compounding

________ @CTERM(int,fv,pv) *Compounding periods*, number of periods required for present value *pv* to increase to desired future value *fv* at stated interest rate *int*. The cell entry **@CTERM(12%/12,2000,1000)** would be used to determine how many months it would take for $1000 to double in value if invested at 12%, compounded monthly. (The result is 69.66 months.)

________ @RATE(fv,pv,term) *Periodic interest*, the rate necessary for the present value *pv* to grow into the future value *fv* over the number of periods in the *term*. The cell entry **@RATE(2000,1000,60)** would be used to determine the investment rate necessary for $1000 to double in value over a period of five years, compounded monthly. (The result is `.011619`, which, multiplied by 12, is 13.94% per annum.)

Depreciation

________ @DDB(cost,salvage,life,period) *Double declining balance depreciation*, the depreciation amount in a specific *period*, given the initial *cost*, *salvage* value, and *life* of the item.

________ @SLN(cost,salvage,life) *Straight-line depreciation*, which is the same amount for each period, given the initial *cost*, *salvage* value, and *life* of the item.

________ @SYD(cost,salvage,life,period) *Sum-of-the-years' digits depreciation*, for a specified *period*, given the initial *cost*, *salvage* value, and *life* of the item.

Date and Time Functions

Lotus calculates dates by counting the number of days that have elapsed between the date in question and January 1, 1900. To Lotus, year 00 is 1900, year 85 is 1985, and year 150 is 2050. The following three functions yield a *serial date number*:

________ @DATE(year,month,day) *Serial number of a given date*, where **@DATE(00,01,01)** [January 1, 1900] is number 1 and **@DATE(199,12,31)** [December 31, 2099] is number 73049.

________ @NOW *Current date and time*, assuming you set the proper date when you started or reset the system. This returns both date (integer) and time (fractional) components. To see both current date and time, have two **@NOW** entries; one formatted as date and the other as time. We like to include these in our worksheets so we can see exactly when a given printout was produced. @NOW is updated whenever the worksheet is recalculated.

________ @DATEVALUE(date string) *String to date*, converts a string to a serial date number, for example **@DATEVALUE("16-Feb-87")** yields `31824`.

The results of @DATE, @NOW, and @DATEVALUE must be formatted using the /**R**ange**F**ormat command before they are meaningful. You can use these functions in formulas, e.g., **@NOW+7** is one week from today.

Lotus 1-2-3 Release 2 also gives you the ability to calculate time as a fractional serial number, with midnight being 0 (zero) and noon being 0.5. Use the /**R**ange**F**ormat command to format the result as time. If the @NOW function is formatted to Time, then the current time is displayed. You can also use either of the following two functions:

________ @TIME(hr,min,sec) *Serial time number*, computes a time number.

_______ @TIMEVALUE(time string) *String to time*, converts a string to a serial time number, for example **@TIMEVALUE("6:06 PM")** yields 0.754166.

The other date and time functions yield a number:

_______ @DAY(date) *Day of the month* of the given date. If today is May 21, 1985, then **@DAY(@NOW)** yields 21.

_______ @MONTH(date) *Month number* of the given date. If today is May 21, 1985, then **@MONTH(@NOW)** yields 5.

_______ @YEAR(date) *Year number* of the given date. If today is May 21, 1985, then **@YEAR(@NOW)** yields 85.

_______ @HOUR(time number) *Hour value of time number.* If the time is now 8:08:25, then **HOUR(@NOW)** yields 8.

_______ @MINUTE(time number) *Minute value of time number.* If the time is now 8:08:25, then **@MINUTE(@NOW)** yields 8.

_______ @SECOND(time number) *Second value of time number.* If the time is now 8:08:25, then **@SECOND(@NOW)** yields 25.

Statistical Functions

_______ @AVG(list) The *average value* of the items in the list. If the list contains @NA or @ERR, then the average will be @NA or @ERR. (@NA and @ERR are special functions discussed with Lotus logic in Part 3.) The cell entry **@AVG(-5,8,3/12,(-6-2))** yields the result 1.1875, which is the average of the values. **@AVG(A1,B5,C8)** would compute the average of the current values of those three cells.

_______ @COUNT(list) The *number of items* in the list. Every non-blank cell in a range counts, whether it contains a value or a label.

_______ @MIN(list) The *minimum value* in the list. The cell entry **@MIN(-5,8,3/12,(-6-2))** yields the result −8, which is the smallest of the values. **@MIN(A1,B5,C8)** would display the smallest of the current values of those three cells.

_______ @MAX(list) The *maximum value* in the list. The cell entry **@MAX(-5,8,3/12,(-6-2))** yields the result 8, which is the largest of the values. **@MAX(A1,B5,C8)** would display the largest of the current values of those three cells.

_______ @STD(list) The *standard deviation* of the items in the list (N weighted).

_______ @SUM(list) The *sum* of the items in the list. If the list contains @NA or @ERR, then the sum will be @NA or @ERR. **@SUM(A1,B5,C8)** would display the sum of the current values of those three cells.

_______ @VAR(list) The *variance* of the items in the list (N weighted).

Database Statistical Functions

In the definitions below, *input,offset,criterion* are the means by which Lotus knows which fields (columns) of which records (rows) to average, sum, etc.

Input is a named or specified range that contains all rows of interest and columns containing criterion fields and the field to be averaged, summed, etc.

Offset identifies the specific field relative to the leftmost column. An offset of 0 (zero) indicates the leftmost column; an offset of 5 indicates the sixth column from the left. The offset column is the column that is summed, averaged, etc.

Criterion is a named or specified range that contains selection criteria.

________ @DAVG(input,offset,criterion) *the average value* of the items in *offset* column of *input* range that meet the *criterion.* For example, **@DAVG(A1..D39,3,F1..F2)** will average the values of those cells in the range D2..D39 which meet the criterion established in F1..F2.

________ @DCOUNT(input,offset,criterion) *the number of items* in the *offset* column of *input* range that meet the *criterion.* For example, **@DCOUNT(A1..D39,2,F1..F2)** will count the number of non-empty cells in the range C2..C39 which meet the criterion established in F1..F2.

________ @DMIN(input,offset,criterion) *the minimum value* in the *offset* column of *input* range that meets the *criterion.* For example, **@DMIN(A1..D39,2,F1..F2)** will display the minimum value of those cells in the range C2..C39 which meet the criterion established in F1..F2.

________ @DMAX(input,offset,criterion) *the maximum value* in the *offset* column of *input* range that meets the *criterion.* For example, **@DMAX(A1..D39,2,F1..F2)** will display the maximum value of those cells in the range C2..C39 which meet the criterion established in F1..F2.

________ @DSTD(input,offset,criterion) *the standard deviation* (N weighted) of the items in the *offset* column of *input* range that meet the *criterion.* For example, **@DSTD(A1..D39,3,F1..F2)** will display the standard deviation statistic for those cells in the range D2..D39 which meet the criterion established in F1..F2.

________ @DSUM(input,offset,criterion) *the sum* of the items in the *offset* column of *input* range that meet the *criterion.* For example, **@DSUM(A1..D39,3,F1..F2)** will display the sum of those cells in the range D2..D39 which meet the criterion established in F1..F2.

________ @DVAR(input,offset,criterion) *the variance* (N weighted) of the items in the *offset* column of *input* range that meet the *criterion.* For example, **@DSTD(A1..D39,3,F1..F2)** will display the variance of those cells in the range D2..D39 which meet the criterion established in F1..F2.

String Functions

Strings can be the result of a logical formula, and the label contents of a cell can be referred to by another cell. Labels can be entered as usual in cells, but labels used in formulas must be enclosed in double quotation marks (" . . . "). Two labels are combined (*concatenated*) with the & operator.

Several functions are provided to further enhance use of string data. Since many readers of this book are familiar with the string functions of the BASIC programming language, equivalent BASIC statements are included where possible.

________ @CHAR(x) *character whose ASCII value is x.* This is often used to create characters that are not directly accessible on the keyboard. For instance, @CHAR(189) will display ½ on the screen. [Same as BASIC CHR$(189)]

________ @CODE(string) *ASCII value of first character in string.* [Same as BASIC ASC(string$)]

________ @EXACT(string1,string2) *exact equivalence of two strings*, where exact equivalence includes capitalization. Use of the = operator also checks for equivalence, but ignores capitalization. For instance, if C35 contains *'Polish* and J35 contains *'polish*, then **@IF(C35=J35,@TRUE,@FALSE)** is TRUE; while **@EXACT(C35,J35)** is FALSE.

________ @FIND(search string,string,start number) *location of search string in another string.* This is used to determine position of the *search string* in the *string*, starting with character at *start number.* [Same as BASIC INSTR(n,string1$,string2$)]

________ @LEFT(string,n) *first n characters of string.* [Same as BASIC LEFT$(string$,n)]

________ @LENGTH(string) *number of characters in string.* [Same as BASIC LEN(string$)]

________ @LOWER(string) *lower case conversion.* This converts all characters in *string* to lower case and displays the result. It could be used before an @EXACT comparison. Following above example, **@EXACT(@LOWER(C35),J35)** is TRUE.

________ @MID(string,start number,length) *middle characters from string*, starting at *start number*, proceeding for *length* characters. [Same as BASIC MID$(string$,n,m)]

________ @N(range) *label to value conversion.* This converts label in upper left corner of range to numeric type, with value of 0 (zero), allowing numeric formulas to reference cells that can or can not contain labels. This is often a problem in accounting worksheets, where a balance is computed by adding the previous balance to the current net. In the first period, the cell that would normally contain the previous balance contains a label. If the balances are in row 15 and the net amounts are in row 14, the following formula would compute the proper balance for column B and could be copied across the worksheet: **@N(A15..A15)+B14** Because A15 is a single cell range, it must be entered as **!A15** or **A15..A15.** Regardless of how it is entered, Lotus will convert the range to A15..A15 for storage. This function converts only one cell, the upper left cell in the range, regardless of the size of the range specified. See also @VALUE.

_______ @PROPER(string) *proper capitalization.* This capitalizes the first letter of each word in *string.* See example in next function.

_______ @REPEAT(string,n) *repeat string.* This repeats the *string, n* times. The following example is inspired by the Reference Manual:

@PROPER("SHE LOVES YOU, "&@REPEAT("YEAH ",3)) yields
`She Loves You, Yeah Yeah Yeah`

_______ @REPLACE(original string,start number,n,new string) *replace text in string with new string.* This replaces *text* in original string, beginning at character *start number*, for *n* characters, with *new string.*

_______ @RIGHT(string,n) *last n characters in string.* [Same as BASIC RIGHT$(string$,n)]

_______ @S(range) *value to label conversion.* This turns values into empty labels so they can be used in string functions. The only use of this function appears to be prevention of an error caused by referencing a value cell with a string function or operator. As with @N and @CELL, single cell ranges require special notation. This function converts only one cell, the upper left cell in the range, regardless of the size of the range specified. See @STRING for conversion of value to string data.

_______ @STRING(value,n) *value to label conversion.* This creates a string out of a number, allowing specification of *n* decimal places. [Similar to BASIC MKS$(x)] For instance, if cell X13 contains the current year as a value (e.g., 1987), you could concatenate that to a label entry: **+"Results for "&@STRING(X13,0)**

_______ @TRIM(string) *remove excess spaces.* This removes leading and trailing space characters, and converts multiple embedded spaces to single spaces.

_______ @UPPER(string) *upper case conversion.* This converts all characters in string to upper case and displays result.

_______ @VALUE(string) *label to value conversion.* This will convert any of the following to values that can be used in numeric computations: **@VALUE("13 3/5")** yields `13.6`; **@VALUE(K9)** yields `10` if cell K9 contains '10; **@VALUE("TV")** yields ERR (error).

Cell and Range Reference Functions

The functions in this group are used to determine information about the cells and ranges of a worksheet.

_______ @@(cell address) *value of cell referenced by cell at cell address.* This allows one cell to reference another cell which contains a value. For instance, if F9 contains the label entry **'K9**, and cell K9 contains the value **100**, then a cell containing the function **@@(F9)** would also display the value `100`.

_______ @CELL(attribute,range) *attribute of range*, where range attributes include type of data, contents of cell, numeric format, protection status, and several others.

Consult the reference manual for more information and a list of all the attributes. If you want information about a single cell, the *range* must be specified as either **A1..A1** or **!A1**, e.g., **@CELL("FORMAT",!A1)**.

________ @CELLPOINTER(attribute) *attribute of current cell*, i.e., the attribute (such as address) of the cell in which the cell pointer was at the time of the last recalculation.

________ @COLS(range) *number of columns in a range*: most useful when used with named ranges.

________ @ROWS(range) *number of rows in a range*: again, most useful when analyzing named ranges.

LOTUS FEATURES

Lotus 1-2-3 contains several idiosyncratic features that provide improved operation but are confusing to those who have worked with other spreadsheet software. Features that are important to the examples discussed in this book are presented below.

Relative, Absolute, and Mixed Cell Addresses

A cell address included in a formula can be one of three types:

- *Relative address* (normal).
- *Absolute address.*
- *Mixed address.*

The type of address is important when the formula is copied. Some software packages allow the user to control adjustment of cell reference when the /Copy or equivalent command is issued. In Lotus, this control is obtained by the type of cell address in a formula.

For example, to put the sum of cells A2 and B2 into cell A1, we enter the formula *+A2+B2* in that cell. Lotus does not remember this as *+A2+B2*, however, but rather as + *down-1* + *down-1 & right-1*. If we /Copy the formula from cell A1 to another place on the worksheet, say cell F25, then Lotus will still remember the formula as + *down-1* + *down-1 & right-1*. In F25, the formula will read *+F26+G26*.

Relative Cell Addresses. The example above illustrates how Lotus normally handles cell addresses in formulas: as relative movements from the cell in which the formula resides. *Relative addressing* occurs irrespective of the method used to input the formula. Both pointing and typing methods yield a relative address.

If you never /Copy the formula, then relative addresses are fine. On many occasions, however, you will build a set of formulas that you want to duplicate elsewhere in the spreadsheet. In some cases, relative addresses will be acceptable, but in other cases they will not be acceptable.

Absolute Cell Addresses. When an *absolute cell address* appears in a formula, that address does not change as the formula is copied to other places in the spreadsheet. For instance, you might put a percentage value in cell A2 that will be used in several places in your worksheet. As you /Copy formulas from one place to another, you do not want the reference to cell A2 to change.

To indicate to Lotus that cell A2 is an absolute rather than a relative address, it must be entered into the formula as **$A$2**. The $ sign tells Lotus that this is an absolute address: not to be changed in a /Copy procedure.

Following our earlier example, if cell A1 contains the formula *+$A$2+B2*, and we /Copy that formula to cell F25, then the result will be *+$A$2+G26*. Notice that the relative component of the address (B2) changes (to G26), but the absolute ($A$2) does not change.

Mixed Cell Addresses. A third possibility is that you wish to hold the row (or column) absolute while allowing the column (or row) to vary relative to the address. This is called a *mixed cell address*, and is obtained by putting the $ prior to the item that does not vary:

$A2 *column A is constant, row varies;*

A$2 *row 2 is constant, column varies.*

Continuing with our example, if cell A1 contains the formula *+$A2+B2*, and we /Copy that formula to cell F25, then the result will be *+$A26+G26*. Notice that the relative component of the first address (row 2) changes (to row 26), but the absolute (column A) does not change.

Range Names

The named-range capability of Lotus 1-2-3 provides a quick method of referring to specific portions of the worksheet.

Naming Ranges. To name a range, move the cell pointer to the upper left corner of the range to be named, give the /**R**ange**N**ame**C**reate command, and indicate the lower right corner of the range. You can remove the name from a specific range using /**R**ange**N**ame**D**elete, and from all ranges with /**R**ange**N**ame**R**eset. /**R**ange**N**ame**L**abels can be used to assign names from adjacent cells. And, /**R**ange**N**ame**T**able creates a table in the worksheet with the names and addresses of currently active ranges. If you later add or delete a range, you must use the command again. This is useful for debugging large worksheets.

Using Named Ranges: In Formulas. Many Lotus functions allow the use of range names as arguments. To use a range name as an argument, simply type the range name where you would normally type addresses. In the following examples, assume that you have named the range Q5..Q20 as WEST.

UNNAMED RANGE	NAMED RANGE
@IRR(0.10,Q5..Q20)	@IRR(0.10,WEST)
@SUM(Q5..Q20)	@SUM(WEST)
@DAVG(Q5..Q20,1,A1..B2)	@DAVG(WEST,1,A1..B2)

Using Named Ranges: As a Destination. If you are building a tax form worksheet and name the ranges with names such as FORM1040, SCHEDA, etc., then it is very easy to jump about. Press the F5 {goto} key, then the F3 {name} key and you will be presented with a list of named ranges. Arrow to the desired one and press <CR>. You will jump to the upper left corner of the chosen range.

Using Named Ranges: In Commands. Almost all Lotus commands make use of ranges:

/**R**ange	all subcommands
/**C**opy	FROM and TO ranges
/**M**ove	FROM and TO ranges
/**F**ile	Combine and eXtract operations
/**P**rint	Range
/**G**raph	X and A . . . F ranges
/**D**ata	all subcommands

Cell Protection

Cell protection is used to prevent you or others from making inadvertent changes to protected cells. There are two aspects to cell protection:

1. A given cell is either unprotected or protected.

2. The entire worksheet is either in the protection-on or the protection-off state.

The normal mode is that all cells are protected, but the worksheet is in protection-off state. A given cell's protected state is irrelevant if the entire worksheet is in the protection-off state.

Establishing Protected Cells. The normal sequence of events for using cell protection:

1. As you build the worksheet, make note of those cells that the user will need to change.

2. Either concurrently with step 1, or later, use the /**R**ange**U**nprotect command to make these cells unprotected. If you unprotect the wrong cells, use the /**R**ange**P**rotect command to (re)protect them. The contents of unprotected cells will be displayed in a different intensity or color, and a *U* will be displayed in the control panel area to indicate the cell is unprotected.

3. Change the worksheet to the protection-on state using the /**W**orksheet**G**lobal**P**rotection**E**nable command. To make changes later, use the /**W**orksheet**G**lobal**P**rotection**D**isable command to change the worksheet to protection-off state.

   When this worksheet is /**F**ile**S**aved, the unprotected status of the cells and the protection-on/off status of the worksheet is also saved. When the worksheet is later retrieved, these statuses will still be in effect.

MACROS

Macro commands are used for four main purposes: for a repeated entry (i.e., a label that appears in several places on the worksheet); for a repeated command (i.e., a command such as a format command that will be used in several places on the worksheet); for a repeated procedure (i.e., a series of commands, such as setting width, or setting numeric format and label alignment in a column); and for programming commands (i.e., commands to build a specialized menu and to execute different commands based upon menu choice).

Creating Macro Commands

Before they can be used, macros must be created. Macro creation is a two-step process: enter the macro as a label into one or more spreadsheet cells, then name the range containing the macro. If the macro is lengthy, it can be put into several contiguous cells in the same column; Lotus executes macro instructions from the point of entry until it reaches a blank cell in the column below the point of entry. We usually place macro commands to the right of (<TAB> over one or more screens) or below (PgDn one or more screens) the main worksheet area. *Make sure that the first cell in the column below the macro is blank.*

Naming Macro Commands

Once the macro is entered, the top cell of the macro must be named, using the /**R**ange**N**ame**C**reate command. Most of the time, you will wish to execute the macro from the keyboard. To do so, give the macro a name starting with the \ (*backslash*) character (*not* the / [*frontslash* or *slash*] character!) and one additional character, which is one of the letters of the alphabet. Examples: \A \G \F \c \k etc. The letters can be entered as upper or lower case, Lotus converts them to upper case. The only non-letter character permissible as a macro name is 0 (zero). A macro named \0 will be executed automatically whenever you /**F**ile**R**etrieve the worksheet. If you want to check your macro later, you can locate it quickly by pressing F5 {goto} followed by F3 {name}. The macro ranges appear at the end of the list of range names.

Invoking Macro Commands

Once the macro is created and named, it can be invoked by pressing the Alt key and the letter. (Hold down the Alt key while pressing the letter key.) For instance, to invoke the macro named \Z, you press Alt **Z**. Whatever you have entered into the cell (range) named \Z will be executed.

Programming with Macros

Sophisticated applications are possible with a series of macro programming commands. With these, it is possible to write your own menus and to use conditional logic to determine worksheet operations. The Lotus 1-2-3 Release 2 manual contains a very extensive discussion of programming with macro commands. The discussion that follows provides only an overview of what the commands accomplish. Persons who wish to take full advantage of Lotus macros should consult the reference manual.

Screen Control Commands

________ {beep} This command sounds the computer's "bell."

________ {indicate *string*} This command changes the indicator in the upper right hand corner of the screen to the *string* of your choice.

________ {paneloff} / {panelon} The first command suppresses display in the control panel area during macro execution, which speeds up macro execution. Panel display remains suppressed until the second command is encountered, or the macro terminates.

________ {windowsoff} / {windowson} The command first suppresses display in the window area of the screen; which greatly speeds up macro execution because the screen is not redrawn after each step.

Keyboard Interaction Commands

________ {?} Causes the computer to pause until <CR> is struck, accepts input at current cell location.

________ {breakon} / {breakoff} These commands enable or disable the ability to stop macro execution by pressing the Ctrl-Scroll Lock (Break) key combination. Use {breakoff} in a macro which others will use when you do not want them to be able to stop the macro.

________ {get *location*} This command causes Lotus to pause for a single keystroke, which will be stored in *location.*

________ {getlabel *prompt-string,location*} This displays *prompt-string*, stores input label at *location.* Same as the /**XL** command.

________ {getnumber *prompt-string,location*} This displays *prompt-string*, stores input number at *location.* Same as /**XN** command.

________ {look *location*} This checks to see if a character key has been pressed since the macro began execution, if so, stores the character in *location.*

________ {menubranch *location*} This passes control to menu at *location.* When menu activity is finished, control reverts to *READY* mode unless a {branch} sends it elsewhere. Same as /**XM** command.

________ {menucall *location*} This passes control to menu at *location.* When menu is finished, control will return to statement following (below) the {menucall} command.

________ {wait *time serial number*} This command causes the macro to suspend operation until the specified time is reached. To wait one minute, use the cell entry **{WAIT @NOW+@TIME(0,1,0)}**.

Commands That Control Program Flow

________ {*routine*} Macro execution is sent to the named routine (a named range). Control passes to the statement following this when the routine terminates. Same as **/XC** command.

________ {branch *location*} Macro execution is sent to *location* for further instructions. This is the equivalent of the **/XG** command, and the infamous BASIC language GOTO statement.

________ {define *location:type* . . . } This is used to receive arguments in routines, the discussion of which is too complex for this text.

________ {dispatch *location*} This transfers control to the cell that is named in *location* cell.

________ {for *counter-location,start-number,stop-number,step-number,starting-location*} This command repeatedly executes instructions at *starting-location*, counting the iterations in *counter-location*, according to the sequence in *start-number,stop-number,step-number*. The loop is restarted when a blank cell or a {return} is encountered below *starting-location.*

________ {forbreak} This cancels a {for} loop and transfers control to the statement following the {for}.

________ {if *condition*} When the *condition* is true, macro execution continues on the same line (i.e., in the same cell) as the {if} statement. If the *condition* is not true, macro execution proceeds to the cell below. The *condition* can be another cell, or can be contained in the {if} statement. Read the Lotus manual carefully before trying to get too fancy with these. Same as the **/XI** command.

________ {onerror *branch-location,message-location*} This allows you to write your macro so it will recover from errors. Again, see the Lotus manual for examples.

________ {quit} This stops execution of all macros, including sub- and calling routines. Same as the **/XQ** command.

________ {restart} This is used to cause Lotus to avoid returning to a calling routine from a called subroutine (the name of this command is not particularly descriptive). After this command, the subroutine will continue execution to its own end; then the macro will cease, as if a {quit} had been encountered.

________ {return} This returns to the statement following the {*routine*} or {menucall} statement. This statement is not required if there is a blank cell below the subroutine or menu. Same as the **/XR** command.

Commands for Data Manipulation

________ {blank *location*} This does the equivalent of a /RangeErase of *location*.

________ {contents *destination-location,source-location*} This copies contents of *source-location* cell to *destination-location*, converting value data to label data. Format of the data can be specified: see the Lotus manual.

________ {let *location,number*} This command stores a *number* entry at *location*.

________ {let *location,string*} This stores a *string* entry at *location*.

________ {put *location,col-number,row-number,number*} This stores the *number* in the range *location*, offset from the upper left by *col-number* and *row-number*.

________ {put *location,col-number,row-number,string*} This stores the *string* in the range *location*, offset from the upper left by *col-number* and *row-number*.

________ {recalc *location*} This recalculates a specified *location* of the worksheet, proceeding row by row.

________ {recalccol *location*} This recalculates a specified *location* of the worksheet, proceeding column by column.

Commands Dealing with Files

________ {close} This terminates all further interaction with the currently open file.

________ {filesize *location*} This stores the size of the currently open file, in bytes, in *location*. Used to insure that you do not try to read beyond the end of the file.

________ {getpos *location*} This determines the current position of the file pointer in the open file and stores it in *location*. Used to keep track of where you are in the file.

________ {open *file-name,access-mode*} This opens a file for reading (only); writing as well as reading; or modification. Access mode codes are R, W, and M respectively. Files opened for writing lose any previous contents; files opened for modification retain their previous contents.

________ {read *bytecount,location*} This reads the specified number of bytes from the open file and stores the result in *location*.

________ {readln *location*} This reads a full line (up to a <CR> character) and stores the result in *location*.

________ {setpos *file-position*} This moves the file pointer to *file-position* bytes from the beginning of the file.

________ {write *string*} This writes the *string* to the currently open file, at the file pointer position.

________ {writeln *string*} This writes the *string* to the currently open file, at the file pointer position. The string is terminated by the carriage return-line feed sequence.

TABLE A-1 Special Key Indicators for Macro Commands

Macro Entry	Keyboard Equivalent	Macro Entry	Keyboard Equivalent
~	<CR> key	{up}	<UP> arrow
{down}	<DOWN> arrow	{left}	<LEFT> arrow
{right}	<RIGHT> arrow	{home}	Home key
{end}	End key	{pgup}	PgUp key
{pgdn}	PgDn key	{esc}	Esc key
{del}	Del key	{bs}	<BACKSPACE> key
{edit}	F2 (function key 2)	{name}	F3
{abs}	F4	{goto}	F5
{window}	F6	{query}	F7
{table}	F8	{calc}	F9
{graph}	F10	{~}	~ (not interpreted as <CR>)
{{}	{	{}}	}
{bigright}	<TAB> key	{bigleft}	<SHIFT><TAB>

/X Commands

Lotus 1-2-3 provides a series of /X commands that also allow macro programming. See Table A-2.

TABLE A-2 /X Commands

Programming Commands	
/XI*condition~then*	If . . . then
/XG*location~*	Go to cell or range *location*
/XC*location~*	Call subroutine at cell or range *location*
/XR	Return from subroutine
/XQ	Quit macro
Pause for Input Commands	
{?}	Pause for input and store in current cell
/XM*location~*	Process user-defined menu at cell or range *location*
/XL*message~location~*	Accept label entry and store in cell or range *location*
/XN*message~location~*	Accept number entry and store in cell or range *location*

APPENDIX

B

TRANSFERRING DATA BETWEEN LOTUS 1-2-3 AND dBASE III PLUS

This appendix[1] deals with the specific problem of moving data between a database management system (dBASE III Plus) and a spreadsheet package (Lotus 1-2-3 Release 2) as well as the more general problem of how to transfer data between each of these two packages and other applications software. Both software packages have special features that make the transfer easy, but the user must still have some knowledge of what is to be accomplished. The basic techniques discussed provide a starting point for data interchange with programs other than those discussed in this book.

TYPES OF FILES

Program-Specific

Most applications software programs use a specialized format for storing data in disk files, often with distinctive file extensions (the characters after the period) used to denote the special format. For instance, dBASE III uses the extension .DBF, while Lotus uses .WK1. A number of programs have the ability to store data in the so-called Data Interchange Format, or .DIF, that was developed by the makers of VisiCalc for transfer of numeric data among programs.

In this book, we use two program-specific files:

- Lotus .WK1 Files
- dBASE .DBF Files

---

[1] The material in this appendix is excerpted from two books: S. C. Ross, *Understanding and Using Lotus 1-2-3 Release 2* and S. C. Ross, *Understanding and Using dBASE III Plus*, both published in 1987 by West Publishing Company.

```
                    Lotus Translate Utility  Version 2.01
      Copyright 1985 Lotus Development Corporation  All Rights Reserved

  What do you want to translate FROM?

          1-2-3, release 1A
          1-2-3, release 2
          dBase II
          dBase III
          DIF
          Jazz
          SYMPHONY, release 1.0
          SYMPHONY, release 1.1
          VISICALC

         Move the menu pointer to your selection and press [RETURN].
                Press [ESCAPE] to leave the Translate Utility.
                      Press [HELP] for more information.
```

FIGURE B-1 Specifying the Source File Type

ASCII-Generic

ASCII is the acronym for American Standard Code for Information Interchange. ASCII-generic formatted files are files in which the data is not in a special machine-code, but rather in rows and/or columns of plain text. ASCII-generic files are created by BASIC programs as sequential files (but BASIC random access files are not ASCII-generic). WordStar (in the non-document mode) and MultiMate (using the File Conversion Utilities) create ASCII-generic files. dBASE III and other database managers will write an ASCII-generic file with commands such as **COPY TO . . . SDF** and **COPY TO . . . DELIMITED**. Also, anything you receive *over the wire* that is in text and numbers can probably be converted to an ASCII-generic format. Lotus 1-2-3 generates ASCII-generic files when you use the /**P**rint**F**ile command.

These two types of files are in ASCII-generic format:

- Lotus .PRN Files
- dBASE .TXT Files

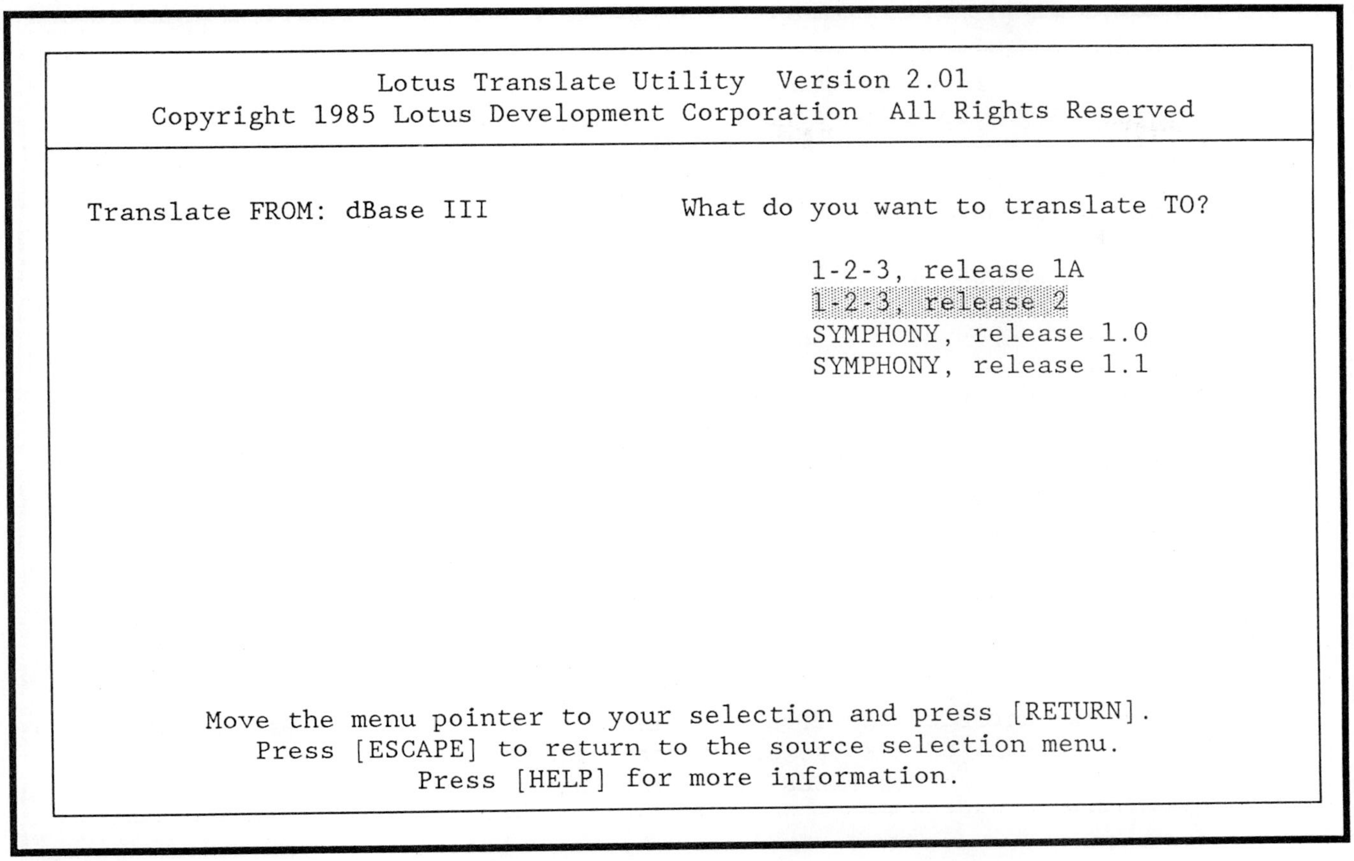

FIGURE B-2 Specifying the Destination File Type

IMPORTING DATA INTO 1-2-3

The data you wish to include in a spreadsheet model can come from a number of sources:

- VisiCalc or some other spreadsheet, for applications created by others.
- dBASE III or dBASE II files, such as a master transaction file.
- BASIC programs that write sequential files.
- WordStar or MultiMate files; these *word processors* are also good for entering text and data into sequential files.
- The Moon, or, at least, a mainframe computer, via a communications package.

The above sources fall into the Program-specific format and ASCII-generic format categories described earlier. The format determines how you will incorporate the file into 1-2-3.

```
                 Lotus Translate Utility  Version 2.01
     Copyright 1985 Lotus Development Corporation  All Rights Reserved

 Translate FROM: dBase III                 Translate TO: 1-2-3, release 2

 Source File: B:\*.DBF

  MIL_BANK DBF   6/25/85   9:34p      5465

         DATEBOOK DBF
         FIN_G004 DBF
         FIN_G005 DBF
         FIN_G006 DBF
         FIN_GOOD DBF
         MAILING  DBF
         MIL_BANK DBF
         —More—

Move the menu pointer to the file you want to translate and press [RETURN].
              Press [ESCAPE] to edit the source specification.
                     Press [HELP] for more information.
```

FIGURE B-3 Selecting the Source File

Program-specific Formats

The kind folks who make 1-2-3 have provided a utility program to transfer data between program-specific formats and Lotus 1-2-3 and Symphony worksheet formats. The various formats that Lotus can translate are listed in Figure B-1.

The transfer is initiated from the Lotus Access System, the menu you see first after typing **LOTUS** at the DOS command prompt. Instead of choosing 1-2-3 (the default), use the <ARROW> key to move over to *Translate* and then press <CR>. Depending on your specific computer system, you may have to switch disks. If this is necessary, 1-2-3 will prompt you.

The screen in Figure B-1 is the first stage of the translate process. The instructions at the bottom of the various translate screens are quite clear, and will guide you through the various steps. The program also lets you change your mind in several places.

Once you indicate the type of file you wish to translate from, the program displays the possible formats that you may translate to (Figure B-2). In this example, we translate from a dBASE III .DBF file to a Lotus 1-2-3 Release 2 .WK1 file.

```
                Lotus Translate Utility  Version 2.01
     Copyright 1985 Lotus Development Corporation  All Rights Reserved

 Translate FROM: dBase III             Translate TO: 1-2-3, release 2

 Source File: B:\MIL_BANK.DBF

 Destination: B:\MIL_BANK.WK1_



  Edit the destination file specification if necessary and press [RETURN].
             Press [ESCAPE] to select a different source file.
                   Press [HELP] for more information.
```

FIGURE B-4 Specifying the Destination File

Next, Translate displays a list of files of the appropriate source-type, e.g., all .DBF files (Figure B-3). Use the <ARROW> keys to move the menu pointer to select the source file. Translate will suggest a destination file name, that you may change or accept (Figure B-4).

Translate then asks you if you wish to proceed. As the file is translated, the program keeps your attention by displaying a bar graph showing progress:

```
Translation in progress... Please wait
```

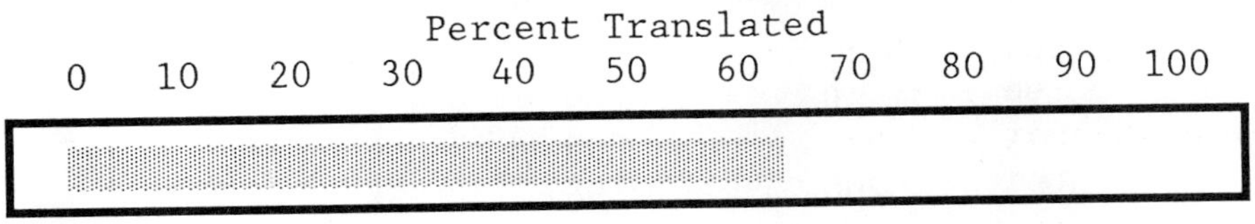

Upon completion, you can perform another translation of the same type, or specify a different type of translation (e.g., from Lotus .WK1 to dBASE .DBF), or exit to the Lotus Access System.

You will now have a .WK1 (or .DBF or whatever) file that is essentially the same as the source .DBF (or .WK1 or whatever) file. Some VisiCalc functions and formulas will not transfer; nor will deleted dBASE records. As you use the program, it informs you via messages on the screen of other conditions that affect the final result.

To use your .WK1 file, simply return to the Lotus Access System menu, select 1-2-3, and then /**F**ile**R**etrieve or /**F**ile**C**ombine. You will probably have to do a bit of cleaning up of formats, and so on, but this is far better than re-entering all the data.

ASCII-generic Formats

If an ASCII-generic file contains both text and numbers that you wish to include in your worksheet, you must edit it before loading it into 1-2-3, or use the /**D**ata**P**arse command discussed below. If you choose to edit the file, enclose text in double quotes (" . . . "), and separate text and numbers by spaces or commas. The file should have a .PRN extension; if it does not, rename it.

Once the file is edited, you are ready to import it into a 1-2-3 worksheet. First, you must be in the 1-2-3 worksheet mode. Move the pointer to the upper left corner of the region you wish the imported file to occupy. Enter the /**F**ile**I**mport command. You are asked if you are importing Text (only) or Numbers (and text-labels). Then you type or point to the file name.

The results depend on whether you specified Text or Numbers. For text, 1-2-3 creates a left-aligned label for each line in the print file. For numbers, 1-2-3 creates a number entry for each number and a left-aligned label for each " . . . " string. Each line in the print (imported) file generates a row on the worksheet. Anything else is ignored. You may need to experiment a bit to get the results you want.

/DataParse and ASCII File Importation

The /**D**ata**P**arse command works in conjunction with the /**F**ile**I**mport**T**ext command to make the importation of ASCII-generic data easier. This command separates (*parses*) imported data into value, date, time, and label entries based on a *format line*, and even helps create the format line. This command is useful to those who create tables and lists of numbers using other applications software (such as word processing, statistical, or database management systems), or who capture data in tabular format from mainframe computers.

For example, say you have a file of inventory data on a disk, with each line of the file beginning with a label followed by three numbers:

Generic Pet Type	Cost	Qty	Price
Parakeet	0.99	10	4.99
Hamster	1.25	15	6.95
Guppy	0.03	200	0.98

You wish to bring these data into Lotus so you can calculate how much you have paid for your inventory and how much money you will make if you sell it all. Before entering Lotus, you renamed this file so it has a .PRN extension.

First, use the /**W**orksheet**E**rase command to give yourself a clean worksheet (remember to /**F**ile**S**ave before erasing). Then /**F**ile**I**mport**T**ext to bring the file in as a series of labels. You will create a column of label entries starting with the cell where the cell pointer was when the command was initiated. Cell A1 will now contain the label

```
'Generic Pet Type            Cost      Qty       Price
```

and A2 will contain the label

```
'Parakeet                    0.99      10         4.99
```

Keeping the cell pointer in the top cell of the column of imported data, give the /**D**ata**P**arse command. You will be presented with the submenu illustrated in Figure B-5. In this instance, we imported data with the cell pointer in A1. (The screen in Figure B-5 was created *after* using the format-line create option discussed in the next paragraph.)

The first step in parsing is to create a format line. The format line is used in subsequent steps to tell Lotus how to divide the text data into label and value *blocks*, with each block occupying a different column in the worksheet after parsing. Lotus creates a "best guess" format line if you select the *Format-Line* option. This option yields two further options, *Create* or *Edit*; choose *Create*. Lotus inspects the label text in the current cell, creates a format line based on the data in that cell, displaces the cell entries one row down, and places the proposed format line in the current cell. You can see the result in Figure B-5. The data imported into cells A1..A4 have been pushed down one cell, and A1 now contains a format line. Format line symbols have the following meanings:

L	*first character of a label block.*
V	*first character of a value block.*
D	*first character of a date block.*
T	*first character of a time block.*
S	*skip the character below when parsing.*
>	*continuation of a block.*
*	*blank space, currently undefined, that can become part of the block to either side in cells below.*

As it creates the format line, Lotus analyzes each character in the input line. Blanks are assumed to separate blocks, and are replaced in the format line by the * character. When a non-numeric character is encountered, a label block is started with the L symbol. When a number is encountered after a blank, a value, date or time block is started with symbols V, D, or T. The block, of whatever type, is continued with > characters until another blank space is encountered.

Format line creation works reasonably well except when there are labels with embedded spaces in the line being analyzed. Note that Lotus separated *Generic Pet Type* into three separate blocks in the initial format line (illustrated in Figure B-5). It was necessary to edit, using the *Format-lineEdit* subcommand, to achieve the proper format line illustrated in Figure B-6. When editing format lines, the default is *overstrike* mode and an *OVR* indicator appears in the bottom right of the screen. Terminate editing by pressing <CR>. When you have label-type column headings over numeric-type data columns, as in this example, it is necessary to create a second format line, as shown in Figure B-6.

```
A1: |L>>>>>>*L>>*L>>>*********L>>>*******L>>******L>>>>                    MENU
Format-Line  Input-Column  Output-Range  Reset  Go  Quit
Create or edit format line at current cell
        A         B         C         D         E         F         G         H
1   L>>>>>>*L>>*L>>>*********L>>>*******L>>******L>>>>
2   Generic Pet Type        Cost       Qty       Price
3   Parakeet                0.99        10        4.99
4   Hamster                 1.25        15        6.95
5   Guppy                   0.03       200        0.98
6
7
8
9
10
11
12
13
14
15
16
17
18
19
20
14-Feb-86  05:28  PM                                   CALC
```

FIGURE B-5 /**D**ata**P**arse Command

Once format lines are created and edited, the *Input-Column* should be specified. The input column is the range containing the format line(s) and all rows of text to be parsed. In this situation, the range was specified as A1..A6. The *Output-Range* is identified by the upper left cell in the output range (in this case, A11). Finally, the *Go* option parses the data according to the format line(s) and fills the output range with the data. We had to adjust the width of Column A (using the /**W**orksheet**C**olumn**S**et-width command) because the labels in that column are wider than the default width. Note, in Figure B-6, that the width of column A is displayed as *[W17]* in the control panel area when the cell pointer points at a cell in that column. In addition, we used the /**R**ange**L**abel**R**ight command on cells B11..D11 to right-justify the headings over those columns.

Although the /**D**ata**P**arse command may seem difficult, it is by far the easiest way to import tabular ASCII data. On the other hand, when the source of the data creates output in a delimited form (quotes ["] around labels, and commas [,] between data items), /**D**ata**P**arse is not necessary: the data may be directly imported using the /**F**ile**I**mport**N**umbers command. Both dBASE and BASIC have the capability of writing disk files in this format.

```
A11: [W17] 'Generic Pet Type                                        READY

            A               B         C         D         E         F         G
1   L>>>>>>>>>>>>>>>>********L>>>>******L>>>******L>>>>
2   Generic Pet Type        Cost       Qty       Price
3   L>>>>>>****************V>>>*******V>*******V>>>
4   Parakeet                0.99        10        4.99
5   Hamster                 1.25        15        6.95
6   Guppy                   0.03       200        0.98
7
8
9
10
11  Generic Pet Type     Cost      Qty     Price
12  Parakeet             0.99       10      4.99
13  Hamster              1.25       15      6.95
14  Guppy                0.03      200      0.98
15
16
17
18
19
20
14-Feb-86  05:29  PM
```

FIGURE B-6 Result of /**D**ata**P**arse Command and Additional Editing

EXPORTING DATA FROM 1-2-3

There are two ways to export data from Lotus 1-2-3 worksheets. The first uses Translate, discussed above. The second uses /**P**rint**F**ile to create an ASCII-generic file that can be directly imported into word processors such as WordStar. These files can also be imported into dBASE III and other database managers if both worksheet and database are structured alike.

/**P**rint**F**ile works just like the more common /**P**rint**P**rinter command. It is generally best, however, to set *OptionsOtherUnformatted* before printing to eliminate margins and page breaks in the output. These usually cause problems when the file is later read by the other program.

OUTPUT FROM dBASE III

The **COPY** command may be used to extract data from a file that will be used by a word processing program such as WordStar MailMerge to print form letters and other applications. This command can also extract data for further analysis by a spreadsheet program such as VisiCalc, Multiplan, or Lotus 1-2-3, or for input to a programming language such as BASIC. The output file can be constrained using a **{field list}** or **{condition}**.

```
. copy to sdf_ex for cost>.10 sdf
      3 records copied
. type sdf_ex.txt
0007sesame seed bun    0.1240019851008
0016apple pie          0.1634619850815
0017cherry pie         0.1420019850919

. copy to delim_ex for cost>.10 delimited
      3 records copied
. type delim_ex.txt
"0007","sesame seed bun",0.12,400,19851008
"0016","apple pie",0.16,346,19850815
"0017","cherry pie",0.14,200,19850919

. _
Command Line    |<B:>|RAW_MATL              |Rec: EOF/19      |      |

                 Enter a dBASE III PLUS command.
```

FIGURE B-7 Variations of the **COPY** Command
Note: Items entered by the user are in **boldface**.

To make the data available to other software, the output of the command must be either a file in *ASCII text* or a file with special information recognized by the specific program. First, we will discuss the creation of ASCII text files for word processors and computer languages (such as BASIC), then we will discuss the creation of specially-coded spreadsheet files.

ASCII Text Output

ASCII text might also be called plain text; it is not coded in any special way by dBASE. Most applications software can read ASCII text, so it is a good way (if not an especially efficient method) to move data among programs. The dBASE III command **TYPE {filename.ext}** may be used to display the contents of an ASCII file on screen or printer.

Notice, in Figure B-7, that two variations of the **COPY** command produce ASCII files.

- **COPY TO {filename} SDF** creates a file in ASCII text of the entire database (or, a portion of the database if you use a **{field list}** or a **{condition}**). Fields are aligned similar to the output of the **LIST** command. This is useful when you want to include a table of data into a text document being edited by a word processor.

- **COPY TO {filename} DELIMITED** creates a file in ASCII text of the entire database (or, a portion of the database if you use a **{field list}** or a **{condition}**). Character-type fields are enclosed in quotation marks and all fields are separated by commas.

DELIMITED output is almost always preferred, but you may use **SDF** (*Structured Data Format*) output if your applications program is written in FORTRAN or COBOL and requires a structured format.

Finally, notice how dBASE III converts date-type fields for ASCII output. Your application program may or may not be able to make use of such a format.

A default extension of .TXT is assigned unless you specify otherwise.

WordStar MailMerge Users: Use the **DELIMITED** form: **COPY TO OUTPUT DELIMITED**. You will be able to use the file as a MailMerge data file without editing.

BASIC Language Programmers: Use the **DELIMITED** form: **COPY TO OUTPUT DELIMITED**. You will be able to read the file as a sequential file with **INPUT #** statements without editing.

Spreadsheet File Output

dBASE III Plus (but not the original dBASE III) allows you to output a file that can be directly read by three of the most popular spreadsheet programs: VisiCalc, Multiplan, and Lotus 1-2-3. Records are placed in rows, with fields in columns. The basic forms of the command are as follows:

copy to {filename} type dif	*Creates a file in VisiCalc format.*
copy to {filename} type sylk	*Creates a file in Multiplan format.*
copy to {filename} type wks	*Creates a file in Lotus 1-2-3 format.*

Example for Lotus 1-2-3. To test this feature, we opened the file RAW_MATL and then issued the command

copy to raw_matl type wks

A file named RAW_MATL.WKS was created on the default disk. Then, we **QUIT** dBASE III and entered Lotus 1-2-3. We used the Lotus /**F**ile**R**etrieve command to load the worksheet file. The result appears in Figure B-8.

Note that the Lotus column widths are set to the dBASE field widths, resulting in a line of ******* across the INVENTORY field column and the hiding of part of the field name. This can be easily corrected by setting the column width to a larger number (in Lotus, or in dBASE before making the copy). The numeric format of the COST field also needs to be changed. No information is lost: but some information is hidden because of the differing uses of column widths and numeric formats by the two programs.

Finally, the dates are copied as a label (character string), that may be converted by a Lotus 1-2-3 Release 2 function. For instance, to convert the date in E2 to a Lotus-style date, you could use the following function in cell F2 (all three lines are one cell entry).

```
A2: [W4] '0014                                                          READY


      A        B             C     D  E        F        G        H
1   RMIDDESC               COST    INVLAST_ORDER
2   001412 oz. cup            0 ***19871004
3   001516 oz. cup            0 ***19870928
4   00184 oz. fry pack        0 ***19871019
5   00196 oz. fry pack        0 ***19871015
6   00138 oz. cup             0 ***19871006
7   0011Coca Cola (oz.)       0 ***19871013
8   0012Sprite (oz.)          0 ***19871012
9   0001all-beef patty        0 ***19871001
10  0016apple pie             0 ***19870815
11  0009catsup (oz.)          0 ***19871010
12  0006ch. onion (oz.)       0 ***19871010
13  0004cheese slice          0 ***19871009
14  0017cherry pie            0 ***19870919
15  0010fren. fry (oz.)       0 ***19871012
16  0003lettuce leaf          0 90 19871003
17  0005pickle slice          0 ***19870915
18  0008regular bun           0 ***19871003
19  0007sesame seed bun       0 ***19871008
20  0002sp. sauce (oz.)       0 ***19870930
25-Mar-87  08:55 AM
```

FIGURE B-8 A Lotus 1-2-3 Worksheet Created by the **COPY . . . TYPE WKS** Command

@DATE(@INT((@VALUE(E2)-19000000)/10000),
    @INT(@MOD((@VALUE(E2)-19000000),10000)/100),
    @MOD(@INT(@MOD((@VALUE(E2)-19000000),10000)),100))

It would be less cumbersome, however, to add three fields to the database before it is copied: one for year, one for month, and one for day. Then, use the **REPLACE** command as follows (this is one command, do not separate it with <CR> into two lines).

replace all year with year(last_order), month with month(last_order), day with day(last_order)

After this, the dBASE **COPY** command will create a Lotus column for each of year, month, and day, and the Lotus function @DATE(F2-1900,G2,H2), placed in I2 and copied down column I, should work nicely.

INPUT TO dBASE III

The transfer of data from other applications software, such as a word processor or spreadsheet, is essentially the reverse of the process to output data to those programs. The **APPEND FROM** command is used, with the basic forms:

append from {filename} delimited	*For data in delimited format.*
append from {filename} sdf	*For data in structured format.*
append from {filename} type dif	*For data in a VisiCalc spreadsheet.*
append from {filename} type sylk	*For data in a Multiplan spreadsheet.*
append from {filename} type wks	*For data in a Lotus 1-2-3 worksheet.*

where **{filename}** is an ASCII text file, or a file in the appropriate spreadsheet format. dBASE assumes a .TXT file extension for ASCII text files (or, you may specify a different extension), and the appropriate extension for each of the spreadsheet types. Examples:

append from ws_file delimited	*For data separated by commas, with character strings enclosed by " (quotation) marks.*
append from lot_file.prn sdf	*For structured data created by a Lotus /***P***rint***F***ile command.*
append from lot_file type wks	*For data from a Lotus 1-2-3 Release 1A worksheet.*
append from lot_file.wk1 type wks	*For data from a Lotus 1-2-3 Release 2 worksheet; because Lotus has changed the default worksheet file extension (to* .WK1*), it must be specified.*

Before appending from an another file, you must **CREATE** a data file to hold the incoming data. The structure you create must match the type and width of the data being imported. The receiving data file is then opened with the **USE** command, and the appropriate version of **APPEND FROM** is given.

Word Processor Users: You may create the file with commas separating data elements and use the **DELIMITED** form, or you may carefully align the data in columns and use the **SDF** form.

BASIC Programmers: Use the **WRITE #** statement to create delimited output, then import with the **DELIMITED** qualifier.

Spreadsheet Users: Make sure that the type of data is the same in each column (i.e., all character or all numeric). Before leaving the spreadsheet program, make careful notes of width, data type, and number of decimal places in each column. Also, remove column headings and anything else that is not part of the data to be imported by dBASE. (You may want to work with an extra copy of the file.)

You now have two choices:

- From within the spreadsheet program, you may use the command that creates an ASCII output file (e.g., /**P**rint**F**ile in Lotus 1-2-3) to put the data on a disk file. When you are in dBASE, create a file structure that matches the spreadsheet columns and use the **SDF** option on input. (Because some spreadsheet programs automatically assign extensions to ASCII output files, you may have to specify the extension as part of the command: **APPEND FROM LOT_FILE.PRN SDF**.)

- Exit the spreadsheet and enter dBASE. Create a file structure that matches the spreadsheet columns, and then use the appropriate **APPEND FROM . . . TYPE . . .** command. (If you are using the original dBASE III, this choice is not available, and you must use the SDF option above.)

APPENDIX

C

RANDOM NUMBERS AND PROBABILITY DISTRIBUTIONS

This appendix covers the basic principles for generating random numbers and testing to see if the numbers are random. Random numbers are used to generate random observations from arbitrary discrete and continuous probability distributions and from the well-known exponential and normal probability distributions. The purpose of this appendix is to supply the additional tools needed to work with random numbers and probability distributions in Lotus 1-2-3.

GENERATING RANDOM NUMBERS

A number is said to be random if its chance of occurring is the same as that of any other number. If you were selecting numbers between 1 and 100, you would expect as many to be between 1 and 10 as are between 21 and 30, or 44 and 53, for example. We say that random numbers are equally likely, or that they come from a *uniform probability distribution.*

Lotus 1-2-3 includes a function, @RAND, that produces a pseudo-random number. It generates a number that "acts like" a random number but is actually determined by a formula that depends on a particular "seed" or starting point. Unlike some other random number generators, the one in Lotus 1-2-3 does not use a user-controlled seed. Each time you load and run Lotus 1-2-3 (Release 1A), you start with the same random-number seed and you obtain the same first random number from the @RAND function (0.1475065968). The sequence of "random" numbers generated within a particular spreadsheet will be the same. In Lotus 1-2-3 (Release 2), you get a different random number each time you load and run Lotus 1-2-3. Therefore, it is impossible to generate the same sequence of random numbers using the @RAND function in Release 2. If you wish to repeat the same sequence of random numbers, 1-2-3 can be restarted (from the DOS prompt) in Release 1A, or you can create a separate table of random numbers which can then be used in another spreadsheet to provide repeatability. If you are comparing several alternative policies or procedures that depend on some random variables, you would like the results to reflect only the effects of the different policies. If you do not use the same set of random numbers, some of the variation in the results will be due to random variation. Using the same set of random numbers, then, allows you to control for the random variation.

Contributed by Robert L. Armacost

```
A1: 'COUNT                                                                   READY


          A         B         C          D         E         F         G         H
1   COUNT          21              /RNCCOUNT~B1~/RNCLIMIT~B2~{GOTO}LIMIT~
2   LIMIT          20              /XNENTER NO. OF RANDOM NOS. DESIRED  ~LIMIT~
3                                  /RNCTABLE~A15..B15~/REA15..B2048~/WGRM~
4                                  {GOTO}$COUNT~0~+$COUNT+1~/RNCLOOP~D5~
5                                  {CALC}~
6                                  {GOTO}A14~{DOWN}~+LIMIT-COUNT+2{EDIT}{CALC}~
7                                  {RIGHT}~+@RAND{EDIT}{CALC}~
8                                  /WIR~
9                                  /XICOUNT<=LIMIT~/XGLOOP~
10                                 {GOTO}TABLE~/RNCTABLE~.{END}{UP}~
11                                 {GOTO}A14~"INDEX~{RIGHT}RANDOM_NO~
12                                 {GOTO}{HOME}~COUNT~{DOWN}LIMIT~
13
14      INDEX RANDOM_NO
15
16          1 0.472762
17          2 0.725215
18          3 0.663530
19          4 0.697482
20          5 0.937345
```

FIGURE C-1 Random Number Table Generator

A macro program that generates a table of random numbers is illustrated in Figure C-1, in the range D1..D12. The table of random numbers starts in A16..B16; the quantity of numbers generated is input by the user. Column A contains a sequential index number and column B contains the random number. The table is a named range called TABLE that can be /FileCombined with another file. If you want only the random numbers, then you have to modify the named range (TABLE) to include only column B. The macro is complete as written and defines all of the necessary ranges in the program except the name of the macro. Use the /RangeNameCreate command in cell D1 to name the macro with a name such as \R (for Random).

TESTING A RANDOM NUMBER GENERATOR

This section contains two tests. The first is a method for you to test your particular spreadsheet package to determine whether the initial seed is constant, user-controlled, or random. The second is used to test whether a set of random numbers could have come from a uniform distribution.

Random Number Seed Test

Whether or not you are not using Lotus 1-2-3 (because the software may have changed since we wrote this book), you should determine whether the initial seed is constant, user-controlled, or random. You can perform a simple observational test following these steps:

1. Find the description of the random number function in your software package documentation. In some cases, the function will require or permit an argument that is the random number seed. In other cases, the documentation will state whether the seed is constant or variable. *Do not believe everything you read: we have found one instance where the documentation stated that the seed was constant but, in fact, was not constant as determined by the test described here!*

2. Start the software from the DOS (or other operating system) prompt. Generate a random number (e.g., in Lotus 1-2-3, enter @RAND in A1) before doing anything else. Record the value of the random number on a piece of paper. Generate three more random numbers (in Lotus and similar spreadsheet packages, use the *recalculate* command or function key), recording each. Where the software allows a user-controlled seed as an argument, supply a number that is approximately the mid-point of the allowable range.

3. Exit to the operating system.

4. Repeat step 2. (If the software allows a seed, use the same number as before.) If you obtain the same series of random numbers, then the seed is probably constant (or user-controlled). If you obtain a different series of numbers, the seed is probably random.

Goodness-of-Fit Test

Random numbers must each be equally likely to occur. In statistical terms, they must come from a uniform probability distribution. To test whether a set of random numbers could have come from a uniform distribution, the *chi-square goodness-of-fit test* is used. The data are divided into a number of intervals or classes (n). The number of observations one would expect (E) in a given interval if the data did come from a uniform distribution is calculated, and the number of observations actually occurring (O) in that interval is counted. The chi-square statistic is then calculated according to the following formula:

$$\text{Chi-Square} = \sum[(O - E)^2/E]$$

The calculated chi-square value is compared to the test value at the given level of significance with n-1 degrees of freedom. (The degrees of freedom may be different when other distributions are tested.) Figure C-2 contains a spreadsheet for the goodness-of-fit test.

Several tasks must be accomplished before the macro that performs the goodness-of-fit test is invoked. The numbers to be tested must be entered in column A, by importing them from another source (such as the random number generating spreadsheet described above), by calculating them directly in this spreadsheet, or by manually entering them. Name cell A1 as RNTABLE. Enter the various labels in the cells indicated in Figure C-2. The spreadsheet illustrated in Figure C-2 is set up for ten classes, thus 10 must be entered in D2. The number of points, D1, is computed by the macro and may be left at 0 for now. Enter the upper limits of the ten classes in cells B7..B16 or use /DataFill based on information in cell D2. The

```
D1: @COUNT(RNTABLE)                                                        READY


          A          B          C          D          E          F          G          H
1   0.472762               POINTS         20                /RNCDIST~B7..B16~
2   0.725215               CLASSES        10                /RNCPOINTS~D1..D1~
3   0.663530                                                /RNCCLASS~D2..D2~
4   0.697482                                                /RNDRNTABLE~{GOTO}A1~
5   0.937345                                                /RNCRNTABLE~{END}{DOWN}~
6   0.704439     LIMIT        OBS        EXP     CHI-SQ {GOTO}D1~+@COUNT(RNTABLE)~
7   0.178575       0.1          2          2        0.0 /DDRNTABLE~DIST~{CALC}~/XQ~
8   0.062679       0.2          3          2        0.5
9   0.688185       0.3          0          2        2.0
10  0.375249       0.4          1          2        0.5
11  0.130148       0.5          3          2        0.5
12  0.869768       0.6          0          2        2.0
13  0.655470       0.7          5          2        4.5
14  0.748348       0.8          3          2        0.5
15  0.454472       0.9          2          2        0.0
16  0.006453       1.0          1          2        0.5
17  0.895124                    0
18  0.690568    CALCULATED CHI-SQUARE             11.00
19  0.414100    TEST CHI-SQUARE
20  0.147506              ALPHA=.05, DF=9         16.919
```

FIGURE C-2 Random Number Test

expected frequency is calculated in column D: enter the formula $D$1/$D$2 in cell D7 and copy it through cell D16. In cell E7 enter the formula (C7-D7)^2/D7 and copy it through cell E16. These cells will display ERR until the macro is run. The chi-square statistic is computed in cell E18 with @SUM(E7..E16). The test value of the chi-square statistic is found in a chi-square table for the appropriate number of degrees of freedom and a specified significance level and entered as shown in cells B19..E20.

The macro contained in F1..F7 is named \G. When invoked, it names several ranges, determines the number of (random number) points, and uses the /**D**ata**D**istribution command to find the observed frequency in each class, placing the frequencies in column C of the table. The chi-square statistic is then computed by the formulas entered earlier.

With a few modifications, the goodness-of-fit test can be used to test if a set of data comes from any other specified distribution. The primary modification is that the expected frequencies must be manually entered because they are usually difficult to calculate. If the number of classes is changed (e.g., increased to reflect a more complex distribution) or the number of population parameters to be estimated changes, then additional modifications are required to the defined ranges and the test statistic. Consult a standard statistics textbook for guidance.

PROBABILITY DISTRIBUTIONS AND RANDOM VARIABLES

On many occasions you need observations from particular probability distributions. To generate values of those random variables, you generally use random numbers in conjunction with a cumulative probability distribution. In Unit 11 we used random numbers to generate observations from discrete distributions for motorcycle, snowmobile, and ATV quarterly demands. In many cases you are required to generate observations from continuous distributions.

Exponential Distribution

A common continuous distribution used in various decision support models is the *exponential distribution.* Often the interarrival time or the service time at a service facility (e.g., bank teller, checkout cashier) can be characterized by an exponential distribution. The only parameter required to define a unique exponential distribution is the average (mean) of the distribution (AVG). The cumulative exponential distribution that provides the probability that the service time is less than or equal to a specific time t is given by the following formula:

$$F(t) = 1 - e^{-(t/AVG)}$$

This function provides the basis for generating exponentially-distributed time values. Because F(t) is a probability, we can substitute a random number RN for F(t):

$$RN = 1 - e^{-(t/AVG)}$$

Solving this expression for t, we obtain

$$t = -AVG \ln(1 - RN)$$

Because 1 - RN is also a random number, this equation can be simplified to

$$t = -AVG \ln(RN)$$

Therefore t is a random observation from an exponential distribution with a mean of AVG. The Lotus 1-2-3 expression for this equation is

```
-AVG*@LN(@RAND)
```

This expression can be used wherever an exponential random variable is required. Note, however, that each time the spreadsheet is recalculated a new value appears because the @RAND function generates a new random number. The alternative is to generate a separate table of random numbers using a procedure similar to that in Figure C-1. The following changes must be made. In D4, the range named LOOP is D6. Insert a new row 5 to provide for the input of AVG. Use the formula

```
{RIGHT}~-AVG*@LN(@RAND){EDIT}{CALC}~
```

to compute the exponential random number in row 8. Change row 12 to enter the label EXP_RANDOM_NO. Refer to Figure C-3 for the complete macro.

```
A2: 'LIMIT                                                         READY


       A          B          C          D         E         F         G         H
1   COUNT            21             /RNCCOUNT~B1~/RNCLIMIT~B2~{GOTO}LIMIT~
2   LIMIT            20             /XNENTER NO. OF RANDOM NOS. DESIRED  ~LIMIT~
3                                   /RNCTABLE~A15..B15~/REA15..B2048~/WGRM~
4                                   {GOTO}$COUNT~0~+$COUNT+1~/RNCLOOP~D6~
5   AVG =           3.5             /RNCAVG~B5~{GOTO}A5~AVG =~/XNENTER AVG ~AVG~
6                                   {CALC}~
7                                   {GOTO}A14~{DOWN}~+LIMIT-COUNT+2{EDIT}{CALC}~
8                                   {RIGHT}~-AVG*@LN(@RAND){EDIT}{CALC}~
9                                   /WIR~
10                                  /XICOUNT<=LIMIT~/XGLOOP~
11                                  {GOTO}TABLE~/RNCTABLE~.{END}{UP}~
12                                  {GOTO}A14~"INDEX~{RIGHT}EXP_RANDOM_NO~
13                                  {GOTO}{HOME}~COUNT~{DOWN}LIMIT~
14       INDEX EXP_RANDOM_NO
15
16           1 2.622064
17           2 1.124503
18           3 1.435632
19           4 1.260972
20           5 0.226460
```

FIGURE C-3 Exponential Random Number Generator

General Continuous Distributions

Because the cumulative distribution function is available in an analytic functional form for the exponential distribution, it can be "inverted" to find the value of the random variable for a given cumulative probability (random number). For most continuous distributions, this luxury is not available and some other scheme must be used to generate random variates.

For the discrete distribution in Unit 11, we used a partitioning scheme with the cumulative distribution function. Suppose that the motorcycle demand depicted in Figure 11-2 was actually a continuous variable, and that the points on the graph were points drawn from that continuous cumulative probability distribution. The resulting piecewise linear curve that approximates the continuous cumulative distribution is plotted in Figure C-4.

Using this continuous distribution, a random number equal to 0.15 does not yield a demand of 1050 units but rather a demand between 950 and 1050 units. The exact number is found by linear interpolation:

$$\text{Demand} = 950 + [(0.15 - 0.05) / (0.20 - 0.05)] \times [1050 - 950]$$
$$= 1016.67 \text{ units}$$

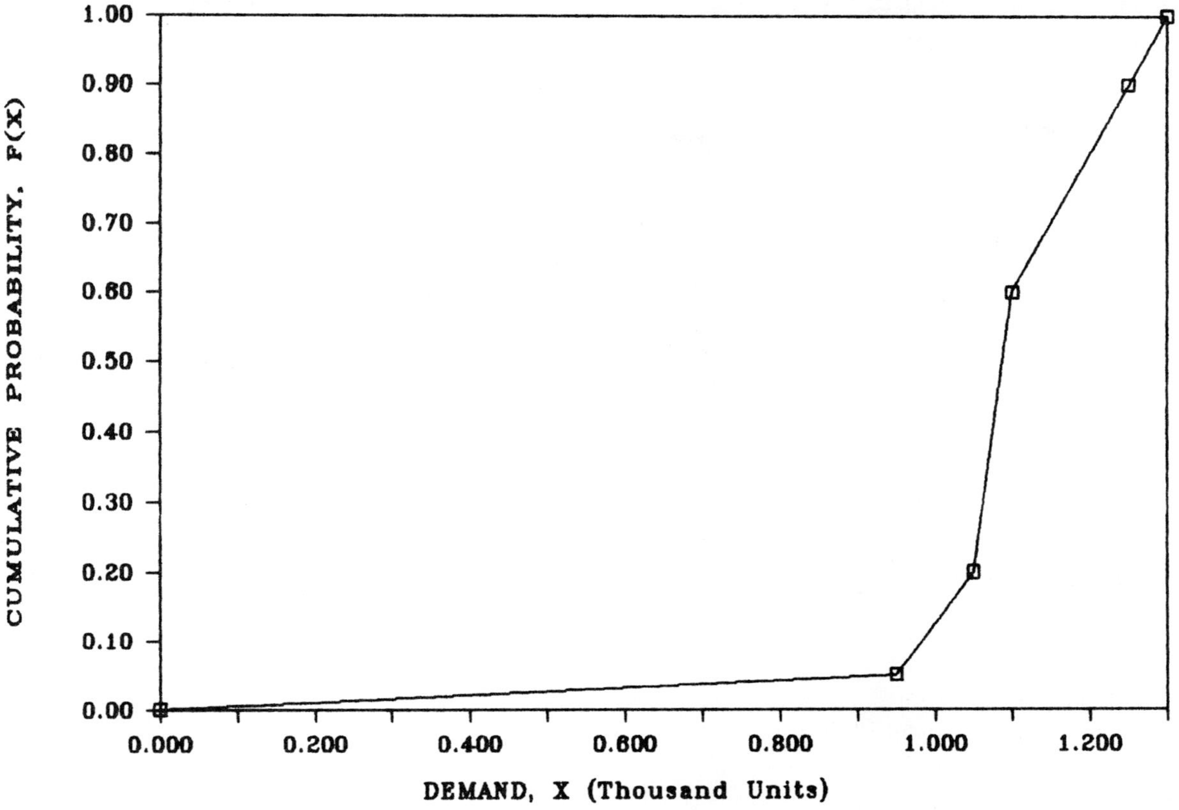

FIGURE C-4 Cumulative Continuous Probability Distribution

In Unit 11, we used the @VLOOKUP function to find the demand with the random number as the index. With a continuous distribution, we still use the @VLOOKUP function with the random number as the index, but now the distribution is entered differently. Recall that the @VLOOKUP function selects values from the row where the index column value is less than or equal to the index argument. To interpolate, we must also know the differences in index column values and demand column values between the chosen row and the row below it. Rather than imbed those values in another table, it is simpler to calculate the intervals and include them in the lookup table.

The modified lookup table and lookup function are illustrated in Figure C-5 using the first quarter motorcycle demand data from Unit 11. The cells A4..D9 are a named range called PQ1M. The value in cell C4 is calculated by the formula A5 - A4, and that formula is copied to cells C5..C8. Similarly, the value in cell D4 is calculated by the formula B5 - B4 and that formula is copied to cells D5..D8. Cell C12 contains the function @RAND and is a named range called RN. The random demand is calculated using linear interpolation with the @VLOOKUP function. Only part of the formula is shown at the top of Figure C-5. The complete formula is

```
@VLOOKUP(RN,PQ1M,1)+(RN-@VLOOKUP(RN,PQ1M,0))/@VLOOKUP(RN,PQ1M,2)*@VLOOKUP(RN,PQ1M,3)
```

Enter labels as shown in the figure.

```
C14: @VLOOKUP(RN,PQ1M,1)+(RN-@VLOOKUP(RN,PQ1M,0))/@VLOOKUP(RN,PQ1M,2)*@    READY


         A          B          C          D          E          F          G          H
1    Motorcycle Demand:
2           Q1
3        Index     Demand     RN Int  Dmnd Int
4         0.00          0       0.05       950
5         0.05        950       0.15       100
6         0.20       1050       0.40        50
7         0.60       1100       0.30       150
8         0.90       1250       0.10        50
9         1.00       1300
10
11
12   Random Number        0.228899
13
14   Random Demand        1053.612
15
16
17
18
19
20
```

FIGURE C-5 Continuous Random Variable

In the illustration, the @RAND function was used to generate the random number directly. As an alternative, the random number could be drawn from a table generated by the macro in Figure C-1. This macro could be modified to generate a table of random demands from this distribution. The lookup procedure illustrated above could also be used directly in the aggregate planning simulation model.

Normal Distribution

A frequently used continuous probability distribution is the *normal distribution* characterized by the familiar bell-shaped curve. A useful characteristic of the normal distribution is that any given normal distribution can be described in terms of its mean and standard deviation. The *standard normal distribution*, with a mean equal to zero and a standard deviation equal to one, is used as the basis for all calculations of normal variates. A number called the standard score (Z) describes a given point, x, as being some number of standard deviations away from the mean. If the standard score is positive, then x is larger than the mean. If the standard score is negative, then x is smaller than the mean. The standard score is calculated by the following formula.

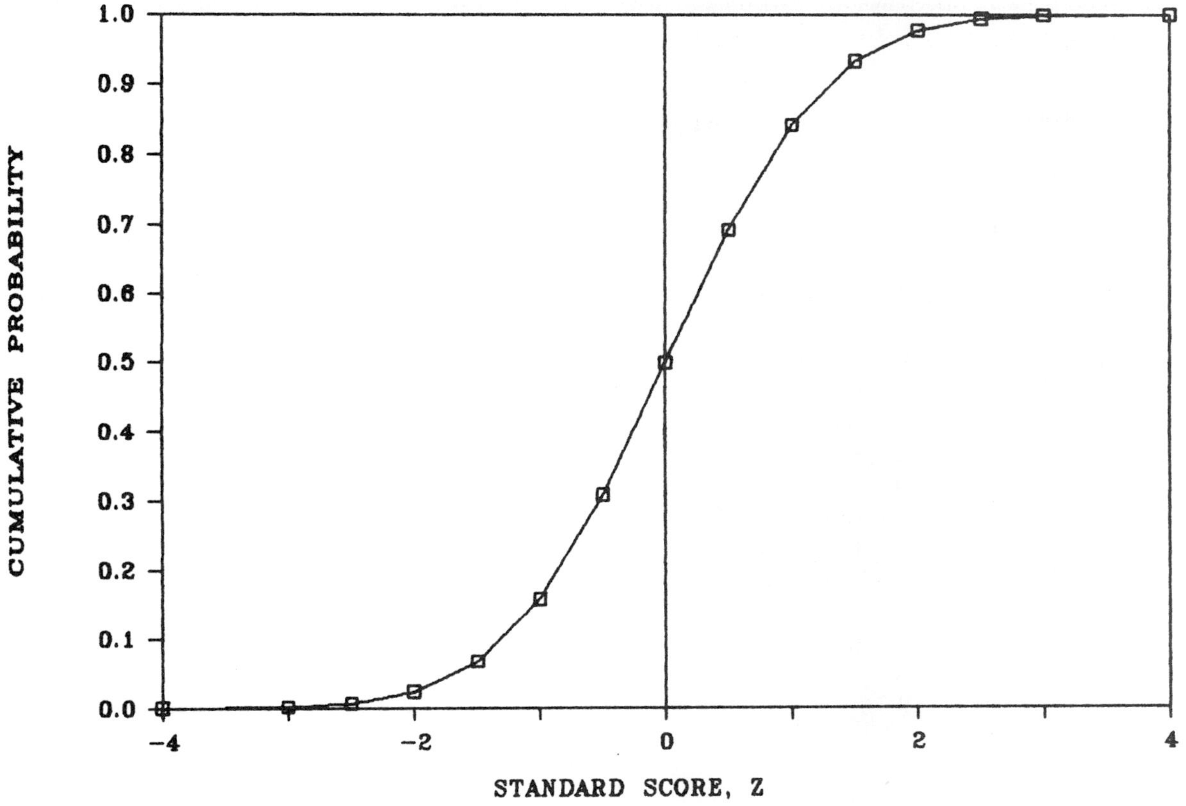

FIGURE C-6 Cumulative Normal Probability Distribution

Z = (x - mean) / standard deviation

To obtain values of the normal random variable x, you need only generate values for Z from the standard normal distribution and calculate x using the following formula:

x = mean + (Z)(standard deviation)

There are several ways to generate a value for Z. One is to "discretize" the normal distribution, that is, divide the normal distribution into a number of discrete intervals, each of which has a specific cumulative probability of occurring. In Lotus 1-2-3, generate a random number and calculate the appropriate value of Z from a direct table lookup as was done in Unit 11.

A second approach is to "linearize" the cumulative probability distribution, as in Figure C-4. This is illustrated in Figure C-6 using an interval between points of 0.5 standard deviations. In Lotus 1-2-3, use a table lookup interpolating between the various points, as discussed below.

G15: +G10+G13*G11 READY

	A	B	C	D	E	F	G	H
1	Standard Normal Distribution							
2								
3	Index	Z-Score	RN Int	Z Int				
4	0.00000	-4.0	0.00135	1.0				
5	0.00135	-3.0	0.00486	0.5				
6	0.00621	-2.5	0.01659	0.5				
7	0.02280	-2.0	0.04400	0.5				
8	0.06680	-1.5	0.09190	0.5				
9	0.15870	-1.0	0.14980	0.5				
10	0.30850	-0.5	0.19150	0.5		Mean	1150	
11	0.50000	0.0	0.19150	0.5		Std. Dev.	98.7	
12	0.69150	0.5	0.14980	0.5		Random Number	0.746051	
13	0.84130	1.0	0.09190	0.5		Z-Score	0.682081	
14	0.93320	1.5	0.04400	0.5				
15	0.97720	2.0	0.01659	0.5		Random Variable	1217.321	
16	0.99379	2.5	0.00486	0.5				
17	0.99865	3.0	0.00135	1.0				
18	1.00000	4.0						
19								
20								

FIGURE C-7 Normal Random Variable

A normal distribution lookup table and lookup function are illustrated in Figure C-7. Assume that the first quarter motorcycle demand data from Unit 11 is normally distributed. The mean demand is 1150 units and the standard deviation, calculated from the data, is 98.7 units. Enter these values and associated labels. The cells A4..D18 are a named range called NORM. The intervals are calculated as before. Cell G12 contains the function @RAND and is a named range called RN. The (random) Z-Score is calculated in cell G13 using the @VLOOKUP function as follows:

```
@VLOOKUP(RN,NORM,1)+(RN-@VLOOKUP(RN,NORM,0))/@VLOOKUP(RN,NORM,2)*@VLOOKUP(RN,NORM,3)
```

Finally, the (normal) random demand is calculated in cell G15 using the formula shown at the top of Figure C-7.

The normal distribution can be integrated into any model using the above linearization and table lookup procedure. Whether the lookup table is included in the particular program or the normal random numbers are generated and placed in a separate table is up to the user; the choice is influenced by repeatability considerations as well as programming considerations.

In addition to the discretization and linearization approaches, standardized normal variates can be produced yet another way. The *central limit theorem* provides that the sum of n independent identically distributed random variables tends to be normally distributed as n becomes large. In fact, normality is approached rapidly, even for small values of n. This means that you can approximate the normal distribution by computing the sum of uniform random variables. The sum of n uniform random variables is approximately normally distributed with a mean equal to n/2 and a variance equal to n/12. When n = 12, the resulting random variable is approximately normally distributed with a mean equal to 6 and a standard deviation equal to 1. Thus, if you let n = 12, the standard normal Z-Score is calculated as follows:

$$Z = RN_1 + RN_2 + \ldots + RN_{12} - 6$$

This standard score is then multiplied by the standard deviation and the product added to the mean to calculate an observation from the given normal distribution. This approach is much simpler than discretization and linearization, but it requires that you use twelve uniform random numbers to get one normal random observation.

Other Probability Distributions

The approaches used above apply to other probability distributions as well. If you know what the correct distribution is, you can use these techniques directly. The only requirement is that you be able to specify the cumulative probability distribution, either as a function or in table form.

When you are working with data, you often do not know which probability distribution is appropriate. The common approach in such cases is to plot the data to see the general shape, calculate the mean and standard deviation, guess what kind of distribution might apply, and then use the chi-square goodness-of-fit test to see if the data could have come from the hypothesized distribution. Then estimate the cumulative probability distribution and apply a technique such as linearization to generate random observations from that distribution.

ADDITIONAL READING

The standard normal distribution and the chi-square goodness-of-fit test are discussed in standard statistics textbooks; see, for example,

Anderson, D. R., D. J. Sweeney, and T. A. Williams. *Statistics for Business and Economics*, 3rd edition. St. Paul: West, 1987.

Generation of random numbers is discussed in

Pritsker, A. A. B., and C. D. Pegden. *Introduction to Simulation and SLAM.* New York: Wiley, 1979.

APPENDIX

D ANSWERS TO REVIEW QUESTIONS

UNIT 1 AN INTRODUCTION TO DECISION SUPPORT ON PERSONAL COMPUTER SYSTEMS

1. Briefly state the general differences among EDP, MIS, and DSS.

   Electronic Data Processing (EDP) is concerned with the efficient processing of data, usually to maintain files or to produce routine output such as payroll checks. Management Information Systems (MIS) are designed to extract data from organizational records to provide reports such as job status and staff utilization. Decision Support Systems (DSS) are developed to assist in making decisions by retrieving data and analyzing it according to a model. EDP deals with current operations, MIS deals with control, and DSS deals with future direction of the organization.

3. What are the technological levels of a DSS?

   - DSS Tools — the hardware components.
   - DSS Generators — software used to build the system.
   - Specific DSS — the combination of data, model, and user interface designed to support a particular decision or set of decisions.

5. Outline the different types of decision-making models that are used in DSS, listing pairs of alternatives and how they differ.

   - *Data Inquiry* versus *Computational Modeling* — Data inquiry focuses on data retrieval and simple data analysis while computational models require extensive mathematical calculations.
   - *Stochastic* versus *Deterministic* — In a stochastic decision-making situation, a variety of possible outcomes exist for each alternative and the decision maker assigns probabilities to each of those outcomes occurring. In a deterministic situation there is no uncertainty regarding outcomes.

- *Single Criterion* versus *Multi-criterion* — Single criterion models focus on one measure of effectiveness while multi-criterion models are those that attempt to satisfy a number of objectives simultaneously.

- *Generic* versus *Specific* — Generic decision support models can be used to analyze a wide variety of situations in all of the functional areas of a business. Specific decision support models are designed and used to analyze fairly unique decision-making situations.

- *Heuristic* versus *Optimizing* — A heuristic model generally uses a "rule of thumb" to produce an adequate solution. An optimizing model is one that produces the best possible solution under the stated conditions of a problem.

UNIT 2 SOFTWARE FOR DECISION SUPPORT APPLICATIONS

1. What are the three components of a decision support system?

   - The analytical *models*.
   - The *data* to be analyzed.
   - The *user interface*.

3. What are the features of database management software?

   Database management systems software usually includes facilities for data input, editing, and output (including report writing). Usually included in these features are means for selecting only certain records, managing multiple files at once, and interfacing with other types of software.

5. What other types of software are used as DSS generators? Give an example of how each may be used.

   - Word Processing, for creation of memoranda and reports, also programming.
   - Outlining, for arrangement of ideas in project development and reporting.
   - Communications, for moving data over distances.
   - Quantitative Analysis, for model building and analysis.
   - Graphics, for communicating relationships among data.
   - Programming Language, for development of systems with intricate logic and heuristics.

UNIT 3 DATABASES FOR DECISION SUPPORT APPLICATIONS

1. What is an attribute? What is a record structure? Describe the products carried in a grocery store, listing the attributes and organizing them in a record structure.

   An attribute is a characteristic of an object, event, idea, or phenomenon selected for recording purposes. A record structure is a hierarchically organized list of attributes that describes a set of similar events, ideas, or phenomena. A typical record structure for the products in a grocery store is:

```
PRODUCT
   PRODUCT_ID_NUMBER (UPC)
   PRODUCT_NAME
   PRODUCT_UNIT_COST
   PRODUCT_SHELF_PRICE
   PRODUCT_SHELF_LOCATION
   PRODUCT_SUPPLIER*
      SUPPLIER_ID
   PRODUCT_STORAGE_LIFE
   .
   .
   .
```

3. Define one-to-one, many-to-one, one-to-many, and many-to-many relationships. What is a functional relationship?

   Let A and B be two attributes. For every value of A, if the value corresponds to one and only one value of B, and vice versa, then these two attributes have a one-to-one relationship. If each value of A corresponds to several values of B, and no value of B corresponds to more than one value of A, then we say A and B have a one-to-many relationship. If we exchange A and B in the above definition, we have a many-to-one relationship. If each of the values of A corresponds to several values of B and each of the values of B corresponds to several values of A, then we say A and B have a many-to-many relationship. One-to-one relationships and many-to-one relationships are functional relationships.

4. Identify all the attributes in data stores DEALERSHIP_FILE and PENDING_ORDER_FILE in this unit. What are the key attributes in DEALERSHIP_FILE and PENDING_ORDER_FILE, respectively?

   Attributes in the DEALERSHIP_FILE are:
      DEALERSHIP NAME, DEALER_ID_NUMBER, BUILDING_NUMBER, STREET, CITY, STATE, ZIP_CODE, CREDIT_LIMIT, and OUTSTANDING_BALANCE.

   Attributes in the PENDING_ORDER_FILE are:
      ORDER_NUMBER, O_D_DAY, O_D_MONTH, O_D_YEAR, DEALER_NAME, BUILDING, STREET, CITY, STATE, ZIP_CODE, MODEL_NUMBER, QUANTITY, S_D_D_DAY, S_D_D_MONTH, S_D_D_YEAR, UNIT_PRICE, ITEM_PRICE, and ORDER_TOTAL_PRICE.

UNIT 4 COST ALLOCATIONS — WHO ABSORBS THE OVERHEAD?

1. Why are cost allocations necessary?

   Some manufacturing costs cannot be traced directly to products or departments. However, these costs must be included in the cost of the product for balance sheet (inventory valuation) and income statement purposes. Since there is no way to directly trace the proper amount of cost to be assigned, allocations of cost are necessary.

3. Why may cost allocations be characterized as being partially an art form?

   While allocations require precise computations, there are several choices involved in terms of how the computations are made. Since there are no hard-fast rules for making these choices, judgment is required as it is in art.

5. Describe the step-down method.

   The allocation begins with the first service department whose costs are allocated to producing departments and other service departments where appropriate. The costs of other service departments are then allocated, in turn, until all service department costs have been allocated to producing departments. Once a service department's cost has been allocated, however, no cost from other service departments is allocated back to that service department.

7. Suggest a suitable basis for allocating the following service department costs in a manufacturing firm.

   a. employee cafeteria — number of employees in department.

   c. inventory control — direct material cost incurred in department.

UNIT 5 PRODUCTION ANALYSIS — PUTTING RESOURCES TO WORK

2. Define the following terms as they are used in this unit.

   d. returns to scale — the proportionate return in total product to an increase in scale of operations.

   e. marginal revenue product — the monetary value to the employer of the marginal product (additional output produced) of each worker. It is the value which the employer compares to the wage when deciding on the number of workers to employ. It is found by multiplying the marginal product of the input by the value (selling price) of the good being produced.

   h. marginal product — the increase in total product caused by an additional unit of an input being added to a set of inputs already being employed.

3. How are historic data used to calculate production relationships?

Using a data regression feature of an advanced spreadsheet, the historic relationships between various input levels and the corresponding output levels are estimated (computed numerically). These numbers are then used to simulate the production system to see how certain input levels could be expected to produce certain output levels.

7. How can changes in production scale (proportional changes in all inputs) be analyzed?

The sum of the output elasticities is the elasticity measure of returns to scale, which thus measures equiproportional changes in all inputs.

UNIT 6 AGGREGATE PLANNING — MATCHING SUPPLY AND DEMAND

2. What are the basic strategies used in developing an aggregate plan?

There are two basic strategies that are used in developing an aggregate plan: level and chase. With a pure level strategy, the firm maintains a constant workforce and allows the variations in demand to be absorbed by variations in inventory and backorder levels. A level strategy is typically used when the workforce is unionized or highly skilled. With a pure chase strategy, the firm varies the workforce by hiring workers in the peak of the demand cycle and firing or laying them off in the trough. In this situation, the workforce is used to absorb demand fluctuations. A chase strategy is typically used with an uneducated, unskilled, non-unionized workforce.

3. Define the following terms as they relate to aggregate planning:

   b. fixed workforce — typically associated with a pure level aggregate planning strategy in which the workforce remains constant while the firm builds inventory and incurs backorders in the process of matching supply and demand.

   d. subcontracting — a mechanism for increasing output in the peak of a demand cycle in which a firm that needs additional output to satisfy its demand contracts with a competitor to produce it.

   f. backordering — a mechanism for deferring customer demand from an earlier to a later period. Firms use backordering in their aggregate plans when there is little market competition for their product.

5. Which types of graphs are most useful for illustrating aggregate planning solutions?

Line charts are most useful for illustrating aggregate planning solutions. Other types of charts are also used, for instance, bar charts to compare relative levels.

UNIT 7 INVENTORY ANALYSIS – HOW MUCH DO WE ORDER? WHEN?

3. What is the effect of a 20% error in inventory carrying rate on order quantity? A 50% error?

   To examine the effect of errors in the inventory carrying rate consider the EOQ model. Since the relationship between the order quantity and the inventory carrying rate is inversely proportional to the square root, a 20% error in carrying rate will affect the order quantity by approximately 10%. A 50% error rate will affect the order quantity by a greater margin. Thus for small errors in inventory carrying rate the effect on order quantity is negligible and the inventory carrying rate estimate need not be extremely accurate.

4. How does the use of a spreadsheet package such as Lotus 1-2-3 simplify decision making in inventory management?

   Most of the inventory management models can be easily set up on a spreadsheet package such as Lotus 1-2-3. Further, the use of graphs can be exploited. Spreadsheet packages can be used to answer what-if questions in inventory analysis, the repeatability feature (ability to copy formulas) in such packages can allow extension of the analysis to many items.

5. Define the following terms as they are used in inventory analysis:

   a. inventory carrying rate — typically a firm incurs certain costs for keeping an item in stock. The sum of these costs, which include cost of capital, storage, insurance, taxes, and shrinkage, is usually expressed as a fraction of the unit cost of the item, and is known as the inventory carrying rate.

   c. review period — used in a periodic review system, it is the (fixed) time interval between the placing of successive orders.

   e. safety stock — inventory used to protect against uncertainty in demand, supply, and lead time.

   g. stockout — the situation in which the demand for a stock item is not satisfied when it occurs.

   i. economic order quantity — is the order quantity that minimizes the sum of the annual holding and ordering costs, provided certain assumptions such as constant demand rate, no uncertainty in demand, and so on are met.

UNIT 8 DEMAND ANALYSIS – HOW MUCH WILL WE SELL?

2. Define the following terms as they are used in this unit.

   a. a demand function — a mathematical function portraying firm's sales as the result of certain causal variables such as advertising, price, income, and interest.

d. elasticities — the measure of responsiveness of sales to changes in any of the demand variables. It shows the percentage change in sales that is caused by a 1% change in the demand variable. Useful in forecasting the effects of predicted small changes in one demand variable.

3. How are historic data used to calculate demand relationships?

The data representing past values of sales and all the relevant, measurable economic variables that are thought to influence demand are entered on the spreadsheet. The regression feature of the spreadsheet is used to compute the coefficients representing the numerical magnitude of influence of each of the variables.

5. Is it possible to assess the magnitude of influence of any one demand variable on sales? How?

Yes, by examining the coefficient of that variable and by interpreting its impact on sales (e.g., one thousand dollars of advertising budget increase sales by ten units).

7. Is it possible to "predict" sales for the product for past years? How?

Having estimated the demand relationship, it is possible to make *ex post* as well as future predictions with the coefficients. To get a prediction of sales, simply plug in certain values for all the causal variables. If last year's values for the demand variables are used, you have a "prediction" of last years sales.

UNIT 9 BREAKEVEN ANALYSIS — ASSESSING THE PROFITABILITY OF A NEW PRODUCT

1. What form of the income statement provides a suitable framework in which to examine the profitability of a proposed new product? Why?

The contribution margin income statement format provides a suitable framework for this analysis. This form of the income statement provides the required cost classification for breakeven analysis as well as other analysis of the sensitivity of profits to changes in costs, price, or demand.

3. Define the following terms as they are used in new-product analysis:

a. variable costs — those costs which vary in *total* proportionately to the number of units sold. Direct materials is a variable cost. The *per-unit* variable cost is a constant.

b. fixed costs — those costs which do not vary in *total* with respect to the number of units sold. Straight-line depreciation is a fixed cost. The *per-unit* fixed cost decreases as the number of units sold increases.

e. factory overhead — sometimes called burden or factory burden. Costs incurred in the manufacturing effort which are neither raw materials or direct labor.

4. What factors other than the potential financial impact of a new product enter into the decision whether or not to introduce the product?

   A desire on the part of the firm to be a "full-line" supplier. The number and strength of competitors. The potential of product liability suits that may result from the product.

5. Does the breakeven point increase or decrease in each of the following cases?

   b. The unit variable cost is reduced. Decreases.

   d. The selling price is increased and the fixed costs are reduced. Decreases.

UNIT 10 DECISION TREES — ANALYZING ALTERNATIVES

1. Define the following terms as they relate to decision tree analysis:

   a. expected cost — the average cost that can be anticipated for a particular alternative. The average is calculated by summing the product of the probability and its associated cost for all of the outcomes associated with a particular alternative.

   d. present value — the value of a cash flow stream that has been discounted to time zero at a certain discount (interest) rate. The present value of a particular dollar amount can be determined by using the following formula:

   $$PV = FV/(1 + DR)^n$$

   where PV is the present value of the amount, FV is the future value of the amount, DR is the discount rate per period (expressed as a decimal), and n is the number of periods in the future that the transaction occurs.

3. How does single-stage decision making differ from multistage decision making?

   In a single-stage decision making situation, the current decision is unaffected by decisions that may be made in the future. In a multistage decision making situation, future decisions are considered in the context of the current decision.

5. Why can the time value of money be important in decision tree analysis?

   When the time frame of the decision is quite long (i.e., greater than 2 years) the time value of money can be important in decision tree analysis because dollars transacted in the future are worth less than those transacted today. Present value analysis discounts the value of future transactions (using an interest rate called a discount rate) and establishes the value of those transactions in the present (i.e., their present value). Three situations — the longer the time frame of the decision, the higher the discount rate, and the more frequently the high dollar amounts occur far in the future — make consideration of the time value of money an important factor in making a decision. When the time value of money is not considered, it is assumed that dollars are worth the same regardless of when they are transacted.

UNIT 11 SIMULATION — EXPERIENCE IS THE BEST TEACHER

3. How can sequences of random numbers be repeated with a spreadsheet package?

   The ability to repeat a sequence of random numbers depends on how the random numbers are generated by the particular spreadsheet package. There are three general possibilities.

   First, there is a user-controlled seed that "starts" the random number generator. In such a case, you only have to use the same seed and you will obtain the same sequence of random numbers.

   A second situation is similar to Lotus 1-2-3 Release 1A where the spreadsheet package uses the same seed each time the program is entered. To generate the same sequence of random numbers then requires that you simply restart the spreadsheet program each time you want to repeat the sequence of random numbers.

   The third situation is similar to Lotus 1-2-3 Release 2 where the spreadsheet package generates a different initial random number each time the program is entered. In this case, the only method for repeating a sequence of random numbers is to generate the random numbers and write the sequence of random numbers to a table as generated. Then, when the simulation program runs, go to the table you developed and select the random number in the sequence in which it was generated. Since the random numbers are stored in a table, you can repeat the sequence of random numbers by simply going back to the same starting point in the table.

5. How can the effect of a random number be preserved in a spreadsheet model?

   Random numbers are often generated by spreadsheet software using a system function (e.g., @RAND in Lotus 1-2-3). When this function is used in a cell, a random number is returned. However, each time the spreadsheet is recalculated, a new random number is generated in that cell. In order to keep the value of the random number for a given cell from changing, you have to generate the random number using the function, copy that function (and value) to another cell, then edit the intermediate cell to convert the function to a number. The number can then be used where needed. In Lotus 1-2-3 Release 1A, this is accomplished using {edit}{calc}. Lotus 1-2-3 Release 2 and some other spreadsheet software packages have a command that permits you to copy the value of a formula directly, eliminating the intermediate step.

7. How are repeated loops programmed?

   Most spreadsheet software packages do not have functions or programming commands that can be used directly to repeat a particular set of statements (called a loop). Therefore, you have to use other commands to accomplish this function. The elements of the loop are a counter (variable/cell), an ending value of the counter (how many times you want to go through the loop), a cell which increments the counter (increases its value by one for each pass through the loop), and a means to test the counter to see if it has reached the ending value. When you enter the loop, you initialize the counter. You can perform the test at the beginning or end of the loop; where you perform the test affects what initial value you use and how you increment the counter. When the test (using something like the /XI command in Lotus 1-2-3) indicates that the counter exceeds the desired number of passes through the loop, you move to another cell outside of the loop.

UNIT 12 WEIGHTED FACTOR APPROACH — DECISION ANALYSIS USING MULTIPLE CRITERIA

1. Define the following terms as they relate to the facility-location problem:

   b. satisficing - producing a solution that is satisfactory (but usually less than optimal) under the stated constraints.

   d. center of gravity method - a single-criterion satisficing technique in which the location of a facility is established at the "center of gravity" of the system. The technique uses the volume of product moved, the distance that the product is moved, and the movement cost per unit distance to establish the location.

   e. population-distance matrix - a matrix that is used to identify service locations that are near to population centers and, thus, require few people to travel long distances to use the service.

   g. weighted factor approach - a satisficing technique that allows the decision maker to consider both quantitative and qualitative criteria simultaneously in arriving at a decision. It is a "generic" decision making technique because it can be used in virtually any decision-making situation, including facility location.

   i. normalized factor score - a unitless number that establishes the relative preference of various location alternatives according to a given criterion.

2. Identify the primary criterion that is typically used to solve the following facility-location problems:

   a. warehouse - storage cost minimization

   c. distribution center - distribution cost minimization

   e. manufacturing plant - production cost minimization

4. How does a spreadsheet package simplify use of the weighted factor approach model?

   A spreadsheet package simplifies the what-if analysis of the weighted factor approach model, allowing the decision maker to quickly and accurately assess the impact of changes in the model parameters (such as the list of sites, the list of factors, the factor weights, and the factor scores).

UNIT 13 FINANCIAL ANALYSIS — ANALYZING THE RETURN ON AN INVESTMENT

1. Define relevant and irrelevant costs and give an example of each.

   A relevant cost is a cost that must be taken into account when deciding whether or not to replace an old machine. Any maintenance costs that will be incurred over the expected life of the new machine are relevant costs. An irrelevant cost does not have to be taken into account in the replacement decision since it has no effect on the outcome. The original cost of the old machine is an irrelevant cost in this case.

3. How does the use of the sum-of-the-years digits method of depreciation impact upon the net present value of machine replacement?

   Other things being equal, the sum-of-the-years-digits method will produce a higher net present value than the straight-line method. This results from the larger tax savings in the earlier years of the machine's life under the sum-of-the-years-digits method.

5. Why would a firm use an assumed or target rate of return in the analysis, such as the 10% used by EZRydr? Where does the 10% come from?

   There are usually more opportunities for capital investments than there are funds. The 10% may be somewhat arbitrarily selected by management as a lower limit in view of the other opportunities available. In this case projects that do not meet the 10% requirement would be eliminated from further consideration. Theoretically, the 10% represents the firm's cost of capital — a rather complex measure that one can find presented and discussed in financial management texts.

7. What specific cost savings might be included in the estimate of savings generated by the new machine for each period? Who might provide these estimates?

   Some possibilities include:

   - reduced machine cycle times.
   - reduced defectives and rework
   - reduced operator times
   - reduced set-up times

   These estimates would probably be provided by the engineering unit of the operations management function.

UNIT 14 RESOURCE ALLOCATION — MAKING THE RIGHT CHOICES

1. What are the basic criteria that must be satisfied in order to use a linear programming model?

   Four criteria must be satisfied before a linear programming model can be used. The degree to which they are not satisfied is a measure of the degree of approximation provided by using an LP model. The criteria are:

Proportionality. This means that a particular change in a decision variable will result in a proportional change in the resources consumed, profit generated, and so on. In economic terms, this implies "constant returns to scale."

Additivity. This means that the resources consumed, profit generated, and so on by different activities (decision variables) can be added together. There are no interactions or cross-effects. With proportionality, additivity defines linearity.

Divisibility (Continuity). This means that the activities (decision variables) can take on fractional values. They are divisible. The decision variables are continuous variables.

Deterministic Coefficients. This means that the coefficients or parameters in the problem are determined or known with certainty. If the coefficients are actually realizations of a random variable, this criterion is violated.

4. What are the limitations in using a spreadsheet in solving a linear programming problem?

The biggest limitation in most spreadsheet software packages is that there is no way to directly solve an LP. The solution-by-inspection approach, while workable for small problems, is cumbersome even for moderate size problems. This is an interactive approach and therefore requires the ability to see the problem on the display, which therefore limits the size of problems that can be addressed effectively. Entering the problem, defining inequalities, developing temporary storage areas, and all of the other steps are tedious and time-consuming. Additionally, they are sources of potential error. While these limitation apply to "solving" an LP problem, they are not so severe when applied to describing an LP and doing sensitivity analysis.

INDEX

Notes

Notes

Notes